lords of the ring

The greatest fighters since 1950

lords of the ring

The greatest fighters since 1950

PETER ARNOLD
BOB MEE

HAMLYN

lords of the ring

First published in Great Britain in 1998 by Hamlyn
an imprint of Reed Books Limited Michelin House,
81 Fulham Road, London SW3 6RB and Auckland,
Melbourne, Singapore and Toronto.

ISBN 0 600 59520 X

A catalogue record for this book is available from
the British Library.

Printed and Bound in Great Britain.

CONTENTS

INTRODUCTION

In the second half of the 20th century, television has brought famous sporting personalities into the homes of fans. Prior to the advent of television the public may have been aware of them but would not have felt that they knew them or even that they wanted to know about their lives. That sort of interest was reserved for the film stars met in the intimate darkness of the cinema. The exploits of the great boxers before the Second World War, like Jack Dempsey and Henry Armstrong, were seen on flickering newsreels, and interviews were so formal little was given away. It was impossible for the ordinary fan, even if he or she went to the occasional show, to establish much rapport with the star men, or have much idea what they were like in private. Enormous interest was generated in Britain in 1937 by the effort of Tommy Farr to win the world heavyweight title from Joe Louis at the Yankee Stadium, New York. The live fight commentary was broadcast by radio in Britain in the small hours of the morning. The General Post Office was swamped with requests for 2.30 a.m. telephone alarm calls, and it was reckoned that two million fans gave up their sleep to listen to the crackling voice giving them perhaps an over-rosy description of Farr's progress. But how many of them were aware of the personality of Farr, or if it came to that, of Joe Louis, the brilliant new heavyweight champion? How many would even have recognised Farr in the street?

Things are completely different in the television age, which began in earnest in Britain in the 1950s, with the coronation of Queen Elizabeth. Nowadays people feel as if they almost know personally such TV-exposed boxers as Naseem Hamed or Nigel Benn, Mike Tyson or George Foreman. They certainly know their mannerisms. The incomparable Muhammad Ali, who fought in the 1960s and 1970s, was said to be the most recognisable man in the world, something which could not have been said about Jack Johnson, his counterpart of 50 or so years earlier.

This book is intended to give the follower of boxing an idea of the lives, backgrounds and careers of some 43 champions who have made big impressions since 1950. The object of restricting the number is to be able to give a little more insight into their lives than the potted biographies of two or three paragraphs usually found in the boxing encyclopaedias.

It is common practice in books of this kind to state that of course every reader will have his or her own idea of the 43 greatest boxers since 1950 and be amazed at some of the men included or left out, and that one can only make a personal choice, etc. With this in mind, the authors, in making that choice, have given preference to those boxers who have presented the highest profiles, attracted most interest from the public or have led the more interesting lives. Those readers who rue the omission from the 43 of artists like Azumah Nelson, Salvador Sanchez or Pernell Whitaker will find details of these men and many others in a chapter at the end of the book which rounds up the other prominent fighters of the period.

The book is in three parts, the first being a short history of boxing which outlines the developments which brought the sport and its champions into their current end-of-millennium prominence, and notes the contributions of some of the great heroes of the past to boxing's history.

Statistics are accurate to the end of May 1998.

Peter Arnold and Bob Mee

HISTORY OF BOXING TO 1950

Unorganised fighting with the fists must be as old as humanity itself. An early record of boxing as a formal test of strength and skill was found on slabs in a temple near Baghdad. It shows Sumerians of around 5,000 years ago fighting with their fists tied in leather thongs. The wearing of thongs on the fists continued through the years of the Ancient Greeks and Romans. Boxing became a brutal spectator sport in the last few hundred years before the birth of Christ when the Romans introduced metal spikes or studs into the thongs. The device was called a *caestus* and the gladiatorial battles would be to the death.

Boxing was first introduced into the Olympic Games in 688 BC, when a fighter called *Onamastus* was champion. This was a more civilised form (the boxers wore earguards), but later a contest called the *pancratium* was introduced – this allowed almost anything short of eye-gouging and biting (Mike Tyson please note). Eventually even the Romans could see that the savagery of the *caestus* was pointless (it produced a few great warriors, but only at the expense of killing others) so it died out, and when the Roman Emperor Theodosius the Great banned the Olympic Games in 393 AD boxing as a sport disappeared for nearly 1300 years before it took hold again in 17th century England.

It was linked with fencing and the use of the popular weapons of the day such as the backsword and quarterstaff. The masters of these weapons, while giving exhibitions and teaching the 'noble science of defence' began to teach the use of the fists. Soon there was a kind of professional boxing, when strong men, handy with their fists, would begin to roam the countyside fairs and village greens to issue challenges to the locals to fight them for a guinea, say. Soon these men would travel in groups, so that if nobody had the courage to challenge they could fight each other and raise a collection. Spectators would be asked to hold a rope and form a ring with it for the combatants, hence the boxing 'ring', although nowadays the ring is, of course, square. A challenger would 'throw his cap into the ring', one of many phrases to enter the language from the early days of boxing.

Initially there were no rules, of course, and in the rough and tumble exchanges the fighters could get away with whatever the spectators would allow. Gradually, certain things became universally outlawed, such as biting, gouging, hitting a man when he was down and hitting below the waist. Many other things, like wrestling, grabbing the hair, throwing, even strangling remained legitimate until the end of bare-knuckle fighting and the gradual adoption of the Queensberry Rules from 1867.

Champions began to be patronised or employed by local squires and aristocracy. The first report of 'a match of Boxing' to appear in the press (*The Protestant Mercury* of January 1681), tells of a butcher who beat the footman of His Grace the Duke of Albemarle. Gambling was a big part of the attraction of the prize ring, as it was with the other still practised sports then supported by rich land-owners – cricket and horse-racing. The followers of boxing were called 'the Fancy' – there was even a journal of this name.

As order became imposed on the prize ring, certain conventions arose. Surging spectators holding the ropes were replaced by stakes driven into the ground and the 'ring' became square. The purse holding the bets would be attached to one of the stakes. A boxers' remuneration is still called his 'purse', and betting money in all sports is still called the 'stakes'. The names of world-famous horse races like the Derby Stakes, and the innocent office sweepstakes held on these races are reminders of the old boxing matches. Boxers met at the centre of the ring where a line was scratched in the earth (they 'came up to scratch' or 'toed the line') and a round would last until a man was put down. There was then a 30-second interval during which his backers (seconds) had to revive him and get him to the line for the next round, otherwise he lost (failed to come up to scratch). For big matches a second ring was built round the first, thus forming a corridor all round in which men used whips to discourage spectator interference, and afterwards to encourage spectators to contribute to a collection for the boxers (hence the 'whip-round').

England was called 'The Cradle of Pugilism' and from 1719 a national champion was acknowledged. The first was James Figg, an expert at backsword and quarterstaff, who opened an academy in Tottenham Court Road and took on all-comers. One of his successors, Jack Broughton, drew up the first set of published rules in 1743, appalled at the death of one of his challengers, to whom he'd given a beating. These rules were for observance at his amphitheatre, but came to be accepted universally until superseded in 1838 by the London Prize Ring Rules, prompted by another fatality. Before 1838 a boxer's seconds had been allowed to help, even carry, him to the scratch-line for a new round – the new rules specified he had to get there unaided.

Bare-knuckle fighting, despite drawing huge crowds, was illegal, and organisers had to go to great lengths to keep arrangements from police, even though there was a long tradition of royal patronage. King George IV even had a guard of honour at his coronation in 1821 formed entirely of 20 leading pugilists from champion John Jackson's

Pugilistic Club. It was not until a test case in 1901 (over the death of another boxer) that boxing and legal authorities in England came to a working arrangement whereby police do not interfere with matches properly run under the auspices of a controlling body, currently the British Boxing Board of Control. This is not the same thing as boxing being a legal activity and organisers of 'unofficial' contests could still be prosecuted today.

There were many great bare-knuckle champions, so famous that many have huge monuments erected to their memories e.g. 'Bold Bendigo' in Nottingham, Tom Cribb in Woolwich, John Jackson, who taught the poet Lord Byron, in Brompton cemetery, and Tom Sayers in Highgate cemetery. Jack Broughton has a paving slab in Westminster Abbey.

British sailors and tradesmen spread boxing abroad, and it was embraced with particular enthusiasm in America, especially after a surge in British and Irish immigration in the early 19th century. The first American champion is held to be Tom Hyer, who was acknowledged as champ after beating George McChester in New York after 101 rounds (2 hours 55 minutes) in 1841.

Although a black American slave, Tom Molineux, had been brought across the Atlantic to challenge Tom Cribb for the championship in 1810 (a little gamesmanship by Cribb's seconds spoilt his chance), the first really big international contest took place in 1860, when the American champion, John C. Heenan, arrived with a huge press contingent to try to take the title from Tom Sayers. After 2 hours 20 minutes a draw was declared when police intervened. After this, with the law getting stricter, many British pugilists transferred their activities to America, and the USA has been the dominant boxing nation ever since.

The last great bare-knuckle champion was John L. Sullivan (born 1858, Roxbury, Massachusetts), the 'Boston Strong Boy'. He was the son of Irish immigrants and became the most famous fighter in the land. A roistering braggart who liked his drink, it was he who first boasted in bars that he could 'lick any son-of-a-bitch in the house'.

Bare-knuckle days were ending, however. John Sholto Douglas, the eighth Marquess of Queensberry (famous also for his part in the downfall of Oscar Wilde) published the famous Queensberry Rules in 1867. These rules were devised by John Graham Chambers of the London Athletic Club to cover amateur boxing. He persuaded the Marquess of Queensberry, an amateur boxer who had been a student with him at Cambridge University, to sponsor them and lend his name to them. There were 12 rules originally, of which the last was that 'the contest in all other respects to be governed by revised rules of the London Prize Ring'. The London rules had been updated the year before, and for a time both sets of rules were in operation, until eventually the Queensberry Rules were adopted for boxing everywhere.

The four main innovations of the Queensberry Rules were revolutionary. They were that boxers must wear padded gloves, that rounds would last three minutes, with a minute's rest between each, that wrestling would not be allowed, and that a boxer who was knocked down must rise within 10 seconds or the referee could declare his opponent the winner (the first concept of the 'knockout'). These rules still apply. There was no provision, however, for a contest to be restricted in its length. Matches continued to be fought to a finish. The decision to limit them to a certain number of rounds came gradually, with the number of rounds becoming part of the contract for a fight agreed in advance by the promoter and the two parties. Over a hundred championship contests under Queensberry Rules lasted for 20 rounds or more, the last being in 1923. It was not until 1988 that all ruling bodies agreed that contests should not last longer than 12 rounds.

The Queensberry Rules had a civilising effect on boxing and even the great Sullivan himself, who feared no man, became convinced of the advantages of using gloves, and did so. Some historians regard him as the first modern heavyweight champion of the world, but most regard his defeat by James J. Corbett (born 1866, San Francisco) as the beginning of heavyweight championship boxing. Their bout took place on 7 September 1892 at New Orleans, and Corbett, a dapper dresser who worked as a bank clerk, won with a 21st-round knockout. He was never forgiven for dethroning the man Americans regarded almost as a deity. But Corbett studied boxing and brought to the ring skill, speed and science, qualities which overcame the raw strength and endurance of the great bare-knuckle maestro. The enforced rests between rounds of the Queensberry Rules facilitated the use of speed and skill, while the padded gloves reduced the effectiveness of the bare-knuckle, teeth-crunching swipe to the jaw. Gradually the tempo of boxing, even the stance of the boxers, changed.

Bare-knuckle fighting was against the law in the United States as well as Britain, and in 1900, in New York, the Horton Law was passed which made gloved boxing illegal as well, unless it took place in members-only clubs. The object was to get rid of a criminal element which followed the boxing for gambling, inevitably leading to bribery and corruption. But since membership rules are easily circumvented, a Frawley Law of 1911 allowed boxing in public again but prohibited points decisions. Most states of America followed New York's example. It did not cure the gambling, as a method of reaching decisions based on the 'newspaper verdicts' evolved. It did mean that American boxers' records of the period are littered with 'no decision' contests. Some modern historians try to eliminate them by converting them to the newspaper decisions. So far as championships were concerned, a challenger could only take a champion's title by knocking him out, or stopping him, since a points win was not allowed. This practice was ended by the Walker Law of 1920 which legalised boxing altogether. The dates given apply to New York, and apparent discrepancies in boxers' records arise as other states changed their laws at different times.

The New York State Athletic Commission became immensely powerful in American boxing in so far as they decreed what were or weren't world championship bouts. This irritated the boxing commissions of other states, and 13 banded together in 1920 to form the National Boxing Association. In 1927, they began recognising world champions who differed from the New York champions. In 1962 this body reformed itself as the World Boxing Association with members from 51 states and cities. In 1963 the World Boxing Council was formed in opposition. It incorporated bodies from all round the world including the British Boxing Board of Control, and the New York Commission worked closely with it. In 1983 the International Boxing Federation was formed from a breakaway faction of the WBA and quickly gained equal status with the other two bodies. The formation of the World Boxing Organisation followed in the late 1980s, and although this body is more recognised in Britain than the USA, there are now four well recognised sanctioning bodies who, more than ever, recognise a different champion for each weight. There are other bodies too, but these failed to gain much recognition.

It means that whereas in the early days of the century there were eight world champions, there could now be 68. This is because the number of weight divisions, as well as the number of sanctioning bodies, has proliferated. The National Sporting Club, the unofficial governing body in Britain from the end of the 19th century until the formation of the British Boxing Board of Control, largely from NSC members, in 1929, did most to establish the original classic eight weight divisions in 1909. Previously champions would fiddle around the weight limits to suit themselves. Since 1909 a new weight has been inserted between each of the old divisions, with two below flyweight: light-fly and strawweight. Different bodies call these in-betweens by different names, thus light-middle, junior middle and super-welter are all the same division.

This proliferation of weight classes and authorities is the despair of the traditional fan, who is deprived of a 'real' world champion, since the champions of the various bodies rarely meet, but many in the industry are very happy with the situation. Boxers are happy, since far more can be a 'world' champion and promoters are happy, since many more contests can be labelled as for 'world' championships. With television providing more and more of boxing's revenue, it is becoming almost necessary for a contest to be a world title fight before it will be considered of interest.

There have been great world champions, acknowledged by the fight fan if not by all the sanctioning bodies, ever since boxing began. On 1 January 1900 there were only six world champions in all, as the light-heavy and flyweight divisions were not established until 1903 and 1909 respectively. James J. Jeffries ruled the heavyweights, Tommy Ryan the middleweights, the beautifully named Mysterious Billy Smith the welters, Frank Erne the lightweights, George Dixon, the first black world champion, the feathers, and Terry McGovern the bantams.

James J. Jeffries (born 1875 in Carroll, Ohio) was a true great, who in his day was a giant at 6ft 2in and 220lb. He had been a sparring partner of Corbett, and he beat off a challenge from Corbett after taking the championship in 1899 from Bob Fitzsimmons.

Jeffries retired in 1910 undefeated, having won 15 of 20 contests by knockout. Unfortunately this proud record was spoiled when in 1905 he was persuaded to return to the ring to recapture the heavyweight championship which had fallen into the hands of the hated (by whites) Jack Johnson, and Johnson inevitably beat him. Others of those 1900 champions are among the best-ever. The real name of Tommy Ryan (born 1870, Redwood, New York) was actually Joseph Youngs. He had a French father and English mother. He retired as unbeaten middleweight champion having suffered only three losses in a career of 105 bouts. George Dixon (born 1870, Halifax, Nova Scotia) won the bantamweight championship in England in 1890 and the featherweight title in America in 1892. An extremely skilful boxer, he probably fought as many as 800 contests, including exhibitions. Dixon was only 5ft 3in, and was called 'Little Chocolate'. His defeat of Jack Skelly in a world title fight in 1892 at the Olympia Club, New Orleans, caused racial disquiet, and the club declined to stage further black/white matches. Sadly Dixon died penniless only two years after retiring in 1906.

Bob Fitzsimmons (born 1863, Helston, Cornwall) was not a champion when the century started, but he was world middleweight champion from 1891 to 1894, having won the title from Jack Dempsey the 'Nonpareil', he was heavyweight champion from 1897 to 1899, having beaten Corbett with a punch to the solar plexus, and in 1903 to 1905 he was the third man to hold the championship of the new light-heavyweight division. He was the first man to win world titles at three weights. Born in England, he went as a boy to New Zealand, began his career in Australia and went to America to win his titles. Freckled, red-haired, spindly, with thin legs, Fitzsimmons looked nothing like the athletes seen today, but his training as a blacksmith gave him immensely powerful back and shoulder muscles.

Jack Johnson (born 1878, Galveston, Texas) was an all-time great heavyweight champion, who took the title from Tommy Burns in 1908. He was a masterly defensive boxer who was denied a title shot until he was over 30 because he was black. By pursuing Burns to Australia he won the championship in Sydney on Boxing Day with an arrogant display of skill. Americans couldn't stand the idea of a black man being heavyweight champion, especially an uppity one who consorted with white women, and Jim Jeffries was persuaded out of retirement to 'wipe the smile from his face'. Unfortunately the resulting humiliation of Jeffries led to prolonged race riots across America, in which on the first day there were 19 deaths with thousands injured, 250 or so seriously, and there were 5,000 arrests. Johnson was forced into exile, lost his title to giant cowboy Jess Willard in Cuba, and on his return was arrested and served a prison sentence for transporting women across state lines for immoral purposes, an offence against the *Mann Act*. He died crashing one of his fast cars in 1948.

A man who fought Johnson for his heavyweight title was one of the greatest middleweights of all time, Stanley Ketchel (born 1886, Grand Rapids, Michigan). Of Polish descent, Ketchel was a very tough character who won a $1000 reward as a teenager by capturing a murderer who shot at him. Ketchel feigned death to grab his man. He won the title in 1908 by knocking out Jack Twin Sullivan in the 20th round. He faced Johnson in 1909 in a match in which Johnson had agreed to 'carry' Ketchel, but Ketchel surprised Johnson in the 12th round by knocking him down. An angry Johnson, who outweighed Ketchel by 35lb, got up to knock Ketchel out with a blow so hard that some of Ketchel's teeth were later found embedded in his glove. The hard-drinking, womanising Ketchel was shot dead while on a farm holiday in 1910, by a farmhand whose girlfriend he dabbled with. The 24-year-old Ketchel was at the height of his powers.

The first of the great lightweights, Joe Gans (born 1874, Baltimore, Maryland) was black and came up in an era when black boxers, to get lucrative fights, were expected to 'lay down' occasionally, hence some of the eight defeats on his 156-fight record. When he did win a good purse he would wire home to his poor family that he was 'bringing home the bacon'. He was so good he was known as the 'Old Master'. Gans fought in the first promotion of the greatest of all promoters, Tex Rickard, who paid him $10,000 to defend his lightweight title in Goldfield, Nevada. He paid the challenger, Battling Nelson, who was white, $20,000. The $30,000 total purse was unheard of for lightweights in 1906, but Rickard did it to publicise Goldfield, a desert town, putting the cash in coins in the window of his saloon. He built an arena to hold 8,000 spectators and filled it, taking $69,715 at the gate and making Goldfield a temporary boom town. The fight was scheduled for 45 rounds in scorching heat which made Gans, who broke his hand and took several low blows from the crude Nelson, sick over the ropes. Gans won when Nelson, demoralised, deliberately fouled in the 42nd round and was disqualified. Nelson later did manage to take Gans' title but by then Gans was already suffering from the consumption which killed him in 1910, less than 18 months after his last fight.

Promoter Rickard's biggest drawing card was Jack Dempsey (born 1895, Manassa, Colorado) who became world heavyweight champion in 1919 with a demolition of the holder, Jess Willard, the Giant Cowboy. Dempsey had been helped to the fore by a cunning manager, Jack 'Doc' Kearns, who bet Dempsey's whole purse for the title fight on Dempsey winning in the first round. He thought he'd won when Willard was downed seven times, the last time for the count, but the bell had rung during the count, and Dempsey, who was leaving the ring, was recalled. He had to wait till the third round to win, when the brave Willard, who outweighed Dempsey by 58lb, was forced to retire with a smashed jaw and broken ribs.

Three great Welsh fighters were in action at the time of the First World War. Jimmy Wilde (born 1892, Tylorstown) was a tiny man of 5ft 2in who popularised the flyweight class, where he remains the greatest ever practitioner. In fact he was too small even for that smallest of classes, hardly ever weighing more than 102lb, a strawweight by today's standards. Yet Wilde, who built up the strength in his matchstick arms by working in the narrow seams in the coalmines, was often forced to fight bantams and even feathers. He probably had the hardest punch for his size of any boxer, ever, and was called the 'Ghost with a Hammer in his Hand'. He was world flyweight champion from 1916 to 1923. Wilde learned his trade in the boxing booths, and claimed to have had 854 contests. His official record shows 145, with only three defeats. Of his 136 victims, 99 were knocked out or stopped. He died in 1969, after four years of not knowing who he was, the result of a beating-up by thugs on Cardiff railway station when he was 72.

Jim Driscoll (born 1881, Cardiff) was a classical straight-left, upright, British-style boxer, who was so commanding that he was called 'Peerless' Jim. He was never recognised in America as featherweight champion, despite thoroughly outclassing the holder, Abe Attell, in a no-decision contest in New York. Attell never would meet him in a real title fight. Driscoll had to be content with British and European recognition as world champion. He too, fought hundreds of times in the booths. He lost only three of his 69 official bouts, including his last, to Frenchman Charles Ledoux in 1919. He already had tuberculosis, and died just over five years later. One of Driscoll's three defeats was on a foul to Freddie Welsh (born 1886, Pontypridd, real name Frederick Thomas), who was British, European and Empire lightweight champion before becoming world champion from 1914 to 1917. He fought mostly in America and lost only five times in 163 contests, although half of these were 'no-decision' bouts.

The 1920s was a golden age of boxing, in which promoter Rickard and champion Dempsey set the fashion for million-dollar gates. The first was at Boyles Thirty Acres, Jersey City, on 2 July 1921, when Rickard pitched Dempsey, perceived then as a war-slacker, against the handsome, decorated French war hero Georges Carpentier (born 1894, Lens). Carpentier was a boxing prodigy who had started as a 13-year-old flyweight. He rose up the weights, being a French champion at two of them, and a European champion at four, before he became light-heavyweight champion of the world in 1920, knocking out Battling Levinsky. He was a very skilful boxer with a devastating right-hand punch, but he broke his hand on Dempsey's head early in their fight and thereafter lacked the power to trouble the 16lb heavier Dempsey, who knocked him out in the fourth round. Dempsey took part in the first five contests to take $1 million at the gate, the highest grosser being the 1927 return with the man who took his title, Gene Tunney (born 1897, New York City). Tunney was a cool, studious boxer who won Dempsey's title in a rain-soaked 1926 match in Philadelphia, and then beat him again at Soldier Field, Chicago, where the attendance of 104,943 shattered previous gate money figures by paying $2,658,660. Tunney suffered only one defeat in 83 contests, and was the first to retire from the ring as heavyweight champion and resist all pleas to make a comeback. He married an heiress and became a successful businessman.

The man who beat Tunney, and put him in hospital, was Harry Greb (born Pittsburg, 1894), the world middleweight champion 1923-26. He was an amazing all-action fighter, called 'The Human Windmill', who demolished his opponents with glee and ferocity, sometimes with methods which stretched the rules. He hardly trained, but had 299 contests, so didn't need to. He had 40 fights in 1919 alone. Most of his contests were no-decision, but he won 105 and was reckoned to have won the newspaper decision in another 159. He lost eight times. In 1921 he suffered a detached retina, but was back in the ring three weeks later. It is thought he fought his last 83 contests, including nine for the world title, while blind in one eye. He was having routine surgery for facial injuries after a car accident when he died in 1926, only a month after fighting for the world title.

In the 1920s and 1930s three men won world titles at three weights, the most remarkable being the great Henry Armstrong (born 1912, Columbus, Mississippi, real name Henry Jackson), who held the undisputed featherweight, lightweight and welterweight titles simultaneously in 1938, a unique achievement. Had the super-feather and light-welter championships not been in disuse at the time, he could have held five. Armstrong's secret was a slow heartbeat which allowed him to keep up a non-stop whirlwind attack for the whole of 15 rounds. He was called 'Hurricane Hank'. Incredibly, in less than two years between May 1938 and May 1940, he took part in 21 world title fights, including a challenge for the middleweight title, which he drew.

Armstrong won the welterweight crown from Barney Ross (born 1909, New York City, real name Beryl Rosofsky), another who won world titles at three weights: light, light-welter and welter. Ross was from an Orthodox Jewish family opposed to boxing, but when his father, a grocer, was killed in a hold-up, he persuaded his mother he could support the family best with his fists, and he proved he could. His first titles, at light and light-welter, were won from Tony Canzoneri (born 1908, Slidell, Louisiana), who as he had previously been featherweight champion, was another triple world champion. These great boxers, Armstrong, Ross and Canzoneri, had 437 contests between them, of which 66 were world title fights.

The dominant fighter of the 1930s and 1940s was Joe Louis, the heavyweight champion (born 1914, Lafayette, Alabama, real name Joseph Barrow). The only blot on his rise to the top was a surprise knockout by former champion Max Schmeling of Germany in 1936. Louis overcame this to win the world title from James J. Braddock a year later, politics having ensured Schmeling was side-stepped. However, in 1938 Louis chose to defend against Schmeling in a contest which became mixed up in the propaganda surrounding the forthcoming Second World War. Louis became an American hero after winning it emphatically. He defended his title through the war on what became known as a 'Bum-a-Month' campaign, and established a world record with 25 successful defences of his title. He retired as champion in 1948, but financial problems, mostly concerned with tax, forced him to make a comeback in which he suffered two more defeats. His 1941 defence against the light-heavyweight champion Billy Conn, which he won by a 13th-round knockout after being outpointed throughout, was one of the classic fights of all time.

Two of boxing's most vicious and exciting series of scraps began in the late 1940s. Tony Zale, the middleweight champion, retained his crown after three legendary battles with Rocky Graziano in 1946 to 1948, and featherweights Willie Pep and Sandy Saddler had a series of four ill-tempered, foul-filled wars which lasted from 1948 to 1951.

Other boxers established in the 1940s, such as Sugar Ray Robinson, Archie Moore, Jersey Joe Walcott and Ezzard Charles, did enough in the 1950s to be included in the second part of this book . . .

EZZARD CHARLES

THE CINCINNATI FLASH

Mass public adulation is not usually reserved for modest, unassuming family men. Neither do writers find themselves inspired by respectable gents who could be found handing out hymn books in church or chatting to neighbours.

Even worse, if that churchgoing, unassuming family man happens to deprive the world of an icon, a superstar whose greatness has taken him beyond his peculiar craft into the realm of society hero, then he is likely to be slaughtered by writers and scoffed at by his public.

So it was with Ezzard Charles, one of the finest boxers of the century, who once said he would like to be remembered as 'a simple, square sort of fellow who believed in playing the game by the rules'.

In effect, Charles twice deprived the world of Joe Louis, the fabled Brown Bomber who had been there for the people from the Depression through Second World War and into the years of joy and optimism which followed it. Nobody wanted Louis to lose. And while those who thought about it were happy for him to retire, anybody unlucky enough to be asked to succeed him as champion could never hope for public acceptance.

Charles knew that, but boxing is a business. When the opportunity came to fight for the title vacated by Louis, of course he took it. And when he outpointed Jersey Joe Walcott in Chicago in June 1949, he was sensitive to the fact that whatever recognition he received was qualified. He knew he would have to prove himself over time by defeating the best challengers available to him.

However, it must have hurt horribly when Nat Fleischer, the decisive editor of the disproportionately influential *Ring* magazine, slaughtered him. Before Charles beat Walcott, Fleischer said: 'Louis left boxing a legacy of toil and brilliant action, but his heirs are about as seedy a lot as ever were assembled in quest for world honours'. After the fight, Fleischer dismissed the victory. 'Charles Not A Champion Of Any Place,' blared the *Ring* headline.

Yet a look at films of Charles in action shows he was a far more accomplished boxer than all of the heavyweight champions of the 1930s except Louis. Historians now place him ahead of Max Baer (one of Fleischer's heroes), James J. Braddock, Primo Carnera, Jack Sharkey and Max Schmeling.

Even when Charles outpointed Louis, when the latter came out of retirement in 1950, the public could not accept him. The man he beat bore Joe Louis's name, but did not resemble the Brown Bomber who had ruled the boxing world for 12 years. At least, Fleischer had no alternative but to recognise him as champion, but the following year the critics were still attacking.

Dan Parker of the *New York Post* dismissed him as 'about as spectacular as a snail and as colorful as an Arctic snowbank'. Charles, dignified and modest, accepted the flak, but how he must have longed for recognition, for someone to say, 'here is a great fighter who has learned his business from first to last, who is a ring artist of the highest order'. For that is what Ezzard Charles was. And it took until he was dead, from multiple sclerosis at the age of 53, for people to begin to speak loudly in his defence.

Ezzard Mack Charles was born in Lawrenceville, Georgia, on 7 July 1921. When his mother, Alberta, separated from his father, she moved to New York and sent Ezzard to Cincinnati, Ohio, where he was raised by grandmother, Maude Foster, and great-grandmother, Belle Russell. Maude also had seven of her own children, and brought them all up to fear God, attend church, and speak with modesty and respect. Ezzard was never a street kid. He graduated from high school before the boxing bug bit him.

Once committed, however, he was single-minded and absorbed all the knowledge he could from the veterans and wise, old trainers whose lives revolved around the Cincinnati gyms.

He was slow to fill out, but compiled a perfect 42–0 amateur record, including the 1939 National AAU middleweight championship. He turned professional in March 1940 when he was 18.

After 20 wins, he was pushed up a little too high and lost on points to the recently deposed world middleweight champion Ken Overlin from Illinois. However, later that year he did outscore another former world titleholder, the Pittsburgh veteran Thaddeus 'Teddy' Yarosz, whose best days were well behind him. It was a good name to have on the record of any young prospect, and Charles moved on quickly.

He knocked out Anton Christoforidis, a former light-heavyweight champ, in three rounds in Cincinnati and then drew a return with Overlin. A defeat by Kid Tunero was a surprise, but then he pulled off two victories that would demonstrate to historians just how good he must have been in his unfilmed youth. In May and June 1942, he twice outpointed the now legendary Charley Burley.

Burley could and should have been world middleweight champion in the 1940s, but nobody would give him a shot. Burley fought from 1936 until 1950, lost only 11 decisions in 98 fights, was never knocked out and was still on a winning roll when he retired in frustration at the age of 32. Yet, Charles was too slick and fast for him and won clearly both times ... and both fights were in Pittsburgh, which was Burley territory.

Working under the nickname of 'The Cincinnati Cobra', Charles also knocked out Jose Basora, who was good enough to draw with Ray Robinson, then ended 1942 with a pair of points wins over future light-heavyweight champion Joey Maxim.

Nevertheless, he was far from the finished article, and he lost a decision to another exceptional but undervalued heavyweight Jimmy Bivins and was for the first time stopped, by heavy hitting light-heavy Lloyd Marshall, in eight rounds in Cleveland in March 1943.

The Second World War then put paid to his boxing ambitions for the next three years. He was a GI in Britain and Europe for the duration. Before he enlisted, he had tried to look after his money by investing in a sports stadium. Unfortunately, when he returned, it was $8,000 in debt. He sold his supposed nest-egg at a loss, and years later was still clearing what he owed. It must have been depressing.

Charles was never much more than a light-heavyweight. When he won the title against Walcott in 1949, he weighed 181¾lb, which is astonishing when compared to the giants who dominate today. Nevertheless, he conceded 32lb to dangerous puncher Joe Baksi and stopped him in the 11th round.

After the war he set his record straight by dominating three subsequent fights with Bivins and twice knocking out Marshall. Also, he beat the great Archie Moore three times. Only a colourful character named Elmer 'Violent' Ray managed to beat him, on points in 1947, and in a rematch in Chicago he knocked out Ray in nine. Sadly, he was also involved in a ring tragedy when opponent Sam Baroudi died after their fight in Chicago in February 1948.

A split decision win over 15 rounds against Maxim confirmed his status, and almost begrudgingly, Fleischer rated him No.1 contender on the retirement of Louis, with Walcott No. 2. Quite why Fleischer should then have been so antagonistic towards them in terms of refusing recognition to the winner is not easy to establish. At first the National Boxing Association wanted Charles to fight Lee Savold, but when it failed to materialise, they paired Charles with Walcott. Savold, meanwhile, accepted an offer for a rival 'world title' fight with Bruce Woodcock in London, although he won it, he was never recognised.

Charles outboxed Walcott with a no-risk approach over fifteen rounds in front of an open-air crowd of 25,392 at Comiskey Park, Chicago, on 22 June 1949. Neither that display, nor his modest 'it was just another fight' admission afterwards endeared him to writers or fans. *Ring* labelled the fight 'a dance of the mediocre'. Fleischer said of Charles: 'He possesses no title – neither American nor world'. But only the New York State Athletic Commission agreed.

The rest of the USA accepted Ezzard, who made a successful first defence seven weeks later in Yankee Stadium, New York, when he stopped former light-heavyweight champ Gus Lesnevich, who retired because of eye injuries at the end of the seventh round. Only 16,630 paid at the turnstiles on the hottest day of the year, but they saw a champion who was stung by the criticism into producing a positive, sometimes fiery performance.

In October 1949, he travelled to San Francisco and knocked out sixth ranked contender Pat Valentino impressively in round eight at the Cow Palace.

He stayed in the West for an exhibition tour, but then sustained a rib injury in sparring which led to fears about a heart condition. He had to wait several months for medical clearance, but returned in August 1950 with a 14th round stoppage of Freddie Beshore in Buffalo. Beshore was stopped because of a horribly swollen ear ... and because he was completely outclassed.

By this time Louis, beset by tax problems, had announced a comeback and, without a warm-up bout, was matched with Charles in Yankee Stadium on 27 September 1950. A small crowd of 13,562 paid, with a disappointing gate of $205,370, but the occasion drew 400 writers from around the world. Charles was so undervalued, and Louis so overrated that many picked the old champion to win, even at the age of 37. Bookmakers were even caught up in the hype: they made old Joe a 2–1 favourite.

Afterwards, large chunks of humble pie were on the menu: in spite of a swollen left eye and conceding 34½lb, Charles systematically outboxed and outpunched an increasingly battered and bewildered Louis for 15 rounds.

Louis' mother watched sadly on television in Detroit, and told reporters: 'You can't go on forever. Joe's done enough. He should stop, but that's up to him.'

Meanwhile, Charles' mother, now Mrs Alberta Moss, was unable to bear hearing even the radio broadcast and spent the hour of the fight in her bathroom. Afterwards she promised to watch her son in future. 'If he's good enough to beat Joe Louis, he's good enough for me not to be scared to look at too.'

Louis had been on the payroll of the International Boxing Club, who promoted the fight, and commanded 35 per cent of the gate, but that was only a gross payday of $71,000. Not enough! He had to go on boxing until Rocky Marciano knocked him out the following year.

Charles earned only $41,000 for the privilege of beating a living legend, while the IBC, who had sold live television rights without imposing a local blackout condition, made a financial killing. Instead of paying at the stadium, fight fans watched it on TV in bars across New York.

Charles defended successfully four more times: he knocked out Nick Barone in round 11, stopped Lee Oma in 10, and outpointed old rivals Walcott and Maxim.

Then it all fell apart on a July night in Pittsburgh in 1951. Of all people, it was Walcott who beat him, knocking him out with one of the great punches in heavyweight history, a perfect left hook to the chin.

They fought once more in Philadelphia in June 1952, and Ezzard suffered a disappointing defeat with the majority of ringside press writers believing he was short-changed. His slide began from that point.

He was robbed in Utah against Rex Layne, whom he had previously stopped, but was genuinely beaten by Nino Valdes and Harold Johnson. He did manage to drag out one more inspired performance when he extended Rocky Marciano, who had succeeded Walcott as champion, for 15 terribly hard rounds in Yankee Stadium in June 1954. Even Fleischer stopped griping, called it Charles' greatest bout, and labelled him 'a fine sportsman and a gallant loser'.

But it was his last great effort. Three months later they met again and he was knocked out in round eight, after ripping open a horrible cut on Rocky's nose. By the following year he was sliding rapidly, and announced his retirement in December 1956 after losing on a pathetic disqualification in London against Dick Richardson.

He returned two years later because he needed the money, but lost four of six fights and quit for good at the end of 1959. He was 38. In 1961 he announced he was broke, and tried to make some kind of a living as a wrestler and a nightclub doorman. A few years later he was stricken by multiple sclerosis, and died in a Chicago hospital on 27 May 1975. He left a widow, Gladys, and three children. He was one of the finest stylists, pound for pound, of his day and one of the best technicians the heavyweight division has ever seen.

CAREER STATISTICS

World heavyweight champion 1949–51
Full name: Ezzard Mack Charles
Cincinnati, Ohio, born Lawrenceville, Georgia, 7 July 1921
1939 National AAU middleweight champion
1939 National Golden Gloves middleweight champion

1940
Mar 15 Medley Johnson w ko 3 Middletown
Mar 20 Jimmy Brown w ko 2 Reading, Pa.
Mar 27 John Reeves w pts 6 Cincinnati
Apr 2 Charley Banks w pts 6 Cincinnati
Apr 10 Kid Ash w ko 3 Portsmouth, Ohio
Apr 16 Charley Banks w ko 2 Cincinnati
Apr 24 Remo Fernandez w ko 6 Cincinnati
May 10 Eddie Fowler w ko 3 Portsmouth
May 17 Pat Wright w ko 4 Middletown
Jun 5 Frankie Williams w ko 7 Cincinnati
Jun 12 John Reeves w ko 4 Columbus
Jun 24 Bradley Lewis w ko 3 San Francisco
Sep 23 Marty Simmons w pts 10 Cincinnati
Oct 3 Billy Hood w ko 2 Cincinnati
Dec 2 Charley Jerome w ko 2 Cincinnati
1941
Feb 10 Billy Bengal w pts 10 Cincinnati
Feb 23 Slaka Cavirch w ko 2 Cincinnati
Mar 10 Floyd Howard w ko 7 Cincinnati
Mar 31 Joe Sutka w pts 10 Cincinnati
May 12 Rudy Kozole w pts 10 Cincinnati
Jun 9 Ken Overlin l pts 10 Cincinnati
Jul 21 Al Gilbert w ko 6 Cincinnati
Oct 13 Pat Mangini w ko 1 Cincinnati
Nov 17 Teddy Yarosz w pts 10 Cincinnati
1942
Jan 12 Anton Christoforidis w ko 3 Cincinnati
Mar 2 Ken Overlin drew 10 Cincinnati
Apr 8 Billy Pryor w pts 10 Cincinnati
May 13 Kid Tunero l pts 10 Cincinnati
May 25 Charley Burley w pts 10 Pittsburgh
Jun 29 Charley Burley w pts 10 Pittsburgh
Jul 14 Steve Mamakos w ko 1 Cincinnati
Jul 27 Booker Beckwith w ko 9 Pittsburgh
Aug 17 Jose Basora w ko 5 Pittsburgh
Sep 15 Mose Brown w ko 6 Pittsburgh
Oct 27 Joey Maxim w pts 10 Pittsburgh
Dec 1 Joey Maxim w pts 10 Cleveland
1943
Jan 7 Jimmy Bivins l pts 10 Cleveland
Mar 31 Lloyd Marshall l ko 8 Cleveland
1944-45 Inactive
1946
Feb 18 Al Sheridan w ko 2 Cincinnati
Mar 25 Tee Hubert w pts 10 Cincinnati
Apr 1 Billy Duncan w ko 4 Pittsburgh
Apr 15 Georgie Parks w ko 6 Pittsburgh
May 13 Tee Hubert w ko 4 Cincinnati

May 20 Archie Moore w pts 10 Pittsburgh
Jun 13 Sheldon Bell w ko 5 Youngstown
Jul 29 Lloyd Marshall w ko 6 Cincinnati
Sep 23 Billy Smith w pts 10 Cincinnati
Nov 12 Jimmy Bivins w pts 10 Pittsburgh

1947

Feb 17 Billy Smith w ko 5 Cleveland
Mar 10 Jimmy Bivins w ko 4 Cleveland
Apr 4 Erv Sarlin w pts 10 Pittsburgh
May 5 Archie Moore w pts 10 Cincinnati
Jul 14 Fitzie Fitzpatrick w ko 5 Cincinnati
Jul 25 Elmer Ray l pts 10 New York
Sep 16 Joe Matisi w pts 10 Buffalo
Sep 29 Lloyd Marshall w ko 2 Cincinnati
Oct 16 Al Smith w ko 4 Akron
Oct 27 Clarence Jones w ko 1 Huntington
Nov 3 Teddy Randolph w pts 10 Buffalo
Dec 2 Fitzie Fitzpatrick w ko 4 Cleveland

1948

Jan 13 Archie Moore w ko 8 Cleveland
Feb 20 Sam Baroudi w ko 10 Chicago
May 7 Elmer Ray w ko 9 Chicago
May 20 Erv Sarlin w pts 10 Buffalo
Sep 13 Jimmy Bivins w pts 10 Washington DC
Nov 14 Walter Hafer w ko 7 Cincinnati
Dec 10 Joe Baksi w ko 11 New York

1949

Feb 7 Johnny Haynes w ko 8 Philadelphia
Feb 28 Joey Maxim w pts 15 Cincinnati
Jun 22 Jersey Joe Walcott w pts 15 Chicago *(vacant world heavyweight title)*
Aug 10 Gus Lesnevich w rsf 7 New York *(World heavyweight title)*
Oct 14 Pat Valentino w ko 8 San Francisco *(World heavyweight title)*

1950

Aug 15 Freddie Beshore w rsf 14 Buffalo *(World heavyweight title)*
Sep 27 Joe Louis w pts 15 New York *(World heavyweight title)*
Dec 5 Nick Barone w ko 11 Cincinnati *(World heavyweight title)*

1951

Jan 12 Lee Oma w rsf 10 New York *(World heavyweight title)*
Mar 7 Jersey Joe Walcott w pts 15 Detroit *(World heavyweight title)*
May 30 Joey Maxim w pts 15 Chicago *(World heavyweight title)*
Jul 18 Jersey Joe Walcott l ko 7 Pittsburgh *(World heavyweight title)*
Oct 10 Rex Layne w rsf 11 Pittsburgh
Dec 12 Joey Maxim w pts 12 San Francisco
Dec 21 Joe Kahut w ko 8 Portland, Oregon

1952

Jun 5 Jersey Joe Walcott l pts 15 Philadelphia *(World heavyweight title)*
Aug 8 Rex Layne l pts 10 Ogden, Utah
Oct 8 Bernie Reynolds w ko 2 Cincinnati
Oct 24 Cesar Brion w pts 10 New York
Nov 26 Jimmy Bivins w pts 10 Chicago
Dec 15 Frank Buford w rsf 7 Boston

1953

Jan 14 Wes Bascom w rsf 9 St Louis
Feb 4 Tommy Harrison w rsf 9 Detroit
Apr 1 Rex Layne w pts 10 San Francisco
May 12 Bill Gilliam w pts 10 Toledo
May 26 Larry Watson w ko 5 Milwaukee
Aug 11 Nino Valdes l pts 10 Miami
Sep 8 Harold Johnson l pts 10 Philadelphia
Dec 16 Coley Wallace w ko 10 San Francisco

1954

Jan 13 Bob Satterfield w ko 2 Chicago
Jun 17 Rocky Marciano l pts 15 New York *(World heavyweight title)*
Sep 17 Rocky Marciano l ko 8 New York *(World heavyweight title)*

1955

Feb 18 Charley Norkus w pts 10 New York
Apr 11 Vern Escoe w ko 3 Edmonton, Alberta
Apr 27 John Holman l ko 9 Miami
Jun 8 John Holman w pts 10 Cincinnati
Jul 13 Paul Andrews w pts 10 Chicago
Aug 3 Tommy Jackson l pts 10 Syracuse
Aug 31 Tommy Jackson l pts 10 Cleveland
Nov 14 Toxie Hall l pts 10 Providence
Dec 6 Toxie Hall w pts 10 Rochester
Dec 22 Bob Albright w pts 10 San Francisco
Dec 29 Young Jack Johnson l ko 6 Los Angeles

1956

Apr 21 Don Jasper w ko 9 Windsor, Ontario
May 21 Wayne Bethea l pts 10 New York
Jun 19 Bob Albright w ko 7 Phoenix
Jul 13 Pat McMurtry l pts 10 Tacoma
Aug 13 Harry Matthews l pts 10 Seattle
Oct 2 Dick Richardson l dis 2 London

1957 inactive

1958

Aug 28 Johnny Harper w pts 10 Fairmont
Sep 30 Alfredo Zuany l pts 10 Juarez
Oct 27 Donnie Fleeman l ko 6 Dallas

1959

Jul 3 Dave Ashley w ko 7 Cincinnati
Jul 30 George Logan l ko 8 Boise, Idaho
Sep 1 Alvin Green l pts 10 Oklahoma City

Fights 122 Won 96 Lost 25 Drawn 1
Died 27 May 1975, Chicago, aged 53

RANDOLPH TURPIN

THE LEAMINGTON LICKER

Older British fight fans still remember 10 July 1951, when Randolph Turpin provided them with just about the most exciting night British boxing has enjoyed since the Second World War. A convincing defeat of the legendary Sugar Ray Robinson, regarded by many then and now as the best pound-for-pound boxer ever, suggested the 23-year-old Turpin would become an all-time great himself. However Robinson just managed to win the return and Turpin's complex private life began to erode his remarkable talent. He still had an outstanding career but never again stood on the heights alongside the immortal Robinson. The depths came when he took his own life less than 15 years after his great victory, when the 18,000 inside the Earls Court arena had spontaneously sung 'For he's a jolly good fellow'.

The bad fortune which seemed to follow Randolph Adolphus Turpin for much of his life did not take long to manifest itself. Only three months after his birth on 7 June 1928 in Leamington Spa, Warwickshire, his father, Lionel Fitzherbert Turpin, died. Lionel had never truly recovered from being gassed on the Somme in the First World War. He had emigrated from British Guiana, and was said to be the first black man to live in Leamington. He had married a local girl, Beatrice Whitehouse, and Randolph was the youngest of their five children. The others, in order, were Dick, Joan, Jackie and Kathy. The three boys were all to become professional boxers. Their grandfather, Tommy Whitehouse, had been a bare-knuckle boxer.

Randolph's mother had a hard time after her husband died. She had the handicap of being partially sighted, and had to scrub floors to earn some cash, while her mother and an aunt helped with the children. After three years of widowhood she married again, to Ernest Manly. Young Randolph, however, had a serious bout of double pneumonia when three, surviving an illness which often proved fatal then. He had one other big setback as a boy, when trapped underwater by weeds when swimming. His eardrum was damaged, and for the rest of his life he was a little deaf.

When Randy was nine, his brother Dick, who was not yet 17, became a professional boxer, and Randy joined the Leamington Boys Club, where a police inspector, Jerry Gibbs, spotted his great talent for boxing. Randolph began an amateur career when 12. He was immediately outstanding, and won junior titles in 1943 at 112 lb, in 1944 at 133lb and in 1945 at 147 lb, at which weight (welter) he also won the ABA title, the youngest man and the first black man to become an ABA champion.

Randy, who had been working since the age of 14 with a builder, now followed his brother Jackie into the Royal Navy. Dick was in the army and both sisters were in the Women's Auxiliary Air Force. Randy continued to box, became Navy and Inter-Services champion and won a second ABA title, at middleweight. When he fought for England against the USA, he knocked out America's star middleweight, Harold Anspach, with a single punch in the first round.

In 1946 both Randy and Jack turned professional and brother Dick's manager, George Middleton, a grocer, looked after all three brothers. Jack was an excellent featherweight, who was to have over 100 pro contests without quite reaching championship class. Randy, however, had immediate success as a professional and at 19 outpointed the British middleweight champion, Vince Hawkins. Randy had built up a magnificent physique by now. He had always been good at sports and his partial deafness had given him a certain self-sufficiency which allowed him to concentrate on his gym work, and cultivate his strength. Broad shoulders and a slim waist gave him a Superman appearance, and the great American boxing writer A. J. Liebling, seeing him in New York for his second meeting with Sugar Ray Robinson, said he had never seen such a big, strong middleweight.

Brother Dick was also doing well, and in May 1948 he knocked out New Zealander Bos Murphy in the first round at Coventry to become British Empire middleweight champion. The following month Dick became British champion by outpointing Vince Hawkins at Birmingham. He was the first to benefit from the British Boxing Board of Control changing their rules after the Second World War to allow black boxers to challenge for British titles.

Randy's private life meanwhile showed signs of turmoil and emotional inadequacy which were never to leave him. At 17 he took a drug overdose when his girlfriend, Mary Stack, threatened to leave him. The navy regarded this as attempted suicide, but he escaped official charges. He subsequently married Mary Stack but the marriage did not last long and ended with accusations on her side that Turpin beat her and kicked her in the stomach while she was pregnant. An assault case was dismissed but Turpin had to admit he had hit his wife, and she divorced him.

The case affected Turpin's boxing and was the first indication that his ascent to greatness would be hindered by his inability to prevent personal upheavals inhibiting his ring performances. Turpin was unable to channel distress and setbacks outside the ring into aggression inside it, as many champions can. Instead, he felt sorry for himself and fought with no heart.

While the case was preying on his mind Turpin fought tamely against Albert Finch, and dropped his first decision when outpointed. Five months later, having won in the meantime, he fought Jean Stock of France. On the very day of the fight, Turpin was told that his wife had been given custody of their son, Randolph junior. He told brother Dick in the dressing room that he had no stomach for the fight and even that he half-expected to lose. In an extraordinary display he was knocked down several times and threw in the towel after five rounds.

This pathetic display could have spelt the end for Turpin, but after a rest he returned with all his former brilliance, notching up a string of impressive wins, notably against a recent European champion, Cyrille Delannoit, of Belgium.

Albert Finch had five contests with one or other of the Turpin brothers, and can be proud of coming out 3–2 ahead, although it was 2–1 to the Turpins in title fights. After beating Randolph, he challenged Dick for the British and Empire titles and lost. But in 1950 he beat Dick twice, taking the British title (Dick had earlier lost the Empire title to Australian Dave Sands). This gave Randy the chance, when his string of wins had earned a British title shot against Finch, to avenge the family, and he took it with vicious punching which decked Finch three times and knocked him out cold in the fifth round.

Four months later Randy added the European title to the British by knocking out the Dutchman, Luc Van Dam, in an electrifying 48 seconds.

Turpin was at the peak of his powers, and on 10 July 1951 had his big opportunity. Sugar Ray Robinson, former unbeaten world welterweight champion and newly crowned middleweight champion, was on a triumphal three-month tour of Europe, during which he warmed up to accept a title challenge from Turpin with six non-title fights, winning the last with an impressive third round knockout of former European champion Cyrille Delannoit.

Robinson was the glamour boy of boxing, and many would argue the greatest champion of all time. In 132 contests, he had been beaten once, a defeat he avenged five times. The 23-year-old Turpin was given very little chance, even by British critics and fans. The experienced radio commentators themselves were so mesmerised by the reputation of the great Robinson that they failed to convey how easily Turpin was winning the fight, so that millions of listeners were robbed of the mounting pleasure and expectation of Turpin's performace. Not so the 18,000 packed into the Earls Court arena in London, who were singing before the end.

Robinson had never met a boxer like Turpin before, a man who crouched low and threw powerful punches with both hands from all angles. He later said: 'Turpin does everything wrong – right'. There was only one winner at the end, and Turpin was emotionally cheered all the way back to the dressing room. Robinson was gracious: 'You were real good. I have no alibis. I was beaten by a better man.' The US fans could hardly credit the news. 'Unbelievable – Robinson beaten' ran the New York newspaper placards.

Turpin was one of the most popular sportsmen in post-war austerity Britain, feted wherever he went, and of course he attracted as many girl friends as he wanted. Robinson, as was standard in those days, had a return clause in his contract, and the return fight took place at the Polo Grounds, New York, only 64 days later. Naturally all Americans wanted to see for themselves boxing's new sensation against the old master. The fight attracted 61,370 spectators, a record for non-heavyweights, and the receipts of $767,626 exceeded the old record by over $300,000. Only nine contests had ever grossed more, all of them heavyweight title bouts. Turpin, with movies and TV revenue, earned over $200,000, a vast sum in 1951.

Turpin began slowly in New York but after nine rounds was almost level and looked likelier to win. In the tenth he split Robinson's left eyebrow so badly that Robinson banked all on a desperate assault. It worked. Turpin was dropped by a right for a count of seven and then Robinson attacked a still groggy Turpin on the ropes with a fusillade of punches. Turpin ducked and swayed and refused to go down again but was not fighting back and the referee Ruby Goldstein stepped in with eight seconds of the round left. Many thought this action premature, as had he lasted the round, Turpin would probably have been in the better condition to continue, with Robinson's eye so badly cut.

Turpin recovered his form well, and took the British and Empire light-heavyweight titles when stopping Don Cockell in the 11th round at the White City, London (Cockell later fought Marciano for the world heavyweight title), then he won the Empire middleweight title from George Angelo of South Africa and successfully defended his European middleweight title against Charles Humez of France.

After eight impressive wins since losing his world title, Turpin returned to New York to try to regain it in a contest with Carl 'Bobo' Olson, Robinson having made a short-lived retirement. It was now that Turpin's final decline began, and the cause was the old one – his inability to control his relationships with women.

In New York, a showgirl whom he had met on his first trip, Adele Daniels, turned up at his hotel and made scenes when Turpin, whose divorce was now final, told her he was engaged to a Welsh girl, Gwenneth Price. Turpin could not cope with the brouhaha and the title contest at the same time. He gave up training and hid himself away. On the night, at Madison Square Garden, he fought with no passion or urgency and was well beaten on points. Adele Daniels then charged him with rape and assault, and Turpin was arrested and had to deposit $10,000 as a surety of return before being allowed home. The case was eventually settled out of court, without Turpin giving evidence. Daniels accepted $3,500 (she had sued for $100,000). Although it was a small payment for her, Turpin's legal bill was not so easily shrugged off.

Turpin's private affairs now got worse. There was a split with brother Dick over Randy's inability to concentrate on boxing. His marriage to Gwenneth estranged more of his family, and although he was happy with Gwenneth, with whom he was to have four daughters, there was more trouble when he was cited as co-respondent in a divorce case. In 1954 he lost his European middleweight title when knocked out in the first round by Tiberio Mitri in Rome. However at times he could reproduce the old flair, and he never did lose his British and Empire titles at both middle and light-heavyweight in the ring. But when, in 1958, he was knocked out by Yolande Pompey, he retired. He was 30. It was his eighth defeat, but it could be claimed that only Sugar Ray Robinson beat him when he was emotionally in the mood to fight.

Turpin's mostly unhappy life dipped much further after he retired. He had no idea of business and his investments were disastrous. A castle in Wales where he had trained for his fights was bought and converted into a hotel, but it failed, as did a Great Orme Holiday Camp which he started. Like other hard-up ex-boxers he was reduced, at one time, to capitalising on his name and wrestling professionally. His financial affairs were not healthy, and in particular income tax had been left unpaid. In 1959, only a year after retiring and eight years after his greatest night, and the adulation that went with it, he was working in George Middleton's scrap yard for around £3 per day, while renting a small transport café that his wife ran, and above which he and his family lived.

In 1962 Turpin was made bankrupt over £17,126 he owed as income tax. Writing in the US magazine *Boxing Illustrated* he said: 'I'm broke, I'm bitter and I've been bled to bankruptcy'. He was by now also beginning to worry about his eyesight, but nevertheless mad two come back appearances in 1963 and 1964 to try to help his situation. Even the local council seemed to be against him in 1964 when a compulsory purchase order was served on the café, which was to be demolished to make way for a car park. In May 1966, while he was still living in the café, a final demand arrived from the Inland Revenue. It was all he could take. Three days later, on 17 May 1966, the man who 15 years earlier had been idolised by the British public wrote some suicide notes and went up to his bedroom with a gun. Sadly, his youngest daughter followed him. He shot her and himself twice each. Fortunately she survived, but Turpin was dead. He had written a surprisingly sensitive poem which included the lines: 'So we'll leave this game, which was hard and cruel/And down at the show, on a ringside stool/We'll watch the next man....'

CAREER STATISTICS

World middleweight champion 1951
Full name: Randolph Adolphus Turpin
Leamington Spa, England, born 7 June 1928
1945 ABA welterweight champion
1946 ABA middleweight champion

1946

Sep 17 Gordon Griffiths w rsf 1 London
Nov 9 Des Jones w pts 6 London
Dec 26 Bill Blything w ko 1 Birmingham

1947

Jan 14 Jimmy Davis w ko 4 London
Jan 24 Dai Jones w ko 3 Birmingham
Feb 18 Johnny Best w rsf 1 London
Mar 18 Bert Hyland w ko 1 London
Apr 1 Frank Dolan w rsf 2 London
Apr 15 Tommy Davies w ko 2 London
Apr 28 Bert Sanders w pts 6 London
May 12 Ron Cooper w rsf 4 Oxford
May 27 Jury VII w pts 6 London

Jun 3 Mark Hart w pts 6 London
Jun 23 Leon Fouquet w ko 1 Coventry
Sep 9 Jimmy Ingle w rsf 3 Coventry
Oct 20 Mark Hart drew 6 London
1948
Jan 26 Freddie Price w ko 1 Coventry
Feb 17 Gerry McCrea w rsf 1 London
Mar 16 Vince Hawkins w pts 8 London
Apr 26 Albert Finch l pts 8 London
Jun 28 Alby Hollister w pts 8 Birmingham
Sep 21 Jean Stock l rsf 5 London
1949
Feb 7 Jackie Jones w rsf 5 Coventry
Feb 21 Doug Miller w pts 8 London
Mar 25 Mickey Laurent w rsf 3 Manchester
May 3 William Poli w dis 4 London
Jun 20 Cyrille Delanoit w rsf 8 Birmingham
Aug 22 Jean Wanes w rsf 3 Manchester
Sep 19 Roy Wouters w rsf 5 Coventry
Nov 15 Pete Mead w rsf 4 London
1950
Jan 31 Gilbert Stock w pts 8 London
Mar 6 Richard Armah w rsf 6 Croydon
Apr 24 Gustave Degouve w pts 8 Nottingham
Sep 5 Eli Elandon w ko 2 Watford
Oct 17 Albert Finch w ko 5 London
(British middleweight title)
Nov 13 Jose Alamo w ko 2 Abergavenny
Dec 12 Tommy Yarosz w dis 8 London
1951
Jan 22 Eduardo Lopez w ko 1 Birmingham
Feb 27 Luc Van Dam w ko 1 London
(vacant European middleweight title)
Mar 19 Jean Stock w rsf 5 Leicester
Apr 16 Billy Brown w ko 2 Birmingham
May 7 Jan de Bruin w ko 6 Coventry
Jun 5 Jackie Keough w rsf 7 London
Jul 10 Ray Robinson w pts 15 London
(World middleweight title)
Sep 12 Ray Robinson l rsf 10 New York
(World middleweight title)
1952
Feb 12 Alex Burton w rsf 7 London
Apr 22 Jacques Hairabedian w ko 3 London
Jun 10 Don Cockell w rsf 11 London
(vacant Empire light-heavyweight title)
Oct 21 George Angelo w pts 15 London
(vacant Empire middleweight title)
1953
Jan 19 Victor D'Haes w ko 6 Birmingham
Feb 16 Duggie Miller w pts 10 Leicester
Mar 17 Walter Cartier w dis 2 London
Jun 9 Charley Humez w pts 15 London
(European middleweight title)
Oct 21 Carl Olson l pts 15 New York
(vacant World middleweight title)
1954
Mar 30 Olle Bengtsson w pts 10 London
May 2 Tiberio Mitri l rsf 1 Rome
(European middleweight title)
1955
Feb 15 Ray Schmidt w dis 8 Birmingham
Mar 8 Jose Gonzalez w ko 7 London
Apr 26 Alex Buxton w ko 2 London
(British & Empire light-heavyweight titles)
Sep 19 Polly Smith w pts 10 Birmingham
Oct 18 Gordon Wallace l ko 4 London
1956
Apr 17 Alessandro D'Ottavio w rsf 6 Birmingham
Jun 18 Jacques Bro w ko 5 Birmingham
Sep 21 Hans Stretz l pts 10 Hamburg
Nov 26 Alex Buxton w rsf 5 Leicester
1957
Jun 11 Arthur Howard w pts 15 Leicester
(British light-heavyweight title)
Sep 17 Ahmed Boulgroune w rsf 9 London
Oct 28 Sergio Burchi w rsf 2 Birmingham
Nov 25 Uwe Janssen w rsf 8 Leicester
1958
Feb 11 Wim Snoek w pts 10 Birmingham
Apr 21 Eddie Wright w rsf 7 Leicester
Jul 22 Redvers Sangoe w rsf 4 Oswestry
Sep 9 Yolande Pompey l ko 2 Birmingham
1959-62 inactive
1963
Mar 18 Eddie Marcano w ko 6 Wisbech
1964
Aug 22 Charles Seguna w rsf 2 Malta

Fights 75 Won 66 Lost 8 Drawn 1
Died 17 May 1966, Leamington, aged 37

JERSEY JOE WALCOTT

THE CREAM

Master of Ceremonies Michael Buffer once announced Jersey Joe Walcott as 'so great he had an entire state named after him'!

OK, so Michael was telling a white lie. But there never was much point in calling Jersey Joe by his real name: the altogether more prosaic Arnold Raymond Cream!

Arnold was a down-to-earth family man with a wife and six kids. But Jersey Joe was the heavyweight champion of the world, and for a time one of the most romantic of all boxing heroes.

He was from fighting stock – his uncle Jeff Clarke fought the legendary Sam Langford an amazing 13 times between 1910 and 1921 – and as a boy Arnold was raised on tales of the great black stars of the early years of the century. His father, who was West Indian, loved one old-timer in particular: 'The Barbados Demon', the original Joe Walcott, who was world welterweight champion from 1901 until 1904.

Arnold was born in Merchantville, New Jersey, on 31 January 1914 and raised in Camden, just over the river from Philadelphia. He married his wife Lydia when they were teenagers and by the age of 19 had a son to support. Eventually, there were six children: Arnold jnr, Elva, Doris, Ruth, Vincent and Carol. He had a job as a garbage collector, although at 16 he had earned $7.50 in his professional boxing debut. One fight is recorded in Vineland, New Jersey, and there might have been two or three others, which passed unrecorded, but then he drifted away from the sport until 1933, when he travelled over the bridge to Philadelphia and linked up with Jack Blackburn, who had been a world class lightweight before doing time for killing a man.

Blackburn, who ran the Arcadia gym, liked what he saw in the young man who wanted to name himself after one of the greatest black fighters of them all, but Jersey Joe fell ill with typhoid before they could establish any long-time relationship or deal. While he was ill, Blackburn moved to Detroit to teach the young Joe Louis.

Arnold's uncle, Jeff Clarke, was a beautiful boxer known as 'The Joplin Ghost' – he lived in Joplin, Missouri – and had also taught his nephew to use his feet and to box on the move. The combined attentions of Clarke and Blackburn gave Arnold a style that was made to last.

Jersey Joe Walcott, as he was known, was fighting again by 1935, but in spite of his ability made little impression ... or money. When he was knocked out by a body shot from a good fighter, Al Ettore, in Camden in January 1936, he was weak from hunger. He took a pounding before going down. Everything he managed to scrape together went on to the family table, and if that meant going without himself, then that's what he did.

In March 1936 he outpointed Willie Reddish, who later trained Sonny Liston, and the following year knocked out Elmer 'Violent' Ray in three rounds. He also beat Phil Johnson, whose son Harold would also become a Walcott victim 14 years later and yet who would go on to win the light-heavyweight crown. Against that, Jersey Joe was knocked out by Tiger Jack Fox and outpointed by Billy Ketchell and George Brothers.

When he was knocked out in six rounds by the giant Abe Simon in Newark in 1940, he looked ready for the scrapheap, and as the Second World War bit deeper into the country's resources, he drifted away from boxing, sometimes earning what he could in shipyards and munitions plants, but otherwise relying on $9.50 a week in state welfare handouts. He had a couple of low-key fights in 1944, and was almost 31 when he decided to take one last shot at fighting for a living, following a visit from local manager Felix Boccacchio, a Camden numbers runner, who was fronted by a promoter named Vic Marsillo.

Jersey Joe wasn't interested in fame or titles; all he wanted was food on the table and coal on his fire. The day after they shook hands Boccacchio had both delivered to the Walcott door.

In August 1945 Boccacchio and Marsillo lured the big former miner from Wilkes-Barre, Pennsylvania, Joe Baksi, to Camden to fight Walcott. It was the turning point of Jersey Joe's career. Baksi was only 25, and had never been knocked out in 52 fights going back five years. He had won two out of three with Lee Savold, and had beaten former world title challengers Gus Dorazio and Lou Nova. Baksi was told Walcott was a harmless club fighter who was only there to earn a few dollars, but was outboxed all the way. Walcott won on points.

From then on, he was a changed man. Mrs Cream and all the young Creams had enough money to live comfortably, if not with excess, and the pressure was taken from him for a while. He fought with more ambition and belief, and in an unbeaten run of a dozen fights he beat quality operators like Jimmy Bivins and Lee Oma.

Two points defeats at the end of 1946 by Joey Maxim and Elmer Ray seemed to set him back, but he reversed both at the start of 1947 and then beat Maxim in a decider to put himself high in world class.

Even so, when Joe Louis looked around for an opponent for a ten round exhibition at Madison Square Garden in December 1947, critics did not give old Jersey Joe a second thought. He was just the fall guy employed to help boost the good cause of the night, the Mrs Randolph Hearst Milk Fund.

Then the New York Commission spoiled the plot. They did not recognise 10-round exhibitions. It would have to be six rounds or a full length, 15-round title fight. Eventually, Louis and promoter Mike Jacobs settled on the latter. The result, of course, was considered a formality. Pressmen, cynical about Walcott's age, labelled him 'Pappy'.

When British writer Peter Wilson visited Louis at his Pompton Lakes training camp, however, he felt the 33-year-old champion seemed more worried than usual, not about Walcott, but about himself. For the last week, Jersey Joe locked the doors on his critics at his Grenloch training camp in New Jersey, hiding from the seemingly perpetual enquiries about how nervous he felt and concentrating on the biggest break he had ever received. There were also rumours that, because of his connections with Boccacchio, he would 'fight in invisible handcuffs'; that is, he would fight within himself and not take any opportunities that might arise.

Walcott was reticent, suspicious and short on explanations. When Wilson asked him if he might freeze on the big night, the challenger grinned and said he had been down the aisle to the ring too often to lose his nerve. He told another enquirer: 'I think I can win'. Nobody else did.

The Garden opened its doors to 18,194 paying fans who paid $216,477, a house record at the time. The customers saw one of the most dramatic fights in ring history. Louis hurt Walcott with a right hand in the first round, but Jersey Joe fought back and dropped the champion with a left hook.

Walcott had Louis on the floor again, more heavily, in round four and by the halfway point the champion looked old. Louis kept plodding forward, won some rounds but could never subdue a challenger who could slide away like an old fox in undergrowth, and who had a shuffle that looked like a break dance. In the last round Walcott, convinced he had points to spare, retreated and survived.

Then came the verdict: referee Ruby Goldstein for Walcott, judges Frank Forbes and Marty Monroe for Louis, the winner by a split decision. Walcott believed for the rest of his life that he had been robbed. New York columnist Jimmy Cannon declared that if it had not been Louis who was on the receiving end of the verdict, there would have been a public enquiry. The Garden crowd booed long and loud. 'I'm sorry, Joe,' said Louis, who explained later that he was merely apologising for a bad fight.

The New York Commission lent its weight to a campaign for a rematch, which was hot business and too big for the Garden. It was staged outdoors before more than 40,000 fans at Yankee Stadium in June 1948. Again, Walcott dropped Louis early in the fight, this time in round three. Again, he could not keep him down.

By the tenth round it had become boring as Louis plodded hopefully forward without leading, and Walcott waited to counter. But then, in round 11, Walcott was nailed by a right hand and under the follow-up attack went down for the count. They gave the old champ a standing ovation, while Walcott left to rue his second failure in a world championship fight. At least he had a payday of more than $150,000 which allowed him to buy his brothers and sisters a house each.

The following March, Louis wrote to the National Boxing Association, and formally announced what he had promised his mother immediately after the second Walcott fight. He would not fight again, he said.

Apart from a brief exhibition in his home town, Walcott had done nothing since Louis knocked him out, but was still rated No. 2. Eventually, the NBA matched him with Ezzard Charles for the vacant title in Chicago in June 1949. He was 35, and Charles was too slick for him. Walcott's camp complained at the verdict, but nobody else did.

Two months later he knocked out Swedish contender Olle Tandberg in five rounds in a Stockholm soccer stadium before a crowd of 43,000.

'Through the years they have interred Jersey Joe half a dozen times, but he keeps coming back,' wrote Sid Feder for *Ring*, adding: 'No member of the feline species ever had more lives than this wizened old graybeard from South Jersey'.

In February 1950, Walcott stopped Harold Johnson in three rounds in Philadelphia. Johnson, a 21-year-old who would go on to win the world light-heavyweight title, had lost only to Archie Moore, a 10-round decision, in 29 fights. Still rated the leading contender for Charles, Jersey Joe kept up the pressure with victories over Omelio Agramonte, Johnny Shkor and the German hope Hein Ten Hoff.

At that time the champion's future was in doubt because of a heart problem as a result of a sparring injury, but when Charles did return to action, Walcott found himself sidestepped. Then in the Garden in November 1950, he was beaten by the strong Utah hopeful Rex Layne.

As so often happens, a defeat actually helped him, and in March 1951 in Detroit, he was given a fourth world title shot only for Charles to beat him again. This time it was close, but the unanimous decision went to the champion.

Boccacchio did a great job of yelling injustice and finally Charles gave Walcott another chance at Forbes Field, Pittsburgh, on 18 July 1951. And amazingly, the old man finally pulled out a punch when it mattered: a clean left hook to the chin in round seven which dismantled Ezzard's senses and left him sprawling on the canvas. Jersey Joe was to remain the oldest heavyweight champion in history – 37 years and five months – until George Foreman knocked out Michael Moorer in 1994.

In Camden they gave him a street parade welcome home, and suddenly all the years of gruelling work, all the hard times, had brought their reward.

Inevitably, Charles was given a revenge chance in Philadelphia in June 1952, but Jersey Joe outpointed him in spite of beginning as a betting outsider. Of 41 ringside pressmen polled, 24 felt Walcott was lucky. The *New York Mirror* ran a bold headline: 'Walcott Retains Title Via Unanimous Gift In Dull, Dirty Scuffle'.

By now the leading contender was the Italian-American star from Brockton, Massachusetts, Rocky Marciano, but hopes that the fight would happen in New York came to nothing because Boccacchio was refused a licence there, barred as an influence 'detrimental to boxing'.

The position was unchangeable and so New York was out. They signed to box at the Municipal Stadium in Philadelphia on 23 September 1952, with Walcott solemnly believing that the strong, unbeaten, but technically raw Marciano did not belong in the same ring. 'He wouldn't have qualified for Joe Louis's Bum of the Month club,' he said in a rare show of arrogance.

A combination of Walcott's fans from Philadelphia and Camden, and the multitudes who followed Marciano, produced a terrific crowd of 40,379, and they saw one of the classic championship fights. In round one Marciano was on the floor from a left hook which also raised a bump by his eye. By round 12 Walcott had boxed into a good lead of three or four points on all cards, but in the 13th Marciano found what he was looking for: a perfect right hand, flush on the chin.

Walcott slid slowly down the ropes, trapped by one arm entangled through them, and Marciano gave him an extra cuff for good measure before the champion fell to the canvas for the count.

Jersey Joe was given a return for a 'pension' payday of $250,000, but that one punch had taken everything out of him. His effort in Chicago in May 1953 was pathetic. He went down in round one, misjudged the count and rose too late. He was booed from the ring.

In retirement he enjoyed the rewards he had reaped so late in his career, but stayed busy by working with young criminals, refereed once in a while – most famously the Muhammad Ali–Sonny Liston rematch in 1965 – and was also the New Jersey State Athletic Commissioner in the 1980s.

He retired when he suffered a fall from a ring apron in his 70s, and died in Camden on 26 February 1994, aged 80.

CAREER STATISTICS

World heavyweight champion 1951-52
Camden, New Jersey, born Merchantville, NJ., 31 January 1914
Full name: Arnold Raymond Cream

1930
Sep 9 Cowboy Wallace w ko 1 Vineland, NJ
1931-32 inactive
1933
DNA Bob Norris w ko 1 Camden
Jul 28 Henry Taylor w ko 1 Camden
Nov 16 Henry Taylor l pts 6 Philadelphia
1934 Inactive
1935
DNA Al Lang w ko 1 Camden
DNA Lew Alva w ko 3 Camden
Oct 1 Pat Roland w ko 4 Camden
Oct 29 Joe King w ko 1 Camden
Nov 26 Roxie Allen w ko 7 Camden
1936
Jan 21 Al Ettore l ko 8 Camden
Mar 16 Willie Reddish w pts 10 Philadelphia

Apr 28 Joe Colucci w ko 4 Camden
Jun 16 Lou LaPage w ko 6 Coney Island
Jun 22 Phil Johnson w ko 3 Philadelphia
Jul 14 Billy Ketchell drew 10 Camden
Aug Carmen Passarella w pts 8 Camden
Aug Billy Ketchell w pts 10 Camden
Sep 1 Billy Ketchell l pts 10 Pensauken

1937

May 22 Tiger Jack Fox l ko 8 New York
Sep 3 Joe Lipps w ko 2 Atlantic City
Sep 25 Elmer Ray w ko 3 New York
Oct 9 George Brothers l pts 8 New York

1938

Jan 10 Freddie Fiducia w pts 8 Philadelphia
Jan 20 Jim Whitest w pts 8 Philadelphia
Mar 25 Art Sykes w ko 4 Philadelphia
Apr 12 Lorenzo Pack w ko 4 Camden
May 10 Tiger Jack Fox l pts 10 Camden
Jun 14 Ray Lazer l pts 8 Fairview, NJ
Dec 23 Bob Tow w pts 8 Camden

1939

Aug 14 Al Boros w pts 8 Newark
Nov 18 Curtis Sheppard w pts 8 New York

1940

Jan 19 Tiger Red Lewis w ko 6 Philadelphia
Feb 12 Abe Simon l ko 6 Newark

1941

Jun 27 Columbus Gant w ko 3 Memphis

1942-43 inactive

1944

Jun 7 Felix Del Paoli w pts 8 Batesville
Jun 28 Ellis Singleton w ko 3 Batesville

1945

Jan 11 Jackie Saunders w ko 2 Camden
Jan 25 Johnny Allen l pts 8 Camden
Feb 22 Austin Johnson w pts 6 Camden
Mar 15 Johnny Allen w pts 8 Camden
Aug 2 Joe Baksi w pts 10 Camden
Sep 20 Johnny Denson w ko 2 Camden
Oct 23 Steve Dudas w ko 5 Paterson
Nov 12 Lee Murray w dis 9 Baltimore
Dec 10 Curtis Sheppard w ko 10 Baltimore

1946

Jan 30 Johnny Allen w ko 3 Camden
Feb 25 Jimmy Bivins w pts 10 Cleveland
Mar 20 Al Blake w ko 4 Camden
May 24 Lee Oma w pts 10 New York
Aug 16 Tommy Gomez w ko 3 New York
Aug 28 Joey Maxim l pts 10 Camden
Nov 15 Elmer Ray l pts 10 New York

1947

Jan 6 Joey Maxim w pts 10 Philadelphia
Mar 4 Elmer Ray w pts 10 Miami
Jun 23 Joey Maxim w pts 10 Los Angeles
Dec 5 Joe Louis l pts 15 New York
(World heavyweight title)

1948

Jun 25 Joe Louis l ko 11 New York
(World heavyweight title)

1949

Jun 22 Ezzard Charles l pts 15 Chicago
(vacant world heavyweight title)
Aug 14 Olle Tandberg w ko 5 Stockholm

1950

Feb 8 Harold Johnson w ko 3 Philadelphia
Mar 3 Omelio Agramonte w ko 7 New York
Mar 13 Johnny Shkor w ko 1 Philadelphia
May 28 Hein Ten Hoff w pts 10 Mannheim
Nov 24 Rex Layne l pts 10 New York

1951

Mar 7 Ezzard Charles l pts 15 Detroit
(World heavyweight title)
Jul 18 Ezzard Charles w ko 7 Pittsburgh
(World heavyweight title)

1952

Jun 5 Ezzard Charles w pts 15 Philadelphia
(World heavyweight title)
Sep 23 Rocky Marciano l ko 13 Philadelphia
(World heavyweight title)

1953

May 15 Rocky Marciano l ko 1 Chicago
(World heavyweight title)

Fights 69 Won 50 Lost 18 Drawn 1
Died 26 February 1994, aged 80

KID GAVILAN

THE BOLO PUNCH KID

Kid Gavilan was a beautiful boxer who made up for his lack of a devastating punch with speed, brilliant ringcraft and an iron chin. In his day, he was considered, pound for pound, second only to Ray Robinson in terms of combination punching and pure skills. In 143 fights spread over 15 years, nobody ever knocked him out. As a man, he was the life and soul of any party, and a natural showman who loved to dance as much as fight. In his prime he was not averse to driving regally around the Manhattan streets in his Cadillac.

Gavilan – 'Sparrowhawk' in Spanish – was born in Berrocal, in Camaguey, Cuba, on 6 January 1926. His family were sharecroppers on a sugar plantation. His actual name was Gerardo Mauras, but after his parents split up, his mother remarried and from then on he used Gonzalez, the name of his stepfather. But it was as Kid Gavilan that he became famous.

By the age 12 he had finished his formal schooling and worked in the cane fields. Later he would use his past as a publicity gimmick, claiming his bolo punch was developed from the action of cutting cane. Maybe, maybe not. He also learned to box, developing his skills as an amateur before adding to the family income by fighting professionally at the age of 17. He called himself 'Gavilan' after the bar of his manager Fernando Balido, and worked his way up from the four-round class from 1943.

He was a bantamweight when he began, but in July 1945 he won the Cuban lightweight title by knocking out Jose Pedroso in four rounds in Havana. Losing his unbeaten record to a Mexican named Carlos Malacara in Mexico City in September 1945 hardly mattered, for within six weeks he had reversed the verdict in Havana.

He made his American debut in New York in November 1946 with a fifth-round knockout of Johnny Ryan, and made repeated trips from Havana to the East Coast fight centres – New York, Philadelphia, Baltimore, Newark – for the next couple of years.

In 1948 he fought two of the greatest boxers of all time, Ike Williams and Ray Robinson, respectively the world lightweight and welterweight champions. Both outpointed him, but on each occasion he made a significant impression. Williams gave him a hammering, but he took it stoically and battled on to reach the final bell. Robinson also outboxed him, but in a closer fight.

When he fought Williams again in January 1949, Ike was still world lightweight titleholder, and began a clear favourite. But Gavilan demonstrated how much he had improved by winning a fast display of educated boxing on points. *Ring* magazine installed him as leading contender for Robinson's welterweight crown, and featured him on the front cover of their May 1949 issue.

In July 1949, Gavilan challenged Robinson in the Municipal Stadium, Philadelphia, and went down on points over 15 rounds before a 35,000 crowd. Robinson staged a masterful exhibition, and demonstrated what a brilliant welterweight he was. Gavilan hung in and fought well, and his Cuban fans were angry at the decision, which was eminently fair. Gavilan decided early on that he could not outbox Robinson and so fought him. Without a heavy punch, he knew he was unlikely to knock the champion out, but concentrated on a high workrate in the hope of wearing him down. It didn't quite succeed, but it was a good fight and enhanced the Kid's reputation.

Two months later Gavilan was back in New York, where he outpointed the popular Rocky Castellani, and then outscored former lightweight champ Beau Jack in Chicago.

He lost a decision here and there, to Lester Felton in Detroit, Billy Graham in New York, Robert Villemain in Montreal, George Costner in Chicago and Eugene Hairston in Scranton, but then he boxed often and his fights usually went the full 10 rounds. Usually, of course, he won. He beat Graham and Hairston, who was a deaf mute nicknamed with what now seems appalling insensitivity 'Dummy', in rematches, and also defeated top contenders like Tony Janiro and Joe Miceli.

Finally in May 1951, Robinson having moved up to become middleweight champ, Gavilan was matched with the man the National Boxing Association recognised as welterweight champion, Johnny Bratton of Chicago. Originally from Little Rock, Arkansas, Bratton was a clever 23-year-old veteran of more than 60 fights. He had won NBA recognition by outscoring Charley Fusari in Chicago two months earlier. Gavilan was plainly superior, but the brave and proud Bratton defied a broken jaw to last the distance. The decision was unanimous and clear. At 25, the Cuban Hawk was world welterweight champion.

After a non-title appearance in Milwaukee, Gavilan defended against Billy Graham from New York's East Side in one of the most controversial fights of the decade. He had given a $2,000 guarantee to the New York Commission that he would give Graham first shot if he beat Bratton, and honoured the commitment at Madison Square Garden in August 1951. Their first two fights had finished in a split decision either way, but it was this third meeting which caused tremendous controversy. After 15 fiercely contested rounds, judge Artie Schwartz saw it 9–6 in rounds to Gavilan, while Frank Forbes had them level, but gave Graham the advantage point. Referee Mark Conn's scorecard decided it. Like Forbes he had them level, but he gave the edge to Gavilan ... and the crowd reacted angrily. Debris rained down on the ring and Conn was assaulted as he left ringside.

Apart from local bias towards a New York favourite, the problem was that Gavilan had been well in front at halfway, only to fade as Graham finished strongly. The crowd remembered Graham's later superiority and forgot how far adrift he was early on. Others said the decision was bent ... and the result of mob control. Underworld supremo Frankie Carbo, it was said, had a piece of Gavilan. Teddy Brenner, who was making matches at the Garden and St Nicholas Arena in Brooklyn in the 1950s, wrote in his book *Only The Ring Was Square* that a few days before the fight Carbo asked Graham's manager Irving Cohen for 20 per cent of the fighter. According to Brenner, who from ringside made Graham the winner, Cohen and Graham discussed it and turned him down. Carbo told Cohen that in that case Gavilan would get the verdict.

'I remember the way Graham stood in the center of the ring, dumbfounded as his supporters came out of their seats into the aisles, waving their fists ... screaming threats ...' wrote Brenner. He also said that Artie Schwartz, when on his deathbed in hospital, told Cohen he had given his verdict on mob orders. True or false? Who knows, but Gavilan remained champion, earned well in non-title fights and then retained his title in February 1952 by outpointing Bobby Dykes in Miami.

Gavilan was under-trained and Dykes, a 23-year-old from San Antonio, Texas, who was on a roll of 15 consecutive wins in the previous 12 months, ran him to another split decision. Dykes, who was living in Miami at the time, was ahead by three points according to referee Eddie Coachman, but judge Mark Erwin from Miami saw it 142–141 for Gavilan and a Cuban official, Ladislad Nodarse, made his compatriot a 145–139 winner, which was considered outrageous. *Ring* felt Gavilan scraped home, thanks to a knockdown he scored in round two.

Two close decisions in two defences was not exactly a perfect start, but he was far more impressive in defence No. 3 in July 1952, when he stopped highly respected and hard hitting Gil Turner from Philadelphia in 11 rounds. Gavilan opted to go into Turner's home town and at the Municipal Stadium, in front of almost 40,000 fans, inflicted the first defeat on Gil's record after 31 straight professional wins and an unbeaten amateur career.

A three-fight non-title tour to Argentina put a few more dollars in the bank account and then he beat Graham in their rematch, which this time took place in Havana on Gavilan's territory. A crowd of 35,000 turned out and the decision after 15 rounds was unanimous. He punched too hard for college graduate and TV favourite Chuck Davey in a February 1953 defence in Chicago, stopping the 26-year-old southpaw from Michigan in the tenth round.

Gavilan's iron jaw and big heart were tested fully by Carmen Basilio in Syracuse, New York, in September 1953 in another fight which was considered controversial and raised some eyebrows. Gavilan suffered a rare knockdown in the second round, closed Basilio's right eye, and fought grimly to hold on to his title on another split verdict.

Two months later a rematch with Bratton in Chicago saw Gavilan back to his magnificent best. He dazzled Bratton with barrages of blows from all kinds of angles and only the challenger's angry insistence prevented the corner from pulling him out.

Gavilan's time as a champion was running out. For all his brilliant skills, his struggle to make the welterweight limit of 10st 7lb (147lb) was no secret. For a non-title fight early in 1954, he scaled 11st 3lb (157lb). It was not a huge surprise when in April 1954 he took a calculated gamble by moving up to challenge world middleweight champion Carl 'Bobo' Olson in Chicago. Gavilan came in at 155lb, conceding just four pounds to a champion who was respected but not considered in the highest class. In fact, he was sluggish and Olson outworked him on the inside, denying him leverage in his punches and using his extra strength to shove him around.

Gavilan, who said afterwards he had a damaged right hand, fought proudly but was beaten on a majority decision in which the judging again seemed strange. One official saw the fight level while the others had Olson six and eight points ahead.

The gamble having failed, he had no alternative but to grind himself down to welterweight again to face Johnny Saxton from Newark, New Jersey, who was known as 'The Fighting Orphan' and whose manager was the notorious Frank 'Blinky' Palermo.

Gavilan believed, or knew, that he could not get the decision over Saxton, in effect that his time had come. Even so, he forced himself down to 145½lb; well inside the limit. True enough, the verdict for Saxton was unanimous, and bitterly disputed. But perhaps worse than that, the Pennsylvania Commission – the fight was in Philadelphia – hauled both boxers before them for lack of effort. The action had been dreary.

The Cuban Hawk's complaints were ignored. He had survived close calls himself, and some felt it a case of poetic justice.

He was only 28, but slipped from the top quickly. He never stopped being a world class performer, but the verdicts began to go the wrong way. He lost four out of eight in 1955, one of them a rematch with Dykes, and five out of nine in 1956, including a controversial decision to British champion Peter Waterman in London. They met again two months later and Gavilan won.

He ended his career in Miami in 1958 when a West Indian middleweight, Yama Bahama, whose real name was William Butler, outpointed him.

His manager Yamil Chade persuaded him to retire, he did some coaching and moved to his farm in Camaguey. He was a friend of the Cuban president Fulgencio Batista and in his heyday was given an honorary appointment as a major in the police force.

However, the country he returned to was changing. A socialist student leader named Fidel Castro was rising rapidly to power and in January 1959, Batista was overthrown and fled into exile. As Castro's policies polarised and moved from socialism to Marxist-Leninism, life in Cuba changed dramatically. There was no place for professional boxing, or old friends of 'unmentionables'. Gavilan stayed on his farm and eventually became a Jehovah's Witness, which meant he was arrested repeatedly for preaching. His car and passport were confiscated, but in 1968 the authorities relented and allowed him to leave. He settled in Miami, where he has lived for the past 30 years.

His health suffered – he had two operations for cataracts and three strokes – but he remained a ready-smiling, easy-going man who enjoyed times like the annual reunions of the International Boxing Hall of Fame in New York State.

CAREER STATISTICS

World welterweight champion 1951-54
Camaguey, Cuba, born 6 January 1926
Real name: Gerardo Gonzalez

1943
Jun 5 Antonio Diaz w pts 4 Havana
Jun 12 Bartolo Molina w pts 4 Havana
Aug 7 Valeriano Dustet w pts 6 Havana
Sep 10 Sergio Prieto w ko 5 Havana
1944
Oct 1 Juan Villalba w ko 9 Havana
Nov 25 Esmerido Salazar w pts 10 Havana
Dec 23 Miguel Acevedo w pts 10 Havana
1945
Feb 10 Esmerido Salazar w pts 10 Havana
Mar 10 Jose Pedroso w pts 10 Havana
Apr 21 Santiago Sosa w ko 9 Havana
May 13 Kid Bebo w ko 4 Cienfugos
May 26 Yucutan Kid w pts 10 Havana
Jun 23 Pedro Ortega w pts 10 Havana
Jul 7 Jose Pedroso w ko 4 Havana
(Cuban lightweight title)
Aug 4 Julio Jimenez w pts 10 Mexico City
Aug 26 Pedro Ortega w ko 6 Mexico City
Sep 22 Carlos Malacara l pts 10 Mexico City
Nov 5 Carlos Malacara w pts 10 Havana
Nov 17 Johnny Suarez w pts 10 Havana
1946
Jan 26 Kid Bururu w pts 10 Havana
Feb 9 Kid Bururu w pts 10 Havana
Mar 2 Jose Zorilla w ko 4 Bayamo
Mar 9 Santiago Sosa w pts 10 Havana
Apr 5 Tony Mar l pts 10 Mexico City
Jun 25 Chico Varona w pts 10 Havana
Aug 4 Hankin Barrow w ko 7 Havana
Aug 24 Jack Larrimore w ko 3 Havana
Sep 7 Hankin Barrow w pts 10 Havana
Nov 1 Johnny Ryan w ko 5 New York
Dec 2 Johnny Williams w pts 10 New York
Dec 13 Johnny Williams w pts 10 New York
1947
Jan 28 Julio Pedroso w pts 10 Havana
Feb 8 Jose Garcia Alvarez w pts 10 Havana
Feb 22 Pablo Roca w pts 10 Havana
Mar 12 Nick Moran w pts 10 Havana
Apr 26 Vince Gambill w ko 2 Havana
Aug 11 Charlie Williams w pts 10 Newark
Aug 18 Bobby Lee w pts 10 Baltimore
Sep 2 Doug Ratford l pts 10 Newark
Sep 15 Charley Millan w ko 1 Baltimore
Sep 18 Billy Justine w pts 8 Philadelphia
Oct 23 Billy Nixon w pts 8 Philadelphia
Nov 3 Bee Bee Wright w rsf 10 Baltimore
Dec 29 Buster Tyler drew 10 New York
1948
Jan 12 Gene Burton drew 10 New York
Jan 23 Joe Curcio w rsf 2 New York
Feb 13 Vinnie Rossano w pts 10 New York
Feb 27 Ike Williams l pts 10 New York
Apr 13 Doug Ratford l pts 10 Brooklyn
Apr 26 Tommy Bell w pts 10 Philadelphia
May 28 Rocco Rossano w ko 1 New York
Jul 22 Roman Alvarez w pts 10 New York
Aug 12 Buster Tyler w pts 10 New York
Sep 23 Ray Robinson l pts 10 New York
Oct 21 Vinnie Rossano w rsf 6 Washington DC
Nov 12 Tony Pellone w pts 10 New York
Dec 11 Ben Buker w pts 10 Havana
1949
Jan 28 Ike Williams w pts 10 New York
Apr 1 Ike Williams w pts 10 New York
May 2 Al Priest w pts 10 Boston

Jun 7 Cliff Hart w ko 2 Syracuse
Jul 11 Ray Robinson l pts 15 Philadelphia
(World welterweight title)
Sep 9 Rocky Castellani w pts 10 New York
Oct 14 Beau Jack w pts 10 Chicago
Oct 21 Lester Felton l pts 10 Detroit
Nov 21 Laurent Dauthuille w pts 10 Montreal
Dec 17 Bobby Lee w pts 10 Havana

1950

Feb 10 Billy Graham l pts 10 New York
Mar 6 Otis Graham w pts 10 Philadelphia
Mar 20 Robert Villemain l pts 10 Montreal
May 8 George Costner l pts 10 Philadelphia
May 26 George Small w pts 10 New York
Jun 8 Mike Koballa w pts 10 Brooklyn
Jun 19 Bobby Mann w pts 10 Hartford
Jul 2 Sonny Horne w pts 10 Brooklyn
Jul 13 Phil Burton w pts 10 Omaha
Aug 15 Johnny Greco w ko 6 Montreal
Oct 23 Tommy Ciarlo drew 10 New Haven
Oct 30 Eugene Hairston l pts 10 Scranton
Nov 17 Billy Graham w pts 10 New York
Dec 4 Tony Janiro w pts 10 Cleveland
Dec 22 Joe Miceli w pts 10 New York

1951

Jan 26 Paddy Young w pts 10 New York
Feb 19 Tommy Ciarlo w pts 10 Caracas
Mar 10 Tommy Ciarlo w rsf 8 Havana
Mar 30 Eugene Hairston w pts 10 New York
Apr 20 Aldo Minelli w pts 10 New York
May 18 Johnny Bratton w pts 15 New York
(vacant world welterweight title)
Jul 16 Fitzie Pruden w pts 10 Milwaukee
Aug 29 Billy Graham w pts 15 New York
(World welterweight title)
Oct 4 Bobby Rosado w rsf 7 Havana
Nov 7 Tony Janiro w rsf 4 Detroit
Nov 28 Johnny Bratton drew 10 Chicago
Dec 14 Walter Cartier w rsf 10 New York

1952

Feb 4 Bobby Dykes w pts 15 Miami
(World welterweight title)
Feb 28 Don Williams w pts 10 Boston
May 19 Ralph Zianelli w pts 10 Providence
May 28 Fitzie Pruden w rsf 6 Indianapolis
Jul 7 Gil Turner w rsf 11 Philadelphia
(World welterweight title)
Aug 16 Mario Diaz w pts 10 Buenos Aires
Sep 6 Rafael Merentino w rsf 9 Buenos Aires
Sep 13 Edward Lausse w pts 10 Buenos Aires
Oct 5 Billy Graham w pts 15 Havana
(World welterweight title)

1953

Jan 13 Aman Peck w pts 10 Tampa
Jan 21 Vic Cardell w pts 10 Washington DC
Feb 11 Chuck Davey w rsf 10 Chicago
(World welterweight title)
Apr 14 Livio Minelli w pts 10 Cleveland
May 2 Danny Womber l pts 10 Syracuse
Jun 10 Italo Scortichini w pts 10 Detroit
Jul 15 Ramon Fuentes w pts 10 Milwaukee
Aug 26 Ralph Jones w pts 10 New York
Sep 18 Carmen Basilio w pts 15 Syracuse
(World welterweight title)
Nov 13 Johnny Bratton w pts 15 Chicago
(World welterweight title)

1954

Feb 23 Johnny Cunningham w pts 10 Miami
Mar 8 Livio Minelli w pts 10 Boston
Apr 2 Carl Olson l pts 15 Chicago
(World middleweight title)
Oct 20 Johnny Saxton l pts 15 Philadelphia
(World welterweight title)

1955

Feb 4 Ernie Durando w pts 10 New York
Feb 23 Hector Constance l pts 10 Miami
Mar 16 Bobby Dykes l pts 10 Miami
Jun 2 Luigi Cemulini w ko 3 Santa Clara
Jul 23 Cirilo Gil w pts 10 Buenos Aires
Aug 13 Juan Bautista Burgues w ko 7 Montevideo
Sep 3 Eduardo Lausse l pts 12 Buenos Aires
Dec 3 Dogomar Martinez l pts 10 Montevideo

1956

Feb 7 Peter Waterman l pts 10 London
Mar 29 Germinal Ballarin l pts 10 Paris
Apr 24 Peter Waterman w pts 10 London
May 13 Louis Trochon drew 10 Marseille
Aug 18 Jimmy Beecham w pts 10 Havana
Oct 13 Tony DeMarco l pts 10 Boston
Nov 13 Chico Vejar w pts 10 Los Angeles
Dec 4 Walter Byars l pts 10 Boston
Dec 20 Ramon Fuentes l pts 10 Los Angeles

1957

Feb 26 Vince Martinez l pts 10 Newark
Apr 24 Del Fianagan l pts 10 St Paul
Jun 17 Vince Martinez l pts 10 Jersey City
Jul 31 Gaspar Ortega w pts 10 Miami
Oct 22 Gaspar Ortega l pts 12 Los Angeles
Nov 20 Walter Byars w pts 10 Chicago

1958

Feb 19 Ralph Jones l pts 10 Miami
Apr 4 Ralph Jones w pts 10 Philadelphia
Jun 18 Yama Bahama l pts 10 Miami

Fights 143 Won 107 Lost 30 Drawn 6

ROCKY MARCIANO

THE BROCKTON BLOCKBUSTER

Rocky Marciano hardly had an amateur career as a boxer, and was laughably crude when he began as a professional. But trainer Charlie Goldman instilled enough discipline and purpose into him to allow him to make the most of his strength, determination and powerful punch. The mix was enough to take Marciano to the very top, the only world heavyweight champion to retire with a 100 per cent record, the winner of all his fights. Rocky, who retired over 40 years ago, was the last great white heavyweight champion.

Rocky Marciano's parents had emigrated to the USA independently from Italy, his mother Pasqualena during the First World War, and his father, Pierino Marchegiano, soon afterwards. Pierino had fought in the war and had been involved in a gas attack, the effects of which he suffered for the rest of his life. They met and married in Brockton, Massachusetts and Rocky, or Rocco, to give him his real name, was the first-born of their five children. He arrived on 1 September 1923.

There was a strong Italian community in and around Brockton but times were hard for them. In the American Depression years they suffered more in comparison to the large Irish community, and were treated with suspicion by many. When Rocky was born two young Italian so-called anarchists, Sacco and Vanzetti, were in prison awaiting execution for double murder at a local factory, having been convicted in 1921 for what many thought political considerations. They were finally executed, although palpably innocent, in 1927. The case made a strong impression on Rocky's father, because Nikola Sacco, like himself, was a shoemaker.

Young Rocco Francis Marchegiano nearly failed to survive his second year. He had been given up by the doctor when suffering severely from pneumonia at 19 months. The family were awaiting his death when he was put on the way to recovery by an action of a great aunt, Paolina Mangifesti, who trickled warm water into his mouth from a spoon. She was 90 years old and was following a custom from her young days back in Italy. Rocky, who had taken nothing for days, responded, and slowly began to recover.

Rocky grew into a strong boy, mad on baseball. He dreamed of being a star, and was keen to develop his muscles, in which his Uncle John, Pasqualena's brother, encouraged him. Rocky would say that his general strength came from his mother, who was a big, strong, woman, while his father provided his strength of will. Poor Pierino was little more than a welterweight in boxing terms and struggled hard with his breathing difficulties in the sweatshop of the shoe factory to support his growing family.

Rocky was one of the best baseball players on the Brockton High School and St Patrick's Church teams. After leaving school, he had several jobs, the most satisfactory being in a construction crew, where he could develop his muscles, before he was drafted into the army in 1943. He discovered a liking for boxing, and is alleged to have demonstrated his prowess in a pub fight in Cardiff, near where he was stationed during the war.

A pal of Rocky's from his schooldays, Allie Colombo, also served in the army, where he met a boxer, Dick O'Connor, and he and another of Rocky's uncles, Uncle Mike, began to think of a boxing career for Rocky. A local promoter, who was to become Rocky's first manager when he turned pro, Gene Caggiano, arranged a fight. Rocky was untrained and was tired and losing badly when he kneed his opponent in the groin and was disqualified. Rocky felt utterly humiliated in front of his friends, and made sure from then on that he was always fit for a contest. He also lost badly in the final of a tournament at Portland, after injuring his left thumb in the semi-final.

On discharge from the army, Rocky was digging trenches for the Brockton Gas Company when his pal Allie arranged a pro fight in Holyoke, Massachusetts, on St Patrick's Day, 1947. They called him Rocky Mack to preserve his amateur status. Rocky beat Lee Epperson by a knockout in the third round, through brute force rather than skill. This encounter has now gone into the records as the first professional contest of Rocky's career.

Rocky was much more interested in being a baseball star, however, and he and five of his Brockton baseball pals were granted a month's trial by the Chicago Cubs, but Rocky was rejected after only three weeks. He was a strong batter, but in the field he was slow and, remarkably for a man who was to demonstrate one of the hardest punches ever seen, he had a weak throw. He was unsuccessful in getting on any other team's squad and, back in Brockton, entered the Golden Gloves tournament for amateur boxers. He lost in the semi-finals of the New York tournament, and also failed to get into the US Olympic team for 1948, when the thumb injury sustained during his army days recurred. This injury also cost him his trench-digging job. At 24, Rocky decided that a professional boxing career was his best option.

At his age, and with only 12 amateur bouts, four lost, there seemed hardly any hope of much success. Allie Colombo wrote to New York manager Al Weill asking for a trial for his friend, lying a little about his age and accomplishments. Charlie Goldman, Weill's trainer, had a look and told Rocky: 'If you done anything right, I didn't see it'. Weill declined to manage Rocky, but on Goldman's favourable view of Rocky's punching power, promised to get him fights. On the strength of this, the busy Allie obtained jobs for them both as labourers for Brockton's highways department and Rocky began to train hard.

On 1 July 1948, some 16 months after his previous pro debut, Rocky began again – and impressively – knocking out Harry Bilazarian at Providence, Rhode Island. Rocky built up a string of quick wins. In less than a year he had achieved a record of 16 straight knockout wins, only one getting beyond the third round (the fifth), and nine finishing in the first. Then, in May 1949 Don Mogard took him the 10-round distance. Rocky was by now fit enough to go 10 rounds easily.

He was also extremely popular, guaranteeing the fans some heavy hitting. Weill decided to be his manager after all. He met some opposition from Rocky when he decided 'Marchegiano' was too much of a mouthful for an up-and-coming boxer and suggested cutting out three letters, 'heg', and making it Marciano. Rocky was proud of his name and his family, but finally agreed it was for the best. Weill's contract specified a 50 per cent share of receipts between him and Rocky, Goldman and Allie Colombo being on salaries. It was a to be very profitable deal.

In December 1949, Rocky made his debut at Madison Square Garden, a second round knockout of Pat Richards. However, his second fight there would haunt him for many years. His opponent, another promising American-Italian with a big punch and as popular as Rocky, Carmine Vingo, was knocked out in the sixth round after both men had been down and battered earlier in the contest. Vingo was taken away unconscious and his life was in danger for days. He never fought again. Rocky shared the young family's grief and did what he could to help.

The standard of Rocky's opponents was now improving, and Roland LaStarza, his next, was a clever boxer and hard hitter, unbeaten in 37 contests. He was favourite in the betting, and a favourite at the Garden. After ten brilliant rounds the score cards were 5–5, 5–4–1 and 4–5–1, under normal scoring a draw. But a new supplementary points system was being tried out to break such draws, and it was announced that on this basis, Marciano was the winner. LaStarza's connections were furious.

Rocky continued to win, nearly always by knockout, and was now earning considerably too. By the middle of 1951, when he was approaching 28, he had reached contender class and began meeting boxers with names recognisable to the general public. Because of Rocky's late start, some were much younger than him. For instance Rex Layne was five years younger and had fought one more fight than Rocky when the two met at Madison Square Garden. Rocky won again, by a sixth-round knockout. Rocky went to training camp for this fight, another sign that he was considered a serious fighter. Then, after knocking out the experienced Freddie Beshore, who had recently challenged for the title, Rocky met the great former champion Joe Louis, now 37. Louis, on a comeback trail, was made 8–5 favourite, but Marciano's power was all too much, and the 'Brown Bomber' was knocked out in the eighth round and retired from boxing.

After four more title hopefuls had lasted only 11 rounds between them, Rocky got a shot at the heavyweight title, and stepped into the ring at the Municipal Stadium, Philadelphia, against champion Jersey Joe Walcott. Exactly 26 years earlier in the same stadium, Gene Tunney had surprised the boxing world by taking the title from Jack Dempsey. On that day the boxer beat the slugger. Tunney was present to see if the outcome would be the same. For a long time it seemed as if it would be. Old-stager Walcott, with years of experience behind him, outboxed Rocky from the start and was well ahead on all the scorecards when the 13th round began. Then Marciano caught Walcott with a terrific short right flush on the chin, one of the most famous punches in boxing history, and Walcott sank to the canvas face down as the count was completed. Marciano was the champion of the world.

His terrific right-hand punch, which Marciano often delivered with a slightly 'over-arm' action, he nicknamed his 'Suzy-Q'. Marciano was extraordinary for a modern heavyweight in that he stood only 5ft 10½ in and weighed, for his title-winning fight, 184lb. He had short, stubby arms. Forty-five years later it is inconceivable that a man of his size could win the heavyweight title. Nowadays 6ft 3in and 220lb would be the more likely attributes for an aspiring champ. Marciano had to be tough to achieve what he did.

He was very relaxed and could sleep in the dressing room right up to a big fight, usually after eating a large, rare, steak. He was concerned about his appearance and later would wear a toupee when out in public. He wore one for a filmed 'fight' with Bob Hope for charity, and also for the film of his computer fight with Ali just before he died, which the computer decided he'd won. He was notoriously close with money, and wouldn't spend a dollar on anything luxurious, like cab-fare. He often collected his purse money in cash, and hid it away.

Marciano was a great crowd-puller, and would fight all-comers. Walcott was knocked out in the first round of a return in Chicago, obviously apprehensive of Marciano's power. As Henry Cooper observed, nobody who fought Marciano was ever quite the same man again. Roland LaStarza, his unlucky opponent of over three years earlier, got a title chance at New York's Polo Grounds and put on a great show before being bludgeoned into defeat in the 11th round, when the referee stopped it. LaStarza outboxed Rocky completely, but Rocky, the most gentle man outside the ring, was no respecter of rules inside it, and a lot of poor LaStarza's wounds were caused by Marciano's head and elbows.

Ezzard Charles, a former champion, and himself not much more than a light-heavy, gave Rocky two of his hardest title fights. The first, before nearly 48,000 fans at the Yankee Stadium, went the full 15 rounds, and Rocky got ahead only in the later stages when his heavier punching had slowed down Charles, who had outscored him easily early on. In the return at the same venue, Rocky showed his tremendous courage. Charles, down in the second, split Rocky's nose so badly in the sixth that it gushed blood and a stoppage seemed inevitable. Rocky fought desperately to save his title in the seventh, but another blow split the skin around his left eye. Realising the next round was probably his last, Marciano poured everything into it and finally sank Charles twice – the second time Charles was still on his knees as the count reached 10.

British champion Don Cockell was the next to get the treatment as handed out to LaStarza. In the small ring at the Kazar Stadium, San Francisco, Marciano got away with all the fouls in the book, and after an even opening finally clubbed Cockell to submission in the ninth round. Light-heavyweight champion Ancient Archie Moore, aged 41, was the next to try to show that scientific boxing could overcome the tearaway, and 61,574 fans at the Yankee Stadium nearly saw him succeed, at least according to Archie himself. Moore put Marciano down in the second round, and Marciano foolishly leapt up at two while still groggy. Referee Harry Kessler, no friend of Moore, now incorrectly gave Marciano a helpful standing count of eight while Moore itched to get at him. Rocky recovered, and floored Moore in the sixth, eighth and ninth, the third time for the full count.

Moore had reopened the cuts on Marciano's nose and eye that Charles had inflicted a year earlier and now Marciano announced his retirement. Another factor in his decision might have been that he was convinced that Weill had swindled him of a lot of money, particularly in relation to the Cockell fight. By now Marciano had a wife, Barbara, who did not like him boxing, and he had a daughter, Mary-Anne. Also he liked his food. He vowed never to make a comeback and he never did. He behaved in retirement much as he had when champion: amiable, always willing to help a pal, but not necessarily with money, which he liked to store up in a number of obscure places. He loved to dabble in business ventures, usually with friends, but he was a poor businessman and usually ended up losing his investment. He was on his way to a business appointment in a friend's aeroplane on 31 August 1969, the day before his 46th birthday, when the plane crashed and the three on board died. Just before his death, he and Barbara adopted a baby boy, Rocky Kevin, who was 17 months old when Rocky died. Sadly, much of the fortune he had earned in the ring was never recovered from where he hid it, or from where he had invested or loaned it.

CAREER STATISTICS

World heavyweight champion 1952-56
Brockton, Massachusetts, born 1 September 1923
Full name: Rocco Francis Marchegiani

1947
Mar 17 Lee Epperson w ko 3 Holyoke, Ma.
1948
Jul 12 Harry Bilazarian w rsf 1 Providence
Jul 19 John Edwards w ko 1 Providence
Aug 9 Bobby Quinn w ko 3 Providence
Aug 23 Eddie Ross w ko 1 Providence
Aug 30 Jimmy Weeks w rsf 1 Providence
Sep 13 Jerry Jackson w rsf 1 Providence
Sep 20 Bill Hardeman w ko 1 Providence
Sep 30 Gil Cardione w ko 1 Washington DC
Oct 4 Bob Jefferson w rsf 2 Providence
Nov 29 Pat Connolly w ko 1 Providence
Dec 14 Gilley Ferron w rsf 2 Philadelphia
1949
Mar 21 Johnny Pretzie w rsf 5 Providence
Mar 28 Artie Donato w ko 1 Providence
Apr 11 James Walls w ko 3 Providence
May 2 Jimmy Evans w rsf 3 Providence
May 23 Don Mogard w pts 10 Providence
Jul 18 Harry Haft w ko 3 Providence
Aug 16 Pete Louthis w ko 3 New Bedford
Sep 26 Tommy DiGiorgio w ko 4 Providence
Oct 10 Ted Lowry w pts 10 Providence
Nov 7 Joe Dominic w ko 2 Providence
Dec 2 Pat Richards w rsf 2 New York
Dec 19 Phil Muscato w rsf 5 Providence
Dec 30 Carmine Vingo w ko 6 New York
1950
Mar 24 Roland La Starza w pts 10 New York
Jun 5 Eldridge Eatman w rsf 3 Providence
Jul 10 Gino Buonvino w rsf 10 Boston
Sep 18 Johnny Shkor w ko 6 Providence
Nov 13 Ted Lowry w pts 10 Providence
Dec 18 Bill Wilson w ko 1 Providence
1951
Jan 29 Keene Simmons w rsf 8 Providence
Mar 20 Harold Mitchell w rsf 2 Hartford
Mar 26 Art Henri w rsf 9 Providence
Apr 30 Red Applegate w pts 10 Providence
Jul 12 Rex Layne w ko 6 New York
Aug 27 Freddie Beshore w rsf 4 Boston
Oct 26 Joe Louis w ko 8 New York
1952
Feb 13 Lee Savold w rsf 6 Philadelphia
Apr 21 Gino Buonvino w ko 2 Providence
May 12 Bernie Reynolds w ko 3 Providence
Jul 28 Harry Matthews w ko 2 New York
Sep 23 Jersey Joe Walcott w ko 13 Philadelphia
(World heavyweight title)
1953
May 15 Jersey Joe Walcott w ko 1 Chicago
(World heavyweight title)
Sep 24 Roland La Starza w rsf 11 New York
(World heavyweight title)
1954
Jun 17 Ezzard Charles w pts 15 New York
(World heavyweight title)
Sep 17 Ezzard Charles w ko 8 New York
(World heavyweight title)
1955
May 16 Don Cockell w rsf 9 San Francisco
(World heavyweight title)
Sep 21 Archie Moore w ko 9 New York
(World heavyweight title)

Fights 49 Won 49 KOs 43
Died 31 August 1969, Aged 44

SANDY SADDLER

FEATHER OF DESTRUCTION

Mentally tough, with a wiry frame, long arms and a vicious punch, Sandy Saddler was one of the most ruthless featherweights of all. His great rival Willie Pep was more popular and had dazzling skills, but Saddler hit harder and beat the 'Will o'the Wisp' three times out of four.

It irked Saddler that when they were both introduced in later years, it was Pep who was given star billing. At least those who saw him at his peak almost half a century ago, and those who now see him on film, know just how great he was. He held the featherweight crown twice – interrupted by his only defeat by Pep – and was also recognised as the 130lb champion, although the super-featherweight division was barely recognised then.

He was born Joseph Saddler in Boston, Massachusetts, on 23 June 1926 (although he once insisted it was three years earlier). When he was three years old, his family moved to Harlem, New York, where he grew up, and by his teens he was boxing at the local Police Athletic League gym. The legendary manager Jimmy Johnston spotted him and persuaded his reluctant parents to let him take their son under his wing. Eventually he used the licence of his brother Bill to turn Saddler pro.

Aged 17, he made his professional debut in Hartford, Connecticut, over eight rounds against New England champion Earl Roys. Saddler won on points, and agreed to a return a fortnight later. However, Roys pulled out and a tough prospect named Jock Leslie, whom he had met on the train to Hartford, substituted. Saddler was beaten in three rounds – the only time he was stopped or knocked out in his entire career.

Six days later Saddler, back in action in Holyoke, Massachusetts, knocked out his opponent, Al King, in two rounds, and got down to the job of learning his new craft. He quickly developed into a sensational talent. By the time of his 20th birthday, in June 1946, he was on the brink of world class. Only a couple of decisions had gone against him since the Leslie fight, and he had scored almost 50 wins. Jimmy Johnston died, and Bill Johnston handed the contract on to another brother, Charley, who remained Sandy's manager until his retirement in 1957.

Phil Terranova, a stocky New Yorker, had been recognised as featherweight champion by the National Boxing Association. Although his claims disappeared because of points defeats by Sal Bartolo and Willie Pep, in 1946 he was still a world class operator. When Saddler tried to use Terranova as a stepping stone in Detroit, he was outfought over 10 rounds. Nevertheless, it was priceless experience.

In 1947 he fought two men who would go on to win the lightweight title: Joe Brown and Jimmy Carter. He knocked out Brown in three rounds in New Orleans and drew with Carter in Washington DC.

By the time he was matched with Pep for the undisputed world title in October 1948, he was a 22-year-old veteran of 94 fights, of which he had lost only half a dozen. Pep was a clear pre-fight favourite, but took a pounding from the start. He went down twice in round three and twice more in the fourth for a knockout defeat.

Saddler had gambled on winning, for Pep had demanded a guaranteed fee of $25,000, which left the challenger doing only marginally better than breaking even after expenses. Part of the deal he signed also promised Pep a rematch, an arrangement which he honoured four months later. Again it was at Madison Square Garden, which was packed with almost 20,000 fans, who paid an indoor featherweight record of $87,563.

This time, it was Pep's turn to show what a great fighter he was. For the full 15 rounds he boxed beautifully, defying cuts around both eyes and a terrific right hand from Saddler in round 10, eventually running out a clear winner.

Saddler kept busy with non-title fights, including an appearance at White City Stadium in London in June 1949 as the chief support to the heavyweight fight between Bruce Woodcock and Freddie Mills, which drew a crowd of 46,000. Saddler knocked out Irish lightweight Jim Keery in four rounds, flooring him four times with body punches.

A third fight with Pep was an obvious attraction, but took time to negotiate and plan. As he waited, Saddler stayed busy, fighting anywhere he could get well paid. His best wins were a points decision over Harold Dade, the former world bantamweight champion, and a ninth round stoppage of Paddy De Marco, who would go on to be world lightweight champion.

In December 1949, Saddler also collected the lightly regarded 130lb championship, known in those days as the junior-lightweight title, by outpointing Orlando Zulueta in a 10-rounder in Cleveland. Not even Saddler took much notice of the title, even when he retained it by stopping another future champion Lauro Salas in the ninth round in Cleveland in April 1950.

What he wanted was Pep, and the featherweight title. Finally, Charley Johnston managed to negotiate a settlement and they met in Yankee Stadium, New York, on 8 September 1950. It was an amazing attraction, with 38,781 fans paying to watch one of the biggest fights of the era. The gate was more than a quarter of a million dollars.

For two rounds it looked as if Pep would repeat his brilliant performance of the previous year, but in round three Saddler connected with a left hook and dropped him. Pep kept on the move, boxing superbly but Saddler kept working the body.

Pep boxed well in round seven, but then quit on his stool, claiming his shoulder had been dislocated in a clinch at the end of the session. 'I couldn't raise my arm,' he complained. New York Commission doctor Vincent Nardiello confirmed there was damage to the shoulder and sent Pep to hospital for an X-ray. This showed neither dislocation nor fracture, but did reveal a slight swelling.

A fourth fight was a must, but again this took time to organise. Saddler was in the ring for a non-title fight a month after regaining the title, and kept up a steady schedule from then on. In February 1951 he retained his 130lb belt with a second-round knockout against Diego Sosa in Havana, and altogether had 14 bouts between the third and fourth Pep fights in 10 months. It was hectic and he lost a couple of decisions along the way, including the final fight before he met Pep, which was over 10 rounds against Paddy De Marco in Milwaukee, Wisconsin.

But in September 1951, he and Pep stepped out to take their series a step further at the Polo Grounds. This was a foul-filled brawl almost from the start, with Pep forsaking his boxing ability to maul and wrestle whenever he could; a crazy policy against a man as physically strong as Saddler, although Pep accused the champion of the rougher tactics, claiming he was holding and hitting. Saddler smashed and slashed away until Pep quit again, claiming eye problems, at the end of round nine. Both were hauled before the New York State Athletic Commission and when neither could come up with a satisfactory explanation of their behaviour, both lost their licences.

It was an incredible incident. Saddler was actually reprieved quickly enough to box a non-title 10-rounder with Paddy De Marco, known as the Brooklyn Bull, three months later in the Garden. Before the fight both were warned to fight cleanly, and De Marco went on to win a controversial decision. Saddler and Johnston complained angrily that the champion had been discriminated against in his own city.

Saddler was out of sorts and generally discontented with the business – and it showed. He lost on points to Rhode Island lightweight prospect George Araujo in Boston, and was disqualified against Armand Savoie in a bizarre fight in Montreal. A rough, all-action battle was in its fourth round when, to general astonishment, the local commissioner ordered the fight stopped. It was announced that Saddler, who had already had two points deducted, had been disqualified for fouls.

Saddler seemed to be losing his edge and suspicions that his career was going downhill were increased when he was knocked down by a tough, but relatively unskilled Irish-American, Tommy Collins in Boston. Saddler got up to win in round five, and before much more theorising could be done, he was called up to serve in the US Army in Korea. He was still only 25. He could not pick up the threads of his career until January 1954 when he stopped Bill Bossio of Pittsburgh in nine rounds at St Nick's Arena in New York.

His two-year stint in the army was officially ended in April 1954, by which time Percy Bassett of Philadelphia had been declared 'Interim Champion'. Nobody took that seriously. Once Saddler was back in action, he was regarded as the world titleholder, although Charley Johnston warned it would take time for him to get in top fighting shape. He was given time, and not until February 1955 did he defend the title – his first championship fight for three and a half years. He outpointed Teddy 'Red Top' Davis – who had beaten Bassett – over 15 rounds to retain his title.

The years were wearing him down, however. He defended for the final time against Filipino southpaw Gabriel 'Flash' Elorde in San Francisco in January 1956. Elorde had previously outpointed him in a non-title bout in Manila, but Saddler was still good enough when it mattered and slammed away for a 13th round stoppage victory.

Three months later he lost a decision to Larry Boardman in Boston, and in July 1956 he was in a taxi in New York when it crashed. He received a serious eye injury when his head hit the door of the cab. After six months of hoping for a miracle he was forced to announce his retirement on 21 January 1957. Doctors had warned him that if he boxed again, he could go blind. 'I love to fight,' he said, sadly. 'It's the only thing I know.'

He became a trainer of amateurs at the National Maritime Union gym in New York before health worries prompted him to give that up. In the 1990s he lived quietly with his family, one of boxing's respected but rarely sought out elder statesmen.

CAREER STATISTICS

World featherweight champion 1948-49, 1950-56
Boston, Massachusetts, born 23 June 1926

1944
Mar 7 Earl Roys w pts 8 Hartford
Mar 21 Jock Leslie l ko 3 Hartford
Mar 27 Al King w ko 2 Holyoke
Apr 17 Joe Landry w ko 1 Holyoke
May 8 Jose Aponte Torres w pts 6 Trenton
May 15 Jose Aponte Torres w pts 6 Holyoke
May 23 Domingo Diaz w pts 6 Jersey City
Jun 13 Jose Aponte Torres w pts 8 Union City
Jun 15 Lou Alter l pts 6 Hamilton
Jun 23 Lou Alter drew 4 New York
Jul 11 Clyde English w pts 6 Dexter
Jul 18 Benny Saladino w ko 3 Brooklyn
Jul 25 Al Pennino w pts 6 Brooklyn
Aug 8 Georgie Knox w ko 3 Brooklyn
Aug 18 Clifford Smith w pts 6 New York
Nov 11 Manuel Torres w pts 6 Brooklyn
Nov 13 Ken Tompkins w ko 1 Newark
Nov 24 Manuel Torres w ko 5 New York
Nov 28 Percy Lewis w ko 1 Jersey City
Dec 12 Tony Oshiro w ko 2 Jersey City
Dec 16 Earl Mintz w ko 2 Brooklyn
Dec 26 Midget Mayo w ko 3 Newark

1945
Jan 13 Tony Oshiro w pts 6 Brooklyn
Jan 15 Mickey Johnson w ko 1 Newark
Jan 22 Joey Puig w ko 1 New York
Jan 26 Benny May w pts 6 New Brunswick
Feb 19 Joey Gatto w ko 1 New York
Mar 10 Harold Gibson w pts 8 Brooklyn
Mar 19 Joe Montiero w ko 4 New York
Mar 22 Georgie Knox w ko 4 Camden
Apr 2 Jimmy Allen w ko 1 Newark
Apr 19 Willie Anderson w ko 5 Detroit
Apr 30 Chilindrina Valencia w ko 9 Detroit
Jun 18 Caswell Harris w ko 3 Baltimore
Jun 25 Bobby Washington w ko 2 Allentown
Jun 29 Leo Methot w ko 1 New York
Jul 23 Herbert Jones w ko 3 Baltimore
Jul 24 Joe Montiero w ko 5 Brooklyn
Jul 30 Luis Rivera w ko 4 New York
Aug 16 Louis Langley w ko 1 Brooklyn
Aug 20 Bobby English w ko 3 Providence
Aug 27 Earl Mintz w ko 1 Providence
Sep 21 Richie Myashiro w pts 6 New York
Dec 3 Benny Daniels w pts 6 Holyoke
Dec 14 Joe Montiero w pts 8 Boston
Dec 21 Filberto Osario w pts 6 New York

1946
Jan 17 Sam Zelman w ko 1 Orange, NJ
Feb 18 Bobby McQuillar l pts 10 Detroit
Apr 8 Ralph La Salle w ko 1 New York
Apr 11 Johnny Wolgast w pts 8 Atlantic City
Apr 25 Pedro Firpo w pts 8 Atlantic City
Jun 13 Cedric Flournoy w ko 4 Detroit
Jul 10 George Cooper w ko 7 Brooklyn
Jul 23 Phil Terranova l pts 10 Detroit
Aug 5 Dom Ameroso w ko 2 Providence
Aug 22 Pedro Firpo w pts 10 Brooklyn
Oct 10 Jose Rodriguez w ko 3 Atlantic City
Nov 12 Art Price w pts 10 Detroit
Dec 9 Clyde English w ko 3 Holyoke
Dec 26 Luis Marquez w ko 2 Jamaica
Dec 30 Leonard Caesar w ko 2 Newark

1947
Jan 20 George Brown w ko 4 Holyoke
Jan 27 Humberto Zavala w ko 7 New York
Feb 7 Larry Thomas w ko 2 Asbury Park
Mar 8 Leonardo Lopez w ko 2 Mexico City
Mar 29 Carlos Malacara w pts 10 Mexico City
Apr 14 Charley Lewis w pts 10 New York
May 2 Joe Brown w ko 3 New Orleans
May 9 Melvin Bartholomew w pts 10 New Orleans
Jun 3 Jimmy Carter drew 10 Washington DC
Jul 26 Oscar Calles w ko 5 Caracas
Aug 14 Leslie Harris w ko 5 Atlantic City
Aug 29 Miguel Acevedo w ko 8 New York
Sep 17 Angelo Ambrosano w ko 2 Jamaica
Oct 3 Humberto Sierra l pts 10 Minneapolis
Oct 13 Al Pennino w ko 4 New York
Oct 26 Lino Garcia w ko 5 Caracas
Nov 9 Emilio Sanchez w ko 5 Caracas
Dec 5 Lino Garcia w ko 3 Havana
Dec 13 Orlando Zulueta w pts 10 Havana

1948
Feb 2 Charley Noel w pts 10 Holyoke
Feb 9 Joey Angelo w pts 10 New York
Mar 5 Archie Wilmer w pts 8 New York
Mar 8 Thompson Harmon w rsf 8 New York
Mar 23 Bobby Thompson w pts 10 Hartford
Apr 10 Luis Monagas w ko 3 Caracas
Apr 17 Jose Diaz w ko 8 Caracas
Apr 26 Young Tanner w ko 5 Aruba

May 24 Harry LaSane w pts 10 Holyoke
Jun 29 Chico Rosa l pts 10 Honolulu
Aug 16 Kid Zefine w ko 2 Panama City
Aug 23 Aguilino Allen w ko 2 Panama City
Oct 11 Willie Roache w rsf 3 New Haven
Oct 29 Willie Pep w ko 4 New York
(World featherweight title)
Nov 19 Tomas Beato w ko 2 Bridgeport
Nov 29 Dennis Brady w pts 10 Boston
Dec 7 Eddie Giosa w ko 2 Cleveland
Dec 17 Terry Young w ko 10 New York

1949

Jan 17 Young Flanagan w ko 5 Panama City
Feb 11 Willie Pep l pts 15 New York
(World featherweight title)
Mar 21 Felix Ramirez w pts 10 Newark
Apr 18 Ermano Bonetti w ko 2 Philadelphia
Jun 2 Jim Keery w ko 4 London
Jun 23 Luis Ramos w ko 5 New York
Jul 15 Gordon House w rsf 5 New York
Aug 2 Chuck Burton w ko 5 Pittsfield
Aug 8 Johnny Rowe w ko 8 Brooklyn
Aug 24 Alfredo Escobar w ko 9 Los Angeles
Sep 2 Harold Dade w pts 10 Chicago
Sep 20 Proctor Heinold w ko 2 Schenectady
Oct 28 Paddy De Marco w rsf 9 New York
Nov 7 Leroy Willis w pts 10 Toledo
Dec 6 Orlando Zulueta w pts 10 Cleveland
(World junior-lightweight title)

1950

Jan 16 Paulie Jackson w ko 1 Caracas
Jan 22 Pedro Firpo w ko 1 Caracas
Feb 6 Chuck Burton w ko 1 Holyoke
Feb 20 Luis Ramos w rsf 3 Toronto
Apr 10 Reuben Davis w rsf 7 Newark
Apr 18 Lauro Salas w rsf 9 Cleveland
(World junior-lightweight title)
Apr 29 Jesse Underwood w pts 10 Waterbury
May 25 Miguel Acevedo w rsf 6 Minneapolis
Jun 19 Johnny Forte w ko 3 Toronto
Jun 30 Leroy Willis w rsf 2 Long Beach
Sep 8 Willie Pep w rtd 7 New York
(World featherweight title)
Oct 12 Harry LaSane w pts 10 St Louis
Nov 1 Charley Riley w pts 10 St Louis
Dec 6 Del Flanagan l pts 10 Detroit

1951

Jan 23 Jesse Underwood w pts 10 Buffalo
Feb 28 Diego Sosa w ko 2 Havana
(World junior-lightweight title)
Mar 27 Lauro Salas w rsf 6 Los Angeles
Apr 3 Freddie Herman w rsf 5 Los Angeles
May 5 Harry LaSane w pts 10 Hershey, Pa.
Jun 2 Alfredo Prada w ko 4 Buenos Aires
Jun 16 Oscar Flores w ko 1 Buenos Aires
Jun 22 Mario Salinas w ko 5 Santiago
Jun 30 Angel Olivieri w ko 5 Buenos Aires
Aug 20 Hermie Freeman w rsf 5 Philadelphia
Aug 27 Paddy De Marco l pts 10 Milwaukee
Sep 26 Willie Pep w rtd 8 New York
(World featherweight title)
Dec 7 Paddy De Marco l pts 10 New York

1952

Jan 14 George Araujo l pts 10 Boston
Mar 3 Armand Savoie l dis 4 Montreal
Mar 17 Tommy Collins w rsf 5 Boston

1953 Inactive

1954

Jan 15 Bill Bossio w rsf 9 New York
Mar 4 Charlie Slaughter w rsf 4 Akron
Apr 1 Augie Salazar w rsf 7 Boston
May 17 Hoacine Khalfi l pts 10 New York
Jul 5 Libby Manzo w ko 10 New York
Aug 30 Jackie Blair w rsf 1 Caracas
Sep 27 Baby Ortiz w rsf 3 Caracas
Oct 25 Ray Famechon w rsf 6 Paris
Dec 10 Bobby Woods w pts 10 Spokane

1955

Jan 17 Lulu Perez w ko 4 Boston
Feb 25 Teddy Davis w pts 15 New York
(World featherweight title)
Apr 5 Kenny Davis w rsf 5 Butte
May 24 Joe Lopes l pts 10 Sacramento
Jul 8 Shigeji Kaneko w rsf 6 Tokyo
Jul 20 Flash Elorde l pts 10 Manila
Dec 12 Dave Gallardo w rsf 7 San Francisco

1956

Jan 18 Flash Elorde w rsf 13 San Francisco
(World featherweight title)
Feb 13 Curley Monroe w rsf 3 Providence
Apr 14 Larry Boardman l pts 10 Boston

Fights 162 Won 144 Lost 16 Drawn 2

SUGAR RAY ROBINSON

THE ORIGINAL SUGAR RAY

During his career Ray Robinson, who had the 'Sugar' added to his name because he was said to box 'as sweet as sugar', was often described as the best pound-for-pound boxer the world has ever seen. Since then only Muhammad Ali has emerged to put in a challenge to Robinson for this description. Sugar Ray had 202 contests over more than 25 years. Only heat exhaustion when facing a world champion from a heavier division caused him to fail to finish a contest. He was undefeated as the world welterweight champion, and won the world middleweight title a record five times. He dropped some decisions in the twilight of his career, but only one man, Jake LaMotta, was to beat him in his first 132 contests, and Robinson beat LaMotta five times. Robinson had everything: skill, speed, courage and punch, and at the end of his long career the dancing master was as handsome and unmarked as the day he started.

Robinson's real name was Walker Smith, his father's name, and he was born on 3 May 1921 in a part of Detroit known as Black Bottom. It was a poor area. His parents had moved from Georgia, where 'Pop' Smith picked cotton, to Detroit, where he worked as a labourer on construction jobs, mixing cement, etc. Young Walker weighed in at 7lb 12 oz, but on the day he was born Pop decided that he would have to be called 'Junior', so Junior it was, to everybody. Junior's two older sisters, Marie and Evelyn, had been born before the move to Detroit. When Junior was five, continued arguments among his parents about drink, and Pop's expenditure on it in particular, caused his mother, Leila, to take the children back to Georgia for a year. She returned to Black Bottom only to obtain a divorce.

Back in Detroit, Junior would go to the Brewster Center, where youngsters could meet and play sports, and it was there he got his interest in boxing. An older local boy, Joe Louis Barrow, who was at school with Marie, was already an amateur boxer with a big reputation, and Junior idolised him, even to the extent of carrying his bag for him. Barrow, of course, under the name Joe Louis, would become famous as heavyweight champion of the world. Junior began practising the boxing moves himself. When

Junior was 11 the family moved to New York and Junior, with his sister Evelyn, took tap-dancing lessons, which were to teach him how to move, and would become useful in his later boxing career. Two years later, when the family moved to Harlem, a school friend of Junior was the nephew of George Gainford, who ran the Salem-Crescent Athletic Club in the basement of a church. Junior was taken along and introduced to Gainford. Gainford was also involved in 'bootleg' boxing shows, where so-called amateurs boxed for a little cash.

Junior, whose best boxing talent was his footwork, which helped him avoid punches, began an amateur career by accident. He volunteered to stand in when a promotion was short of a flyweight. Gainford agreed, and provided him with the necessary Amateur Athletic Union identity card. It belonged to a bootleg boxer two years older than Junior, who had packed in the sport to become a bartender. His name was Ray Robinson. Junior boxed, won, and sold his prize, a gold watch, back to the promoter for $10, no doubt for use again. This is how the bootleg shows worked, and over the next few months Junior earned himself a tidy few dollars. When Ray Robinson's licence expired, Junior renewed it, and thus acquired a boxing name.

Robinson proved a very proficient boxer and when 18 he won the National Golden Gloves championship at featherweight. The following year he won the title at lightweight and was already famous. He was also a husband and father. He had made a high-school friend, Marjie, pregnant. The families got together and agreed the two should be married, but wouldn't live together. So they did, and eventually son Ronnie was born. Soon afterwards the marriage was quietly annulled. Robinson had also acquired an extension to his name. He got very excited when he scored his first knockout, especially as his opponent was previously unbeaten. The sports editor of the local paper in Waterton, New York, told Gainford that he had a sweet fighter in that Robinson. A lady at ringside said: 'As sweet as sugar'. Next day the editor, Jack Case, referred in his report to 'Sugar Ray Robinson', and the name caught on.

Sugar Ray decided it was time to turn pro and make sure his mother had a house of her own, when she had to move house again, for non-payment of rent. He and George Gainford and a millionaire brewer, Curt 'Pop' Horrmann, who had come to take an interest in Robinson's boxing and occasionally slipped him a $20 bill, made the arrangements. Horrmann was to be manager, on 33 per cent of income. Gainford was trainer, on 10 per cent. So in the summer of 1940 Robinson, aged 19, with a sweet amateur career of 85 bouts, all wins, including 69 knockouts, 40 in the first round, made the smooth transition to the pro ranks.

Success came fast for Sugar Ray. He made his debut at Madison Square Garden, a second round knockout of Joe Echevarria. After eight contests, Sugar Ray fought George Zengaras as main support bout when his friend Joe Louis defended his heavyweight title against Red Burman. Robinson went to training camp with Louis, and Jack Blackburn, Louis's trainer, got Robinson to build up his arm muscles with rowing.

Before he had been a pro a year, Robinson outpointed NBA lightweight champion Sammy Angott in a non-title contest over ten rounds, which earned him his biggest purse to date, enough for him to start making his mother's life more comfortable.

One of his bigger earlier successes was when he outpointed future middleweight champion Jake LaMotta, a man he was to meet six times in all. Robinson was already a serious contender for the welterweight crown, with 40 straight victories to his credit. He was an intelligent man who had resisted the attempts of the Mob to get him to fix results, and he also realised he knew more about the fight game than his manager Curt Horrmann, who was taking 33 per cent of his earnings, so he bought Horrmann out of his contract and decided to manage himself, with the assistance of Gainford, who would be the manager off record.

Sugar Ray's first contest in 1943, a return with LaMotta, brought a surprise defeat. Unfortunately for Sugar Ray, the fight was in his home town of Detroit, before 18,930 fans, many of them his old pals from Black Bottom. In the build-up around town he over-played the conquering hero role, especially, he thought, with various old girl-friends, and overlooked the fact that LaMotta was a tough, capable fighter. Two punches from the Bronx Bull dumped Sugar Ray on the ring apron in the eighth round, and made sure he took the decision. Sugar Ray just had time to reverse the decision three weeks later in Detroit before he was inducted into the army.

Robinson's army service lasted little more than a year before he was honourably discharged. A fall on his head which caused a spell of amnesia was the cause. He had teamed up with his pal Joe Louis again, giving boxing exhibitions to the troops. He also got married again, to Edna Mae Holly, a beautiful nightclub entertainer.

His brief war service hardly interrupted Robinson's boxing career. Mike Jacobs, the Madison Square promoter, and the most powerful man in boxing in view of his control of the heavyweight championship through his contract with Joe Louis, fixed up lucrative bouts for Sugar Ray, including two more in 1945 with Jake LaMotta, both won on points to make the score 4–1 in Robinson's favour. In 1946 Sugar Ray was scheduled to challenge Marty Servo for the world welterweight championship but Servo was forced to retire after middleweight Rocky Graziano broke his nose in a warm-up fight, and Sugar Ray instead met Tommy Bell for the vacant crown. He'd beaten Bell before, and comfortably did so again for the title. He celebrated in style four days later when his café, Sugar Ray's, opened on Seventh Avenue. Sugar Ray did not believe in leaving earnings idle in the bank. He was still only 25.

Sugar Ray had a terrible experience on the first defence of his title. He dreamt beforehand that his opponent, Jimmy Doyle, had died after being knocked out. So vivid an impression did this dream make that he did his best to get the fight cancelled, but of course without success. Doyle was indeed knocked down in the eighth round, cracking his head on the boards. He didn't recover consciousness and died next day in hospital.

There were no welterweights around, not even Kid Gavilan – whom Sugar Ray outpointed in 1948 and again in 1949 in a title bout – who could seriously threaten his championship. Sugar Ray continued to pile up the wins, and also to live the life of the prosperous business-man. There was his office, Ray Robinson Enterprises, to run, and there were his businesses: the café, the cleaning business, the lingerie shop in Edna Mae's name and the barber shop in George Gainford's. There were the suits, the golf, the Cadillac, which he had had painted 'flamingo pink', and the famous entourage who travelled with him wherever he went, including a tour of Europe: wife, sister Evelyn, trainer, friend, secretary, barber-cum-valet and a court jester, a man who became attached to the entourage after amusing him in Paris. In November 1949 he also acquired a son, Ray Junior.

Sugar Ray, who made five successful defences of his welterweight championship, was now looking to the middleweight division to further his boxing ambitions. By outpointing a Frenchman, Robert Villemain, who had beaten the new middleweight champion, Jake LaMotta, Robinson was recognised by the Pennsylvania Boxing Commission as the world champion. Nobody else took any notice, but Robinson happily defended this 'title' until he could be ignored no more and was given a shot at Jake LaMotta's otherwise undisputed title. Robinson had to wait because he refused to deal with the Mob, controlling boxing at the time through the International Boxing Club. In fact gangster Frankie Carbo tried to fix a deal with Robinson, which involved Sugar Ray losing to LaMotta, winning a return and then fighting for the title in earnest after the Mob had cashed in with betting on the crooked fights.

Having already established superiority over LaMotta, it was no surprise that Sugar Ray stopped him in the 13th round of a bloody battle which inevitably, because it was on 14 February in Chicago, was called the St Valentine's Day Massacre, after the notorious Al Capone-inspired shootout of 1929.

As the new middleweight champion, with only one defeat in 124 contests, Sugar Ray enlarged his entourage for another trip to Europe, during which he took his number of contests to 132, although there was one hiccup when he was disqualified for kidney-punching in Berlin, but the result was quickly altered to 'no contest'.

Robinson's tour ended in London with a challenge for his title from Randolph Turpin. To everybody's amazement, Turpin thoroughly outpointed Robinson, who lost his title on his first defence. But 64 days later at the Polo Grounds, New York, Sugar Ray won it back again when, with his eye split and the fight seemingly headed for a stoppage, he produced an attack of such fierce, fast punching that the referee stepped in to rescue Turpin with eight seconds of the tenth round remaining. 'It was do or die,' said Robinson.

After that Sugar Ray beat his next two challengers, Carl 'Bobo' Olson on points, and former champion Rocky Graziano by knockout. Then, trying to make quick money before retiring, he challenged Joey Maxim for the light-heavyweight title. At the weigh-in Maxim outweighed Robinson by 15½lb. The temperature in the Yankee

Stadium was the hottest for 25 June in New York history, probably over 100 degrees F during the fight.

Sugar Ray, naturally the faster, was outpointing Maxim comfortably when the heat got to him. From the ninth on he lost knowledge of what was happening. In the 13th he missed Maxim with a punch and collapsed on the canvas. He got up, but was taking punches on the ropes at the bell. He had to be helped to his corner and could not come out for the 14th. He lost 16lb during the fight. It was his third defeat and, six months later, without boxing again, he announced his retirement.

Sugar Ray returned to his tap-dancing studies and, through an impresario friend, began getting lucrative engagements in New York and Las Vegas, dancing, telling jokes, being MC, even doing some of his old training regime with a skipping rope. But his businesses started to decline and after two-and-a-half years out of the ring he returned to make some money. He was nearly 34. On his second comeback fight he lost clumsily. Boxing opinion was that he should give up. Only gradually did the old timing return. In December 1955, at Chicago, he challenged new champion Carl 'Bobo' Olson for his old world middleweight title and won it back by knocking out Olson in the second round. Robinson was now under contract to the gangster-influenced, monopolistic IBC, so matches came easily, and a return contest with Olson five months later in Los Angeles also ended quickly, Robinson winning by a fourth-round knockout.

But there were more calls to Robinson to retire when on his next defence he couldn't cope with the pace and ferocity of Gene Fullmer's attacks and was well outpointed. However, four months later, in the return bout two days before Robinson's 36th birthday, he knocked out Fullmer, a man who had never been down before, with one punch. Sugar Ray had identified a weakness in Fullmer's defence, and when the opening arrived in the fifth round, a perfectly timed left hook knocked out Fullmer with such finality that when he recovered he didn't even realise the fight was over.

Robinson then accepted a challenge from welterweight champion Carmen Basilio. The fight turned out to be 15 rounds of vicious cut-and-thrust before 38,072 fans in the Yankee Stadium, New York. Basilio was 4½ inches shorter and 7 lb lighter, but he was seven years younger than Robinson, and as tough as they come. At the end of what Robinson thought was his toughest fight, it was a split decision, with Basilio getting it by two to one.

There had to be a return, and it was held at the Chicago Stadium. Robinson was found to have a high temperature at the weigh-in, and it was only because the Commission doctor was co-operative that he was allowed to fight at all. At the end it was another split decision, but referee Frank Sikora, who gave it to Basilio, was booed. Most fans agreed with the two judges who made Robinson a clear winner.

Sugar Ray had now won the world middleweight championship for the fifth time. He thus set a record unprecedented in any division. The fact that he won it five times is not itself a measure of his greatness, because he could not achieve this without having lost it three times as well (once he relinquished it). The way he swapped the title with Fullmer and Basilio argued, on the contrary, that he had declined. But it was a stupendous feat that, in his 37th year and with 150 bouts behind him, he was still able to beat the best middleweights in the world in gruelling 15-round contests. It was proof that as a boxer Robinson had no weaknesses. He could cope with any style of opponent; he had the skill to inflict his own will, he had supreme footwork, as his show-business dancing career confirmed, he had a tremendous punch, as his dispatch of 109 opponents inside the distance testified, he could take a punch himself, and he possessed the aggression, heart and instinct of a boxer, as proved by his comeback against Turpin to snatch victory from the brink of defeat.

Robinson now lost his claim to be undisputed champion as the NBA stripped him for not granting a third match with Basilio. There was little love lost between the two men in their fighting days. Sugar Ray fought only once in 1959, and next defended his title, still recognised in New York and Europe, against Paul Pender, an underrated fighter from Boston. Pender suffered problems throughout his career with his hands, and was not in love with boxing, but he found the way to beat the 38-year-old Robinson. He flicked his left jab and danced away from any meaningful encounters. For once Sugar Ray's legs didn't allow him to catch up with Pender. The referee gave it to Robinson 8–4–3, but the two judges gave it to Pender. The fight was in Pender's home town of Boston. Gainford was outraged, but he and Sugar Ray accepted Pender had got a 'home-town' decision, and awaited the return. Unfortunately they had to accept this was also to be in Boston. The fight was a repeat of the first, and so was the verdict. Once more the referee thought Robinson had done enough, but the two judges voted for Pender. Robinson was 39. This was the first time he had lost twice to the same man.

At this point, as with others which were to follow, perhaps Robinson should have retired. His older sister, Marie, died. Robinson had another preoccupation; he was developing a friendship with another woman, Millie Bruce, and he split with his wife, Edna Mae. Their relationship over the years had not always been the most cordial. Also, Robinson was having trouble with unpaid back taxes, and with his businesses failing he felt obliged to carry on. There would also now be alimony to pay to Edna Mae, and support for Ray junior.

Another reason to continue was that later in 1960 he got a shot at the other half of the world title, the NBA crown, held by his old adversary Gene Fullmer. The fight was at the Sports Arena at Los Angeles, Millie Bruce's home town. Sugar Ray fought well, and thought he'd won. The referee thought so, too, by the enormous margin of 11–4. One judge scored 9–5 for Fullmer, and the other scored it a draw. This made the verdict a draw, and Fullmer kept his crown. This was a big disappointment to Robinson. He was given a return in March 1961, as his 40th birthday approached, but was well outpointed. The Las Vegas Convention Center ring was only 17 feet square, instead of 20, a difference of over 100 square feet, making it much more suitable for the younger man's bustling in-your-face style then Robinson's classical boxing. It was the last of Sugar Ray's 25 world title fights (including the California-recognised ones), and again it was an obvious point to retire.

Unfortunately, although still comfortably off if not extremely wealthy (the pink Cadillac, the entourage, had gone; the businesses either sold or soon would be) Sugar Ray still felt obliged to earn a little more, and in fact he continued boxing for nearly five more years, and 45 more contests, 10 of which he lost. The most recognisable names among these opponents were former world champion Terry Downes, who outpointed him in London on one of Sugar Ray's trips to Europe, and future champion Joey Giardello, who outpointed him in Philadelphia. His final contest was with contender Joey Archer, who beat him in Pittsburgh in 1965. He was more than halfway through his 45th year. In the last six months of his career he had 10 contests, losing five.

He was given a splendid retirement ceremony in December 1965, when he entered the Madison Square Garden ring in his boxing gear and gown, still looking as handsome and sprightly as in his younger days. He was supported by Basilio, Olson, Fullmer and Turpin, similarly attired. Jake LaMotta was there but the New York Commission denied him access to the ring on account of an old misdemeanour.

In retirement, Robinson was able to cash in a bit on his popularity, of course, and initially he got plenty of show business work, including an occasional acting part, such as in the well-known *Run for Your Life* (*The Fugitive*) TV serial with Ben Gazzara. He married Millie Bruce, and in 1969 they went to live in Los Angeles, where Sugar Ray gave his name to the Sugar Ray Robinson Youth Foundation, where youngsters are encouraged in sports and the arts. In the 1980s he began to suffer from Alzheimer's disease, and gradually lost the ability to recognise friends or remember his own glorious career. He said on retirement that he had no regrets, not even for the bad and the hurting times. His first inspiration, Joe Louis, called him: 'The greatest fighter ever to step in the ring'. Another great heavyweight, Muhammad Ali, who sought his advice and absorbed some of his skills, said: 'He was the greatest boxer of all time'. Sugar Ray died in his Los Angeles home on 12 April 1989, approaching 68. Nearly 10 years later he still commands the 'best pound-for-pound ever' tag.

CAREER STATISTICS

World welterweight champion 1946-51
World middleweight champion five times between 1951 and 1960
New York, born Detroit 3 May 1921
Full name: Walker Smith, Jnr.

1940
Oct 4 Joe Echevarria w rsf 2 New York
Oct 8 Silent Stafford w ko 2 Savannah, Ga.
Oct 22 Mistos Grispos w pts 6 Bronx
Nov 11 Bobby Woods w ko 1 Philadelphia
Dec 9 Norment Quarles w rsf 4 Philadelphia
Dec 13 Oliver White w rsf 3 New York
1941
Jan 4 Henry LaBarba w rsf 1 Brooklyn
Jan 13 Frankie Wallace w ko 1 Philadelphia
Jan 31 George Zengaras w pts 6 New York
Feb 8 Benny Cartagena w rsf 1 Brooklyn
Feb 21 Bobby McIntyre w pts 6 New York
Feb 27 Gene Spencer w rsf 5 Detroit
Mar 3 Jimmy Tygh w ko 8 Philadelphia
Apr 14 Jimmy Tygh w rsf 1 Philadelphia
Apr 24 Charley Burns w ko 1 Atlantic City
Apr 30 Joe Ghnouly w rsf 3 Washington DC
May 10 Vic Troise w rsf 1 Brooklyn
May 19 Nick Castiglione w ko 1 Philadelphia
Jun 16 Mike Evans w ko 2 Philadelphia
Jul 2 Pete Lello w rsf 4 New York
Jul 21 Sammy Angott w pts 10 Philadelphia
Aug 27 Carl Guggino w rsf 3 Long Island City
Aug 29 Maurice Arnault w ko 1 Atlantic City
Sep 19 Maxie Shapiro w rsf 3 New York
Sep 25 Marty Servo w pts 10 Philadelphia
Oct 31 Fritzie Zivic w pts 10 New York
1942
Jan 16 Fritzie Zivic w rsf 10 New York
Feb 20 Maxie Berger w rsf 2 New York
Mar 20 Norman Rubio w rsf 8 New York
Apr 17 Harvey Duba w rsf 6 Detroit
Apr 30 Dick Banner w ko 2 Minneapolis
May 28 Marty Servo w pts 10 New York
Jul 31 Sammy Angott w pts 10 New York
Aug 21 Ruben Shank w ko 2 New York
Aug 27 Tony Motisi w ko 1 Chicago
Oct 2 Jake La Motta w pts 10 New York
Oct 19 Izzy Jannazzo w pts 10 Philadelphia
Nov 6 Vic Dellicurti w pts 10 New York
Dec 1 Izzy Jannazzo w rsf 8 Cleveland
Dec 14 Al Nettlow w rsf 3 Philadelphia
1943
Feb 5 Jake La Motta l pts 10 Detroit
Feb 19 Jackie Wilson w pts 10 New York
Feb 26 Jake La Motta w pts 10 Detroit
Apr 30 Freddie Cabral w ko 1 Boston
Jul 1 Ralph Zannelli w pts 10 Boston
Aug 27 Henry Armstrong w pts 10 New York
1944
Oct 13 Izzy Jannazzo w rsf 2 Boston
Oct 27 Lou Woods w rsf 9 Chicago
Nov 17 Vic Dellicurti w pts 10 Detroit
Dec 12 Sheik Rangel w rsf 2 Philadelphia
Dec 22 Georgie Martin w rsf 7 Boston
1945
Jan 10 Billy Furrone w rsf 2 Washington DC
Jan 16 Tommy Bell w pts 10 Cleveland
Feb 14 George Costner w ko 1 Chicago
Feb 24 Jake La Motta w pts 10 New York
May 14 Jose Basora drew 10 Philadelphia
Jun 15 Jimmy McDaniels w ko 2 New York
Sep 18 Jimmy Mandell w rsf 5 Buffalo
Sep 26 Jake La Motta w pts 12 Chicago
Dec 4 Vic Dellicurti w pts 10 Boston
1946
Jan 14 Dave Clark w rsf 2 Pittsburgh
Feb 5 Tony Riccio w rsf 4 Elizabeth
Feb 15 O'Neill Bell w ko 2 Detroit
Feb 26 Cliff Beckett w ko 4 St Louis
Mar 4 Sammy Angott w pts 10 Pittsburgh
Mar 14 Izzy Jannazzo w pts 10 Baltimore
Mar 21 Freddy Flores w ko 5 New York
Jun 12 Freddy Wilson w ko 2 Worcester
Jun 25 Norman Rubio w pts 10 Union City
Jul 12 Joe Curcio w ko 1 New York
Aug 15 Vinnie Vines w ko 6 Albany
Sep 25 Sidney Miller w ko 3 Elizabeth
Oct 7 Ossie Harris w pts 10 Pittsburgh
Nov 1 Cecil Hudson w ko 6 Detroit
Nov 6 Artie Levine w ko 10 Cleveland
Dec 20 Tommy Bell w pts 15 New York
(World welterweight title)
1947
Mar 27 Bernie Miller w rsf 3 Miami
Apr 3 Fred Wilson w ko 3 Akron
Apr 8 Eddie Finazzo w rsf 4 Kansas City
May 16 Georgie Abrams w pts 10 New York
Jun 24 Jimmy Doyle w rsf 8 Cleveland
(World welterweight title)
Aug 21 Sammy Secreet w ko 1 Akron

Aug 29 Flashy Sebastian w ko 1 New York
Oct 28 Jackie Wilson w rsf 7 Los Angeles
Dec 10 Billy Nixon w rsf 6 Elizabeth
Dec 19 Chuck Taylor w rsf 6 Detroit
(World welterweight title)

1948

Mar 4 Ossie Harris w pts 10 Toledo
Mar 16 Henry Brimm w pts 10 Buffalo
Jun 28 Bernard Docusen w pts 15 Chicago
(World welterweight title)
Sep 23 Kid Gavilan w pts 10 New York
Nov 15 Bobby Lee w pts 10 Philadelphia

1949

Feb 10 Gene Buffalo w ko 1 Wilkes-Barre
Feb 15 Henry Brimm drew 10 Buffalo
Mar 25 Bobby Lee w pts 10 Chicago
Apr 11 Don Lee w pts 10 Omaha
Apr 20 Earl Turner w rsf 8 Oakland
Jun 7 Freddie Flores w rsf 3 New Bedford
Jun 20 Cecil Hudson w rsf 5 Providence
Jul 11 Kid Gavilan w pts 15 Philadelphia
(World welterweight title)
Aug 24 Steve Belloise w ko 7 New York
Sep 9 Benny Evans w rsf 5 Omaha
Sep 12 Charley Dotson w ko 3 Houston
Nov 9 Don Lee w pts 10 Denver
Nov 13 Vern Lester w ko 5 New Orleans

1950

Jan 30 George La Rover w rsf 4 New Haven
Feb 13 Al Mobley w rsf 6 Miami
Feb 22 Aaron Wade w ko 3 Savannah
Feb 27 Jean Walzack w pts 10 St Louis
Mar 22 George Costner w ko 1 Philadelphia
Apr 21 Cliff Beckett w rsf 3 Columbus
Apr 28 Ray Barnes w pts 10 Detroit
Jun 5 Robert Villemain w pts 15 Philadelphia
Aug 9 Charley Fusari w pts 15 Jersey City
(World welterweight title)
Aug 25 Jose Basora w ko 1 Scranton
Sep 4 Billy Brown w pts 10 New York
Oct 16 Joe Rindone w ko 6 Boston
Oct 26 Carl Olson w ko 12 Philadelphia
Nov 8 Bobby Dykes w pts 10 Chicago
Nov 27 Jean Stock w rsf 2 Paris
Dec 9 Luc Van Dam w ko 4 Brussels
Dec 16 Jean Walzack w pts 10 Geneva
Dec 22 Robert Villemain w rsf 9 Paris
Dec 25 Hans Stretz w ko 5 Frankfurt

1951

Feb 14 Jake La Motta w rsf 13 Chicago
(World middleweight title)
Apr 5 Holley Mims w pts 10 Miami
Apr 9 Don Ellis w ko 1 Oklahoma City
May 21 Kid Marcel w rsf 5 Paris
May 26 Jean Wanes w pts 10 Zurich
Jun 10 Jan de Bruin w rsf 8 Antwerp
Jun 16 Jean Walzack w rsf 6 Liege
Jun 24 Gerhard Hecht nc 2 Berlin
Jul 1 Cyrille Delannoit w rsf 3 Turin
Jul 10 Randolph Turpin l pts 15 London
(World middleweight title)
Sep 12 Randolph Turpin w rsf 10 New York
(World middleweight title)

1952

Mar 13 Carl Olson w pts 15 San Francisco
(World middleweight title)
Apr 16 Rocky Graziano w ko 3 Chicago
(World middleweight title)
Jun 25 Joey Maxim l rtd 13 New York
(World light-heavyweight title)

1953-54 inactive

1955

Jan 5 Joe Rindone w ko 6 Detroit
Jan 19 Ralph Jones l pts 10 Chicago
Mar 29 Johnny Lombardo w pts 10 Cincinnati
Apr 14 Ted Ollis w rsf 3 Milwaukee
May 4 Garth Panter w pts 10 Detroit
Jul 22 Rocky Castellani w pts 10 San Francisco
Dec 9 Carl Olson w ko 2 Chicago
(World middleweight title)

1956

May 18 Carl Olson w ko 4 Los Angeles
(World middleweight title)
Nov 10 Bob Provizzi w pts 10 New Haven

1957

Jan 2 Gene Fullmer l pts 15 New York
(World middleweight title)
May 1 Gene Fullmer w ko 5 Chicago
(World middleweight title)
Sep 23 Carmen Basilio l pts 15 New York
(World middleweight title)

1958

Mar 25 Carmen Basilio w pts 15 Chicago
(World middleweight title)

1959

Dec 14 Bob Young w rsf 2 Boston

1960

Jan 22 Paul Pender l pts 15 Boston
(World middleweight title)
Apr 2 Tony Baldoni w ko 1 Baltimore
Jun 10 Paul Pender l pts 15 Boston
(World middleweight title)
Dec 3 Gene Fullmer drew 15 Los Angeles
(NBA middleweight title)

1961

Mar 4 Gene Fullmer l pts 15 Las Vegas
(NBA middleweight title)
Sep 25 Wilf Greaves w pts 10 Detroit

Oct 21 Denny Moyer w pts 10 New York
Nov 20 Al Hauser w rsf 6 Providence
Dec 8 Wilf Greaves w ko 8 Pittsburgh

1962

Feb 17 Denny Moyer l pts 10 New York
Apr 27 Bobby Lee w ko 2 Port of Spain
Jul 9 Phil Moyer l pts 10 Los Angeles
Sep 25 Terry Downes l pts 10 London
Oct 17 Diego Infantes w ko 2 Vienna
Nov 10 Georges Estatoff w rsf 6 Lyon

1963

Jan 30 Ralph Dupas w pts 10 Miami
Feb 25 Bernie Reynolds w ko 4 Santo Domingo
Mar 11 Billy Thornton w ko 3 Lewiston
May 5 Maurice Robinet w ko 3 Sherbrooke
Jun 24 Joey Giardello l pts 10 Philadelphia
Oct 14 Armand Vanucci w pts 10 Paris
Nov 9 Fabio Bettini drew 10 Lyon
Nov 16 Emile Saerens w ko 8 Brussels
Nov 29 Andre Davier w pts 10 Grenoble
Dec 9 Armand Vanucci w pts 10 Paris

1964

May 19 Gaylord Barnes w pts 10 Portland
Jul 8 Clarence Riley w rsf 6 Pittsfield
Jul 27 Art Hernandez drew 10 Omaha
Sep 3 Mick Leahy l pts 10 Paisley, Scotland
Sep 28 Yolande Leveque w pts 10 Paris
Oct 12 Johnny Angel w rsf 6 London
Oct 24 Jackie Cailleau w pts 10 Nice
Nov 7 Jean Baptiste Rolland w pts 10 Caen
Nov 14 Jean Beltritti w pts 10 Marseille
Nov 27 Fabio Bettini drew 10 Rome

1965

Mar 6 Jimmy Beecham w ko 2 Kingston
Apr 4 Earl Basting w ko 1 Savannah
Apr 28 Rocky Randall w ko 3 Norfolk
May 5 Rocky Randall w pts 8 Jacksonville
May 24 Memo Ayon l pts 10 Tijuana
Jun 1 Stan Harrington l pts 10 Honolulu
Jun 24 Harvey McCullough w pts 10 Richmond
Jul 12 Fred Hernandez l pts 10 Las Vegas
Jul 27 Harvey McCullough w pts 10 Richmond
Aug 10 Stan Harrington l pts 10 Honolulu
Sep 15 Bill Henderson nc 2 Norfolk, Va.
Sep 23 Harvey McCullough w pts 10 Philadelphia
Oct 1 Peter Schmidt w pts 10 Johnstown, Pa.
Oct 5 Neil Morrison w rsf 2 Richmond
Oct 20 Rudolph Bent w ko 3 Steubenville
Nov 10 Joey Archer l pts 10 Pittsburgh

Fights 202 Won 175 Lost 19 Drew 6 No Contests 2
Died 12 April 1989, Aged 67

INGEMAR JOHANSSON

THE HAMMER OF THOR

Ingemar Johansson was an unusual boxer. He had little regard for what many fans see as courage. Everything in his career, he said, was shaped by cautiousness. He was scornful of 'brave' boxers who take risks in the ring, and said a boxer must distinguish between bravery and stupidity. Twice during his career he was widely accused of cowardice. But in fact he proved that he was a skilful fighter with a tremendous punch and the courage to make the most of his talent whatever people said. He became the heavyweight champion of the world, and the only two fights he lost in his whole career were world title fights.

Ingemar Johansson was born in Gothenburg, Sweden, on 16 October 1932. He says in his autobiography, *Seconds Out of the Ring*, that he had no outstanding experiences that he can remember until he was 13 years old, although in fact he had watched his first boxing contest when he was 12. He was brought up in a happy if slightly strict home in which his father Jens, a street paver, and his mother Ebba insisted the boys (brother Henry was two years older and Rolf four years younger) contribue a little to their keep, and from the age of 11 he had to do afternoon jobs such as delivering groceries for a shopkeeper. He was a big lad from the start, and at five had already overtaken Henry in size.

What happened to him at 13 was that, walking home from an errand, he discovered the open door of the Redbergslid's Boxing Club, and was attracted to the ambience –the sparring, the skipping, the sweaty and dusty atmosphere. A coach spoke to him and gave him a membership card. He said it was the greatest moment of his life till then. From then on his schooling and the jobs he got later became subsidiary to his boxing training and his ambition to make boxing his career. At 13 he already weighed 140lb, but he had none of the toughness of older boys of his size, and was a docile youth, apart from his determination to box.

At 14, before he had had any formal amateur contests, he was chosen for the Swedish Boxing Association's training camp, where he was the youngest, heaviest and fastest taking part. At 15, he sparred with professionals at Eddie Ahlqvist's gym. Ahlqvist was a publisher and promoter who became Johansson's adviser, and one winter he worked for Ahlqvist's company. Other jobs he did when he finished school at 15 were shifting bananas in the docks, and sweeping snow.

Johansson began his amateur career as a 15-year-old in February 1948 and won the Gothenburg district junior championship. He weighed 180lb. He lost in the Swedish junior championships at the end of the year but won the title in 1950 and was already being spoken of as Sweden's next great heavyweight. International honours came his way but there was already something different being noticed about him. He would take no risks against tough opponents, which often led to dull fights. A report of a contest against a rock-hard Norwegian read: 'The only man to strike a blow in the first two rounds was the man with the gong'. Because Johansson's precocious size meant he sometimes fought fully grown men while still little more than a youth himself, he developed an ultra-cautious attitude.

After he had become world champion, he wrote: 'It is my unshakeable opinion that no prize is worth boxing injuries ... No man in his senses stands in front of a train, but that is almost what many 'brave' boys do who take the craziest risks in the ring.'

Of course, this at times made him very unpopular. When a European team went to the USA in 1951, Johansson knocked out his heavyweight opponent in Chicago (there were 16 million watching on TV), but hurt his left hand in doing so. He refused to box in Washington in a second match but the trainer thought he could persuade him at the last minute. So when Johansson was announced from the ring but didn't appear, it looked as if he'd been frightened off. He was accused in the press of faking injury to avoid taking a beating. The International Boxing Association (the European body) wanted him banned for three months, but the Swedish authorities refused. Johansson spent weeks with his hand in plaster.

Ingemar's amateur career consisted of 71 contests, of which he won 61 and lost ten. It ended in August 1952 with the Helsinki Olympic Games. Johansson won three bouts on points to reach the final against an American, Ed Sanders, a big puncher who had laid out his opponents impressively. Sanders and Johansson were both counterpunchers. The 19-year-old Johansson considered he lacked the condition and skill to attack Sanders and decided to lie in wait for two rounds and perhaps sneak it in the third. Unfortunately Sanders also waited for Johansson to attack. Both were warned to fight at the end of the first round, but nothing happened in the second either, during which the French referee repeatedly warned Johansson. At the end of the round the referee conferred with the judges and disqualified Johansson for 'not giving of his best'. Ingemar was disgraced and not awarded the silver medal. The Swedish newspapers were almost unanimously severe: 'fleeing rat', 'cowardice', 'ashamed', were words used. The public scorned him. His professional prospects were said to be finished.

Johansson had no regrets about his performance and considered the criticism unfair.

His caution and defensive boxing as a young amateur gave him the chance to learn his trade, he said. He claimed he wasn't ripe to mix it with Sanders, but was prepared to counter Sanders' attacks, which didn't come. He withstood all the contempt heaped upon him, and began a professional career. In 1982, long after he'd been champion of the world, the International Olympic Committee gave him his silver medal. Tragically his opponent in that Helsinki final, Ed Sanders, died of a brain haemorrhage two years later after being knocked out in his ninth professional contest.

After he'd been boxing professionally for a while, Ingemar cultivated a more aggressive approach, but his style remained basically one where he felt out the opposition with his left while awaiting an opportunity to deliver his hugely powerful right. Johansson's left was never much more than a flick to distract attention but his right dealt destruction.

He waited for the furore over his Olympic debacle to die down a bit before his first pro fight, in December 1952, a fourth-round knockout of Frenchman Robert Masson in his home town of Gothenburg. The hall was full, and there were one or two jeers from the 5,500 fans as Ingemar climbed into the ring. Damage to his right hand, entailing a nine-month layoff, and national service in the navy in 1954 meant that in his first two years he had only six bouts, all won. He showed his independent nature in the service when he did his best to get out of going to sea and suffered punishments for insubordination. Finally he went absent without leave, which earned him 30 days close arrest.

Resuming his career, Johansson won the European championship in 1956 with a 13th round knockout of Franco Cavicchi of Italy in Bologna. Three of Ingemar's next four opponents were British, and he knocked out all of them: Peter Bates, Henry Cooper and Joe Erskine. The fights with Cooper, in Stockholm, and Erskine, in Gothenburg, were defences of the European title, and Cooper was knocked out in the fifth and Erskine in the 13th.

The fight which really set up Johansson's career was with American Eddie Machen, who was a leading contender for Floyd Patterson's world title. It was a fight Ingemar himself was doubtful about, but it took place on 14 September 1958, at the Nya Ullev in Gothenburg before 33,864 fans. Machen's connections severely underestimated Ingemar, whose right connected with his opponent's chin in the very first round, knocking him to the canvas. He rose, but was hammered down twice more for a first-round knockout. Suddenly, Ingemar found himself a leading contender, and his next fight, nine months later, was for the undisputed championship of the world.

Ingemar was a sensation in New York when he arrived to challenge Floyd Patterson at the Yankee Stadium. The boxing scribes had seen nothing like it. Ingemar had with him a family entourage comprising his parents, brother Rolf, cousin Ernest, sister Eva and sister-in-law Annette, who gave birth in Grossinger's training hostelry where Johansson trained. Adviser Eddie Ahlqvist, who was never officially manager, although he acted as such, second Nils Blomberg, and American adviser Whitey Bimstein were also in the main party as well as the beautiful Birgit Lundgren, secretary and fiancée. It was Ms Lundgren who captured the attention, particularly when Ingemar's training seemed to centre round the swimming pool and the dance hall with Birgit as the main sparring partner. Rocky Marciano was astounded: 'I used to wake up to see trainer Charley Goldman looking mean and unshaven ... Ingemar has this beautiful doll to keep his eye sharpened.' In all the papers 'playboy' Ingemar's chances were written off. The stories of the humiliating Olympic final and the 'runaway' of his US amateur fight were recycled. He was 5–1 in the betting.

What was hushed up in the brouhaha about Birgit was that Johansson was already a father of two children. He had married as a teenager and subsequently divorced.

With hindsight, the build-up to this much-publicised fight could have been an early example of the kidology an 'psyching out' of opponents that goes on today. The media latched on to the 'travelling circus' aspect of the Swedish contingent; somebody recollected Johansson's poor performance in the Olympics seven years previously – and complacency settled comfortably upon the Patterson camp.

What they should have been considering very closely was Ingemar's recent record of six knockouts in his seven victories (no defeats) within the past three years, particularly the first-round annihilation of Eddie Machen nine months earlier.

On the night, the contest was delayed because of a downpour. Even so 18,125 were present and for the first time receipts from closed-circuit TV grossed over $1 million. After two feeling-out rounds, Ingemar's right connected for the first time in the third round and Patterson hit the deck. He got up at the count of nine, but was so bemused and bewildered that he went to a neutral corner, because he believed that he had knocked Johansson down. Six more times in the next two minutes Patterson was bludgeoned down by a right. He kept getting up but he didn't know where he was or what was happening. Finally referee Ruby Goldstein took mercy on him. Johansson was the first Swede to be a world boxing champion, and only the third from the Continent (after Schmeling and Carnera) to be heavyweight champion. The press rushed to christen this fabulous right-hand punch. The posh papers remembered their mythology and called it 'The Hammer of Thor'; to the tabloids it was 'Ingo's Bingo'.

Ingemar enjoyed a year as champion, making a couple of movies, and making the usual celebrity appearances in public and on television. He then returned to New York for a return at the Polo Grounds. The attendance rose this time to 45,000. Johansson was a couple of pounds lighter than before at 194lb. He shook Patterson with his right in the second round, but Patterson took over in the third and in the fifth dropped Johansson for nine and then knocked him out. Patterson became the first heavyweight to recover the world title.

Nine months later there was the rubber match in Miami Beach Convention Hall. This meant in effect that nobody but Johansson and Patterson fought for a heavyweight title for over two years. Patterson was a favourite at 4–1 on, the fans believing that Johansson's bubble had burst. Ingemar weighed the highest of his career at 206lb,

12lb more than Patterson. There were 16,000 'live' spectators and another big closed-circuit TV audience. In this contest a mandatory eight count was in operation for the first time. Patterson was down twice in the first round before an over-eager Johansson chased him across the ring only to be dropped himself as Patterson bounced off the ropes with a left hook. Rounds were even until a clash of heads in the fifth left Johansson with a cut on the eyebrow. Suddenly in the sixth a right from Patterson caught Johansson behind the ear and he fell awkwardly face first. He fell to one side as he attempted to rise and was counted out. Johansson's world title days were over. The three fights had earned him around $2 million – OK for 1961.

However, Ingemar's career continued. On 17 June 1962 he regained the European crown, which he had relinquished to fight for the world title, with an eighth-round knockout of champion Dick Richardson from Britain. In fact Johansson showed a liking for British heavyweights, and during his career – as well as Richardson – he beat Joe Bygraves, Henry Cooper, Joe Erskine and Brian London, all of whom had spells as British champion. He was stripped of the European title for failing to defend it, so he then decided on a change of strategy. Sonny Liston had won the world heavyweight title in September 1962, with a first-round knockout of Floyd Patterson and Ingemar started his road to another world title challenge in April 1963 with a fight in Stockholm against Brian London. In what should have been a routine contest Johansson was slightly ahead in a dull fight with less than 10 seconds to go when London toppled him with a hard punch to the chin. It would have been the knockout blow had the bell not rung when the count reached four. Ingemar won the fight, but retired from the ring. Floyd Patterson had been the only man to beat him in his career.

Ingemar married the famous Birgit, but that marriage, too, ended in divorce. After dabbling in various businesses in Europe, Ingemar went to live in Miami, where he opened a successful motel which later on his son ran for him. His daughter lived in London. Ingemar kept fit (he ran in the New York marathon in the 1980s) and eventually returned to Sweden, where he became a TV commentator and pundit on the big fights.

CAREER STATISTICS

World heavyweight champion 1959-60
Gothenburg, Sweden, born 16 October 1932
1952 Olympic heavyweight silver medal

1952
Dec 5 Robert Masson w ko 4 Gothenburg
1953
Feb 7 Emil Bentz w ko 2 Gothenburg
Mar 6 Lloyd Barnett w pts 6 Gothenburg
Mar 12 Erik Jensen w pts 6 Copenhagen
Dec 8 Ray Innocenti w ko 2 Gothenburg
1954
Nov 5 Werner Wiegand w ko 5 Stockholm
1955
Jan 5 Ansel Adams w pts 8 Gothenburg
Feb 13 Kurt Shiegl w ko 5 Stockholm
Mar 5 Aldo Pellegrini w dis 5 Gothenburg
Apr 3 Uber Baccilieri w pts 8 Stockholm
Jun 12 Gunter Nurnberg w ko 7 Dortmund
Aug 28 Hein Ten Hoff w ko 1 Gothenburg
1956
Feb 24 Joe Bygraves w pts 10 Gothenburg
Apr 15 Hans Friedrich w pts 10 Stockholm
Sep 30 Francesco Cavicchi w ko 13 Bologna
(European heavyweight title)
Dec 28 Peter Bates w ko 2 Gothenburg
1957
May 19 Henry Cooper w ko 5 Stockholm
(European heavyweight title)
Dec 13 Archie McBride w pts 10 Gothenburg
1958
Feb 21 Joe Erskine w ko 13 Gothenburg
(European heavyweight title)
Jul 13 Heinz Neuhaus w ko 4 Gothenburg
Sep 14 Eddie Machen w ko 1 Gothenburg
1959
Jun 26 Floyd Patterson w rsf 3 New York
(World heavyweight title)
1960
Jun 20 Floyd Patterson l ko 5 New York
(World heavyweight title)
1961
Mar 13 Floyd Patterson l ko 6 Miami
(World heavyweight title)
1962
Feb 9 Joe Bygraves w ko 7 Gothenburg
Apr 15 Wim Snoek w ko 5 Stockholm
Jun 17 Dick Richardson w ko 8 Gothenburg
(European heavyweight title)
1963
Apr 21 Brian London w pts 12 Stockholm

Fights 28 Won 26 Lost 2

ARCHIE MOORE

THE OLE MONGOOSE

Archie Moore's career lasted 27 years. He had 235 contests and at least eight managers, but more or less managed himself. He was already old (39) when he won the world light-heavyweight championship, so they called him 'Ancient Archie'. He was also called 'The Ole Mongoose', because he said he'd like to fight like one. He was a month short of his 49th birthday when he took on the 20-year-old heavyweight sensation Cassius Clay.

Early record books give Archie Moore's birthdate as 13 December 1916, but this was a date supplied by Archie himself. In 1960, when he wrote his autobiography, he stuck to this date. But his mother insisted he was born in 1913, and modern record books agree with her. The place is not in doubt: Benoit, Mississippi. His real name is Archie Lee Wright. His mother, Lorena, was only 17 when Archie was born, and she already had a two-year-old daughter, Rachel. Lorena separated from her husband, Thomas Wright, when Archie was 18 months old and Archie and Rachel were sent to St Louis, where uncle Cleveland Moore and his wife Willie Pearl Moore brought them up. For convenience, both children took the name 'Moore' and Archie kept it forever.

Archie had two passions as a teenager. A friend's brother was a boxer and Archie happened to see a prizefight. He enjoyed fighting himself, and fancied being a great champion. He also dreamed of playing a trumpet in a jazz band (he would do so later in life). He indulged in petty thieving to save for a trumpet, and when Uncle Cleveland died he began stealing in earnest.

A sentence of three years in reform school forced Archie, who was an intelligent boy and good at his lessons, to see the light, and he got out after 22 months. He worked for the Civilian Conservation Corps, clearing sites for roads. Archie, who had decided at the last minute to spend his ill-gotten gains on boxing gloves instead of a trumpet, had developed his boxing skills in reform school, and now in the CCC camp in Missouri, he raised a camp boxing team. He had many amateur bouts in these years, and others were no doubt professional. A payment of $3 for a fight by a promoter-manager named Kid

Bundy became known to the Amateur Athletic Union, who revoked his amateur licence, thus removing his chance of getting into the 1936 Olympic team. Moore turned professional with Cal Thompson as his manager.

Felix Thurman, a friend from St Louis, sold his garage to finance a trip to California for him and Moore in order to look for fights. Thurman thus became Moore's next manager. In March 1938 their car overturned in an accident. Moore severed an artery in his wrist punching through the windscreen and his life was saved only by the luck of a following car containing doctors from the local hospital.

Jack Richardson bought Moore's contract from Thurman for $250 by promising a tour of Australia. Moore married San Diego girl Mattie Chapman on New Year's Day 1940 on the strength of it, only to find that Richardson would not allow her on the trip, for which the boat sailed five days later. Moore fought seven times in Australia, all wins, and earned a big reputation there, but in the last match he broke his hand and the party returned. Sadly the nine months or so of absence had cooled his wife's feelings for him. They soon separated and divorced.

He found his performances in Australia made it no easier to get fights in America, and he was sweeping leaves for a living when, in 1941, he developed peritonitis. Having survived this dangerous illness, he was back in hospital with acute appendicitis. At one time his weight dropped to flyweight level and he was out of boxing for almost a year.

Moore then married for the second time and started a business, Archie Moore's Chicken Shack, which became such a success that he could have become a lifelong chicken fryer. But the pull of boxing was such that he went to New York to try his luck with promoter Jimmy Johnston. Jimmy's brother Charley Johnston became manager and Moore was able to train at the famous Stillman's Gymnasium and to fight better opposition. He was now a light-heavyweight, and lost a few fights, particularly three to Ezzard Charles, another great black light-heavyweight.

There was another hiatus in Moore's career in 1950, when Jimmy Johnston died and Charley could get him only two fights. He went on tour to Argentina in 1951 with Charley and the featherweight champion Sandy Saddler. By now Moore had been the leading contender for the light-heavyweight crown for years, and he at last got his title shot in 1952. This owed much more to the business acumen of the champion's manager, Jack 'Doc' Kearns (former manager of Jack Dempsey) than it did to any notions of fair play to Archie. Moore had been running a clever press campaign demanding a title shot, while champion Joey Maxim instead tried for the heavyweight crown (losing to Ezzard Charles) and defended lucratively against middleweight Sugar Ray Robinson (who lost through heat exhaustion). Then Maxim's manager Kearns gave Moore his chance (Moore made $800 to Maxim's $100,000), provided Kearns had a subsequent share in Moore's management. Moore wanted his parents at the title fight, and sought out his father, Thomas Wright, with whom he had a tearful reunion.

Given his chance, he seized it, inflicting a painful 15 rounds ordeal on Maxim and winning an easy decision. Kearns seized his chance, too, and matched his two fighters twice more for the title, taking his percentage from both. There was no danger that Maxim would win. Moore was briefly married for a third time around now, a messy and bitter affair in which his wife accused him of failing to support her, leading to his purse for the third Maxim fight being withheld for a while.

Moore defended against good challengers in Harold Johnson and middleweight champion Carl 'Bobo' Olson, and in September 1955 challenged Rocky Marciano for the heavyweight title. This was the biggest disappointment of his life. He put Marciano down in the second round, and when Marciano rose at the count of two, Moore wanted to finish him, but Harry Kessler, a referee who crossed Moore more than once in his life, mistakenly gave the groggy Marciano a standing eight count and Moore lost the chance. He was knocked out in the ninth. But Archie at last made decent money, to be precise $270,000 for this fight, and he even felt safe enough to sell his Chicken Shack to Felix Thurman.

Archie had another shot for the heavyweight title a year later, fighting Floyd Patterson for it when Marciano retired, but he lost once more. Again he was disappointed, because he thought he could win, and guessed he'd overtrained. However, he did well considering he was twice Patterson's age: 42 to 21.

On 10 December 1958 at The Forum, Montreal, Moore really captured the public imagination in a big way, when he defended his title for the seventh time. His opponent was Yvon Durelle, a hard-punching Canadian ex-fisherman. Moore was all but knocked out in the first round, taking three counts and just beating the count of ten the third time. Moore had just about recovered his poise by the fifth, when a hard right dropped him again. But once more Ancient Archie fought back, turning the tables by decking Durelle in the seventh. Moore finally got on top and three more knockdowns saw Durelle counted out in the 11th round. It was a remarkable recovery and the fight is remembered as one of the all-time great contests.

Moore by now was married again, and this time he and his wife, formerly Joan Hardy, formed a happy and long-lasting partnership.

There was little more for Archie to do in the ring. He beat Durelle in a return, was stripped by the NBA for failing to defend for over a year, retained the New York and European versions of the title in 1961 by outpointing Guilio Rinaldi, and then in February 1962 was stripped of these titles for failing to meet NBA champion Harold Johnson, a man he had beaten four times in five meetings. However it must be admitted that Johnson, at 15 years younger, would have been a big threat.

For the last seven years of his career, Archie had slimmed down for his light-heavyweight defences, fighting normally at nearly 200lb. He was 197lb when he lost to Cassius Clay. After that defeat, he retired on a winning note by stopping heavyweight Mike DiBiase. He was three months past his 49th birthday.

In the end Archie's long struggle for recognition paid off and he finally made the sort of money and earned the lifestyle he deserved. An interview he gave when he beat Yvon Durelle so impressed Hollywood that he was invited to play the slave Jim in the film *The Adventures of Huckleberry Finn*. He was a great success and other film roles followed. His knowledge was also in great demand in fight circles and he appeared in the corners of several champions, including heavyweight champion George Foreman in the 1970s. He successfully came through a triple heart bypass operation in 1995, when 82, and remains a regular and highly popular visitor at the International Boxing Hall of Fame celebrity weekends.

CAREER STATISTICS

World light-heavyweight champion 1952-62
Born Benoit, Mississippi, 13 December 1913
Real name: Archibald Lee Wright

1936

Jan 31 Polo Kid w ko 2 Arkansas
Feb 7 Dale Richards w ko 1 St Louis
Feb 18 Ray Halford w ko 3 St Louis
Feb 20 Willie Harper w ko 3 St Louis
Feb 21 Courtland Sheppard l pts 6 St Louis
Mar - Kneibert Davidson w ko 2 "Not known"
Mar - Ray Brewster w ko 3 "Not known"
Mar - Billy Simms w ko 2 "Not known"
Mar - Johnny Leggs w ko 1 "Not known"
Apr 15 Peter Urban w ko 6 Ohio
Apr 16 Frankie Nelson l pts 6 Ohio
May 4 Tiger Brown l pts 6 St Louis
May 18 Thurman Martin w pts 6 St Louis
Jul 14 Murray Allen w pts 6 Quincy, Il.
Aug 1 Sammy Christian drew 6 Quincy
Aug - Julius Kemp w ko 3 "Not known"
Aug - Four H. Posey w pts 6 "Not known"
Oct 9 Sammy Jackson w pts 5 St Louis
Nov - Dick Putnam w ko 3 "Not known"
Dec 8 Sammy Jackson drew 6 St Louis
Dec 30 Sammy Christian w ko 6 "Not known"

1937

Jan 5 Demetrius Payne w ko 1 St Louis
Jan 18 Johnny Davis w ko 3 Quincy
Feb 2 Joe Huff w ko 2 St Louis
Mar 23 Ham Pounder w ko 2 Punca City
Apr 9 Charley Dawson w ko 5 Indianapolis
Apr 23 Karl Martin w ko 1 Indianapolis
May - Frank Hatfield w ko 1 "Not known"
Jun - Al Dublinsky w ko 1 "Not known"
Jul - Murray Allen w ko 2 Keokuk, Iowa
Aug 19 Deacon Logan w ko 3 St Louis
Sep 1 Billy Adams l pts 8 Cincinnati
Sep 9 Sammy Slaughter w pts 10 Indianapolis
Sep 17 Charley Dawson w ko 5 St Louis
Nov 16 Sammy Christian w pts 8 St Louis
Dec - Sammy Jackson w ko 8 Missouri

1938

Jan 7 Carl Lautenschlager w ko 2 St Louis
May 20 Jimmy Brent w ko 1 San Diego
May 27 Ray Vargas w ko 3 San Diego
Jun 24 Johnny Romero l pts 10 San Diego
Jul 22 Johnny Sykes w ko 4 San Diego
Aug 5 Lorenzo Pedro w pts 10 San Diego
Sep 2 Johnny Romero w ko 8 San Diego
Sep 16 Frank Rowsey w ko 3 San Diego
Sep 27 Tom Henry w ko 4 Los Angeles
Oct - Bob Llanes w ko 2 Missouri
Nov 22 Ray Lyle w ko 2 St Louis
Dec 8 Bob Turner w ko 2 St Louis

1939

Jan 20 Jack Moran w ko 1 St Louis
Mar 2 Domenic Ceccarelli w ko 2 St Louis
Mar 16 Marty Simmons w pts 10 St Louis
Apr 20 Teddy Yarosz l pts 10 St Louis
Jul 21 Jack Coggins nc 8 San Diego
Sep 1 Jack Coggins w pts 10 San Diego
Sep 22 Bobby Seaman w ko 7 San Diego
Nov 13 Freddie Dixon drew 8 Phoenix
Nov 27 Billy Day w ko 1 Phoenix
Dec 7 Honeyboy Jones w pts 10 St Louis
Dec 29 Shorty Hogue l pts 6 San Diego

1940

Mar 20 Jack McNamee w ko 4 Melbourne
Apr 18 Ron Richards w rsf 10 Sydney
May 9 Atilio Sabatino w ko 5 Sydney
May 12 Joe Delaney w ko 7 Adelaide
Jun 2 Frank Lindsay w ko 4 Tasmania
Jun 27 Fred Henneberry w ko 7 Sydney
Jul 11 Ron Richards w pts 12 Sydney
Oct 18 Pancho Ramirez w ko 5 San Diego
Dec 5 Shorty Hogue l pts 6 San Diego

1941

Jan 17 Clay Rowan w ko 1 San Diego
Jan 31 Shorty Hogue l pts 10 San Diego
Feb 21 Eddie Booker drew 10 San Diego

1942

Jan 28 Bobby Britton w ko 3 Phoenix
Feb 27 Guero Martinez w ko 2 San Diego
Mar 17 Jimmy Casino w ko 5 Oakland
Oct 30 Shorty Hogue w ko 2 San Diego
Nov 6 Tabby Romero w ko 2 San Diego
Nov 27 Jack Chase w pts 10 San Diego
Dec 11 Eddie Booker drew 12 San Diego *(Californian middleweight title)*

1943

May 8 Jack Chasse w pts 15 San Diego *(Californian middleweight title)*
Jul 22 Willard Hogue w rsf 5 San Diego
Jul 28 Eddie Cerda w ko 3 San Diego
Aug 2 Jack Chase l pts 15 San Francisco *(Californian middleweight title)*
Aug 16 Aaron Wade l pts 10 San Francisco
Nov 5 Kid Hermosollo w ko 5 San Diego
Nov 26 Jack Chase w pts 10 Los Angeles

1944

Jan 7 Amado Rodriguez w ko 1 San Diego
Jan 21 Eddie Booker l ko 8 Los Angeles
Mar 24 Roman Starr w rsf 2 Los Angeles
Apr 21 Charley Burley l pts 10 Los Angeles
May 19 Kenny LaSalle w pts 10 San Diego
Aug 11 Louis Mays w ko 3 San Diego
Aug 18 Jimmy Hayden w ko 5 San Diego
Sep 1 Battling Monroe w ko 6 San Diego
Dec 18 Nate Bolden w pts 10 New York

1945

Jan 11 Joey Jones w ko 1 Boston
Jan 29 Bob Jacobs w ko 9 New York
Feb 12 Nap Mitchell w ko 6 Boston
Apr 2 Nate Bolden w pts 10 Baltimore
Apr 23 Teddy Randolph w ko 9 Baltimore
May 21 Lloyd Marshall w pts 10 Baltimore
Jun 18 George Kochan w ko 6 Baltimore
Jun 26 Lloyd Marshall w rsf 10 Cleveland
Aug 22 Jimmy Bivins l rsf 6 Cleveland
Sep 17 Cocoa Kid w ko 8 Baltimore
Oct 22 Holman Williams l pts 10 Baltimore
Nov 12 Odell Riley w ko 6 Detroit
Nov 26 Holman Williams w rsf 11 Baltimore
Dec 13 Colion Chaney w ko 5 St Louis

1946

Jan 28 Curtis Sheppard w pts 12 Baltimore
Feb 5 Georgie Parks w rsf 1 Washington DC
May 2 Verne Escoe w rsf 7 Orange, NJ
May 20 Ezzard Charles l pts 10 Pittsburgh
Aug 19 Buddy Walker w ko 4 Baltimore
Sep 9 Shamus O'Brien w ko 2 Baltimore
Oct 23 Billy Smith drew 12 Oakland *(Californian light-heavyweight title)*
Nov 6 Jack Chase drew 10 Oakland

1947

Mar 18 Jack Chase w ko 9 Los Angeles *(Californian light-heavyweight title)*
Apr 11 Rusty Payne w pts 10 San Diego
May 5 Ezzard Charles l pts 10 Cincinnati
Jun 16 Curtis Sheppard w pts 10 Washington DC
Jul 14 Bert Lytell w pts 10 Baltimore
Jul 30 Bobby Zander w pts 12 Oakland *(Californian light-heavyweight title)*
Sep 8 Jimmy Bivins w rsf 9 Baltimore
Nov 10 George Fitch w ko 6 Baltimore

1948

Jan 13 Ezzard Charles l ko 8 Cleveland
Apr 12 Dusty Wilkerson w ko 7 Baltimore
Apr 19 Charley Williams w ko 7 Newark
May 5 Billy Smith w pts 10 Cincinnati
Jun 2 Leonard Morrow l ko 1 Oakland *(Californian light-heavyweight title)*
Jun 28 Jimmy Bivins w pts 10 Baltimore
Aug 2 Ted Lowry w pts 10 Baltimore
Sep 20 Billy Smith w ko 4 Baltimore
Oct 15 Henry Hall l pts 10 New Orleans
Nov 1 Lloyd Gibson l dis 4 Washington DC
Nov 15 Henry Hall w pts 10 Baltimore
Dec 6 Bob Amos w pts 10 Washington DC
Dec 27 Charley Williams w ko 7 Baltimore

1949

Jan 10 Alabama Kid w ko 4 Toledo
Jan 31 Bob Satterfield w rsf 3 Toledo
Mar 4 Alabama Kid w ko 3 Columbus
Mar 23 Dusty Wilkerson w ko 6 Philadelphia
Apr 11 Jimmy Bivins w ko 8 Toledo
Apr 26 Harold Johnson w pts 10 Philadelphia
Jun 13 Clinton Bacon l dis 6 Indianapolis
Jun 27 Bob Sikes w rsf 3 Indianapolis
Jul 29 Esco Greenwood w ko 2 N. Adams
Oct 4 Bob Amos w pts 10 Toledo
Oct 24 Phil Muscato w rsf 6 Toledo
Dec 6 Charley Williams w ko 8 Hartford
Dec 13 Leonard Morrow w ko 10 Toledo

1950

Jan 31 Bert Lytell w pts 10 Toledo
Jul 31 Vernon Williams w ko 2 Chicago

1951

Jan 2 Billy Smith w rsf 8 Portland, Or.
Jan 28 John Thomas w ko 1 Panama City
Feb 21 Jimmy Bivins w rsf 9 New York
Mar 13 Abel Cestac w pts 10 Toledo
Apr 26 Herman Harris w rsf 4 Flint
May 14 Art Henri w rsf 4 Baltimore

Jun 9 Abel Cestac w rsf 10 Buenos Aires
Jun 23 Karel Sys drew 10 Buenos Aires
Jul 8 Alberto Lovell w ko 1 Buenos Aires
Jul 15 Vicente Quiroz w ko 6 Montevideo
Jul 26 Victor Carabajal w rsf 3 Cordoba
Jul 28 Americo Capitanelli w rsf 3 Tucuman
Aug 5 Rafael Miranda w rsf 4 Argentina
Aug 17 Alfredo Lagay w ko 3 Bahia Blanca
Sep 5 Embrell Davison w ko 1 Detroit
Sep 24 Harold Johnson w pts 10 Philadelphia
Oct 29 Chubby Wright w rsf 7 St Louis
Dec 10 Harold Johnson l pts 10 Milwaukee

1952

Jan 29 Harold Johnson w pts 10 Toledo
Feb 27 Jimmy Slade w pts 10 St Louis
May 19 Bob Dunlap w ko 6 San Francisco
Jun 26 Clarence Henry w pts 10 Baltimore
Jul 25 Clint Bacon w rsf 4 Denver
Dec 17 Joey Maxim w pts 15 St Louis
(World light-heavyweight title)

1953

Jan 27 Toxie Hall w ko 4 Toledo
Feb 16 Leonard Dugan w rsf 8 San Francisco
Mar 3 Sonny Andrews w rsf 5 Sacramento
Mar 11 Nino Valdes w pts 10 St Louis
Mar 17 Al Spaulding w ko 3 Spokane
Mar 30 Frank Buford w rsf 9 San Diego
Jun 24 Joey Maxim w pts 15 Ogden
(World light-heavyweight title)
Aug 22 Reinaldo Ansaloni w rsf 4 Buenos Aires
Sep 12 Dogomar Martinez w pts 10 Buenos Aires

1954

Jan 27 Joey Maxim w pts 15 Miami
(World light-heavyweight title)
Mar 9 Bob Baker w rsf 9 Miami
Jun 7 Bert Whitehurst w ko 6 New York
Aug 11 Harold Johnson w rsf 14 New York
(World light-heavyweight title)

1955

May 2 Nino Valdes w pts 15 Las Vegas
Jun 22 Carl Olson w ko 3 New York
(World light-heavyweight title)
Sep 21 Rocky Marciano l ko 9 New York
(World heavyweight title)

1956

Feb 20 Howard King w pts 10 San Francisco
Feb 27 Bob Dunlap w ko 1 San Diego
Mar 17 Frankie Daniels w pts 10 Los Angeles
Mar 27 Howard King w pts 10 Sacramento
Apr 10 Willie Bean w rsf 5 Richmond, Ca.
Apr 16 George Parmenter w rsf 3 Seattle
Apr 26 Sonny Andrews w ko 4 Edmonton
Apr 30 Gene Thompson w rsf 3 Tucson
Jun 5 Yolande Pompey w rsf 10 London
(World light-heavyweight title)
Jul 25 James J. Parker w rsf 9 Toronto
Sep 8 Roy Shire w rsf 3 Ogden
Nov 30 Floyd Patterson l ko 5 Chicago
(vacant world heavyweight title)

1957

May 1 Hans Kalbfell w pts 10 Essen
Jun 2 Alain Cherville w rsf 6 Stuttgart
Sep 20 Tony Anthony w rsf 7 Los Angeles
(World light-heavyweight title)
Oct 31 Bob Mitchell w rsf 5 Vancouver
Nov 5 Eddie Cotton w pts 10 Seattle
Nov 29 Roger Rischer w ko 4 Portland

1958

Jan 18 Luis Ignacio w pts 10 Sao Paulo
Feb 1 Julio Neves w ko 3 Rio de Janeiro
Mar 4 Bert Whitehurst w rsf 10 San Bernardino
Mar 10 Bob Albright w rsf 7 Vancouver
May 2 Willi Besmanoff w pts 10 Louisville
May 17 Howard King w pts 10 San Diego
May 26 Charlie Norkus w pts 10 San Francisco
Jun 9 Howard King w pts 10 Sacramento
Aug 4 Howard King drew 10 Reno
Dec 10 Yvon Durelle w ko 11 Montreal
(World light-heavyweight title)

1959

Mar 9 Sterling Davis w rsf 3 Odessa, Tx
Aug 12 Yvon Durelle w ko 3 Montreal
(World light-heavyweight title)

1960

May 25 Willi Besmanoff w rsf 10 Indianapolis
Sep 13 George Abinet w rsf 3 Dallas
Oct 25: Stripped of NBA light-heavyweight title.
Oct 29 Giulio Rinaldi l pts 10 Rome
Nov 28 Buddy Turman w pts 10 Dallas

1961

Mar 25 Buddy Turman w pts 10 Manila
May 12 Clifford Gray w ko 4 Noagales
Jun 10 Giulio Rinaldi w pts 15 New York
(World light-heavyweight title)
Oct 23 Pete Rademacher w rsf 6 Baltimore

1962

Feb 10: New York State Commission & European Boxing Union refused to recognise him as world champion.
Mar 30 Alejandro Lavorante w rsf 10 Los Angeles
May 7 Howard King w ko 1 Tijuana
May 28 Willie Pastrano drew 10 Los Angeles
Nov 15 Cassius Clay l ko 4 Los Angeles

1963

Mar 15 Mike DiBiase w ko 3 Phoenix

Fights 235 Won 197 Lost 27 Drawn 10 No Contests 1

FLOYD PATTERSON

MASTER OF DISGUISE

FLOYD PATTERSON was fast. He could box, punch and had immense determination, but it was his speed that separated him from his rivals. If he didn't have the greatest chin in heavyweight history, nobody worked harder to improve than the one-time lonely boy from the Bedford-Stuyvesant district of Brooklyn, which decades later was to spawn another precocious heavyweight champion, Mike Tyson.

Patterson was an Olympic middleweight gold medallist at 17 and the youngest world heavyweight champion at 21, a record which lasted until the arrival of Tyson. He was also the first man to regain the heavyweight championship.

If his achievements had their detractors, it was because his manager Cus D'Amato took a pragmatic approach to the championship and deliberately steered him away from some contenders. But that wasn't Patterson's fault and over 20 years in the professional business he did eventually fight most of the best heavyweights of his time. In later life, he became a dignified, if unassuming and shy New York State Athletic Commissioner before retiring in 1998.

Patterson was born in Waco, North Carolina, on 4 January 1935. His father worked as a construction labourer for the local railway company, but moved the family to New York a year after Floyd was born. One of 11 children, he developed into a withdrawn child who felt the family's poverty keenly and took to hiding from the world in alleyways, subways, and even in a disused shed by a railway track. Eventually, at the age of 10, he was hauled before a court for truancy from school and petty delinquency, and was sent to a reform school in upstate New York, Wiltwyck School for Boys. There he discovered the joys of a countryside he had never imagined and gradually learned how to make friends. He said he could not remember having fun or even laughing before he arrived in Wiltwyck. He preferred sitting in the dark – even when it was daytime – rather than the light, where people could see and ridicule him.

After two years he was sent back to New York City where he attended a special school until his graduation in 1952.

He did a little boxing at Wiltwyck but at the Gramercy Gym in New York he met D'Amato, who was to change his life. Although he lost three of his first four amateur bouts, he improved rapidly and at 17 won the National AAU middleweight title. Then he won the Olympic trials and, out of the country for the first time, the gold medal at the Helsinki Olympics. He knocked out Vasile Tita of Romania in the first round.

Patterson turned professional with D'Amato training and managing him in September 1952, stopping Eddie Godbold in the fourth round at the St Nicholas Arena in New York. He scaled 164 ½lb – still only a big middleweight.

In his sixth fight he scraped past a tough pro, Dick Wagner, on a majority decision, and although he stopped him in round five in the rematch, he never forgot how sore he was after their first meeting. He also stopped Gordon Wallace in three rounds and outpointed Yvon Durelle. Both would hold the British Empire title, and Durelle would twice fight Archie Moore for the world light-heavyweight crown.

Patterson's first defeat was on a close eight-round decision to former world light-heavy champ Joey Maxim at the Eastern Parkway Arena in Brooklyn in June 1954. All three officials scored for Maxim, including world class referee Ruby Goldstein, and yet all 11 newspaper correspondents at ringside felt the 19-year-old Patterson had won.

It didn't matter much. Had he won, even though he was restricted to eight rounds in New York State, because of his age, and scaled 168lb, he would have been a leading contender for Archie Moore's light-heavyweight title. As it was, with only 14 fights behind him, *Ring* magazine rated him No. 6.

The following month he was on the floor in the opening round before battering Jacques Royer-Crecy to a standstill after seven rounds, and then demolished Tommy Harrison of Los Angeles in 89 seconds. He was back on track – and growing fast. At the end of 1955 he weighed a career-heaviest 178½lb when he stopped Jimmy Slade in seven rounds.

In April 1956, world heavyweight champion Rocky Marciano announced his retirement, and two months later a 12-round points win over Tommy 'Hurricane' Jackson put Patterson high in the queue for a shot at the vacant crown. It was a split decision and Floyd still weighed only 178lb, but the heavyweight division was in a dire state. The Cuban, Nino Valdes, was past 30 and temporarily fading, and Bob Baker, a big, easygoing character from Pittsburgh, who would have been in line to fight Marciano early in 1956, blew his chance when he lost a disputed decision to Jackson. The stars of the late 1950s like Sonny Liston, Eddie Machen, Zora Folley and Ingemar Johansson were only just emerging.

Patterson needed time for a broken right hand to mend, but then a match was made for the vacant championship with 42-year-old Moore, who still held the world light-heavyweight title.

Ray Robinson voiced the fears of many boxing purists when he said Floyd's tendency to leap in with his punches could be like putting him in a tank with a shark when he fought Moore. Ancient Archie was a big favourite when the bookmakers began business, but a strange, late rush of money brought the final odds down to almost evens ...

Patterson won the heavyweight championship at Chicago Stadium on 30 November 1956 when he knocked out Moore in the fifth round. Moore was floored by a clean left hook, hauled himself up at nine, only to be dropped again by a right that was little more than a shove. He was spent.

Patterson's share was 30 per cent of the total gate, including television rights. He collected $116,274, while Moore picked up 35 per cent, or $126,734. The stadium grossed almost a quarter of a million dollars, with which to pay the undercard and its overheads. A nice night's work!

A million-dollar gate was forecast for a showdown between Patterson and Marciano, but 'The Rock' issued a statement, emphatically rejecting any offer to come out of retirement.

The day after his win, the new champion was in a New York hospital ... visiting his wife Sandra, who had given birth to their first child, daughter Seneca Elizabeth, on the day of his greatest triumph. On the following Sunday, he attended Mass at the Church of the Holy Rosary in Brooklyn, near his boyhood home.

As 1956 drew to a close, the leading contenders were Jackson, Machen, Folley, Willie Pastrano, and the thunderous punching Cleveland Williams, who was on a comeback after two years out. Sonny Liston was in jail and another rising star, Harold Carter, was in the army.

D'Amato chose Jackson as the safest option, and Floyd stopped him in the tenth round at the Polo Grounds in July 1957. Jackson, an unorthodox whirlwind of a fighter with no discernible defence, took a pasting.

Then D'Amato set off on his policy of avoidance, and began with perhaps the most ludicrous of all heavyweight title fights: a defence against 1956 Olympic champion but professional debutant Pete Rademacher at the aptly named Sick's Stadium in Seattle. It was only 24 days since the win over Jackson, but apart from one shock, flash knockdown in round two, Patterson had the desired comfortable night. Rademacher was knocked down seven times and was counted out in round six.

Boxing can be bizarre. Patterson earned less than $50,000 for beating Jackson, who had earned his chance, and five times that amount against Rademacher.

When Patterson fought again, 12 months had passed. Behind him, the division was buzzing. There were a handful of dangerous, legitimate contenders in Machen (unbeaten in 25 fights) Folley (two defeats in 45) Williams (40 wins in 42) and Liston, menacing again with 22 wins in 23 contests. Even old Valdes was on a winning roll at the age of 33 and seemed to have regained his zest for the business.

Who was selected? Roy Harris, a schoolteacher from the small Texan town of Cut N' Shoot, a tough, but relatively inexperienced fighter who had beaten Willie Pastrano and Bob Baker in 1957, but who was still some way adrift of the others.

Patterson's defensive frailties were exposed as Harris put him down in round two, but once he had warmed up he outclassed the Texan, dropping him four times before the fight was stopped at the end of round 12.

Nine months passed before the champion boxed again. Good careers were going to waste, and the public groaned once more when his next opponent was announced: Brian London, who had already lost his British title to Henry Cooper. The British Boxing Board of Control fined London for accepting the fight, but it wasn't his fault. What else was he supposed to do? Patterson knocked him out in the 11th round of a one-sided fight in Indianapolis in May 1959.

At last, on 29 June 1959, he fought a leading contender – the Swede, Ingemar Johansson – who had knocked out Machen in one round and like Floyd was a veteran of the Helsinki Olympics. (He had been disqualified in the heavyweight final against American Ed Sanders.)

Before a modest paying crowd of only 18,215 at Yankee Stadium in New York, Patterson's reign disintegrated. Johansson blasted home right hands to floor him seven times before referee Ruby Goldstein stopped the fight in round three. D'Amato had at least driven a hard bargain for Patterson, who grossed somewhere around $500,000. The deposed champion hid away at home, before eventually returning to training as the contracted return fight was finally signed for 20 June 1960 at the Polo Grounds.

Nobody had regained the heavyweight title, but Patterson boxed brilliantly to knock out Johansson in the fifth and rewrite the history books. He was still only 25.

Nine months later he knocked out Johansson in the sixth round of an exciting decider in Miami. He had proved himself.

By then Liston was the obvious contender, but D'Amato instead chose for their next opponent, Tom McNeeley from Boston, a tough but raw former footballer who had no right to a title shot. They fought in Toronto in December 1961, with McNeeley down ten times before the end came as a merciful release in round four.

Against D'Amato's wishes, Patterson insisted that Liston be given the next chance. He wanted to be an honourable champion ... but his dignity and sense of justice cost him the world title. For in Chicago's Comiskey Park, where Joe Louis had knocked out James J. Braddock a quarter of a century earlier, Charles 'Sonny' Liston blew away Patterson in two minutes six seconds of controlled mayhem.

Floyd left the arena in false beard and glasses and drove home. There was no shame in losing to Liston, but Patterson regressed into his boyhood behaviour and took time to be coaxed back to normality.

He insisted on the rematch clause and fought Liston again at the Las Vegas Convention Center in the summer of 1963. He promised to last longer. And he did – four seconds longer.

He worked his way back over the next couple of years, ironically outpointing Machen in Stockholm in July 1964, and in November 1965, challenged Liston's successor, the brash, flashy Muhammad Ali in Las Vegas. Slowed by a pre-fight back injury, Patterson was in serious pain as the 22-year-old Ali, formerly known as Cassius Clay, danced around him and picked him apart. The slaughter was allowed to go on to round 12 as Ali, angered by Patterson's refusal to address him by his Muslim name, handed out what amounted to a ritualised torture.

A fourth round knockout of Henry Cooper re-established Patterson in 1966, and when Ali was exiled for refusing the draft, the old champ took part in the elimination tournament organised by the World Boxing Association. He lost to Jerry Quarry, but was then given first shot at the tournament winner, Jimmy Ellis, in Stockholm in 1968. He thought he had won. The judges didn't.

He retired for two years, then came back, working his way steadily into world class. He best win was a 10-round decision over the rugged Argentine brawler Oscar Bonavena in February 1972, but when he fought Ali in a match nominally for the North American championship in Madison Square Garden in September 1972, he was stopped in seven rounds.

That was his 64th and last fight at the age of 37 and a full 20 years after his professional debut.

Patterson had his flaws, but was a marvellously talented heavyweight who deserved the chance to defend his title against the best men of his era. He might have beaten anybody but Liston.

In retirement he stayed fit, ran several marathons, and became a trainer and manager. He guided his adopted son, Tracy Harris Patterson to the WBC super-bantamweight title in 1992, and three years later was appointed New York State Athletic Commission chairman, a post he had first held some years before. He resigned in 1998, following a humiliating court hearing when he failed to respond adequately to questions about basic boxing rules and his own career.

CAREER STATISTICS

World heavyweight champion 1956-59, 1960-62
New York, born Waco, North Carolina 4 January 1935
1952 Olympic middleweight gold medal

1952

Sep 12 Eddie Godbold w rsf 4 New York
Oct 6 Sammy Walker w rsf 2 Brooklyn
Oct 21 Lester Jackson w rsf 3 New York
Dec 29 Lalu Sabotin w rsf 5 Brooklyn

1953

Jan 28 Chester Mieszala w rsf 5 Chicago
Apr 3 Dick Wagner w pts 8 Brooklyn
Jun 1 Gordon Wallace w rsf 3 Brooklyn
Oct 19 Wes Bascom w pts 8 Brooklyn
Dec 14 Dick Wagner w rsf 5 Brooklyn

1954

Feb 15 Yvon Durelle w pts 8 Brooklyn
Mar 30 Sam Brown w rsf 2 Washington DC
Apr 19 Alvin Williams w pts 8 Brooklyn
May 10 Jesse Turner w pts 8 Brooklyn
Jun 7 Joey Maxim l pts 8 Brooklyn
Jul 12 Jacques Royer-Crecy w rsf 7 New York
Aug 2 Tommy Harrison w rsf 1 Brooklyn
Oct 11 Esau Ferdinand w pts 8 New York
Oct 22 Joe Gannon w pts 8 New York
Nov 19 Jimmy Slade w pts 8 New York

1955
Jan 7 Willie Troy w rsf 5 New York
Jan 17 Don Grant w rsf 5 Brooklyn
Mar 17 Esau Ferdinand w rsf 10 Oakland
Jun 23 Yvon Durelle w rsf 5 Newcastle
Jul 6 Archie McBride w ko 7 New York
Sep 8 Alvin Williams w rsf 8 Moncton
Sep 29 Dave Whitlock w rsf 3 San Francisco
Oct 13 Calvin Brad w ko 1 Los Angeles
Dec 8 Jimmy Slade w rsf 7 Los Angeles
1956
Mar 12 Jimmy Walls w rsf 2 New Britain
Apr 10 Alvin Williams w ko 3 Kansas City
Jun 8 Tommy Jackson w pts 12 New York
Nov 30 Archie Moore w ko 5 Chicago
(vacant world heavyweight title)
1957
Jul 29 Tommy Jackson w rsf 10 New York
(World heavyweight title)
Aug 22 Pete Rademacher w ko 6 Seattle
(World heavyweight title)
1958
Aug 18 Roy Harris w rsf 12 Los Angeles
(World heavyweight title)
1959
May 1 Brian London w ko 11 Indianapolis
(World heavyweight title)
Jun 26 Ingemar Johansson l rsf 3 New York
(World heavyweight title)
1960
Jun 20 Ingemar Johansson w ko 5 New York
(World heavyweight title)
1961
Mar 13 Ingemar Johansson w ko 6 Miami
(World heavyweight title)
Dec 4 Tom McNeeley w ko 4 Toronto
(World heavyweight title)
1962
Sep 25 Sonny Liston l ko 1 Chicago
(World heavyweight title)
1963
Jul 22 Sonny Liston l ko 1 Las Vegas
(World heavyweight title)
1964
Jan 6 Sante Amonti w rsf 8 Stockholm
Jul 5 Eddie Machen w pts 12 Stockholm
Dec 12 Charley Powell w ko 6 San Juan
1965
Feb 1 George Chuvalo w pts 12 New York
May 14 Ted Herring w rsf 3 Stockholm
Nov 22 Muhammad Ali l rsf 12 Las Vegas
(World heavyweight title)
1966
Sep 20 Henry Cooper w ko 4 London
1967
Feb 13 Willie Johnson w ko 3 Miami
Mar 30 Bill McMurray w ko 1 Pittsburgh
Jun 9 Jerry Quarry drew 10 Los Angeles
Oct 28 Jerry Quarry l pts 12 Los Angeles
1968
Sep 14 Jimmy Ellis l pts 15 Stockholm
(WBA heavyweight title)
1969 Inactive
1970
Sep 15 Charlie Green w ko 10 New York
1971
Jan 16 Levi Forte w rsf 2 Miami
Mar 29 Roger Russell w rsf 9 Philadelphia
May 26 Terry Daniels w pts 10 Cleveland
Jul 17 Charley Polite w pts 10 Erie, Pa.
Aug 21 Vic Brown w pts 10 Buffalo
Nov 23 Charlie Harris w ko 6 Portland, Me.
1972
Feb 11 Oscar Bonavena w pts 10 New York
Jul 14 Pedro Agosto w rsf 6 New York
Sep 20 Muhammad Ali l rsf 7 New York
(NABF heavyweight title)

Fights 64 Won 55 Lost 8 Drawn 1

SONNY LISTON

BIG BAD SONNY

NOBODY wanted to believe in Sonny Liston. The most dangerous heavyweight of his time had the misfortune to reach his peak when boxing's image was at an embarrassing low. The International Boxing Club, which had governed boxing in the 1950s, had been closed down by a federal ruling, its monopolistic practices exposed. Then Senator Estes Kefauver chaired a commission which investigated the way boxing was run. He looked carefully at the supposed influences behind Liston's career, and heard testimonies about mob-inspired corruption. Former middleweight champion Jake La Motta was one who told what he knew.

Then several businessmen were found guilty in an extortion case surrounding the contract of former welterweight champion Don Jordan. As a result, the ringleader, Frankie Carbo, was jailed for 25 years. Carbo was widely believed to have been the controlling influence in Liston's career. His aides Joe Sica, Frank 'Blinky' Palermo and Louis Dragna, received respective sentences of 20, 15 and five years. Truman Gibson, the former president of the IBC, was given five years, but had that suspended and served it on parole. They were also fined $10,000 each.

Liston was refused a licence in New York, even though there was no evidence that he had anything to do with corrupt practices, and former heavyweight champion Jack Dempsey went public in *Ring* magazine to denounce him.

'Sonny Liston shouldn't get a title shot,' he said. 'No one knows what Liston will do next. He must prove himself. He must prove he has rehabilitated himself.'

Cus D'Amato, the manager of heavyweight champion Floyd Patterson, hid behind Liston's criminal past and alleged connections to avoid him. D'Amato had watched Patterson very astutely throughout his career and knew Liston was the best fighter on the scene. He also knew that Patterson's defence was the weakness that could cost him the title. At one point he claimed that Liston could not be given a title shot until he had cleaned up his situation, whatever that meant. However, public pressure and Patterson's own desire to prove himself led to Liston being given his chance in

Comiskey Park, Chicago, in September 1962. He was booed into the ring. Those who had picked Patterson to beat him included former heavyweight champions Rocky Marciano, James J. Braddock and Ingemar Johansson, and *Ring* editor Nat Fleischer.

And even when Sonny blew the champion away in 126 seconds of the first round with as devastating a display of punching as you could wish to see, there were those who complained, who wanted to ignore the evidence of their own eyes.

Ring magazine felt compelled to run a piece, informing readers that the knockout was authentic, that the fight was not fixed.

Liston received a congratulary telegram from the Mayor of Philadelphia, where he was living, and on the flight home from Chicago he was full of how he would be a credit to black Americans. But when he stepped from the plane, there was no official welcoming party and little public interest. Two weeks later, police stopped him for driving suspiciously.

He left Philadelphia for Denver with his wife Geraldine in 1963 and uttered the memorable line: 'I'd rather be a lamppost in Denver than Mayor of Philadelphia'. In Denver, it was no better. Eventually, the Listons settled in Las Vegas, but he was never freed from his past. He died there, in mysterious circumstances, at the end of 1970.

Geraldine Liston returned home from a week away to find the decomposing body of the former world champion, which was estimated to have lain there for at least six days, in the bedroom. The autopsy suggested heroin had been present in his body and there were track marks on his arms. Yet his friends insisted he had a pathological fear of needles. Various stories suggested he had upset mobsters for whom he had been working and was eliminated. But nobody will ever know.

Sonny Liston's life began on an Arkansas cotton farm, where his mother Helen and father Tobe were sharecroppers. Nobody knows when that was: he was Tobe's 24th child out of 25 and nobody bothered to write it down. His estimate was 8 May 1932, but that was just a guess in spite of a birth certificate he produced in the 1960s. His mother, who could be forgiven for being a little hazy about the details, changed her story more than once. But at one point she insisted it was 22 July 1927.

It was a tough start. 'I had nothing but a lot of brothers and sisters, a helpless mother and a father who didn't care about a single one of us,' he said once.

Helen Liston moved to St Louis, Missouri, during the Second World War, and Sonny, whose given name was Charles, stole enough money for a bus ticket and followed her. She worked in a factory, and tried to guide him, but he was illiterate, could not accept the humiliation that came with attending school, and descended into life as a street thug.

He was arrested for mugging and in 1950 he was convicted of armed robbery and sentenced to five years. After two he was given parole, largely thanks to a priest, Father Alois Stevens, whose patch included Jefferson City prison. It was Stevens who encouraged him to take up boxing – and he took to it, at the same time improving his behaviour to the point when he courted and married his wife, while still incarcerated.

'Charley Liston' made his professional debut in St Louis in September 1953 with a first round stoppage of Don Smith, a novice heavyweight from Louisville, Kentucky.

His fifth fight was on an IBC card in St Louis, a points win over local rival Stan Howlett, after which he switched to Detroit for the rest of the year. He was hyped as a future contender before his first fight there, an eight rounder against Michigan champion Johnny Summerlin, and was apparently the recipient of a lucky decision. 'Perhaps some of the advance publicity had swayed the arbitrators,' wrote Jack Waina in *Ring*. Waina felt Summerlin won clearly, and added: 'Decisions of this type I'll never understand, but a rematch has already been signed'.

The return, in August 1954, brought Liston another points win, this time on a split decision. A month later he lost his unbeaten record when, according to legend, he laughed at a joke made by his opponent, the Michigan light-heavyweight champion Marty Marshall, and took a punch on the open mouth which broke his jaw. He lost a split verdict after eight rounds in which the 15lb lighter Marshall used his experience and speed to frustrate him.

The jaw damage kept him out of the ring for six months. He reappeared in St Louis, and in his second fight back, survived what seems to have been a flash knockdown and stopped Marshall in the sixth round. When they fought a decider in Pittsburgh in March 1956, Liston won on points. It was the first time he had gone ten rounds.

Then his career went on hold for almost two years: Sonny left a policeman lying in his own blood in an alley, with a broken knee and a cut eye. The facts of how that came to be were disputed, but it wound up with Liston getting a nine-month sentence. He served seven, and had his boxing licence suspended by the St Louis commission. The city police targeted him as an undesirable, but eventually his licence was reinstated.

He returned to the ring on an IBC card at Chicago Stadium in January 1958 with a two-round knockout of Bill Hunter. The wheels were in motion again. There were eight fights that year, eight wins, six inside the distance. The best was a 69-second demolition of Wayne Bethea in August. By the end of the year he was in the world top ten, and living in Philadelphia.

He ripped through the ratings in 1959, stopping in turn Mike DeJohn, Cleveland Williams, Nino Valdes and Willi Besmanoff. Williams and Valdes, the most important victims, lasted three rounds each.

By 1960, Liston was beyond much doubt the best heavyweight in the world – but nobody wanted to believe it. Howard King, Williams again, former title challenger Roy Harris and Zora Folley were all knocked out or stopped. He did have trouble with crafty Eddie Machen, but won on points over 12 rounds. Harris, who was stopped in the first round, had given world champ Floyd Patterson an argument before losing in 12 two years earlier. He said Liston was much the superior fighter.

He knocked out King again in three and an overmatched German named Albert Westphal in one, but it took until 25 September 1962 to break down the resistance of

Patterson and D'Amato. Eventually, Patterson was ripped apart by one of the most sustained displays of menace in the history of the heavyweight championship.

A rematch was a crazy idea, but they staged it in Las Vegas on 22 July 1963. This time poor Patterson lasted two minutes ten seconds, an improvement on his previous performance of four seconds! Liston, who was invited to the White House and went on a tour to England, looked a class above every other heavyweight on the scene.

And then into the equation danced Cassius Marcellus Clay.

Liston's suspicion of boxing writers in particular and media people in general, as well as the reticence of many who cannot read or write, made him a tough interview. He cut a brooding, monosyllabic figure, and film of him working out to Duke Ellington's 'Night Train' captures a master of intimidation.

He was taunted and tormented by the brash, boyish Clay, but insisted he would knock him out inside two rounds. Most people believed him – and it seemed they were thinking on the right lines when Clay's bizarre weigh-in rantings left a doctor claiming the young challenger was terrified.

But Clay was acting, and Liston grew old in the six rounds the fight lasted. His face leaked blood from a gash below his left eye. He swiped and hooked, missed far more than he landed, and missed his chance to win when Clay was close to panic because his vision was temporarily impaired. He ran, his eyes cleared and he was on top again when Liston retired on his stool at the end of round six, unable to go on because of a shoulder injury.

A public which saw Liston as one of the hardest men in boxing history inevitably took some persuading that he quit so tamely. Suspicions rose that he threw the fight to suit some strange behind-the-scenes move. And the general lack of trust in the result was not helped when Clay became Muhammad Ali and publicly acknowledged his role in the Black Muslim Movement. Was there nobody around this business who could be seen as a figure of trust?

Inevitably, the return was signed. It was delayed when Ali underwent a hernia operation, and then became the fight that nobody wanted. Eventually, it was condemned to the fringes: Lewiston, Maine, in front of around 2,500 people.

It was a pathetic exhibition. Ali circled, jabbed, prodded, and then stepped in behind a right hand to the temple. Liston went down on his side, referee Jersey Joe Walcott lost control of what was happening and failed to pick up the count. Liston eventually hauled himself to his feet, and as they shaped up and moved around, *Ring* editor Nat Fleischer, whose job was to count the knockdowns, attracted Walcott's attention by banging on the canvas: Liston had been counted out. It was all over in one minute 52 seconds.

Nobody wanted a part of Liston after that. He did not box in the USA again until 1968 (after four wins in Sweden). Although he scored some solid wins, he was not allowed into the heavyweight frame as Ali went into exile and new generation stars

Joe Frazier and Jimmy Ellis argued over who should succeed him.

Liston stopped the talented Californian Henry Clark in seven, outpointed Billy Joiner and stopped a string of second-raters.

He fought his way into contention to the point where he was given a meaningful fight against Leotis Martin in Las Vegas in December 1969. By then, however, he had lost heart. He trained sloppily and, though he was ahead on all three scorecards after eight rounds, was knocked out in the ninth.

Martin sustained eye damage that forced him to retire shortly afterwards, while Sonny had one more fight, when he stopped Chuck Wepner, otherwise known as 'The Bayonne Bleeder', at the end of nine rounds. Wepner needed more than 50 stitches in his face.

There were dark rumours that Liston had refused to obey an instruction from associates to throw the fight. Maybe, maybe not. There were so many stories about him and nobody, probably not even Liston, knew what was true any more.

Six months after the Wepner fight, he was dead.

CAREER STATISTICS

World heavyweight champion 1962-64
St Louis, born St Francis County, Arkansas, 8 May 1932
Real name: Charles Liston

1953
Sep 2 Don Smith w rsf 1 St Louis
Sep 17 Ponce DeLeon w pts 4 St Louis
Nov 21 Ben Thomas w pts 6 St Louis
1954
Jan 25 Martin Lee w rsf 6 St Louis
Mar 31 Stan Howlett w pts 6 St Louis
Jun 29 John Summerlin w pts 8 Detroit
Aug 10 John Summerlin w pts 8 Detroit
Sep 7 Marty Marshall l pts 8 Detroit
1955
Mar 1 Neil Welch w pts 8 St Louis
Apr 21 Marty Marshall w rsf 6 St Louis
May 5 Emil Brtko w rsf 5 Pittsburgh
May 25 Calvin Butler w rsf 2 St Louis
Sep 13 Johnny Gray w rsf 6 Indianapolis
Dec 13 Larry Watson w rsf 4 St Louis
1956
Mar 6 Marty Marshall w pts 10 Pittsburgh
1957 inactive
1958
Jan 29 Bill Hunter w ko 2 Chicago
Mar 11 Ben Wise w ko 4 Chicago
Apr 3 Bert Whitehurst w pts 10 St Louis
May 14 Julio Mederos w rsf 3 Chicago
Aug 6 Wayne Bethea w rsf 1 Chicago
Oct 7 Frankie Daniels w ko 1 Miami
Oct 24 Bert Whitehurst w pts 10 St Louis
Nov 18 Ernie Cab w rsf 8 Miami
1959
Feb 18 Mike DeJohn w rsf 6 Miami
Apr 15 Cleveland Williams w rsf 3 Miami
Aug 5 Nino Valdes w ko 3 Chicago
Dec 9 Willi Besmanoff w rsf 7 Cleveland
1960
Feb 23 Howard King w rsf 8 Miami
Mar 21 Cleveland Williams w rsf 2 Houston
Apr 25 Roy Harris w rsf 1 Houston
Jul 18 Zora Folley w ko 3 Denver
Sep 7 Eddie Machen w pts 12 Seattle
1961
Mar 8 Howard King w ko 3 Miami
Dec 4 Albert Westphal w ko 1 Philadelphia
1962
Sep 25 Floyd Patterson w ko 1 Chicago
(World heavyweight title)
1963
Jul 22 Floyd Patterson w ko 1 Las Vegas
(World heavyweight title)
1964
Feb 25 Cassius Clay l rtd 6 Miami
(World heavyweight title)
1965
May 25 Muhammad Ali l ko 1 Lewiston, Me
(World heavyweight title)
1966
Jun 29 Gerhard Zech w ko 7 Stockholm
Aug 19 Amos Johnson w ko 3 Gothenburg
1967
Mar 30 Dave Bailey w ko 1 Gothenburg
Apr 28 Elmer Rush w rsf 6 Stockholm
1968
Mar 16 Bill McMurray w ko 4 Reno
May 23 Billy Joiner w rsf 7 Los Angeles
Jul 6 Henry Clark w rsf 7 San Francisco
Oct 14 Sonny Moore w rsf 3 Phoenix
Nov 3 Willis Earls w ko 2 Juarez
Nov 12 Roger Rischer w ko 3 Pittsburgh
Dec 10 Amos Lincoln w ko 2 Baltimore
1969
Mar 28 Billy Joiner w pts 10 St Louis
Mar 19 George Johnson w rsf 7 Las Vegas
Sep 23 Sonny Moore w ko 3 Houston
Dec 6 Leotis Martin l ko 9 Las Vegas
(NABF heavyweight title)
1970
Jun 29 Chuck Wepner w rsf 10 Jersey City

Fights 54 Won 50 Lost 4
Died 30 December 1970, Las Vegas, aged 38

EMILE GRIFFITH

THE VIRGIN ISLAND MILLINER

Emile Griffith was one of the cleverest, most enduring of champions. He fought professionally for almost 20 years and spent most of that time in world class. He held the world welterweight title three times and the middleweight championship twice.

Griffith wasn't the biggest of hitters, but had a tight defence, and was a fine all-round boxer, as happy to work on the inside as he was at long range. In short, he was a natural.

A gentle, quietly spoken and sometimes superstitious man, he was also at the centre of a terrible controversy when opponent Benny Paret died in a nationally televised bout in 1962. The tragedy came at a time when boxing was already under the microscope, following the jailing of mobster Frankie Carbo and his henchmen and the Kefauver Commission hearings which posed some embarrassing questions for boxing's defenders to answer.

Boxing was never nearer to being banned in the USA than after Griffith's fatal fight with Paret, and the turmoil must have been hard to bear. He considered retiring, but eventually came to understand that what had happened to Paret might have happened to anyone.

Emile Alphonse Griffith was born in Charlotte Amalie, St Thomas, on the American Virgin Islands on 3 February 1938. His father was a car mechanic, who moved his family – wife Emelda, and eight children, of whom Emile was the eldest – to New York in 1955. Mr Griffith snr. died in 1959, having seen his son's beginnings in the sport which was to make him famous.

Emile broke into boxing almost by accident, when working at his first job as a delivery boy for a New York hat-maker, Howie Albert. He did well enough to move up in the company, which was on West 39th Street, and tried his hand at designing. But Albert was a boxing nut, and Griffith had such a tremendous natural physique – wide shoulders and narrow waist – that he persuaded him to give the sport a try under the wing of his friend, a schoolteacher named Gil Clancy who had managed, among others, pros like middleweight Ralph 'Tiger' Jones, who held a 1955 win over Ray Robinson.

They hit it off immediately and Griffith's talent soon became obvious. He won the 1958 National Golden Gloves welterweight title and in June that year, having lost only twice in 53 amateur contests, decided to try his luck as a professional with Albert and Clancy co-managing him. Billed out of West Side, he won his debut at the St Nicholas Arena with a four-round points win over a fully blown middleweight, Joe Parham from Paterson, New Jersey.

Emelda Griffith was an enthusiastic ringside presence whenever he fought. He topped the bill for the first time, at St Nick's in March 1959, in only his 10th pro fight, outpointing Bobby Shell over 10 rounds. Shell, from Washington DC, was not a particularly severe test – he had won only once in his previous seven fights – but Griffith looked good, which to Clancy and Albert was the important issue.

After climbing the ladder a little further with decisions over Mel Barker, Willie 'Pineapple' Stevenson and the dangerous Cuban, Kid Fichique, the Griffith unbeaten run came to an end in October 1959 when classy middleweight Randy Sandy outpointed him at the Academy of Music Arena in New York.

Sandy, a tough 28-year-old originally from Brooklyn but then living in Harlem, was settling into the role of high-class opponent, but could still teach top grade fighters a trick or two. He was a little too strong and wise for Griffith, but the 21-year-old came out of the fight with credit.

Griffith made his national TV debut in Madison Square Garden in February 1960 when he outsped and outfought Mexican Gaspar 'Indian' Ortega over ten rounds. Surprisingly, it was only a split decision, but the improvement of this bright, church-going hopeful was noted.

In March and April 1960 he won and lost against Denny Moyer, who was to hold the light-middleweight title and fight the best of a generation in a 140-fight career, and then marched into the world title picture with two points wins over Jorge Fernandez, another over Florentino Fernandez, an eighth-round stoppage of Willie Toweel from South Africa, and a decision over Luis Rodriguez.

The outcome was his first world title fight against Benny Paret at Miami Beach Convention Center in April 1961. Paret, a transplanted Cuban, had won the title almost a year earlier by outscoring Don Jordan. He had lost decisions in non-title fights against Moyer and Ortega, and had far from proved himself as a world champion. Griffith outfought him on the inside, whacking away at his ribs, which was Paret's game. Paret, who later admitted he had underestimated Griffith and had neglected his training, had his moments, and the fight was delicately poised when Emile opened up with left hooks from longer range in the 13th and knocked him out.

In June 1961 he stopped Gaspar Ortega in the 12th round of his first defence in Los Angeles, staging a marvellous performance. Ortega, who was down in round seven, fought back but was stopped for the first time in his eight-year, 83-fight career. In fact, he had not deserved his title chance, as he had lost three of his previous four fights, the sequence broken only by a shock decision over Paret. Strangely, Paret had accepted $20,000 step-aside money to let Griffith box Ortega.

Then Griffith gave Paret a rematch in September 1961 in front of a disappointingly low crowd of 4,390 at Madison Square Garden and lost a split decision after 15 hard rounds. Clancy was furious, claiming that they had been the victims of an injustice. *Ring* magazine made Griffith a two-point winner, as did most of the ringside pressmen.

Six months later, they fought their tragic decider. This time Paret insulted Griffith at the weigh-in, touching his behind and calling him a homosexual ('maricon' in Spanish). Griffith was angry, but contained his rage for the fight. Paret had been badly mauled in an attempt to beat world middleweight champion Gene Fullmer, and may well have been carrying a deep-seated injury from that knockout defeat three months earlier. He dropped Griffith in round six, but was then steadily outfought. By round 12 the Cuban, whose wife was watching on television at their Miami home, was exhausted. Griffith pinned him on the ropes, where his arm was trapped, and blasted away in a ferocious two-fisted barrage. Even as referee Ruby Goldstein struggled to stop it, Paret was sliding down the ropes and slipping into unconsciousness. He underwent surgery for the removal of two blood clots, but never recovered, and died ten days later from brain injuries.

Abolitionists had a field day, and even received support from the Pope, but boxing tottered on.

Griffith was distraught, and some say he never again staged as venomous a barrage as he did against Paret. Four months later, Clancy brought him back in a world title defence, feeling that his character would make him respond to the task. They did, however, go away from the pressure of New York, outpointing leading contender Ralph Dupas in Las Vegas. Before the fight, Griffith was trembling with nerves, and unable to stop his right hand shaking for some time. Once the bell rang, however, he settled down to chase the mobile, elusive Dupas out of the ring. Dupas tested him, but was almost stopped in the final round. Griffith won unanimously, by 10, nine and four points, but admitted that when Dupas was on the ropes, his mind flashed back to the Paret fight. 'There were times that I had doubts,' he said. 'There were times I was fighting myself in there.'

Clancy kept him busy with a couple of non-title wins over Moyer and Don Fullmer, and took him to Vienna where he won recognition from the European Boxing Union as world light-middleweight champion by outpointing Ted Wright. More seriously, in December 1962, he retained his welterweight belt by stopping old rival Jorge Fernandez of Argentina with a body shot in the ninth round in Las Vegas. Fernandez claimed it was low, was given five minutes to recover, but could not go on.

Griffith took a payday in Copenhagen to defend his spurious light-middleweight belt with a nine rounds win over Chris Christensen, but then lost the welterweight crown a second time when another exiled Cuban, Luis Rodriguez, outpointed him in the Dodger Stadium, Los Angeles, in March 1963. Griffith raged in the ring afterwards that he had been robbed, but his protests were overshadowed later that night when, in one of three world title fights on the show, Davey Moore collapsed with a brain injury after losing his featherweight crown to Sugar Ramos. Moore died two days later.

A return clause enabled Griffith to have a rematch three months later, and this time he won the split decision and it was Rodriguez's turn to complain.

Griffith ended the year with one of only two stoppage defeats in his entire career: world class middleweight Rubin 'Hurricane' Carter took him out in the first round in Pittsburgh.

In 1964, he went on tour, with non-title fights in Sydney, Rome, Honolulu and London as well as a world championship decider against Rodriguez, which he won, almost inevitably, on a disputed split verdict, and a more conclusive points win over Welshman Brian Curvis at the Empire Pool, Wembley. Even so, he fought the late rounds with cramp and had to be carried from the ring!

There were two more successful defences in the Garden in 1965, when he outboxed Jose Stable, a talented Cuban who lived in New York, and Manuel Gonzalez, a tough Texan who had outpointed him early in the year in a 10-round workout in Houston.

The following year he won the world middleweight title by outscoring defending champ Dick Tiger in front of almost 15,000 fans in the Garden. Yet again, a Griffith verdict was controversial, with the majority of fans booing, and *Ring* magazine declaring boldly: 'They took the title from the legitimate owner and passed it on to the challenger ... it was one of the worst verdicts rendered in New York in years'. Nat Fleischer made Tiger a five-point winner! Tony Castellano saw it even, but Arthur Mercante and the veteran Frank Forbes had Griffith in front by four and one respectively.

Griffith, who weighed only 151½lb even in a middleweight title fight, could probably have continued to fight as a welter, but elected to keep the middleweight crown after a court ruled that he could not hold both. Tiger, however, moved up to light-heavyweight.

By now living in Weehawken, New Jersey, Griffith turned back a couple of challenges from Bronx idol Joey Archer before embarking on a celebrated three-fight series with the talented, enigmatic Italian Nino Benvenuti. Griffith lost the first and third fights in the Garden, and won the second in Shea Stadium, in Flushing.

It was now 1968, he was 30 years old and a former champion, after a total of five world championship reigns. Yet he would go on plying his trade for almost a decade more.

In October 1969, he dropped back to welterweight and challenged the Mexican-based Cuban Jose 'Mantequilla' Napoles for the world title in Los Angeles. He was knocked down in round three and lost clearly on points.

Ten more wins took him to a middleweight title bid against Carlos Monzon in Buenos Aires. He was stopped in the 14th round, his legs weary, bent over at the waist, his gloves cupped around his head. There had been only flashes of his old brilliance. Amazingly, he gave Monzon more of an argument two years later in Monte Carlo, when only the great Argentinian's strength brought him through over the last third for a points win. Griffith was disgusted.

He was 38 when he fought for the WBC light-middleweight title against Eckhard Dagge in Berlin. By then beginning to lose as many decisions as he won, it was a tribute to his longevity, rather than a deserved shot at a major championship. Dagge won a majority decision. The Griffith camp argued about it.

He retired in 1977 after losing a one-sided fight in Monte Carlo against a future world champ, Alan Minter. In retirement he became a widely respected trainer at the Times Square Gym, and worked in Wilfred Benitez's corner on the night he became WBC welterweight champion. He was also with James 'Bonecrusher' Smith on the night the American heavyweight knocked out Frank Bruno in 1984.

He was seriously hurt in 1992 when he was attacked in New York. Details were sketchy, but his kidneys were damaged, and for a time his life was thought to be in danger. Fortunately, he recovered.

CAREER STATISTICS

World welterweight champion 1961, 1962-63, 1963-66
World middleweight champion 1966-67, 1967-68
New York, born St Thomas, Virgin Islands, 3 February 1938
Full name: Emile Alphonse Griffith

1958
Jun 2 Joe Parham w pts 4 New York
Jun 23 Bobby Gibson w pts 4 New York
Jul 21 Tommy Leaks w pts 4 New York
Oct 6 Art Cunningham w pts 6 New York
Nov 18 Sergio Rios w ko 3 New York
Dec 15 Larry Jones w ko 5 New York

1959
Jan 26 Gaylord Barnes w ko 5 New York
Feb 9 Willie Johnson w ko 5 New York
Feb 23 Barry Allison w ko 5 New York
Mar 23 Bobby Shell w pts 10 New York
Apr 27 Mel Barker w pts 10 New York
May 25 Willie Stevenson w pts 10 New York
Aug 7 Kid Fichique w pts 10 New York
Oct 26 Randy Sandy l pts 10 New York
Nov 23 Ray Lancaster w rsf 7 New York

1960
Jan 8 Roberto Pena w pts 10 New York
Feb 12 Gaspar Ortega w pts 10 New York
Mar 11 Denny Moyer w pts 10 New York
Apr 26 Denny Moyer l pts 10 Portland
Jun 3 Jorge Fernandez w pts 10 New York
Jul 25 Jorge Fernandez w pts 10 New York
Aug 25 Florentino Fernandez w pts 10 New York
Oct 22 Willie Toweel w rsf 8 New York
Dec 17 Luis Rodriguez w pts 10 New York

1961
Apr 1 Benny Paret w ko 13 Miami
(World welterweight title)
Jun 3 Gaspar Ortega w rsf 12 Los Angeles
(World welterweight title)
Jul 29 Yama Bahama w pts 10 New York
Sep 30 Benny Paret l pts 15 New York
(World welterweight title)
Nov 4 Stanford Bulla w rsf 4 Hamilton
Dec 23 Isaac Logart w pts 10 New York

1962
Feb 3 Johnny Torres w pts 10 St Thomas
Mar 24 Benny Paret w rsf 12 New York
(World welterweight title)
Jul 13 Ralph Dupas w pts 15 Las Vegas
(World welterweight title)
Aug 18 Denny Moyer w pts 10 Tacoma
Oct 6 Don Fullmer w pts 10 New York
Oct 17 Ted Wright w pts 15 Vienna
Dec 8 Jorge Fernandez w rsf 9 Las Vegas
(World welterweight title)

1963
Feb 3 Chris Christensen w rsf 9 Copenhagen
Mar 21 Luis Rodriguez l pts 15 Los Angeles
(World welterweight title)
Jun 8 Luis Rodriguez w pts 15 New York
(World welterweight title)
Aug 10 Holley Mims w pts 10 Saratoga Springs
Oct 5 Jose Gonzalez w pts 10 San Juan

Dec 20 Rubin Carter l rsf 1 Pittsburgh
1964
Feb 10 Ralph Dupas w ko 3 Sydney
Mar 11 Juan Carlos Duran nc 7 Rome
Apr 14 Stan Harrington w ko 4 Honolulu
Jun 12 Luis Rodriguez w pts 15 Las Vegas
(World welterweight title)
Sep 22 Brian Curvis w pts 15 London
(World welterweight title)
Dec 1 Dave Charnley w rsf 9 London
1965
Jan 26 Manuel Gonzalez l pts 10 Houston
Mar 30 Jose Stable w pts 15 New York
(World welterweight title)
Jun 14 Eddie Pace w pts 10 Honolulu
Aug 20 Don Fullmer l pts 12 Salt Lake City
Sep 14 Gabe Terronez w ko 4 Fresno
Oct 4 Harry Scott w rsf 7 London
Dec 10 Manuel Gonzalez w pts 15 New York
(World welterweight title)
1966
Feb 3 Johnny Brooks w pts 10 Las Vegas
Apr 25 Dick Tiger w pts 15 New York
(World middleweight title)
Jul 13 Joey Archer w pts 15 New York
(World middleweight title)
1967
Jan 23 Joey Archer w pts 15 New York
(World middleweight title)
Apr 17 Nino Benvenuti l pts 15 New York
(World middleweight title)
Sep 29 Nino Benvenuti w pts 15 Flushing, NY
(World middleweight title)
Dec 15 Remo Golfarini w ko 6 Rome
1968
Mar 4 Nino Benvenuti l pts 15 New York
(World middleweight title)
Jun 11 Andy Heilman w pts 12 Oakland
Aug 6 Gipsy Joe Harris w pts 12 Philadelphia
Oct 29 Stan Hayward l pts 10 Philadelphia
1969
Feb 3 Andy Heilman w pts 10 New York
May 12 Stan Hayward w pts 12 New York
Jul 11 Dick Di Veronica w rsf 7 Syracuse
Aug 15 Art Hernandez w pts 10 Sioux Falls
Oct 18 Jose Napoles l pts 15 Los Angeles
(World welterweight title)
1970
Jan 28 Doyle Baird w pts 10 Cleveland
Mar 11 Carlos Marks w pts 12 New York
Jun 4 Tom Bogs w pts 10 Copenhagen
Jul 15 Dick Tiger w pts 10 New York
Oct 17 Danny Perez w pts 10 St Thomas
Nov 10 Nate Collins w pts 10 San Francisco
1971
Mar 23 Rafael Gutierrez w pts 10 San Francisco
Apr 10 Juan Ramos w ko 2 St Thomas
May 3 Ernie Lopez w pts 10 Las Vegas
Jul 26 Nessim Cohen w pts 10 New York
Sep 25 Carlos Monzon l rsf 14 Buenos Aires
(World middleweight title)
Dec 10 Danny McAloon w pts 10 New York
1972
Jan 31 Armando Muniz w pts 10 Anaheim
Feb 21 Jacques Kechichian w pts 10 Paris
Mar 30 Ernie Lopez w pts 10 Los Angeles
Sep 16 Joe De Nucci w pts 10 Boston
Oct 11 Joe De Nucci w pts 12 Boston
Dec 18 Jean-Claude Bouttier l dis 7 Paris
1973
Mar 12 Nessim Cohen drew 10 Paris
Jun 2 Carlos Monzon l pts 15 Monte Carlo
(World middleweight title)
Nov 2 Manuel Gonzalez w pts 10 Tampa
Nov 19 Tony Mundine l pts 10 Paris
1974
Feb 5 Tony Licata l pts 12 Boston
(vacant NABF middleweight title)
May 25 Renato Garcia w pts 10 Monte Carlo
Oct 9 Bennie Briscoe w pts 10 Philadelphia
Nov 22 Vito Antuofermo l pts 10 New York
Dec 10 Donato Paduano w pts 10 Montreal
1975
May 31 Juan Carlos Duran l pts 10 Cali
Jul 23 Leo Saenz w pts 10 Landover
Aug 9 Elijah Makhatini l pts 10 Johannesburg
Nov 7 Jose Chirino w pts 10 Albany
1976
Feb 9 Loucif Hamani l pts 10 Paris
Jun 26 Bennie Briscoe drew 10 Monte Carlo
Sep 18 Eckhard Dagge l pts 15 Berlin
(WBC light-middleweight title)
Oct 24 Dino Del Cid w rsf 4 Cartagena
Dec 4 Frank Reiche w rsf 10 Hamburg
1977
Feb 2 Christy Elliott w pts 10 New York
Apr 15 Joel Bonnetaz l pts 10 Perigeux
Jul 19 Mayfield Pennington l pts 10 Louisville
Jul 30 Alan Minter l pts 10 Monte Carlo

Fights 112 Won 85 Lost 24 Drawn 2 No Contests 1

DICK TIGER

THE SLEEPING TIGER

Fate was very unkind to Dick Tiger. His Ibo people, for whom he cared so much, were cruelly treated in a bitter civil war in Nigeria, and at the height of his fame he was struck down by illness. All his life he seemed to be fighting back. In boxing, he sought his fortune first in England, but lost his first four fights, and when he tried in America, he won only two of his first five. Nevertheless he went on to win undisputed world titles at two weights and was arguably the most successful fighter to come out of Africa. He was well-spoken, modest and sporting, one of the most respected fighters of any time, and it wasn't only the boxing world who mourned his premature death.

Dick Tiger was born in Amaigbo, Orlu, in south-east Nigeria on 14 August 1929. He was from the Ibo tribe, a proud people who had retained their identity during the administrative changes which had beset the region, notably the amalgamation of North and South Nigeria by the British to form a colony in 1914. The Ibo were at the time mainly farming people, with their own language, which remains one of the chief regional languages of Nigeria today.

Tiger's real name was Richard Ihetu, which it amused him to tell friends in Britain and the States is pronounced as 'I-hate-you'. He was initiated into his tribe when 10 years old, and worked on the local farmland while studying at school. When he left school, he went to live in a town called Aba. He got work as a janitor and began boxing as an amateur, giving himself the ring name of Dick Tiger.

He did well and turned professional in October 1952, with his first fight in Lagos, which he won with a second-round knockout. After six more wins in six months, he challenged Tommy West for the Nigerian middleweight championship, but was stopped in the seventh round. A year later, however, he outpointed West to win the title. Five more wins in the year which followed led Jack Farnsworth, an English insurance salesman who had founded the Nigerian Boxing Board of Control, to persuade Tiger to go to England to try his luck. He was sent to train under Peter Benencko in Liverpool, and found a manager in Tony Vaico.

Meanwhile Tiger had married, but his wife Abigail remained behind in Nigeria to see how things would work out for her husband. The answer, at first, was badly. Fighting in Liverpool and Blackpool, Tiger was outpointed in his first four bouts, spread over three months, but then he got a win with a first-round knockout of Dennis Rowley. Then he outpointed Alan Dean, who had been his conqueror in his first English contest.

Tiger was a crowd-pleasing fighter because he was willing to mix it. He was still untutored as a boxer, so had to take plenty of blows from seasoned British professionals. He had taken part in 11 contests in less then 18 months when he first drew serious attention by beating a Londoner with a big reputation, Terry Downes (who was himself to become a middleweight world champion). It was Tiger's second fight in London, and only the third fight of Downes' pro career. Tiger temporarily derailed the 'Paddington Express' by putting him down and stopping him in the fifth round. His purse was £75.

Tiger outpointed Dean in a fifth contest between them, to win the 'rubber' 3–2, and then in Cardiff outpointed Phil Edwards, the Welsh middleweight champion, and drew in a non-title fight with Pat McAteer, the British and British Empire champion. These good performances earned him a shot in March 1958 at McAteer's British Empire title, at the Liverpool Stadium. McAteer's better boxing had him well in front, but he rashly decided to mix it and Tiger got on top and knocked him out in the ninth with a vicious left hook.

However, Tiger was outpointed by two classy Americans, Ellsworth 'Spider' Webb and the oddly named Randy Sandy, although he had a good win against Yolande Pompey, from Trinidad, who had challenged Archie Moore for the world light-heavyweight title. Tiger's loss to Sandy in March 1959 was watched by his wife Abigail, who made her first trip to England. Probably it was during this visit that they decided Tiger should go to the States in order to further his career. He had time first to avenge the defeat by Sandy in May, and then immediately sailed for New York. He had had 28 fights in Britain, but did not fight there again.

Twenty-four days after winning his last fight in England, Tiger was boxing a draw in New York's Madison Square Garden with Rory Calhoun, ranked in the top 10 of the world's middleweights. His new manager was Jersey Jones, a boxing writer recommended to him by his fellow-Nigerian Hogan 'Kid' Bassey, who in 1957 had won the world featherweight championship. Unfortunately, Bassey had just lost it to Davey Moore when Tiger arrived in 1959.

Tiger lost a return in Syracuse with Calhoun then, also in 1959, won and lost against Joey Giardello, another future world champion. Tiger was proving to be a very popular fighter in the States, and although he lost a few, he was still improving because of the class of opposition he met. In 1960, he went to Edmonton, Alberta to defend his British Empire title against Wilf Greaves of Canada and was outpointed over 15 rounds. The result was first announced as a draw, which would mean Tiger would keep the title, but an hour later an error in adding up the cards was discovered and Greaves was given the verdict. Tiger returned five months later to regain the crown with a ninth-round stoppage.

Four wins in 1961 shot Tiger up the rankings and he was ranked No. 3 in the world by *The Ring* magazine when he disposed of the Angelo Dundee-trained Cuban, Florentino Fernandez, in January 1962. Tiger punished him severely and Fernandez retired on his stool after the fifth round suffering from a severely broken nose.

This earned Tiger a shot at Gene Fullmer's NBA title, in October 1962 at Candlestick Park, San Francisco. It was a tremendous battle, with both men swapping punches non-stop. The turning-point came in the ninth, when Fullmer was cut over the left eye. The ringside doctor's inspection held up the fight for three minutes till Fullmer was allowed to continue. He was cut over the right eye as well in the tenth, and slowed the pace in order to last until the 15th, but was clearly outpointed on all three cards, one judge giving him only one round. It was a desperately sad night for Fullmer, as his four-year-old son screamed 'Come on, daddy' throughout, and his father-in-law died of a heart attack at ringside.

Seventeen days after Tiger's win, he was acclaimed undisputed world champion when the New York State Athletic Commission, the European Boxing Union and the British Boxing Board of Control all withdrew recognition of Paul Pender as champion because of his failure to defend their version of the title within a stipulated period.

Tiger had a short holiday back home in Nigeria to celebrate his winning the championship. By now Abigail had given birth to the first four of what were to be the couple's seven children. Tiger, who was already 33 when he became world champion, lived very quietly in New York, sending most of his money back to his family in Nigeria. *The Ring* magazine named Tiger as its Fighter of the Year for 1962, and he was also awarded the Edward J. Neill Trophy, by New York's boxing writers as the person they considered had done most for boxing during the year. Tiger gave Fullmer a return in the Las Vegas Convention Center in February 1963 and Fullmer finished with eye, nose and head cuts. It was announced a draw: 71–67, 69–69, 68–70 (Tiger first).

There was a third match, but Tiger was now able to make it in his homeland, fulfilling both a promise to his people and a personal ambition. The Nigerian government underwrote the fight in August 1963 at the new Liberty Stadium in Ibadan, 75 miles inland from Lagos. Britons promoted and refereed the fight – Jack Solomons and Jack Hart – and Tiger fought like a fury before 30,000 of his fans, destroying Fullmer, whose manager, Merv Jensen, signalled the referee to stop it in the seventh round. It was Fullmer's last fight and he was moved by his reception in Nigeria. He discovered to his surprise that he was popular there, and touched by the fact that over a thousand people waited outside the stadium to cheer him when he left.

Tiger's performance, however, gave an indication of what he might have achieved had he been able to fight more often before his enthusiastic fans, instead of having to build a career alone, thousands of miles from family and friends.

Fullmer had had a hard career, but Tiger, at 34, was two years older. His next challenger Joey Giardello, was himself 33, and had been a contender for ten years. His one chance at the title had been a draw with Fullmer in 1960. Now, with a chip on his shoulder at his lack of opportunities, he fought his heart out on what he saw as his last chance, at the Convention Hall in Atlantic City. And he took the decision, rendered by referee Paul Cavalier only, who saw it 8–5–2, but he did it by hit-and-run tactics and the unmarked Tiger was incensed at the verdict. However, his purse of over £35,000 was a comforting consolation.

Giardello promised Tiger a return, but Tiger little knew it would be nearly two years before he got it. At last he got his chance before 17,064 fans at Madison Square Garden, and gave Giardello such a beating that at times he seemed unlikely to last the distance. By unanimous decision Tiger was once more undisputed world champion. Before he could defend his crown the Nigerian government was overthrown in a military coup. Six months later the new head of state, an Ibo, was assassinated, and wars broke out between the regions, with many Ibo slain. Tiger considered his duty was to continue to earn by his fists and send as much money back as possible to help his family and the freedom fighters.

His first defence in 1966 was against the undisputed world welterweight champion Emile Griffith, an outstanding boxer and more than eight years Tiger's junior. But Griffith had to give away nine pounds. Griffith jabbed and ran and kept out of the way of Tiger's hooks, as Giardello had done two years before, and, like Giardello, he took the decision by a very narrow margin. The fans disagreed with it, and so did the press, by 18–5 in a ringside poll. Griffith, however, with a short right in the ninth, put Tiger down for the first time in his career.

Tiger decided to move up to light-heavyweight, and was immediately given a title shot by Jose Torres, the undisputed world champion who had already defended three times and saw the blown-up ancient middleweight as an easy pay-day. But Torres had been hospitalised with pancreas problems and Tiger, this time himself having to give weight away – eight pounds – attacked to the body instead of the head as he usually did. Torres was hurt in the ninth and eleventh rounds and Tiger ran out an easy winner.

Soon afterwards the new Nigerian leader attempted to bring peace to his country by breaking down the distinctions between the regions, which was unattractive to the Ibo, who attempted to form a new separate nation in the east, called Biafra. This led to a terrible war and more bloodshed. Tiger went to Port Harcourt, some 25 miles from his old town of Aba, in February 1967, when the new state of Biafra was announced, to fight Abraham Tomica in order to raise funds for his people. As the struggle continued over the next three years he sent a private plane full of medicine and food to Biafra, and became a lieutenant in the Biafran army, but he paid a hard price for his involvement as the government took some of his property and many of his relatives were imprisoned. Tiger was disgusted by the support Britain gave to Nigeria during the war, and by

Britain's refusal to recognise Biafra. In protest he returned the MBE awarded him when he became champion in 1962.

In May 1967 Tiger won a narrow split decision over Jose Torres in a title return bout at Madison Square Garden, but a large number of the 12,674 present must have been Puerto Ricans, for a 20-minute riot followed in which any object to hand was thrown into the ring.

Tiger defended successfully against Roger Rouse at the Las Vegas Convention Center, when the ring announcer called his country as 'The Republic of Biafra', but his long championship reign came to an end in May 1968, when Bob Foster, seven inches taller and with an advantage of eight inches in reach, knocked him out in the fourth round with a short hook as Tiger advanced. It was the only time he was ever knocked out. He described it thus: 'I do not see anything. I do not hear anything. Everything is all quiet and it is dark. There is no pain. There is no sound.'

For some time Tiger, now 38, had been feeling pains in his side, but he would not retire from boxing. He continued fighting and supporting his family and friends. He beat some highly ranked men, such as Nino Benvenuti and Andy Kendall, but on 15 July 1970 he was outpointed over 10 rounds by old foe Emile Griffith, who, like him, was now an ex-champion. By now the Biafran dream had ended in disaster. Famine gripped the area as the Nigerians prevented relief getting through and finally the Biafran army was forced to surrender. Many of them lost their lives.

There was no point in Tiger fighting on any more, although he didn't announce his retirement officially for several months. The Nigerian authorities would not allow him to return home.

He got himself a job as a security officer in New York but, little more than a year after his fight with Griffith, his pain was diagnosed as symptoms of liver cancer. It was incurable and the Nigerian authorities at last relented and allowed him to return to Aba to spend his last days there. These days amounted to less than six months during which time he was treated as a hero by visitors from miles around. He was only 42 when he died, having been a bit more than just a fighting machine. As Gene Fullmer said: 'He was a great competitor and champion and, most important, a gentleman.'

CAREER STATISTICS

World middleweight champion 1962-63, 1965-66
World light-heavyweight champion 1966-68
Amaigbo, Nigeria, born 14 August 1929
Real name: Richard Ihetu
The exact days of most of Tiger's early Nigerian contests are not known.

1952

Oct - Simon Eme w ko 2 Lagos
Nov - Easy Dynamite w ko 1 Lagos
Dec - Mighty Joe w pts 8 Lagos

1953

Jan - Lion Ring w rsf 6 Lagos
Feb - Simon Eme w pts 8 Lagos
Mar - Koko Kid w pts 8 Lagos
Apr - Black Power w pts 8 Lagos
May 6 Tommy West l rsf 7 Lagos
(Nigerian middleweight title)
Oct - Bolaji Johnson w pts 8 Lagos

1954
Feb - Robert Nuanne w ko 2 Lagos
May - Tommy West w pts 12 Lagos
(Nigerian middleweight title)
Jul - Roy Fargbemy w pts 8 Lagos
Nov - Peter Okptra w ko 8 Lagos
1955
Jan - Koko Kid w rsf 6 Lagos
Mar - Super Human Power w pts 8 Lagos
May - John Ama w ko 2 Lagos
Dec 8 Alan Dean l pts 8 Liverpool
1956
Jan 27 Gerry McNally l pts 8 Blackpool
Mar 2 Jimmy Lynas l pts 8 Blackpool
Mar 22 George Roe l pts 8 Liverpool
May 3 Dennis Rowley w ko 1 Liverpool
May 10 Alan Dean w pts 8 Liverpool
May 28 Wally Scott w rtd 4 West Hartlepool
Jul 2 Jimmy Lynas w pts 8 West Hartlepool
Oct 18 Alan Dean l pts 6 Liverpool
Nov 9 Alan Dean w pts 8 Blackpool
1957
Apr 29 Johnny Read w rsf 2 London
May 14 Terry Downes w rtd 6 London
Jun 4 Marius Dort w rsf 7 London
Jul 15 Willie Armstrong l pts 8 West Hartlepool
Jul 25 Alan Dean w pts 8 Liverpool
Sep 9 Phil Edwards w pts 10 Cardiff
Oct 21 Jean-Claude Poisson w pts 10 Cardiff
Nov 11 Pat McAteer drew 10 Cardiff
Nov 29 Paddy Delargy w rsf 6 Birmingham
1958
Jan 13 Jean Ruellet w pts 8 Hull
Feb 3 Jimmy Lynas w rsf 7 Manchester
Feb 25 Johnny Read w rsf 6 London
Mar 27 Pat McAteer w ko 9 Liverpool
(Empire middleweight title)
May 1 Billy Ellaway w rsf 2 Liverpool
Jun 24 Ellsworth "Spider" Webb l pts 10 London
Oct 14 Yolande Pompey w pts 10 London
1959
Mar 19 Randy Sandy l pts 10 Liverpool
May 12 Randy Sandy w pts 10 London
Jun 5 Rory Calhoun drew 10 New York
Jul 17 Rory Calhoun l pts 10 Syracuse
Sep 2 Gene Armstrong w pts 10 Camden
Sep 30 Joey Giardello w pts 10 Chicago
Nov 4 Joey Giardello l pts 10 Cleveland
Dec 30 Holley Mims w pts 10 Chicago
1960
Feb 24 Gene Armstrong w pts 10 Chicago
Apr 1 Victor Zalazar w pts 10 Boston
Jun 22 Wilf Greaves l pts 15 Edmonton
(Empire middleweight title)
Nov 30 Wilf Greaves w rsf 9 Edmonton
(Empire middleweight title)
1961
Feb 18 Gene Armstrong w rsf 9 New York
Apr 15 Ellsworth "Spider" Webb w rsf 6 New York
May 15 Hank Casey w pts 10 New Orleans
Dec 16 Bill Pickett w pts 10 New York
1962
Jan 20 Florentino Fernandez w ko 6 Miami
Mar 31 Henry Hank w pts 10 New York
Oct 23 Gene Fullmer w pts 15 San Francisco
(WBA middleweight title)
Nov 9: New York, EBU and Britain recognised him as champion.
1963
Feb 23 Gene Fullmer drew 15 Las Vegas
(World middleweight title)
Aug 10 Gene Fullmer w rsf 7 Ibadan, Nigeria
(World middleweight title)
Dec 7 Joey Giardello l pts 15 Atlantic City
(World middleweight title)
1964
Jul 31 Jose Gonzalez w rsf 6 New York
Sep 11 Don Fullmer w pts 10 Cleveland
Oct 16 Joey Archer l pts 10 New York
1965
Mar 12 Rocky Rivero w rsf 6 New York
May 20 Rubin Carter w pts 10 New York
Oct 21 Joey Giardello w pts 15 New York
(World middleweight title)
1966
Feb 18 Peter Muller w ko 3 Dortmund
Apr 25 Emile Griffith l pts 15 New York
(World middleweight title)
Dec 16 Jose Torres w pts 15 New York
(World light-heavyweight title)
1967
Feb 5 Abraham Tomica w pts 10 Port Harcourt
May 16 Jose Torres w pts 15 New York
(World light-heavyweight title)
Nov 17 Roger Rouse w rsf 12 Las Vegas
(World light-heavyweight title)
1968
May 24 Bob Foster l ko 4 New York
(World light-heavyweight title)
Oct 25 Frank DePaula w pts 10 New York
1969
May 26 Nino Benvenuti w pts 10 New York
Nov 14 Andy Kendall w pts 10 New York
1970
Jul 15 Emile Griffith l pts 10 New York

Fights 81 Won 61 Lost 17 Drawn 3
Died, Nigeria, 14 December 1971, aged 42

CARLOS ORTIZ

PUERTO RICAN FROM MADISON SQUARE

Carlos Ortiz was one of the modern masters of the lightweight division, by some distance the best of his generation. Apart from a seven-month 'interruption' in 1965, he held the world championship for six years.

Ortiz was born in Mayaguez, Puerto Rico, on 9 September 1936, the fourth of eight children of a nightclub waiter. At eight, he was sent with a sister to live with a relative on New York's East Side.

His face first became known to New Yorkers when he was photographed cradling his dying dog in his arms after she had been run over by a car. 'I wept as only a 12-year-old boy could,' he said. The picture, by a *New York Post* photographer, was on billboards all over the city.

He trained as an amateur boxer at the Madison Square Boys Club from the age of 11, and by 14 was earning himself a living as a delivery boy with his own patch. In 1953, he was a part of a New York team which boxed in London – he beat Georgie Guy of East Ham. By 1955, he was a professional, an ambitious 18-year-old intent on increasing the weekly wage he earned from his job in a Bronx warehouse.

He settled to pro fighting quickly and within 18 months was an unbeaten prospect working at the 10-round level. After 20 wins, most against useful opposition, his 100 per cent record went against Lou Filippo in Los Angeles. Down twice in round six, he rallied to put Filippo down with a body shot after the bell to end the ninth. At first he was disqualified, and then the Californian Commission changed it to a 'No Decision', and finally settled on a Technical Draw.

In a rematch a month afterwards Ortiz won on a seventh-round stoppage. Filippo was later a top-class official, who worked more than 70 world title fights in the 1980s and 1990s.

By 1958, Ortiz was world ranked, married and living in a quality apartment in the Bronx. 'Something inside me insists that I'll make good,' he said. In Los Angeles he outpointed former world title challenger Joey Lopes. In New York, he lost on points to

Johnny Busso (his first defeat), but won a rematch three months later. In London, on the last promotion ever staged at the famous Harringay Arena, he outpointed Dartford southpaw Dave Charnley. Ortiz gave Charnley, considered one of the best British fighters never to win a world title, a boxing lesson for 10 rounds. On the last day of the year, in Miami, Ortiz surprisingly lost a majority decision to Michigan southpaw Kenny Lane.

As world lightweight champion Joe 'Old Bones' Brown defended against other contenders, Garden matchmaker Teddy Brenner matched Ortiz and Lane for the long defunct 140lb title, then known as junior-welter and now more commonly known as the light-welterweight title. It was a championship belt, but neither saw it for more than it was: a marketing ploy that might make them all some money.

Ortiz dropped Lane early in the second round and then almost on the bell landed a right hand which tore open a horrible gash over the right eye. The fight was stopped by the doctor during the interval.

Ortiz saw the light-welterweight title as a convenience rather than an honour, but collected a good payday because of it, wearing down the previously unbeaten 18-year-old Mexican, 'Battling' Raymundo Torres, for a tenth-round knockout in Los Angeles in February 1960. 'It means little,' he said. 'I'm a lightweight and I want the lightweight title.'

He defeated stocky Italian Duilio Loi on a split decision in San Francisco, and then accepted a career-best $30,000 payday to fight Loi in Milan. By now a father of three children, Cynthia, Noreen and Carlos jnr, he grabbed the chance, aware that he would almost certainly lose if the fight went the distance. But as he said: 'For that kind of money, I would go to the end of the world'. And 65,000 fans duly watched Loi deprive him of the championship he never really valued much.

It was close enough to merit a return, which meant another good payday. And in May 1961, Loi floored him on the way to a much clearer points win. It didn't worry Ortiz one jot. He had been well paid, and scaled only just over the lightweight limit. It was Joe Brown's much more prestigious lightweight championship that he had always wanted.

It took until April 1962 for Brown, then a month short of his 36th birthday, to give Ortiz his opportunity. The fight had been delayed when the champion fell ill with a throat infection, but when it finally happened Ortiz, who was also a part-time sergeant in the New York National Guard, boxed methodically at long range, refusing to get involved and piling up points for round after round. 'Old Bones' barely won a round. Brown could scarcely believe it. 'I just couldn't get off the ground,' he said. 'I think the real Joe Brown could whip Ortiz.'

Ortiz said: 'It was the easiest fight I ever had. I thought Brown was going to be a lot tougher.'

The new champion returned to his wife Norma and the children in their eight-roomed house in the Bronx, ready to enjoy whatever time they had at the top. A possible fight with Charnley fell through when the Englishman lost to Doug Vaillant of

Cuba. There were non-title paydays in the Philippines and Japan, and then at last a world title defence in Tokyo in December 1962 against Teruo Kosaka. Ortiz won easily in five rounds.

Already he was investing his money in stocks and owned his house. The next payday was in April 1963, and brought him his first fight in his native Puerto Rico. He drew a crowd of 22,000 as he overpowered Doug Vaillant in 13 rounds, and grossed another $40,000. Afterwards he was accused of ducking leading contender Kenny Lane, but his manager Bill Daly said it was a matter of hard money. They could make five times as much by fighting Flash Elorde in Manila. 'We'll make our own fights. We're the champion. Let them strip us of the title.'

Elorde was, indeed, the next challenger, but it took until February 1964 to come about. Ortiz stayed in shape with non-title appearances in Honolulu and London (where he beat Maurice Cullen). Elorde, an experienced southpaw who had fought Sandy Saddler for the featherweight title and held the 130lb belt, represented a considerable risk at home, but Ortiz proved again what a fine champion he was, breaking him down gradually and stopping him in the 14th round.

Two months later he acknowledged his commitment to fight Kenny Lane, and outpointed the Michigan southpaw in San Juan, putting him down in round 14. Lane fought defensively. Daly sneered: 'He kept telling the world that Carlos was running away from him. And when he got in there, he fought like a scared jack-rabbit.' Ortiz was angry too. 'I'll never give him another fight. He's not in my class.'

Meaningful fights were becoming increasingly rare, however, and Ortiz became complacent. It was another 12 months before he boxed Panamanian stylist Ismael Laguna in Panama City, and in his fifth defence he lost a majority decision after 15 good rounds.

Inevitably, they had a rematch, which Bill Daly brought to San Juan in November 1964. This time Ortiz drilled himself into top shape and won unanimously on points. Even so, he came in half a pound overweight and had to walk off the excess. Afterwards Ortiz talked of moving up to welterweight and fighting Emile Griffith. 'The experts buried me after I lost to Laguna. Well, I fooled them all. In Panama I was sick with a virus. In this fight, I was in top shape. It was the same Laguna, but a different Ortiz.'

His leading contender at lightweight, apart from Laguna, was the Argentine defensive master Nicolino Locche. Ortiz agreed to meet him in Buenos Aires ... but only in a non-title 10-rounder, which the judges called a draw. He also entertained fans in Puerto Rico with a public spar against Sugar Ray Robinson, and when back in New York kept a professional eye on his new acquisition, a club named the Tropicano.

In spite of the talk about moving up in weight, he knew his major earning power was as world lightweight champion. He was back in harness, exactly on the 135lb limit, in June 1966 with a 12th round stoppage of Italian-born Johnny Bizzarro in Pittsburgh. Ortiz had trouble subduing Bizzarro and was cut, but was narrowly ahead when he floored and stopped his man. His next defence caused a riot, and forced him to walk the aisle back to the dressing room with his head covered by a bucket! Even then he was kicked in the back. Daly had a couple of ribs broken.The riot came about when the referee – former world light-heavyweight champion Billy Conn – stopped his fight with Mexican-based Cuban Sugar Ramos in the fifth round because of cuts and swellings around the Cuban's left eye. Twice, he had asked the Mexican Commission doctor to examine the injuries. Twice, the doctor had refused. Ortiz had been on the floor in round two, but had fought back. Judging from the film of the fight, Conn seemed correct.

But the 23,000 crowd in the Mexico City bullring tossed debris towards the participants and generally let rip. The World Boxing Council acted disgracefully in attempting to overrule Conn and persuade Ramos to box on. He refused. Then the WBC had the audacity to declare Ramos the winner in a flagrant attempt to pacify local feeling. Fortunately, the rest of the sporting world rose in protest and the WBC backed off, calling the title vacant. Few took that seriously, however, and in effect Ortiz kept the title. A month later he knocked out Flash Elorde in the 14th round of another defence in the Garden.

Ramos was given a rematch in San Juan in July 1967 and this time was hammered to defeat in four rounds. Ortiz earned $75,000, the best payday for a lightweight in history. And then he topped that by demanding $95,000 to face Laguna for the third time in Shea Stadium in Flushing, an hour's drive from New York City on Long Island. Ortiz, who had predicted a one-sided victory inside 11 rounds, won with a supreme display of boxing, but had to go the distance. Laguna was in survival mode long before the finish.

However, Ortiz was running out of road. At 31, he was no longer as dedicated as he should have been, was beginning to lose the fire in his belly and look towards enjoying the rewards of his career. The Boxing Writers of America acknowledged his contribution by voting him Boxer of the Year, but he and Daly were no longer as close. By the time he defended again, in Santo Domingo against the Dominican Republic's Carlos Teo Cruz, he had stopped living the life. He accepted the fight against Daly's advice and the pair parted as soon as it was over. The title had gone anyway – Cruz received a split decision.

Effectively, he retired. There was a fight in November 1969, a majority 10-round points win in the Garden against Brazilian welterweight Edmundo Leite, but it meant little. He laboured, but at least picked up $20,000. Afterwards he talked of fighting welterweight champion Jose Napoles, but that's all it was.

It was more than two years before he boxed again, by which time he had lost the plot. Between December 1970 and August 1971, he won nine fights, eight inside the distance, and there was a flickering hope among his old fans that even at 35 he might be able to win a title again.

But he had outgoings and overheads. He was on his second marriage, and he had a new home in Orangeburg, New York. A fight with Roberto Duran was made, but that fell through and former champion Ken Buchanan was suggested. Ortiz accepted, but had lost patience with the business and struggled to get in shape. Against Buchanan, that was stupid. He was retired after six rounds – the only time he was ever stopped – and there was no more to give.

Sadly, his business ventures failed and he was forced to work as a cab driver and a salesman to make ends meet. It was sad, but he was one of the finest fighters of his time, and that could never be taken away from him.

CAREER STATISTICS

World lightweight champion 1962-65, 1965-68
World light-welterweight champion 1959-60
New York, born Ponce, Puerto Rico, 9 September 1936

1955
Feb 14 Harry Bell w ko 1 New York
Feb 28 Morris Hodnett w ko 1 New York
May 13 Danny Roberts w ko 3 New York
May 30 Juan Pacheco w ko 2 New York
Jun 24 Jimmy DeMura w pts 6 Syracuse
Aug 10 Tony DeCola w pts 6 New York
Aug 22 Armand Bush w pts 6 New York
Sep 19 Hector Rodriguez w ko 2 New York
Oct 3 Leroy Graham w ko 2 New York
Oct 29 Al Duarte w ko 4 Boston
Nov 12 Lem Miller w pts 8 Boston
Dec 10 Charley Titone w ko 2 Paterson
1956
Jan 9 Ray Portillo w pts 8 New York
Feb 17 Ray Portillo w pts 8 New York
May 25 Johnny Gorman w pts 6 New York
Jul 30 Tommy Salem w pts 10 New York
Oct 27 Mickey Northrup w pts 10 Los Angeles
Dec 15 Phil Kim w rsf 9 Los Angeles
Dec 31 Gale Kerwin w pts 10 New York
1957
Jan 23 Bobby Rogers w pts 10 Chicago
Mar 2 Lou Filippo tdraw 9 Los Angeles
Apr 9 Lou Filippo w rsf 7 Los Angeles
May 7 Ike Vaughn w pts 10 Miami
May 29 Felix Chiocca w pts 10 Chicago
Sep 23 Harry Bell w pts 10 New York
1958
Feb 28 Tommy Tibbs w pts 10 New York
May 9 Joe Lopes w pts 10 Los Angeles
Jun 27 Johnny Busso l pts 10 New York
Sep 19 Johnny Busso w pts 10 New York
Oct 28 Dave Charnley w pts 10 London
Dec 31 Kenny Lane l pts 10 Miami
1959
Apr 13 Len Matthews w rsf 6 Philadelphia
Jun 12 Kenny Lane w rsf 2 New York
(vacant world light-welterweight title)
1960
Feb 4 Battling Torres w ko 10 Los Angeles
(World light-welterweight title)
Jun 15 Duilio Loi w pts 15 San Francisco
(World light-welterweight title)
Sep 1 Duilio Loi l pts 15 Milan
(World light-welterweight title)
1961
Feb 2 Cisco Andrade w pts 10 Los Angeles
May 10 Duilio Loi l pts 15 Milan
(World light-welterweight title)
Sep 2 Doug Vaillant w pts 10 Miami
Nov 18 Paolo Rosi w pts 10 New York
1962
Apr 21 Joe Brown w pts 15 Las Vegas
(World lightweight title)
Aug 1 Arthur Persley w pts 10 Manila
Nov 7 Kazuo Takayama w pts 10 Tokyo
Dec 3 Teruo Kosaka w ko 5 Tokyo
(World lightweight title)
1963
Apr 7 Doug Vaillant w rsf 13 San Juan
(World lightweight title)
Sep 18 Pete Acera w ko 7 Honolulu
Oct 22 Maurice Cullen w pts 10 London

1964
Feb 15 Flash Elorde w rsf 14 Manila
(World lightweight title)
Apr 11 Kenny Lane w pts 15 San Juan
(World lightweight title)
Dec 14 Dick Divola w ko 1 Boston
1965
Apr 10 Ismael Laguna l pts 15 Panama City
(World lightweight title)
Nov 13 Ismael Laguna w pts 15 San Juan
(World lightweight title)
1966
Apr 7 Nicolino Locche drew 10 Buenos Aires
Jun 20 Johnny Bizzarro w rsf 12 Pittsburgh
(World lightweight title)
Oct 22 Sugar Ramos w rsf 5 Mexico City
(World lightweight title)
Nov 28 Flash Elorde w ko 14 New York
(World lightweight title)
1967
Jul 1 Sugar Ramos w rsf 4 San Juan
(World lightweight title)
Aug 16 Ismael Laguna w pts 15 New York
(World lightweight title)
1968
Jun 29 Carlos Teo Cruz l pts 15 Santo Domingo
(World lightweight title)
1969
Nov 21 Edmundo Leite w pts 10 New York
1970 inactive
1971
Dec 1 Jimmy Ligon w ko 3 Las Vegas
1972
Jan 8 Bill Whittenburg w ko 7 Miami
Jan 20 Terry Rondeau w ko 4 Portland, Me
Jan 31 Ivelaw Eastman w ko 2 Waltham
Feb 19 Leo DiFiore w ko 2 San Juan
Mar 20 Junior Varney w ko 2 Ponce
May 1 Greg Potter w pts 10 Los Angeles
Jun 3 Gerardo Ferrat w ko 3 Chicago
Aug 1 Johnny Copeland w ko 3 Oklahoma City
Sep 20 Ken Buchanan l rsf 6 New York

Fights 70 Won 61 Lost 7 Drawn 2

NINO BENVENUTI

THE HANDSOME ITALIAN

A polished boxer with a sharp punch, Nino Benvenuti was a brilliant amateur who turned into a quality world middleweight champion in the second half of the 1960s. When he was in his rhythm, he was a difficult man to beat. He could be over-cautious, but there was a grace about his style that always made him attractive to watch. He held the world light-middleweight title from 1965 until 1966, and had two spells as middleweight champion between 1967 and 1970. His three-fight series with Emile Griffith was exceptional, and he also fought world champions Dick Tiger and Luis Rodriguez before his career was ended by Carlos Monzon.

Benvenuti was a fisherman's son from the village of Isole D'Istria, near Trieste. Inspired by Duilio Loi, an immensely popular fighter who was born in Trieste and who would eventually lose only three of 126 contests, Benvenuti took up boxing at 11.

He was a wonderful amateur, who lost once, in Turkey in 1956, in 120 unpaid bouts. The same year he boxed for Rome against London before a 9,000 sellout crowd at the Royal Albert Hall and outpointed Ron Garnett of the Earlsfield club. He won the European amateur light-middleweight gold medal in Prague in 1957 and in Lucerne in 1959. But it was at the Rome Olympics in 1960 that he shone, winning not only the welterweight gold medal but the Val Barker Trophy for the best boxer of the tournament. Considering the light-heavyweight gold went to Cassius Clay, that was a significant acknowledgement of his talent.

Benvenuti turned professional in Trieste in January 1961, outscoring the long-forgotten Ben Ali Allala from Tunis over six rounds. Nerves probably played a part, but it was a start, and he improved on that performance dramatically in his third fight in Naples the following month when he disposed of Allala inside a round.

There were 14 wins in 1961 as he learned the business in the six- and eight-round classes. Benvenuti began his second professional year with an impressive sixth-round win over George Aldridge in Rome. Aldridge won the British middle-weight title later that year.

In Rome in March 1963, Benvenuti knocked out Tommasso Truppi in round 11 for the vacant Italian middleweight title, and retained it by stopping Francesco Fiori in Priverno five months later. Progress was good: he was too big for the stubborn, wily old Mexican Gaspar Ortega over ten rounds, and also overcame worrying cuts to outscore Ted Wright, a world class welterweight from Detroit who had lasted the full 15 rounds with Emile Griffith in Vienna the previous year in a bout which received somewhat eccentric recognition from the European Boxing Union as a world light-middleweight title fight.

Out of the ring, Benvenuti was elected to Trieste City Council, representing the right-wing Italian Social Movement.

Nino retained his Italian championship again in 1964 by outscoring Fabio Bettini over 12 and also proved his right to be considered in top class when he outpointed Denny Moyer, the former world light-middleweight champion, in Rome. When he beat Juan Carlos Duran of Argentina in Milan, he drew 12,000 fans.

This was all an apprenticeship, of course. He was earning enough money to provide his family with a new house, and there were fast cars, but if Benvenuti was to fulfil his magnificent potential, there had to be more. After a repeat stoppage of Tommaso Truppi in another Italian title fight, he moved down to light-middleweight to challenge his popular compatriot Sandro Mazzhingi for the world 154lb belt in Milan's wonderful San Siro soccer stadium.

He worked hard, living in spartan conditions with his gym-mates in what amounted to a training camp, and proved his ability by knocking out Mazzhingi in six rounds before a noisy 40,000 crowd.

His career was twin-pronged. Already a world champ at the lightly regarded light-middleweight limit, he maintained his assault on the middleweight division. By October 1965 he was European 160lb champ, following a sixth-round knockout of Luis Folledo, from Madrid, who had lost only to the clever Hungarian Laszlo Papp in his previous 52 contests. Folledo liked to do some bull-fighting as well as boxing, but Benvenuti turned matador, jarring him repeatedly at long range before applying the finishing blow.

A rematch with Mazzhingi a week before Christmas 1965 saw Benvenuti pelted with fruit and general debris as he boxed cautiously behind his jab for 15 rounds. He won on points, but the 15,000 fans in the Palazzo Dello Sport were unimpressed.

He was cut badly as he outboxed Don Fullmer, the younger brother of former world champ Gene, and retained his European title with a 14th-round knockout of Jupp Elze from Germany. But then he accepted a $35,000 offer to box former amateur rival Ki-soo Kim of Korea in Seoul, in defence of his light-middleweight championship. Kim had staged a silent protest in the Rome Olympics in 1960 when he lost to Benvenuti, sitting motionless in the ring for almost an hour and refusing to leave. If that had been ridiculous, then events in Seoul were even worse. Benvenuti was in control when a broken ring rope caused a ten-minute delay, after which Kim began round 14 by charging across and hitting the Italian as he sat in his corner, his head still in a towel. Kim received a split decision from the judges. Benvenuti's unbeaten record had gone in his 66th bout.

In a run of six wins at middleweight, he outscored Liverpool's exceptionally tough Harry Scott in Rome and retained his European title by stopping compatriot Pascal Di Benedetto in the 11th round.

Then he reached his destiny in April 1967 by outboxing world middleweight champion Emile Griffith over 15 rounds in Madison Square Garden. It was Nino's American debut, and he responded magnificently by flooring Griffith with a right uppercut in round two. Griffith sent him sprawling with a long right hand in the fourth, and was rough with the head on the inside, and also received a warning for using the heel of the glove on the Italian's face. Benvenuti kept his boxing together heroically, however, and in spite of a broken nose, won a deserved decision.

Benvenuti returned home to a magnificent welcome, a civic reception in Rome and an audience with Pope Paul VI. When he reached Trieste, local police officers suspended their own strike to ensure that his parade through the streets passed off smoothly.

The rematch with Griffith was signed, and Benvenuti sailed on an Italian liner, attracting a huge crowd as it docked in New York. They fought in front of 21,000 people at the Shea Stadium in Flushing, but this time Griffith slugged away on the inside, ignoring his boxing skills, and won a brawl. Benvenuti broke a rib in round three.

They were chosen to open the new Madison Square Garden in March 1968, alongside Joe Frazier's New York world title fight with Buster Mathis. And in the decider, it was Benvenuti who prevailed, beginning a partnership with Italian-American trainer Al Silvani. He put Griffith down with two right hands in round nine, and dominated the last third of the fight to clinch the verdict.

After some non-title paydays, Benvenuti outboxed old rival Don Fullmer before what amounted to a studio audience of 2,500 in a San Remo theatre. He took a count in the seventh, but dominated without looking especially good. Nevertheless, it paved the way for a lucrative deal for acting in a spaghetti Western called *Alive Or Preferably Dead*. I am told film critics do not consider it a modern classic!

He returned to New York in May 1969 to take on veteran former two-weight champion Dick Tiger in a 10-round non-title workout at the Garden. At least, for Benvenuti it probably sounded like a comfortable workout. If he won, as he was expected to do comfortably, the Garden were contemplating offering him a shot with light-heavyweight champion Bob Foster. In fact, as he should have known, even at at the age of 39, Tiger was never the kind who could let up on anything or anyone. Benvenuti apparently broke a hand in round one, and Tiger mauled him the rest of the way. For some reason the New York District Attorney's office, which had been showing interest in reported mob activities in boxing, was represented at ringside. Nobody revealed why.

Fraser Scott was a red-headed slugger from Seattle who had a rapid rise and decline. He turned pro in June 1968, and within 16 months had been pushed into a world title fight against Benvenuti. They fought in Naples in October 1969, with Benvenuti being criticised for avoiding leading contender Luis Rodriguez. He seemed to lack motivation, and appeared to struggle to make the weight. A crowd of 44,500 turned out in the San Paolo Stadium and saw a controversial fight. Scott charged in, attempting to break Benvenuti's rhythm, but in the process, ducking low and roughing him up with the head.

The champion looked sluggish, was bustled around, and seemed tired when both fell over in round seven. But then to general amazement, the American was disqualified for use of the head. The crowd complained long and loud, and referee Toni Gilardi was heavily criticised.

When the dust had settled it was another $64,000 in the bank for Benvenuti, but poor Scott completely lost heart. Eventually, he was to write an autobiography, *Weigh-In*, sub-titled *The Selling of a Middleweight*, in which he claimed the dice had been loaded against him.

A month after the supposed warm-up payday against Scott, Benvenuti honoured the commitment to Rodriguez, who was by now 32 but beaten only once in his last 25 fights since moving up from welterweight.

Benvenuti and Rodriguez fought in Rome's Palazzo Dello Sport with 14,000 Italian fans making their feelings known, tossing oranges, apples and general rubbish into the ring when they felt their hero was not living up to his reputation. For three rounds Benvenuti boxed well behind the jab, but then Rodriguez took over and the champion bled from cuts over the left eye and on the bridge of the nose. Benvenuti seemed behind, and then when he needed it most, found one of the finest punches of his whole career, a left hook so perfect that the iron-jawed Rodriguez, who had been stopped once but never knocked out, crashed on to his back for the full count. It was a moment when time stopped its advance and allowed Benvenuti one last moment of genius.

With hindsight, he should have retired then. There were six more paydays, but it was all becoming too much of a struggle.

In Melbourne, Australia, he quit in the eighth round against Tom Bethea, after being floored in round seven. Bethea had taken the job for $3,500 plus flight expenses and a sightseeing tour. In other words, it was a paid holiday. Except that somehow along the way he managed to beat the middleweight champion of the world! For Benvenuti it was another $30,000, but a serious blow to his reputation. Claims that his ribs were broken were not borne out by the X-rays.

Two months later Bethea, with Gil Clancy and Emile Griffith in his corner, was given a title shot in Umag, which was no more than a big village just across the border in Yugoslavia and close to Nino's home town of Trieste. Professional boxing was banned in Yugoslavia, but President Tito gave his personal permission for the contest. The local tourist department managed to find the funding to build a 5,000 seat arena and agreed to pay Benvenuti $100,000. The champion had drilled himself into shape, and this time the gulf in class was apparent. He knocked out Bethea in the eighth round with a right hand to the chin.

There was talk of Benvenuti returning to fight in Madison Square Garden, but nothing came of it. A non-title knockout of Doyle Baird, from Akron, Ohio, was followed by another $100,000 defence against South American champion Carlos Monzon in Rome in November 1970.

Nobody knew much about Monzon. These were the days before video, and he had rarely fought outside Argentina. There were some recognisable names on the record and if anybody had talked to Tom Bethea, whom he had oupointed the previous year, or Bennie Briscoe, who had held him to a draw in 1967, they would probably have learned that he could fight. Benvenuti took a steady beating before folding in round 12, dropping to his knees from a left hook and right hand. He fell forward, hauled himself up, but too late to beat the count.

A points defeat by Jose Chirino in Bologna the following March should have removed him from the picture, but the influence of his manager Bruno Amaduzzi and his own reputation secured him a rematch with Monzon. It was a crazy move, and in Monte Carlo in May 1971, Monzon enjoyed himself. It was all over in round three. 'I wanted to die,' said the old champion.

In retirement he earned well in acting, involved himself in politics, and at one time sent his son to be taught to box by Emile Griffith in New York.

CAREER STATISTICS

World middleweight champion 1967, 1968-70
World light-middleweight champion 1965-66
Full name: Giovanni Benvenuti
Trieste, born Isole d'Istria, Italy, 26 April 1938
1960 Olympic welterweight gold medallist

1961

Jan 20	Ben Ali Allala w pts 6 Trieste
Feb 10	Nicola Sammartino w rsf 3 Rome
Feb 27	Ben Ali Allala w ko 1 Naples
Mar 14	Sahib Mosri w rsf 3 Bologna
Apr 7	Nick Maric w pts 6 Milan
Apr 21	Pierre Mondino w pts 6 Florence
May 3	Daniel Brunet w dis 3 Naples
May 16	Michel Francois w ko 4 Turin
Jun 7	Henri Cabelduc w pts 6 Bologna
Jun 17	Marc Desforneaux w pts 6 Trieste
Oct 2	Retmia Mahrez w rsf 3 Bologna
Nov 1	Angelo Brisci w ko 1 Trieste
Nov 9	Jesse Jones w dis 6 Rome
Dec 20	Giuseppe Catalano w pts 8 Rome

1962

Jan 19	George Aldridge w ko 6 Rome
Feb 19	Jose Riquelme w pts 8 Bologna
Mar 8	Manfred Haas w pts 8 Turin
Mar 17	Gianni Lommi w rsf 5 Milan
Apr 1	Jim Hegerle w rsf 4 Rome
May 1	Hector Constance w pts 10 Trieste
Jun 2	Jean Ruellet w pts 8 Cagliari
Jun 22	Heini Freytag w pts 8 Rome
Jul 12	Gino Rossi w pts 10 Trieste
Aug 2	Mahmout Le Noir w pts 8 Lignano
Aug 30	Giuseppe Gentiletti w rsf 2 Senigallia
Sep 28	Diego Infantes w pts 8 Rome
Oct 18	Daniel Leullier w pts 10 Padua
Nov 30	Isaac Logart w pts 10 Rome
Dec 26	Giampaolo Melis w rsf 2 Bologna

1963

Mar 1	Tommasso Truppi w ko 11 Rome *(Italian middleweight title)*

Apr 5 Georges Estatoff w ko 6 Turin
Apr 24 Jean Ruellet w pts 10 Alessandria
May 23 Jimmy Beecham w pts 10 Rome
Jun 7 Tony Montano w pts 10 Rome
Aug 31 Francesco Fiori w rsf 3 Priverno
(Italian middleweight title)
Sep 16 Willy Niederau w rsf 6 Prato
Sep 27 Victor Zalazar w rsf 2 Rome
Oct 18 Gaspar Ortega w pts 10 Rome
Nov 7 Jackie Cailleau w pts 10 Prato
Nov 15 Lou Gutierrez w rsf 7 Rome
Dec 13 Ted Wright w pts 10 Rome

1964

Feb 28 Guillermo Ayon w ko 5 Rome
Mar 18 Michel Diouf w pts 10 Bologna
Apr 10 Sugar Boy Nando w pts 10 Rome
May 28 Jimmy Beecham w rsf 2 Bologna
Jul 30 Fabio Bettini w pts 12 San Remo
(Italian middleweight title)
Sep 18 Denny Moyer w pts 10 Rome
Oct 9 Abrao De Souza w dis 7 Rome
Nov 27 Aristeo Chavarin w ko 4 Rome
Dec 19 Juan Carlos Duran w pts 10 Milan

1965

Jan 22 Art Hernandez w rsf 3 Rome
Feb 12 Tommasso Truppi w rsf 5 Bologna
(Italian middleweight title)
Feb 26 Mick Leahy w pts 10 Milan
Mar 18 Dick Knight w ko 6 Bologna
Apr 2 Rip Randall w pts 10 Rome
Apr 30 Milo Calhoun w pts 10 Genoa
Jun 18 Sandro Mazzinghi w ko 6 Milan
(World light-middleweight title)
Aug 15 Daniel Leillier w rsf 7 Senigallia
Oct 15 Luis Folledo w ko 6 Rome
(European middleweight title)
Nov 5 Johnny Torres w dis 7 Turin
Nov 15 James Shelton w pts 10 Bologna
Dec 17 Sandro Mazzhingi w pts 15 Rome
(World light-middleweight title)

1966

Feb 4 Don Fullmer w pts 12 Rome
Mar 11 Clarence James w pts 10 Turin
May 14 Jupp Elze w ko 14 Berlin
(European middleweight title)
Jun 25 Ki-soo Kim l pts 15 Seoul
(World light-middleweight title)
Sep 23 Harry Scott w pts 10 Rome
Oct 21 Pascal Di Benedetto w rsf 11 Rome
(European middleweight title)
Dec 2 Fred Hernandez w pts 10 Rome
Dec 23 Renato Moares w ko 9 Rome

1967

Jan 19 Manfred Graus w ko 2 Bologna
Mar 3 Milo Calhoun w pts 10 Rome
Apr 17 Emile Griffith w pts 15 New York
(World middleweight title)
Sep 28 Emile Griffith l pts 15 Flushing, NY
(World middleweight title)

1968

Jan 19 Charley Austin w pts 10 Rome
Mar 4 Emile Griffith w pts 15 New York
(World middleweight title)
Jun 7 Yoshiaki Akasaka w ko 2 Rome
Jul 5 Jimmy Ramos w rsf 4 Turin
Sep 17 Art Hernandez w pts 10 Toronto
Oct 14 Doyle Baird drew 10 Akron
Dec 14 Don Fullmer w pts 15 San Remo
(World middleweight title)

1969

May 26 Dick Tiger l pts 10 New York
Oct 4 Fraser Scott w dis 7 Naples
(World middleweight title)
Nov 22 Luis Rodriguez w ko 11 Rome
(World middleweight title)

1970

Mar 13 Tom Bethea l rsf 8 Melbourne
May 23 Tom Bethea w ko 8 Umag
(World middleweight title)
Sep 12 Doyle Baird w ko 10 Bari
Nov 7 Carlos Monzon l ko 12 Rome
(World middleweight title)

1971

Mar 17 Jose Chirino l pts 10 Bologna
May 8 Carlos Monzon l rsf 3 Monte Carlo
(World middleweight title)

Fights 90 Won 82 Lost 7 Drawn 1

HENRY COOPER

OUR 'ENERY

The most popular British boxer since the Second World War, amiable Londoner Henry Cooper is the only man to win three Lonsdale Belts outright. Yet his fame rests largely on one punch, the left hook which sat the then Cassius Clay on his bottom, glassy-eyed, at Wembley in 1963. Nobody came nearer than that to beating Clay/Ali in his prime. A legend grew that it took some crafty work with a glove in Clay's corner to make sure that 'The Greatest' did not suffer the indignity of a first defeat. This may be embellishing the truth, but Cooper's performance was still worthy enough to secure his place in British boxing. Without his handicap of cutting easily around the eyes, he might have been able to make a bigger impact on the world stage.

Henry Cooper's mother, Lily, had no idea she was to give birth to twins when she went into labour at the Lying-in Hospital, Westminster, on 3 May 1934. It was kept a secret from her. When two boys arrived they were called Henry and George by a nurse, and the family decided to keep these names because by coincidence their father's name was Henry and the paternal grandfather was George. Henry arrived 20 minutes before George, weighing in at 6lb, while George was a little heavier. They had a four-years-older brother, Bernard.

Both parents' families were from the Elephant and Castle area of south-east London. Grandfather George, who died before the twins were born, was a well-known local character whose main business was the horse trade centred in the area – in the 1880s he helped deliver 22 stallions to the Tsar of Russia. He was also on the fringes of the boxing business and a useful middleweight himself. Father Henry also boxed during six years in the army. When the twins were born he was a tram driver.

The family were living in Camberwell Green at the time, but when the Second World War started (father Henry was called up in 1942) they were living on a council estate in nearby Bellingham. The twins' introduction to boxing at the age of nine has a familiar ring - an ex-amateur boxer, Bob Hill, noticed them sparring and took them to the local boxing club, paying their subscription himself. This kindness was not forgotten by the family and when Henry was featured in *This is Your Life* in 1971, the 76-year-old Hill was tracked down by the BBC to surprise the twins. Ex-British lightweight champion Matt Wells taught the boys until at 15 they joined a boxing club at Eltham.

The twins' introduction to amateur competition was inauspicious: they both lost their first four contests. But they improved, and Henry at 17 won the ABA light-heavyweight title, earning selection for the 1952 Olympic Games, where he lost in his first bout on a split decision to a Soviet boxer, Anatoli Perov. The twins were then called up for national service where they did little but boxing training.

On demob, the boys turned professional with Jim Wicks, whom they'd met before joining up, as manager. Wicks had been a bookmaker and boxing promoter before specialising in managing boxers. He was nearly 60 when the Coopers joined him, and had British champions Alex Buxton and Joe Lucy and Commonwealth champion Jake Tuli in his stable. He was called 'The Bishop' because of his sober (for the boxing business) demeanour. He became a friend of the family, managing the twins' whole careers, even, indeed, past their retirements. He died in 1980. Henry's amateur career consisted of 73 wins to 11 defeats as a light-heavy; George, already a heavyweight, won 42 and lost 22. The twins signed their contracts with Wicks on television's *Sportsview*. George had to adopt the professional name of Jim, as there was already a George Cooper boxing professionally.

The twins trained at the famous Thomas A'Becket gym in the Old Kent Road, maintaining their cockney image; trainer was Danny Holland. They made their pro debuts on the same bill at Harringay Arena on 14 September 1954. Both won, Jim notably against the future British champion Dick Richardson. With purses totalling around £100, the boys bought their parents their first television set.

Henry's career began with eight straight inside-the-distance wins, then a points win over future Commonwealth champion Joe Bygraves, then his first defeat, a second round stoppage by the Italian Uber Bacilieri. Blood poured into Cooper's eye from a cut, and although Danny Holland was one of the best cut-men in the business he could not stop the flow. Cooper's prominent eyebrows and the thin layer of skin covering them were to prove his downfall too often during his career. Henry avenged the defeat, then faced Joe Erskine in an eliminator for the British heavyweight title. Henry had a 2–1 record with Erskine as an amateur, and was to finish 3–2 with him as a pro, but on this occasion Erskine, who was shorter than Cooper and pudgy, but very skilful, won on points.

Henry beat another of his regular opponents, Brian London, who had already beaten brother Jim. Henry then beat ponderous Italian Giannino Luise, but afterwards ran into a bad spell of four successive defeats which might have caused him to pack it in altogether. At 21 he had discovered that his best weight was 189–190lb. This was too much for the light-heavyweight division but made him too light for the big heavyweights of the day, who weighed over 200lb. Henry's weight would have been ideal for today's cruiserweight class. The four successive defeats were from September 1956 to September 1958. First Henry lost on a bad cut to Peter Bates, whom he was handling comfortably, then he was knocked out in the ninth round when challenging for the Commonwealth heavyweight title, by Joe Bygraves, whom he had beaten comfortably before. Cooper was 195lb and struggled for breath after being hit in the body. He then challenged for the European heavyweight crown against Ingemar Johansson of Sweden, a man destined to become world champion, and was knocked out by 'Ingo's Bingo' in the fifth round. Henry's next fight was another title contest, his third title shot in a row, when he took on Joe Erskine, who had now won the British title. Again Erskine won, narrowly outpointing Cooper.

After these four losses, Henry now had three contests in Germany to try to put his career on course. He beat Hans Kalbfell very impressively, drew with Heinz Neuhaus, a home-town decision, and was disqualified for a rabbit punch which knocked out Erich Schoeppner, although Henry contends it was a perfectly good punch to the ear which despatched his opponent. Henry thought he'd won all three German fights, and approached his next contest in England in good heart. He took on Dick Richardson, who had drawn with Bygraves for the British Empire title and later was to be European champion. This fight was a turning-point in Cooper's career. Before it, he had won one fight in seven over two years. Richardson was around 20lb heavier than Henry, and cut Henry's eye badly in the first round with his head. A blood-soaked Cooper was on the canvas in the fifth with what seemed to be the end approaching. It was – but for Richardson. Henry caught him with a perfect left hook which lifted him off his feet and knocked him clean out. At the time British fight commentators were talking of Cooper, Richardson, London and Erskine as representing a golden age of British heavyweight boxing. Before he beat Richardson Cooper seemed the least likely to emerge on top, but his next four fights made him indisputably the best.

First, Cooper outpointed the joint number one contender for the world heavyweight title, Zora Folley. Henry thinks his defeat of the tough American at Wembley Pool was his best career performance. It certainly established him as a serious prospect. Then, by outpointing him at Earls Court, he took the British and British Empire titles from Brian London, who had won them from Erskine. Next he defended the Empire title by knocking out Gawie de Klerk in five rounds, then the British title by at last re-establishing his mastery over Joe Erskine, stopping him in the 12th. Erskine was left draped over the bottom rope, with the referee deciding there was no need to count.

So at the end of 1959 Cooper was established as the best of Britain's four top heavyweights. The good times did not stop there as Henry married Albina, who was a Londoner, although she had been born in the foothills of the Italian Apennines. She was the niece of the proprietor of Henry's favourite Italian restaurant. Henry and Albina moved to Wembley, to live in a house which Henry and brother George helped build, as they did all the plastering.

Cooper was moving into line for a world title shot when he fought Zora Folley again, underestimated him and was knocked out in the second. Or perhaps he lost because of the softness of married life, as he himself implied. Son Henry Marco became an addition to the family. Henry got back into winning ways, registered his third and last pro defeat of Joe Erskine in 1962 and knocked out Dick Richardson again before his most famous fight, against Cassius Clay on 18 June 1963.

The still photo of Clay looking as if he didn't know where he was after Henry's left hook had floored him in the fourth round is one of the most used in British boxing. Unfortunately for Cooper it was near the end of the round and Clay rose at three and made it back to his corner where he again looked groggy. His manager, Angelo Dundee, tried to prolong his rest by worsening a little tear in his glove and making a fuss to the referee about changing it.

This has caused a legend to grow which states that Clay had two or three minutes to recover while the argument progressed, or even while the glove was changed. Cooper himself clearly believes this, and repeated it in a television interview in 1998, and Angelo Dundee, in his autobiography, also claims he engineered this long rest for his man. But this is just another boxing myth. It is a good story, but the radio commentary suggests that the interval overran by only five seconds or so. Clay had fully recovered and went on to stop Cooper on cuts in the following round. In his next contest Clay won the world title from Sonny Liston and changed his name to Muhammad Ali.

The punch which knocked Clay/Ali over was Henry's favourite left hook, the punch with which he delivered most of his knockouts. It became known as 'Enery's 'Ammer'. When his proud mother once said that Henry had achieved his fame and standing with his own hands, Henry had to add: 'Yes Mother, but mostly with the left'.

Cooper now unified the British, Empire and European titles by successfully defending the first two against Brian London and at the same time winning the vacant European title. It was a comfortable points verdict. Eight of Henry's next nine opponents were Americans and he lost to four of them. One was his only world title fight, against Muhammad Ali in May 1966 on Arsenal's football ground at Highbury. Ali won on another cut-eye stoppage in the sixth round. Cooper claimed that Ali had never had him in trouble, in either of their fights, apart from cuts. Cooper lost his next contest, to a fourth-round knockout by Floyd Patterson. But he did have the satisfaction in this spell of knocking out in the first round Chip Johnson, the American whose defeat of brother Jim had finally forced Jim to give in.

Henry's last seven contests were for championships. He successfully defended his British and Commonwealth titles against Jack Bodell and Billy Walker, and his European title against Germany's Karl Mildenberger and Italy's Piero Tomasoni. Henry now had a chance to challenge Jimmy Ellis for the WBA version of the world title, Ali having been stripped over his failure to fight in the Vietnam War. The British Boxing Board of Control, being affiliated to the WBC, refused to recognise this as a title fight, and Wicks and Cooper, in their disgust, gave up the British and Commonwealth titles. In the event Cooper was injured in training and the Ellis fight did not take place. Henry was absent from boxing for a year and had to give up the European title too.

In 1970 he came back to recapture his British and Commonwealth titles from Jack Bodell, and his European title from Jose Urtain of Spain. He put all three titles on the line against 21-year-old Joe Bugner on 16 March 1971 at Wembley. Henry was coming up for 37. Most fans, Henry himself and BBC TV commentator Harry Carpenter thought Henry had won comfortably, but referee Harry Gibbs shook the boxing world by raising Bugner's arm. The fans demonstrated and Henry was bitter about the verdict. It was years before he spoke to Harry Gibbs again. Henry retired, although he says he had promised Albina, who hated boxing, that he would retire anyway after this fight, win or lose.

It had been an illustrious career, stretching over 16½ years and 19 title fights. Before losing to Bugner, Cooper had won 10 British title fights, entitling him to keep three Lonsdale Belts. He is the only man to have won three Lonsdale Belts outright. A belt used to be awarded for three successive championship wins but as the BBBC rules are now changed so that a boxer can win only one Lonsdale belt at each weight, it will not be easy for another boxer to equal Henry's feat.

With his down-to-earth no-nonsense cockney personality, Henry became busy as a celebrity after retirement. He made a famous series of advertisements for Brut cosmetics. He captained a team for three series of BBC TV's *A Question of Sport* and also played in celebrity golf tournaments for charity. A venture into the greengrocery business with a Wembley High Street shop failed with losses of £10,000 after two years and he lost a lot of money in the Lloyd's of London insurance crash, but there was plenty of work, and he commented on most of the big fights on television. He surprised many by giving up this work in 1996 after becoming disillusioned over the way boxing was going, in particular the hype that was making it almost as much of a show-business con as a sport.

Henry and Albina had a second son, John Pietro, in 1967 and they enjoy life to the full, including their visits to Italy. That Henry is not going soft, however, was seen on a 1998 television interview when he was linked by satellite with Joe Bugner in Australia. It was clear from a prickly conversation that Henry still thinks he was robbed.

CAREER STATISTICS

Heavyweight
London, born 3 May 1934

1954
Sep 14 Harry Painter w ko 1 London
Oct 19 Dinny Powell w rsf 4 London
Nov 23 Eddie Keith w rsf 1 London
Dec 7 Denny Ball w ko 3 London
1955
Jan 27 Colin Strauch w rsf 1 London
Feb 8 Cliff Purnell w pts 6 London
Mar 8 Hugh Ferns w dis 2 London
Mar 29 Joe Crickmar w rtd 5 London
Apr 18 Joe Bygraves w pts 8 London
Apr 26 Uber Bacilieri l rsf 2 London
Jun 6 Ron Harman w rsf 7 Nottingham
Sep 13 Uber Bacilieri w ko 7 London
Nov 15 Joe Erskine l pts 10 London
1956
Feb 28 Maurice Mols w rsf 4 London
May 1 Brian London w rsf 1 London
Jun 26 Gianni Luise w rsf 7 London
Sep 7 Peter Bates l rtd 5 Manchester
1957
Feb 19 Joe Bygraves l ko 9 London
(British Empire heavyweight title)
May 19 Ingemar Johansson l ko 5 Stockholm
(European heavyweight title)
Sep 17 Joe Erskine l pts 15 London
(British heavyweight title)
Nov 16 Hans Kalbfell w pts 10 Dortmund
1958
Jan 11 Heinz Neuhaus drew 10 Dortmund
Apr 19 Erich Schoeppner l dis 6 Frankfurt
Sep 3 Dick Richardson w rsf 5 Porthcawl
Oct 14 Zora Folley w pts 10 Wembley
1959
Jan 12 Brian London w pts 15 London
(British & Empire heavyweight titles)
Aug 26 Gawie de Klerk w rsf 5 Porthcawl
(Empire heavyweight title)
Nov 17 Joe Erskine w rsf 12 London
(British & Empire heavyweight titles)
1960
Sep 13 Roy Harris w pts 10 London
Dec 6 Alex Miteff w pts 10 London
1961
Mar 21 Joe Erskine w rtd 5 London
(British & Empire heavyweight titles)
Dec 5 Zora Folley l ko 2 London
1962
Jan 23 Tony Hughes w rtd 5 London
Feb 26 Wayne Bethea w pts 10 Manchester
Apr 2 Joe Erskine w rsf 9 Nottingham
(British & Empire heavyweight titles)
1963
Mar 26 Dick Richardson w ko 5 London
(British & Empire heavyweight titles)
Jun 18 Cassius Clay l rsf 5 London
1964
Feb 24 Brian London w pts 15 Manchester
(European, British & Empire heavyweight titles)
Nov 16 Roger Rischer l pts 10 London
1965
Jan 12 Dick Wipperman w rsf 5 London
Apr 20 Chip Johnson w ko 1 Wolverhampton
Jun 15 Johnny Prescott w rtd 10 Birmingham
(British & Empire heavyweight titles)
Oct 19 Amos Johnson l pts 10 London
1966
Jan 25 Hubert Hilton w rsf 2 London
Feb 16 Jefferson Davis w ko 1 Wolverhampton
May 21 Muhammad Ali l rsf 6 London
(World heavyweight title)
Sep 20 Floyd Patterson l ko 4 London
1967
Apr 17 Boston Jacobs w pts 10 Leicester
Jun 13 Jack Bodell w rsf 2 Wolverhampton
(British & Empire heavyweight titles)
Nov 7 Billy Walker w rsf 6 London
(British & Empire heavyweight titles)
1968
Sep 18 Karl Mildenberger w dis 8 London
(European heavyweight title)
1969
Mar 13 Piero Tomasoni w ko 5 Rome
(European heavyweight title)
1970
Mar 24 Jack Bodell w pts 15 London
(British & heavyweight titles)
Nov 10 Jose Urtain w rsf 9 London
(European heavyweight title)
1971
Mar 16 Joe Bugner l pts 15 London
(British, Empire & European heavyweight titles)

Fights 55 Won 40 Lost 14 Drawn 1

KEN BUCHANAN

GREAT SCOT

Voted more than once Britain's best boxer since the war, Ken Buchanan, immensely skilled, hard punching, undisputed lightweight champion of the world, had it all. Except one thing – he never truly received the appreciation he deserved at home - not from fans, press or the Board of Control, until it was all a bit late. At one time he retired unbeaten and returned his Lonsdale Belt in disgust at his lack of progess. But he eventually triumphed to take his place in the pantheon of greats.

Buchanan was born in Edinburgh on 28 June 1945, just as the Second World War was ending. His father Tommy was to play a big part in his boxing career, and his mother, Cathie, also gave him her full support. But it was two aunts, Joan and Agnes, who set him on the way to a boxing career. Stuck for Christmas present ideas when Ken was seven, they saw some boxing gloves in an Edinburgh store, and realising Ken and his cousin, Robert Barr, liked sparring, they bought them a pair each. Ken was more keen on football until his dad took him to see *The Joe Louis Story* at the cinema, which persuaded Ken to join the Sparta Club when he was eight and learn to box. He soon won medals amongst the boys, and when he reached 17 he began winning youth titles. He represented Scotland in the European Championships and won Scottish and ABA titles at featherweight.

At 20 he received many offers to turn professional and accepted one from Eddie Thomas, who was at the time training the future world champion Howard Winstone. Thomas got Ken's signature for £500, but it was possibly a bad decision. Thomas trained in Wales, but agreed Buchanan could live in Edinburgh, and the difficulties posed by the distance between them were never satisfactorily overcome. A complication was that Ken's father, Tommy, had ambitions to train his son, too, and his advice was sometimes opposite to Thomas's, e.g. Thomas wanted Ken to harden the skin on his face by rubbing in urine, Ken's dad wanted him to soften it with Vaseline.

Thomas, who naturally spent more time with his established champion, Winstone, also had the handicap of not being a running mate of a promotional set-up which was all-powerful in British championship boxing – the Harry Levene, Mike Barrett, Jarvis Astaire and Mickey Duff partnership. So Thomas found difficulty in getting Buchanan fights in the big venues.

Buchanan made his debut on 20 September 1965, stopping his opponent, Brian Tonks, in the second round at the National Sporting Club. Many of Ken's early fights were at this venue, in an atmosphere like a gentlemen's club. Thomas taught the skills of the game well, and Buchanan developed into a classy boxer with quick footwork, an accurate and punishing left jab and the ability to punch hard with either hand. He ran up a string of wins and in 1967 took the Scottish Area lightweight title with a points win over John McMillan.

Buchanan was not too happy with his boxing arrangements: living in Edinburgh, travelling to Wales for training with Eddie Thomas and travelling to London for his contests meant he was always journeying around the sides of a large triangle. Nor was he happy about fighting in genteel clubs before restrained, dressed-up members. He wanted the excitement and roar of the normal big-fight crowd.

In 1968 he was given a shot at the British lightweight title, held by 30-year-old Maurice Cullen, a good, canny boxer from Shotton, near Durham, whose success was based largely on a ramrod left-hand jab. Cullen had won the title a few months before Buchanan had turned pro, and had successfully defended four times. The fight was at the Anglo American Sporting Club in London.

Buchanan was not fancied against the much more experienced Cullen but, in a hard fight, he gradually got on top and dropped the champion twice in the sixth and ninth rounds. In the 11th, with Cullen staging a comeback, Buchanan caught him with a couple of sharp punches and knocked him out with a left hook.

The fight critics were very enthusiastic about Buchanan's performance. He had outstanding skills as a boxer and, in addition, a sufficiently hard punch to knock out nearly a third of his opponents, including the British champion. An intelligent man, Buchanan began to realise that he possessed a very special talent. As he confessed in his autobiography, *High Life and Hard Times* (Mainstream Publishing, Edinburgh), he now thought: 'The big money is just around the corner'. But it wasn't.

By now Ken had married girlfriend Carol Howden and had a young son, Mark. He had taken a large mortgage and bought a dream home in Edinburgh. But because Eddie Thomas was not on good terms with the big London promoters, the lucrative fights failed to materialise. He continued winning well, and impressed a national audience when outpointing Frankie Narvaez on BBC television in 1969.

Buchanan had gone over a year without any defence of his British title being planned, and would have been very depressed had it not been for a match arranged for June 1969 at Nottingham with former world lightweight champion Carlos Teo Cruz of the Dominican Republic. Cruz had just dropped the title to Mando Ramos and the contest with Buchanan was being billed as a final eliminator for the world title. It was at last a great opportunity for Buchanan, and his disappointment when Cruz was forced to pull out at the last minute can be imagined. A frustrated Buchanan took less than a round to dispose of the substitute, Jerry Graci.

During the next month, Buchanan reviewed his position. He was down to his last few pounds in the bank, with a big mortgage to pay. He had been a British champion for 18 months, but had not been able to defend the crown (the British Boxing Board of Control were to tell him unofficially that there was nobody good enough to challenge). Eddie Thomas apparently felt that his fighter, approaching 24, wasn't yet ready to try his luck in America. Buchanan felt that all his three years of hard training and travelling, his 34 contests, all impressive wins, had been a waste of time. Impulsively, he packed up his licence and the Lonsdale Belt he held as champion, and sent them back to the Secretary of the British Board, Teddy Weltham, with a note saying he was giving up. The news broke in the press on 1 August 1969, and caused a sensation in the boxing world. The best fighter Britain had produced in years apparently couldn't make a decent living from boxing, and preferred to go back to his old trade of carpentry. Buchanan, who had a love-hate relationship with Eddie Thomas before they finally split up, noted that even at this crisis Thomas did not get in touch.

It was a sad event two months later that brought Ken back to boxing. His mother, Cathie, died. Eddie Thomas travelled to Edinburgh for the funeral, where he and Buchanan and Buchanan's father Tommy discussed his career. Tommy told Ken that his mother would have wanted him to fight on. In truth Buchanan was already regretting his decision. They decided Buchanan would after all fight on, and see out his contract with Thomas.

His second title fight came nearly two years after his first. It was for the European title against a very tough Spaniard, Miguel Velazquez, who had won all but one of his 40 contests. The fight was in Madrid, and resulted in Buchanan's first defeat. It was close and, like all fighters, Buchanan had plenty of excuses, some more plausible than others, but the fact remained he had lost.

It was a temporary setback. Within four months he had defended his British title at last, scoring a convincing knockout over Brian Hudson at Wembley's Empire Pool. And, better still, he then got a world title chance.

At last fortune smiled on Buchanan. Mando Ramos withdrew from a challenge to champion Ismael Laguna of Panama, and a credible but unthreatening substitute was needed. Who could be more suitable than a clever British boxer who had just been outpointed by a Spaniard? There was, however, a minor snag against Buchanan accepting the fight. The WBC stripped Laguna of the title for breaking a contract. The BBBC, affiliated to the WBC, followed suit and declared the world title vacant, advising Buchanan not to meet Laguna for the WBA crown. Buchanan went ahead and, in a temperature of over 100 degrees, took the ring in the Hiron Bithorn Stadium in San Juan for the 2 p.m. start on Saturday, 26 September 1970. Conditions suited the Laguna while the fair Buchanan was soon bothered by the heat. But Jack Solomons, the London promoter who was in Buchanan's corner, borrowed a parasol from a ringside spectator. It was a tough match which went the distance, but Buchanan gradually proved the stronger and shook Laguna in the 12th round. There was anxiety when a split decision was anounced, but Buchanan won by 145–144 (twice) and 144–145.

Buchanan, justly, was cock-a-hoop. He was the first British world lightweight champion since Freddie Welsh in 1917, and the first Briton to win a world title on the other side of the Atlantic since Ted 'Kid' Lewis in 1915. It was a superb performance, and he got a tremendous send-off at San Juan. Two disappointments awaited him back home, though. He imagined a great Edinburgh welcome at the airport. He was met by six people, four of them family. And still the BBBC wouldn't recognise him as champion.

Later in the year Buchanan made the first of six appearances at Madison Square Garden. He was on the undercard of a Muhammad Ali contest, and outpointed an unbeaten Canadian, Donato Paduano, so brilliantly that he won a standing ovation. He had found his boxing home. Buchanan became the first British boxer to win the Edward J. Neill trophy, awarded annually since 1938 by the New York Boxing Writers Association for the person to do most for boxing during the year.

Buchanan's first defence of his title was against the tough American champion, Ruben Navarro in Los Angeles, and again Buchanan put on a master class to win easily. The WBC agreed to recognise this fight, as did the BBBC, so Buchanan was undisputed champion. This time Edinburgh gave him a parade and a civic reception. At 25, he was on top of the world.

However the WBC did not recognise Buchanan for long, because he signed to meet Laguna in a return at Madison Square Garden, while the WBC wanted him to fight Pedro Carrasco. This time the BBBC stood by Buchanan. The Laguna fight was another classic, with Buchanan, in the second round, suffering an injury to his left eye which began to close. Eddie Thomas had to lance the 'mouse' with a razor blade. It gradually got so bad that, before the 13th and 14th rounds, the doctor examined it to make sure Buchanan could continue. But by now he had got on top and with a minute to go the crowd began to applaud a great fight. Buchanan won a unanimous verdict, 10–5, 9–6 and 8–6–1.

Buchanan's contract with Eddie Thomas was coming up for review and by mutual agreement the two split up. Neither man was unreasonable but the circumstances of their partnership were impossible, especially when Buchanan's father, Tommy, took out a manager's licence.

In 1972 came the fight which left Buchanan forever bitter. He was defending his title against Roberto Duran in Madison Square Garden. After the bell to end the 13th round, Duran fought on with Buchanan on the ropes and delivered a blow to the groin which caused the champion to sink to the canvas in agony. Buchanan is convinced it was delivered by Duran's knee. His protector was split, and he was ruled unable to come out for the 14th round and thus forfeited his title. It was the only time he was stopped in his career. He was doubly bitter that Duran, who remained champion for seven years, never granted him a return. In fact Duran soon lost British and New York recognition for not meeting Buchanan.

Buchanan continued to box brilliantly, notably against Jim Watt in a British title challenge, and he won the European title when knocking out Antonio Puddu of Italy in Cagliari in 1974. Both of these titles he gave up undefeated when he retired, but first there was an attempt to regain the WBC part of the world title from Ishimatsu Suzuki (later Guts Ishimatsu) in Tokyo. He lost this contest after an eye wound, acquired in training, reopened in the fifth round. He then defended his European title against Giancarlo Usai in Cagliari, and suffered double vision after the referee had accidentally poked his finger in his eye. He won the fight but retired on the advice of an eye specialist.

Having used his later ring earnings to open a hotel in Edinburgh, and with a nice home and a customised Mercedes Benz with a 123KB number plate, Buchanan turned his attention to business. But the hotel began to fail and his wife left him, taking their two children (a daughter, Karen, had joined son Mark). Buchanan had to sell the hotel in 1980, and with investment in trust companies going wrong, he had to return to his carpentry work. Meanwhile, he made a boxing comeback in 1979, and challenged Charlie Nash for the European title. He lost narrowly on points. Unfortunately he kept going and lost his last four contests, doubling his total career defeats. After retiring again, Buchanan sadly was tempted into two unlicensed bouts.

He took a second wife, Eileen Doherty, and they managed a pub in Dagenham, Essex. But they were divorced in 1986 after his wife had a child by another man. Buchanan returned to Edinburgh to run another pub, and took out a manager's licence, but neither venture came to anything. In 1997 he was confirmed again as one of his country's best when a Sky TV panel of experts debated who was the greatest British fighter of all time. Buchanan was one of the three boxers considered for the final choice, and the other two, Jimmy Wilde and Ted 'Kid' Lewis, were men from First World War days. A few months later *Boxing News* revealed that Ken Buchanan was living on state benefit in a bedsit outside Glasgow. Still only 53, he was continuing to blame Duran for the state he was in, but was reported chirpy and without regrets. 'I enjoyed every minute of it,' he said. 'I still look forward to the future.'

CAREER STATISTICS

World lightweight champion 1970-72
Edinburgh, Scotland, born 28 June 1945

1965

Sep 20 Brian Tonks w rsf 2 London
Oct 18 Vic Woodhall w rsf 2 Manchester
Nov 1 Billy Williams w rsf 2 London
Nov 22 Joe Okezie w rsf 3 London
Dec 13 Junior Cassidy w pts 8 London

1966

Jan 24 Tommy Tiger w pts 8 London
Mar 7 Manley Brown w rsf 4 London

Apr 4 Tommy Tiger w pts 8 London
Apr 19 Chris Elliott w pts 8 London
May 11 Junior Cassidy w pts 8 Manchester
Jul 12 Brian Smyth w rsf 1 Aberavon
Aug 6 Ivan Whiter w pts 8 London
Sep 6 Mick Laud w pts 8 London
Oct 17 Antonio Paiva w pts 10 London
Nov 29 Al Keen w pts 8 Leeds
Dec 19 Phil Lundgren w pts 10 London

1967

Jan 23 John McMillan w pts 10 Glasgow
Feb 14 Tommy Garrison w pts 10 London
May 11 Franco Brondi w rsf 3 Paisley
Jun 28 Winston Laud w pts 8 London
Jul 26 Rene Roque w pts 10 Aberavon
Sep 14 Al Rocca w rsf 7 London
Oct 30 Spike McCormack w pts 12 London

1968

Feb 19 Maurice Cullen w ko 11 London
(British lightweight title)
Apr 22 Leonard Tavarez w pts 8 London
Jun 10 Ivan Whiter w pts 8 London
Oct 23 Angel Garcia w pts 10 London
Dec 11 Ameur Lamine w rsf 3 Hamilton

1969

Jan 2 Frankie Narvaez w pts 10 London
Feb 17 Mike Cruz w rsf 4 London
Mar 5 Jose Luis Torcida w pts 8 Solihull
Jul 14 Jerry Graci w rsf 1 Nottingham
Nov 11 Vincenzo Pitardi w rsf 2 London

1970

Jan 29 Miguel Velasquez l pts 15 Madrid
(European lightweight title)
Feb 23 Leonard Tavarez w pts 10 London
Apr 6 Chris Fernandez w pts 10 Nottingham
May 12 Brian Hudson w ko 5 London
(British lightweight title)
Sep 26 Ismael Laguna w pts 15 San Juan
(World lightweight title)
Dec 7 Donato Paduano w pts 10 New York

1971

Feb 12 Ruben Navarro w pts 15 Los Angeles
(World lightweight title)
May 11 Carlos Hernandez w rsf 8 London
Sep 13 Ismael Laguna w pts 15 New York
(World lightweight title)

1972

Mar 28 Al Ford w pts 10 London
Apr 29 Andries Steyn w rsf 3 Johannesburg
Jun 26 Roberto Duran l rsf 13 New York
(World lightweight title)
Sep 20 Carlos Ortiz w rsf 6 New York
Dec 4 Chang-kil Lee w rsf 2 New York

1973

Jan 29 Jim Watt w pts 15 Glasgow
(British lightweight title)
Mar 28 Hector Matta w pts 10 London
May 31 Frankie Otero w pts 10 Miami
Sep 1 Chu Chu Malave w rsf 7 New York
Oct 11 Frankie Otero w rsf 6 Toronto
Dec 6 Miguel Araujo w ko 1 Copenhagen

1974

Feb 7 Jose Peterson w pts 10 Copenhagen
Apr 4 Joe Tetteh w ko 3 Copenhagen
May 1 Antonio Puddu w ko 6 Cagliari
(European lightweight title)
Nov 21 Winston Noel w rsf 2 Copenhagen
Dec 16 Leonard Tavarez w rsf 14 Paris
(European lightweight title)

1975

Feb 27 Ishimatsu Suzuki l pts 15 Tokyo
(WBC lightweight title)
Jul 25 Giancarlo Usai w rsf 12 Cagliari
(European lightweight title)

1976-78 inactive

1979

Jun 28 Benny Benitez w pts 8 Randers
Sep 6 Eloy de Souza w pts 8 Randers
Dec 6 Charlie Nash l pts 12 Copenhagen
(European lightweight title)

1980

May 15 Najib Daho w ko 7 London
Oct 20 Des Gwilliam w pts 8 Birmingham

1981

Jan 12 Steve Early l pts 12 Birmingham
Apr 4 Langton Tinago l pts 10 Salisbury
Nov 24 Lance Williams l pts 8 London

1982

Jan 25 George Feeney l pts 8 London

Fights 69 Won 61 Lost 8

JOE FRAZIER

SMOKIN' JOE

Joe Frazier fought in an era of great heavyweights, including Muhammad Ali and George Foreman, the only two men ever to beat him. He was world champion for nearly five years – undisputed for three. His name will always be linked with Ali, with whom he had two of the greatest fights of the century. In fact the first, between two unbeaten world champions, was actually billed as 'The Fight of the Century' and in winning Frazier became the first man ever to beat Ali. Their third encounter, which Ali won, 'The Thrilla in Manila', was a superb contest in which both men gave their all, and took so much out of themselves that neither was to be the same force again. Apart from a belated one-fight comeback, Frazier's career lasted 10 years, half as world champion. He is undoubtedly one of the best heavyweights of modern times.

Born on 12 January 1944 in Beaumont, South Carolina, Joe Frazier was the seventh son, and the 12th of the 13 children of the family. Two of the children had died before Joe was born and the last boy died of diphtheria at nine months, leaving Joe the youngest of the 10 survivors. He was called 'Billy Boy' and was his father's favourite. The whole community was very poor, with the only work available being the harvesting of vegetables on the large plantations. Joe's family was particularly handicapped in that his dad, Rubin, had lost his left hand and the use of his arm as a result of being shot by a drunken friend jealous over a girl they both fancied. Joe recalls how he was at work at six years old picking radishes for 15 cents per crate and helping his dad chop down trees. He wouldn't earn a lot even in a 12-hour day. But they did make bootleg liquor. The family lived in accommodation they built themselves, which let in the rain, and life was hard.

The outdoor, physical life certainly would have helped Joe develop his strength and muscles, and early on he took a liking to boxing. He harboured ambitions of being a boxer himself, and rigged up his own punchbag by filling a sack with leaves and hanging it on a tree. Although Joe Louis had retired before Joe became conscious of the heroes of the sport, Joe Louis became his inspiration from the day he heard his Uncle Israel say: 'That boy is gonna be another Joe Louis.'

At 16 Joe married his boyhood sweetheart, Florence Smith, and moved to Philadelphia where they stayed with Joe's Aunt Evelyn. Joe found himself a job in a slaughterhouse at $25 per 12-hour day, but the work was good for his bodybuilding. In fact Joe's body built at such an alarming rate that unkind people called him fat; at 17 he weighed 220lb. Joe's boxing ambitions were such that he went along to the Police Athletic League gymnasium on 23rd Street to learn the trade. The enthusiastic work he put in on the heavy bag under the direction of Police Sergeant Duke Dugent, who ran the gym, soon got his weight under control. It also impressed the veteran trainer Yancey Durham, who gave Joe his nickname by asking to see smoke coming out of the leather as he punched it. Joe's response had everybody calling him Smokin' Joe.

Durham took an interest in Joe's amateur career and taught him the non-stop pressing technique and combination punching that was to become his trademark. Although Joe's weight was well up to heavyweight standard (over 215lb for 'The Thrilla in Manila'), he never grew taller than half-an-inch under 6ft, comparatively short for the heavyweights of his era (Ali and Foreman, his conquerors, were each 6ft 3in). Frazier couldn't afford to stand around and get picked off at long range. Boring in and hooking savagely to the body was to be more his style.

Joe did well as an amateur, winning the Middle Atlantic Golden Gloves at 19 and 20, and earning a place in the trials to pick the US Olympic team for 1964. Unfortunately for Joe, in the final he came up against the only man who'd beaten him till then, Buster Mathis, and lost a close decision. But Joe earned a place as reserve, and when Mathis broke a finger (ironically on Joe's head in an exhibition bout) Joe was in the team. He himself had broken a bone in his right hand by the time of the Olympic final, but won the narrowest decision to take the gold medal.

With a broken hand, however, Joe lost his job back home. By now he and Florence already had three children – son Marvis and daughters Jacquelyn and Weatta (he had also fathered two illegitimate children back in Beaumont). Hard up, he began a pro career without any backers and, on his debut in August 1965, earned $500 for knocking out Woody Goss in the first round. The contest, like his next four – all won with quick knockouts, although Joe himself was decked in the second – was held in Philadelphia.

Eventually a group of Philadelphia businessmen sponsored him to the extent of paying him $100 a week, hoping to recoup (they did!) by taking 35 per cent of earnings, out of which they paid all expenses. Of the other 65 per cent, Joe was to get 50 per cent (half in cash and half in investments) and Durham the other 15 per cent as trainer.

Joe's first big test came in his 12th fight, in New York against Oscar Bonavena, a tough hard-punching Argentinian, who was cut in the first round and, fighting desperately, dropped Frazier twice in the second. Bonavena tried hard for a third knockdown in the round, which would have won the fight under the rules in operation, but Joe held out and eventually won on points over 10 rounds. But it was a close split decision, and it was the first time he had been forced to go the distance.

Frazier's opponents got tougher but he kept winning. Eddie Machen, Doug Jones and George Chuvalo were all stopped, despite Chuvalo having gone the distance with Ali in a title challenge little more than a year earlier.

Soon afterwards, Ali was stripped of his undisputed title over his stance on the Vietnam War, and Frazier was a natural for the WBA's eight-man competition to find a new champion. Indeed Joe was so natural a choice that on Durham's advice he declined to take part. Durham regarded Joe as the top contender and saw no reason to engage in eliminating bouts. It was a wise decision. All seven fights in the WBA's competition were won by the betting underdog, and the man who emerged as WBA champion, Jimmy Ellis, was not seen as an obvious champion by many. Seven weeks before Ellis won the final, the New York Commission decided to recognise the winner of a Madison Square Garden bout between Frazier and his old amateur opponent, Buster Mathis, as champion. Frazier, outweighed by 39 lb by a huge Mathis, caught up with Mathis with an 11th round left hook and won on a stoppage.

The idea of two heavyweight champions was not taken so equably then as it is now and, less than two years after they'd won their titles, Frazier and Ellis met at Madison Square Garden to unify the division. Both had defended well in the meantime, despite Ellis hardly being a true heavyweight, but on the night Joe proved much the stronger, and took the undisputed title when Ellis, dumped to the canvas twice in the fourth round, was too groggy to come out for the fifth.

Having beaten most of his obvious challengers, Joe easily disposed of a challenge from light-heavyweight champion Bob Foster and then prepared to meet Ali, starting a comeback after three-and-a-half years exile from the ring, and of course claiming that he himself was the only true champion. A meeting between the two unbeaten champions was eagerly anticipated, and it was fixed for 8 March 1971 at Madison Square Garden. It was naturally billed as 'The Fight of the Century'. The take of $1,342,951 was a record for an indoor contest. The closed-circuit TV take at $16.5 million was four times the previous highest. About 300 million fans saw the fight worldwide.

Ali and Frazier enjoyed a love-hate relationship, with the emphasis on the 'hate'. The witty, fast-talking Ali taunted the more deliberate Frazier unmercifully, and Frazier, who was not unintelligent but lacked the, glibness and easy self-confidence of Ali, found it difficult to respond. He had to smoulder in silence and save his animosity for the ring.

Among the 20,455 ticket-buying fans at the Garden on the night were previous champions Dempsey, Tunney, Braddock and Louis as well as other celebrities from boxing and all other walks of life. The atmosphere was electric. Having to tolerate Ali's blabber during the final instructions, Frazier merely stared at him and said: 'I'm gonna kill you'.

Frazier certainly gained full revenge for Ali's insults in this match. Ali always had more difficulty with Frazier's style than would be expected. Ali was famously described as 'floating like a butterfly', but he could also be likened to a moth, continually fluttering round the flame of danger. Ali took so many risks that Frazier always made him pay once or twice. In a bitterly contested fight, in which both men took considerable punishment, a left hook from Frazier which got home to Ali's head in the 11th round did most to win it. Ali was shaken. Frazier had the initiative and another left hook in the 15th and last round put Ali down and caused a big instant swelling to his cheek. Ali rose to finish the fight but the decision went to Frazier by 11–4, 9–6 and 8–6–1. Both men went to hospital after the fight. Frazier spent the first night on a bed of ice and remained in the hospital for weeks, while doctors feared he might have a stroke. So far as boxing was concerned he was out of action for 10 months. But the poor boy with short arms but long in spirit was now the undeniable undisputed heavyweight champion of the world. He made two comparatively easy defences in 1972, but then met his nemesis, George Foreman.

Once again both men in a heavyweight title fight were unbeaten when they climbed into the ring in the National Stadium, Kingston, Jamaica, in January 1973. Foreman had succeeded Frazier as Olympic heavyweight champion and had tremendous physical advantages over his opponent. Crucially, he also punched much harder than Ali. As Frazier bored in as usual, a huge right sat him on his pants. There followed a game of jack-in-the-box, with Frazier continually coming forward but meeting a punch which sat him down. Six times it happened in two rounds of boxing, before referee Arthur Mercante called enough.

Frazier, who was just past his 29th birthday, thus met his first defeat in his 30th bout. No need to retire yet. He outpointed Joe Bugner, and then challenged Ali, whose comeback was progressing satisfactorily, for the North American championship. The old animosity was reawakened at a TV studio meeting when, after a particularly nasty insult, Joe tore his ear-plug out and set about Ali, the two grappling on the floor. Joe was fined $5,000. It was a better fight later in the ring at Madison Square Garden, but this time Ali was more successful at keeping Joe at a distance, and took a unanimous decision. Some newspaper reporters agreed with Joe, however, when he claimed he'd won.

Ali continued to flourish and, in 1974, went on to take the heavyweight title back from Foreman. Joe, after knocking out two old adversaries in Jerry Quarry and Jimmy Ellis, took on Ali for the third time at the Araneta Coliseum, Manila, Philippines on 1 October 1975, to try to recapture the undisputed world title. This was billed as The 'Thrilla in Manila' and was one of the hardest contests ever fought. Both men knew this would settle the score between them, and called on all their reserves. Ali won the first four rounds, but after nine there was nothing in it. Ali gradually got on top again from then on, and Frazier's trainer Eddie Futch (he had taken over when Yancey Durham died the previous year) would not let Joe go out for the last round. His face was puffy and swollen and his eyes were closing. Ali himself confessed he had at one stage been on the point of retiring, and claimed he felt near to death. The boxers weren't helped by an air-conditioning failure during the fight.

Both took a long time to recover, and neither was as good a fighter again. They had nearly destroyed each other.

So perhaps Frazier wasn't in a condition to take on George Foreman for a second time nine months later. By now he was having trouble with his eyes and claims he was secretly wearing contact lenses for the fight. Sporting a shaven head, he still could find no way of getting near big George, and suffered another knockout, this time in the fifth round. It was time to retire.

Joe did not forsake the limelight though. He loved jazz and rock and had a huge collection of records. He was now in a position to indulge himself and he had formed a band some time before with himself as singer – Joe Frazier and the Knockouts. He got lots of bookings because of the novelty value, and for a while the Smokin' Joe Frazier Revue toured all over America. But it could not replace boxing for Joe. After five years, aged 38, he made a comeback and fought a draw with Jumbo Cummings. His performance was enough to convince him he wasn't going to find his old magic again. He was persuaded to retire once more by his children, who told him that the smoke was just about out. His physical condition, too, was suffering. As well as a deteriorating right eye, he now had pain in most of his joints, particularly his right shoulder, which he says is 'dying'. But he says he does not regret the sacrifice. It was a small price to pay to become champion, and lead the life he did.

So ended an outstanding fighting career in which only two men ever beat him: Foreman and Ali. Joe never forgave Ali his taunts and insults. In his autobiography, *Smokin' Joe*, the name Ali is found mostly as a cross-reference in the index. Joe calls him 'Clay' throughout the book. He even refers to today's stricken Ali as a ghost, saying: 'Now look at him; he can hardly talk and he's still out there making a noise'. He seems to have had the last word – and it's a bitter one.

In 1985 Joe and Florence were amicably divorced. They shared five children: Marvis, who also boxed, and four daughters. Joe also had a son, Hector, who became a boxer, and a daughter by an early love in Beaumont, and four other sons for whom he took responsibility. In 1976, when Joe had retired the first time, his sponsoring company, Cloverlay, had gone into liquidation, and Joe had acquired their assets including the contracts of a few boxers and a gymnasium in North Broad Street. Philadelphia is famous as a tough boxing city, where world champions learn their trade in hard, well-organised gyms. Joe realised that he would enjoy his later years most if he trained boxers to try to achieve what he did. Among his clients were two sons, Marvis and Hector (who fought as Joe Frazier Junior) and two nephews. Marvis achieved some fame and fought Larry Holmes and Mike Tyson, though he was overmatched on both occasions. Joe also began promoting. He remains proud of Philadelphia, himself, his family and the fight business.

CAREER STATISTICS

World heavyweight champion 1968-73
Philadelphia, born Beaufort, South Carolina, 12 January 1944
1964 Olympic heavyweight gold medal

1965
Aug 16 Woody Goss w ko 1 Philadelphia
Sep 20 Mike Bruce w ko 3 Philadelphia
Sep 28 Ray Staples w ko 2 Philadelphia
Nov 11 Abe Davis w ko 1 Philadelphia
1966
Jan 17 Mel Turnbow w ko 1 Philadelphia
Mar 4 Dick Wipperman w ko 5 New York
Apr 4 Charley Polite w ko 2 Philadelphia
Apr 29 Don Smith w ko 3 Pittsburgh
May 19 Chuck Leslie w ko 3 Los Angeles
May 26 Memphis Al Jones w ko 1 Los Angeles
Jul 25 Billy Daniels w rsf 6 Philadelphia
Sep 21 Oscar Bonavena w pts 10 New York
Nov 21 Eddie Machen w rsf 10 Los Angeles
1967
Feb 21 Doug Jones w ko 6 Philadelphia
Apr 11 Jefferson Davis w ko 5 Miami
May 4 George Johnson w pts 10 Los Angeles
Jul 19 George Chuvalo w rsf 4 New York
Oct 17 Tony Doyle w rsf 2 Philadelphia
Dec 18 Marion Connors w ko 3 Boston
1968
Mar 4 Buster Mathis w ko 11 New York
(New York World heavyweight title)
Jun 24 Manuel Ramos w rsf 2 New York
(New York World heavyweight title)
Dec 10 Oscar Bonavena w pts 15 Philadelphia
(New York World heavyweight title)
1969
Apr 22 Dave Zyglewicz w ko 1 Houston
(New York World heavyweight title)
Jun 23 Jerry Quarry w rsf 7 New York
(New York World heavyweight title)
1970
Feb 16 Jimmy Ellis w rtd 4 New York
(World heavyweight title)
Nov 18 Bob Foster w ko 2 Detroit
(World heavyweight title)
1971
Mar 8 Muhammad Ali w pts 15 New York
(World heavyweight title)
1972
Jan 15 Terry Daniels w rsf 4 New Orleans
(World heavyweight title)
May 25 Ron Stander w rsf 5 Omaha
(World heavyweight title)
1973
Jan 22 George Foreman l rsf 2 Kingston, Jamaica
(World heavyweight title)
Jul 2 Joe Bugner w pts 12 London
1974
Jan 28 Muhammad Ali l pts 12 New York
(North American Boxing Federation heavyweight title)
Jun 17 Jerry Quarry w rsf 5 New York
1975
Mar 1 Jimmy Ellis w rsf 9 Melbourne
Oct 1 Muhammad Ali l rtd 14 Manila
(World heavyweight title)
1976
Jun 15 George Foreman l rsf 5 Uniondale
1977-80 inactive
1981
Dec 3 Floyd Cummings drew 10 Chicago

Fights 37 Won 32 Lost 4 Drawn 1

BOB FOSTER

THE ALBUQUERQUE SHERIFF

TALL, slim with a textbook left hook, Bob Foster was a calm, methodical boxer and a lethal puncher. He was the best light-heavyweight in the world for six years, between 1968 and 1974. Foster was never a success in the heavyweight division, where his height was not outstanding and the weight he had to concede lessened the effect of his power. Nevertheless, at light-heavyweight he was a commanding, imposing figure who turned back 14 challenges and, like Archie Moore, was never beaten in a 175lb title bout.

He was born Robert Lloyd Foster in Albuquerque, New Mexico, on 15 December 1938. He lived with his mother, Bertha, in a tough, poor area of the city. As a boy he learned the trumpet, and was also keen on American Football. He was talented enough at the latter to be offered a scholarship at the University of New Mexico, but decided not to follow it up.

While still at high school, he boxed as well, but was an underdeveloped stringbean of a boy who was not much more than a featherweight. He seemed to have no real future, even though he says he could always punch. Joe Louis Murphy, a local welterweight, who doubled as a youth leader, took him in hand and taught him the basics.

When he left school he joined the US Air Force. He met his wife Pearl at a services dance 86 miles from Washington in York, Pennsylvania. They were married the day after Bob's 18th birthday.

He persuaded the air force coach to let him box, and after a poor start, settled down, found the key to using his reach and power, and put together an unbeaten run of 94 contests. It was an amazing transformation, which took him to four air force titles and a place on the US international team. He also boxed as a heavyweight in England in October 1958, when he won an international services event called the Britannia Shield at Wembley, knocking out English airman Ken Wilson in two rounds. He also trained air force boxers at the Bolling Base near Washington, and he helped develop future top class heavyweights Doug Jones and Billy Daniels. In fact, Jones was to beat him in the professional ranks!

In 1959 he boxed in the Pan-American Games, but he missed out on the Rome Olympic light-heavyweight slot to Cassius Clay! The selectors asked him to make middleweight, which was ridiculous and, his time in the services over, he turned professional instead, managed at first by Billy Edwards, who later became his trainer, when he signed up with the more influential Morris 'Mushky' Salow.

He made his professional debut in Washington DC in March 1961, had a couple of four-round novice bouts in New York, one in Norfolk, Virginia, and three in Canada before the year was out. He made no headlines, but picked up varied experience.

In 1962 he stretched his winning record to nine, but then lost his unbeaten tag to his old air force pupil Doug Jones in Madison Square Garden. He was a substitute for world rated heavyweight Zora Folley and gave Jones all he could handle before being worn down and stopped in the eighth round. He was given a standing ovation, and because of his professional inexperience before that fight, his reputation was enhanced not diminished.

Work was not exactly plentiful, however. He boxed only twice, in minor bouts in Washington DC, in the next 12 months. Then he took a gamble in going to the Peruvian capital of Lima to fight local hero Mauro Mina. Foster apparently won easily, but Mina got the verdict.

He worked his way back with three quick wins, but then was overmatched against world class heavyweight Ernie Terrell in the Garden in July 1964 and was knocked out in the seventh round. Even though he bulked up to 183lb, Foster conceded almost 20lb and was simply not big enough to deal with one of the giants of the division. After six rounds, his boxing ability had kept him level on the scorecards, but he was exhausted and Terrell finished him off in the next.

After that he concentrated on the light-heavyweight division, and made good headway with two wins over respected contender Henry Hank. However, when he lost a decision to Zora Folley in a dull fight in New Orleans in December 1965, he lost heart, and retired to work in a munitions factory in York, Pennsylvania, where he and his wife had lived since their marriage.

But he was still only 27, and Salow persuaded him to try again at the end of 1966. By the following year, he was considered worthy of a light-heavyweight title shot, which was held by the Nigerian veteran Dick Tiger. That view was given credence by a stunning, third-round win over one-time title claimant Eddie Cotton, who had lost on points to then champion Jose Torres the previous year. Cotton was almost 30 years old with more than 80 fights behind him, but was coming off three straight wins and was considered far from finished. Yet Foster blew him away, flooring him three times. Effectively, he finished Cotton overnight.

Pressure mounted on Tiger to defend against him, but the champion drove a hard financial bargain. He valued his title, which he was using to raise funds for the ill-fated Biafran struggle, and was not about to give it away to a dangerous contender. In the end, he demanded and got $100,000 to defend against Foster in Madison Square Garden in May 1968. In an astonishing gamble, Foster and his team had to underwrite Tiger's purse. Defeat would have been a huge setback. As it was they lost a total of $20,800 before expenses ... but took home the championship as Foster pulled out his most explosive left hooks to stretch Tiger flat on his back in round four. 'I knew it was only a matter of time,' Foster said.

Having taken so long to win the championship, he made it pay for him over the following six years. Tiger, who said he didn't know anything until he heard the referee's count reach nine, wanted a rematch, but Foster said: 'Guarantee me $100,000 and you can have one'. Salow, who was barred from holding a licence in New York, said they would take the title on tour, defending against anyone who could pay.

Meanwhile, former heavyweight champion Jack Dempsey paid the new champion high praise. 'That's the best left jab I've seen since Joe Louis,' he said.

Foster's first appearance as champion was a low-key, third-round stoppage of heavyweight Charley Polite in Springfield, Massachusetts. The purse, in fact, was small, with a gate totalling only $16,000.

Next he returned home to Albuquerque for a non-title workout against Eddie Vick, but had the embarrassment of being knocked down in the opening round. He got up to win a surprisingly tough fight in the ninth, but drew a small crowd of 2,500. From there, it was back to his long-time base of Washington DC, where he stopped former world No.1 contender Roger Rouse easily in five.

His non-title 'tour' ended when he signed to meet rank outsider Frank De Paula in Madison Square Garden on 22 January 1969. *Ring* magazine didn't even rank De Paula in their top ten ... and rightly so. De Paula, a popular brawler from Jersey City, brought in paying customers, but had no place in a ring with Foster. The Garden were happy because 16,129 fans paid $189,920 to be there, and De Paula gave a fraction of credibility to the occasion by putting Foster down with a right hand that looked as much shove as punch. But then the champion got down to business, dropped the former nightclub bouncer three times and won on an automatic stoppage on the three-knockdown rule with only two minutes 17 seconds on the clock. De Paula complained: 'I wasn't hurt. My feet went out from under me ...'

After that it was back to West Springfield, Massachusetts, for a second title defence against Andy Kendall, the No. 4 contender from Portland, Oregon. A one-sided fight was stopped in round four. While there was only a small turnout of around 2,500, because ticket prices were too high, Foster was paid $50,000 – the entire television fee. He was happy enough.

The rest of the year saw him enjoy a couple of non-title paydays in Atlanta, a four rounds win over Levan Roundtree, and in New Orleans, a fifth-round stoppage of Chuck Leslie. Two more workouts in Florida against Bill Hardney and Ray 'Cookie' Wallace began 1970, and by the time he defended against Roger Rouse – a man he had already stopped in a non-title fight – in April, he had gone almost a year between defences. Rouse was out of his depth and could not come out for round four.

Afterwards Foster began talking up a showdown with heavyweight champion Joe Frazier, but after taking 10 rounds to knock out a slippery but modestly talented Texan, Mark Tessman, he admitted that he should perhaps take a couple of other heavyweights before fighting for the title.

However, he earned only $14,000 for beating Tessman ... and his bad showing probably helped him clinch the far bigger payday with Frazier. The match was made for the Cobo Hall, Detroit, in November 1970. Foster stung Frazier with two rights in round one, but was floored twice by Smokin' Joe's venomous left hooks in the second round. The second time he was completely out.

In 1971, Foster turned back four light-heayvweight challengers: Hal Carroll, Ray Anderson, Tommy Hicks and Brian Kelly. None of them were even close to his league.

By this time the WBA had stripped him of his title and had established an alternative champion, Vicente Rondon of Venezuela. 'We will fight Rondon wherever they want, whenever,' said Foster's manager Lou Viscusi. Eventually, there were no realistic matches for either of them, and a unification fight was staged in Miami in April 1972. Foster flattened Rondon in two rounds, as ruthless a piece of point-proving as there has ever been.

In June 1972, Mike Quarry challenged Foster, as his brother Jerry waited in the wings to box Muhammad Ali for the NABF heavyweight title. Jerry admitted later he lost concentration on his own job when he saw Mike knocked senseless by Foster's left hook in round four. Quarry was unconscious for more than five minutes. 'When I hit them,' said the champion, 'they lose interest all the way down.'

From there it was on to London and the Wembley Arena for a defence against the 1968 Olympic middleweight gold medallist, crafty southpaw Chris Finnegan. By this time, Foster and his family were living in Albuquerque, where Bob had a 'second' job as a deputy sheriff. Much was made of this by the British writers, who also enjoyed a tale that he had actually booked his own wife for speeding!

Finnegan thoroughly enjoyed himself, preparing for the biggest fight of his life. He grew a beard, claiming he was hiding his chin from Foster. He talked a good fight. 'The geezer's supposed to be 33, and he looks nearer 43. I reckon if I fiddle him around a bit his legs will start to go. I'm not going to hang my chin out for him to hit. Maybe I can wear him out ...'

For 13 rounds, Finnegan gave Foster an argument. He was losing, but was doing well. At the end of the round, he faced a choice: he could either box defensively and last the distance, or go out with all guns blazing and try for a knockout, with the fair chance of being tagged himself. Typically, he chose the latter, and was knocked out by two right hands 55 seconds into the round.

While the paydays were accumulating at light-heavyweight, Foster retained the dream of winning the heavyweight crown. He also knew that he could earn more for one fight against one of the leading heavyweights than he could for three or four 175lb title defences.

When he agreed to fight Muhammad Ali in November 1972, his mind probably went back to their sparring sessions before the Olympics of a dozen years before. Foster put the then-Cassius Clay down once with a left hook, and no doubt hoped he could do the same again. Then, however, they were both light-heavyweights. By 1972, Ali was much the heavier man. Foster did manage to open a thin cut over Ali's eye, but was overpowered, and dropped seven times before the end came in round eight.

Time was running out, but in 1973 he twice outpointed the talented South African Pierre Fourie, once in Albuquerque and once in Johannesburg, a landmark multi-racial championship fight in South Africa.

But after being held to a lucky draw against a rugged Argentine, Jorge Ahumada, in Albuquerque in June 1974, he retired. He could have earned well by defending against Britain's John Conteh, but knew there was nothing left and decided to get out at the top.

Like so many others, he forgot what his body had told him and a year after the Ahumada fight, returned to the ring for a low-key comeback which ended with back-to-back defeats in 1978 by Mustapha Wasajja and Bob Hazelton, neither of whom could have lived with him at his magnificent peak. He was 39 when he retired for good. He remained in his law enforcement job in Albuquerque, and also trained fighters for a time.

CAREER STATISTICS

World light-heavyweight champion 1968-74
Albuquerque, New Mexico, born 15 December 1938

1961
Mar 27 Duke Williams w ko 2 Washington DC
Apr 3 Clarence Ryan w pts 4 New York
May 8 Billy Johnson w pts 4 New York
Jun 22 Ray Bryan w ko 2 Montreal
Aug 8 Floyd McCoy w pts 6 Montreal
Nov 22 Ernie Knox w ko 4 Norfolk
Dec 4 Clarence Floyd w rsf 4 Toronto
1962
May 19 Billy Tisdale w ko 2 New York
Jun 27 Bert Whitehurst w pts 8 New York
Oct 20 Doug Jones l rsf 8 New York
1963
Feb 18 Richard Benjamin w ko 1 Washington DC
Apr 29 Curtis Bruce w ko 4 Washington DC
Nov 6 Mauro Mina l pts 10 Lima
Dec 11 Willi Besmanoff w rsf 3 Norfolk
1964
Feb 25 Dave Bailey w ko 1 Miami
May 8 Allen Thomas w ko 1 Chicago
Jul 10 Ernie Terrell l ko 7 New York
Nov 12 Don Quinn w ko 1 Norfolk
Nov 23 Norm Letcher w ko 1 San Francisco
Dec 11 Henry Hank w rsf 10 Norfolk
1965
Feb 15 Roberto Rascon w ko 2 Albuquerque
Mar 21 Dave Russell w rsf 6 Norfolk
May 24 Chuck Leslie w rsf 3 New Orleans
Jul 26 Henry Hank w pts 12 New Orleans
Dec 6 Zora Folley l pts 10 New Orleans
1966
Dec 6 Leroy Green w ko 2 Norfolk
1967
Jan 16 Jim Robinson w rsf 1 Washington DC
Feb 27 Andres Selpa w ko 2 Washington DC
May 8 Eddie Cotton w rsf 3 Washington DC
Jun 9 Henry Matthews w rsf 2 Roanoke

Oct 25 Levan Roundtree w ko 8 Washington DC
Nov 20 Eddie Vick w pts 10 Providence
Dec 5 Sonny Moore w ko 2 Washington DC
1968
May 24 Dick Tiger w ko 4 New York
(World light-heavyweight title)
Jul 29 Charley Polite w rsf 3 West Springfield
Aug 26 Eddie Vick w rsf 9 Albuquerque
Sep 9 Roger Rouse w rsf 5 Washington DC
1969
Jan 22 Frank De Paula w rsf 1 New York
(World light-heavyweight title)
May 24 Andy Kendall w rsf 4 West Springfield
(World light-heavyweight title)
Jun 19 Levan Roundtree w rsf 4 Atlanta
Nov 2 Chuck Leslie w rsf 5 New Orleans
1970
Feb 24 Bill Hardney w rsf 4 Orlando
Mar 9 Cookie Wallace w ko 6 Tampa
Apr 4 Roger Rouse w rsf 4 Missoula
(World light-heavyweight title)
Jun 27 Mark Tessman w ko 10 Baltimore
(World light-heavyweight title)
Nov 18 Joe Frazier l ko 2 Detroit
(World heavyweight title)
1971
Mar 2 Hal Carroll w ko 4 Scranton
(World light-heavyweight title)
Apr 24 Ray Anderson w pts 15 Tampa
(World light-heavyweight title)
Aug 17 Vernon McIntosh w rsf 3 Miami
Oct 29 Tommy Hicks w rsf 8 Scranton
(World light-heavyweight title)
Dec 16 Brian Kelly w rsf 3 Oklahoma City
(World light-heavyweight title)
1972
Apr 7 Vicente Rondon w ko 2 Miami
(World light-heavyweight title)
Jun 27 Mike Quarry w ko 4 Las Vegas
(World light-heavyweight title)
Sep 26 Chris Finnegan w ko 14 London
(World light-heavyweight title)
Nov 21 Muhammad Ali l ko 8 Stateline
(NABF heavyweight title)
1973
Aug 21 Pierre Fourie w pts 15 Albuquerque
(World light-heavyweight title)
Dec 1 Pierre Fourie w pts 15 Johannesburg
(World light-heavyweight title)
1974
Jun 17 Jorge Ahumada drew 15 Albuquerque
(World light-heavyweight title)
Sep 16 Relinquished world title.
1975
Jun 28 Bill Hardney w ko 3 Santa Fe
1976
May 8 Al Bolden w ko 3 Missoula
Aug 28 Harold Carter w pts 10 Missoula
Sep 25 Al Bolden w ko 6 Spokane
1977
Sep 2 Bob Hazelton w ko 10 Willemstad
1978
Feb 9 Mustapha Wassaja l rsf 5 Copenhagen
Jun 3 Bob Hazelton l rsf 2 Wichita

Fights 65 Won 56 Lost 8 Drawn 1

CARLOS MONZON

KING CARLOS

Carlos Monzon had the soul of a fighter. The product of a reckless, violent youth, he conquered his private nightmares for long enough to become a boxing legend. When he retired he was still world middleweight champion after seven years, and he had not been beaten for 13.

In retirement he seemed to have left the bad days behind him and softened, but then was convicted of the murder of the mother of his son. He was jailed for 11 years, and was on parole when he died in a car crash in January 1995.

'Carlos was always an honourable man,' said the French actor Alain Delon, who had known him since the 1970s. 'He was exceptionally strong as a boxer, a kind of beast in a pure, savage state. All his friends knew his final days would be tragic.'

Perhaps the most telling description of Monzon the fighter came from Fraser Scott, a Seattle middleweight who lost to him in 1971. Scott recalled the moment they walked into the centre of the ring for the customary pre-fight ritual. 'A chill ran down my back. His eyes were dark and frightening. Deep-running rivers filled with sleepless nights and dreams. Reflections of what I once wanted to be.'

Monzon was born in the village of San Javier near Santa Fe, Argentina, on 7 August 1942. From a native Indian background, he was one of ten children, and was still a child when the family moved into the city's sprawling slums. He was a street kid, with little or no education, who scratched his own living selling newspapers, delivering milk, getting by as best he could.

As he grew, he ran into trouble. He was jailed for inciting a riot at a football match, and again for a fight on a bus. He was a pimp. But somewhere along the way, he found his way into a boxing gym and won 73 of 87 amateur contests. When he was 20, he was launched on a professional career by manager Amilcar Brusa.

There was an early 'No Contest' in circumstances which have long been forgotten, and three points defeats by Antonio Aguilar, Felipe Cambeiro and Alberto Massi between August 1963 and October 1964. He avenged them all.

At one point he left Argentina to live in Brazil because of an intensifying of police interest in his activities, but he returned when the heat died down and won the Argentine middleweight title in Buenos Aires in September 1966 by outpointing Jorge Fernandez, who had given Emile Griffith a decent fight for the world welterweight crown in 1962. Monzon outpointed him, dominating from beginning to end.

In a rematch the following year he again outpointed Fernandez in a South American title fight, which came immediately after a 10-round draw against the remarkable Philadelphian, Bennie Briscoe, in Buenos Aires. Briscoe was an avoided man in the USA, and hurt Monzon in a terrific fight, which could have gone either way.

By now in the hands of the No.1 Argentine promoter, Tito Lectoure, Monzon was feared in South America, but disregarded internationally because he rarely fought outside his homeland. He was out of the ring for a few months at the start of 1968 because he was accused of injuring a photographer at a New Year party, although this time he managed to stay out of prison.

Lectoure tried to lure good class Americans to fight Monzon in Buenos Aires, but nobody at the top end of the ladder wanted to risk their position in the Argentine capital when there was nothing to gain beyond the payday. Monzon was in the boxing wilderness for years, before he was acknowledged publicly as the best middleweight in the world.

He remained South American champion through 1969, when his victims also included Tom 'The Bomb' Bethea from New York. Bethea was a big hitting but moderately skilled battler, who would beat Benvenuti in a non-title fight the following year. For Monzon to outpoint him was not a major achievement, but in the light of Bethea's subsequent performance against Benvenuti it had significance. (Bethea was given a rematch with the Italian for the title and was knocked out.)

Lectoure finally persuaded the world boxing authorities to listen to him and Monzon, who was not even ranked in the world top 10 by Nat Fleischer's *Ring*, challenged Benvenuti in Rome in November 1970. He was unbeaten in six years and 60 contests, yet the Benvenuti management team selected him as the safest challenger available! It was a shocking piece of misjudgement. Monzon battered Benvenuti systematically until the 12th round, then knocked him down face-first with a right hand. Italian fans tried to rush the ring in what seemed like a bizarre attack on referee Rudolf Durst, but the world had a new middleweight champion. Monzon picked up only $15,000 but that didn't matter. The years of marking time, with little or no recognition, were over.

After three non-title fights in Argentina, Monzon slaughtered Benvenuti in three rounds in a return in Monte Carlo. Then former champion Emile Griffith was lured to Buenos Aires and stopped in the 14th round at a packed Luna Park. To be effective, Griffith needed to body punch, but Monzon's reach, height and strength prevented him from doing that and he tired to the point where he was bent over in a corner, his gloves cupped around his head, as Monzon punched without reply. The fight was stopped. 'I was going good until the 14th round,' said Griffith.

Monzon could look unexceptional, but somehow he always got the job done. Denny Moyer, a 110-fight former light-middleweight champion from Oregon, protested bitterly when he was the victim of a ridiculously premature stoppage in the fifth round in Rome in March 1972. Three months later, Monzon and French hero Jean-Claude Bouttier sold 35,000 tickets for the open-air Colombes Stadium in Paris and set a new record for gate receipts for a fight in France. Bouttier fought hard in a hectic, sometimes messy battle, but in the tenth round complained of an eye problem and retired after the 12th, claiming he had been thumbed.

Monzon had still not boxed in the USA, but he was now widely respected in Europe. In August 1972, he outclassed Denmark's Tom Bogs in five rounds in a Copenhagen soccer stadium. Bogs was floored three times.

In his fourth defence of the year, he attracted worldwide television interest as he outpointed old rival Bennie Briscoe before 20,000 Argentine fans in Luna Park. Briscoe shook him dramatically with a right hand in round nine, when Monzon was saved by the bell. But in the tenth he showed his smart ring brain by outboxing Briscoe conservatively, taking over again and giving Briscoe a hard time in the 13th. The wide decision in Monzon's favour did not reflect the American's effort and Carlos remembered it as his most difficult defence.

Meanwhile, the champion's relationship with his equally volatile wife Beatriz ended when Mrs Monzon shot her fleeing husband in the back and buttocks! One bullet remained in his back for the rest of his life. He took up with actress Susanna Giminez, but they parted when he retired from the ring in 1977.

Before he outclassed Roy Dale in a non-title fight in Rome, Monzon was told his brother had been killed in a gunfight in Santa Fe. He said nothing at the time, but after knocking out Dale he said quietly: 'Now we go to the funeral'.

In June 1973, Monzon beat Griffith again. Emile was positively elderly by now, but boxed cleverly from an exaggerated crouch, attempting to work the body and smothering, making no attempt to take Monzon on for strength or power. At times it was a stalemate, before Monzon took over down the stretch. He won a deserved unanimous decision, although the crowd in the Louis II Stadium in Monte Carlo didn't like it and Griffith's manager Gil Clancy claimed the scores had been tampered with. Nothing was ever proved.

Bouttier and Monzon fought again in the Roland Garros in Paris; the arena which is more used to staging the French Open tennis event. Bouttier was in the fight for a while, but was floored in each of the last three rounds and Monzon won by margins of three, six and nine points on the official cards.

By now there were plenty who felt Monzon was slipping. Angelo Dundee, who was training welterweight champion Jose Napoles at the time, was hoping they were right.

They were not. Napoles challenged Monzon in Paris in February 1974 and Dundee pulled him out after the sixth. 'Monzon is the complete fighter,' said Dundee. 'He can box, he can hit, he can think and he is game all the way.'

Afterwards, Monzon left the arena without giving the mandatory urine sample and was fined $10,000 by the World Boxing Council, who also instructed him to fight his leading contender, Rodrigo Valdez of Colombia. Never a man to be told what to do, he ignored them and so the WBC stripped him of their title. Valdez beat Briscoe for the vacant championship, while Monzon continued with World Boxing Association recognition only. It didn't really bother him. The $100,000 paydays kept rolling in.

He knocked out Tony Mundine of Australia in seven rounds in Buenos Aires – it seemed he could have won when he liked – and then, in his only appearance in the USA, he stopped Tony Licata in 10. Temperamental Frenchman Gratien Tonna could fight, but could also quit in strange circumstances. Monzon was far too composed and mentally tough for him, and Tonna was counted out in round five of the fight in Paris in December 1975. He claimed he had been hit on the back of the head and crawled around the ring, calling out: 'Scandale!'

Monzon was close to retirement, but knew he should fight Valdez before the end. The match was made for Monte Carlo in June 1976, with both versions of the title at stake. Valdez was a tremendous fighter in his own right and gave Monzon a hard night's work, but a 14th round knockdown swung it the way of the Argentine by margins of two and four rounds on the cards.

He eventually accepted a $500,000 offer to fight Valdez again in Monte Carlo in July 1977. He probably wasn't counting, but it was his 100th fight (some records doubled up on a fight and erroneously made it 101). He promised it would be his farewell appearance at the age of 34 and went out well, outpointing Valdez again. But it was close because, for the first time, he didn't stay the pace well enough. He knew it was the right time to go and officially announced his retirement a month later. 'I think I showed everybody that I was great,' he said.

He was a remarkably popular man in Argentina, and loved to be the centre of attention. He spent his nights in clubs, appeared on television shows, made films and played the part of a celebrity, but in the daytime preferred the company of old men in Mar Del Plata bars, playing for pennies in card schools. His attempts to start businesses came to nothing, and he lost money, but was still a wealthy man when Alizia Muniz, a Uruguayan model and the mother of his six-year-old son Maximiliano, fell to her death from the balcony of Monzon's apartment. An autopsy revealed she was unconscious when she fell, and although the former champion insisted it was an accident, he was found guilty of murder and jailed for 11 years. 'Me and my bad temper are the ones really responsible,' he said.

While in jail, he was visited by actor Mickey Rourke, who was on a day off from filming at the time. Rourke, who would have a brief professional career of his own, thought it would be a good idea if he were to be filmed sparring with Monzon, and so brought along a crew. Monzon agreed and left the actor unconscious, allegedly with a venomous right hand. A member of the film crew sold the stills!

Monzon was returning to prison from a weekend on permitted home leave in January 1995 when his car left the road and overturned 25 miles out of Santa Fe. A woman passenger, Alicia Sesia, survived, but Monzon and a friend, Geronimo Motura, died. Monzon was 52.

Tributes were paid by Argentine president Carlos Menem, by soccer star Diego Maradona and by the head of the national boxing commission. Perhaps more telling was the tribute by the ordinary people who queued for hours to file past the open coffin in Santa Fe town hall, determined to pay their respects to perhaps the finest fighter ever produced in South America.

CAREER STATISTICS

World middleweight champion 1970-77
Santa Fe, Argentina, born 7 August 1942

1963

Feb 6 Ramon Montenegro w ko 2 Rafaela
Mar 13 Albino Veron nc 1 Vila
Apr 9 Albino Veron w rsf 2 Santa Fe
Apr 26 Mario Suarez w rsf 7 Posadas
May 3 Raul Rivas w rsf 5 Posadas
May 31 Juan Rodriguez w ko 5 Parana
Jul 17 Andres Cejas w rsf 4 Buenos Aires
Aug 9 Lisandro Guzman w rsf 3 Cordoba
Aug 28 Antonio Aguilar l pts 10 Buenos Aires
Oct 18 Benito Sanchez w ko 8 Reconquista
Dec 6 Rene Sosa w ko 6 Parana

1964

Jan 17 Roberto Carabajal w ko 8 Parana
Jun 13 Angel Corta w pts 8 Mar del Plata
Jun 28 Felipe Cambeiro l pts 8 Rio de Janeiro
Jul 10 Roberto Carabajal w pts 10 Tostado
Jul 24 Walter Villa w ko 9 Ceres
Aug 14 Juan Diaz w rsf 9 Villa Angela
Sep 4 Americo Vacca w ko 3 Parana
Sep 25 Francisco Olea w rsf 9 Tostada
Oct 9 Alberto Massi l pts 10 Cordoba
Oct 28 Francisco Gelabert w rsf 3 Buenos Aires
Nov 18 Celedonio Lima drew 10 Buenos Aires

1965

Jan 8 Andres Selpa drew 10 Mar del Plata
Mar 11 Andres Selpa w pts 10 Santa Fe
Apr 9 Emilio Ale Ali drew 10 Tucuman
May 19 Anibal Cordoba w pts 10 Buenos Aires
Jul 14 Alberto Rotondo w rsf 8 Buenos Aires
Aug 10 Felix Cambeiro w pts 8 San Pablo
Aug 28 Manuel Severino drew 8 Rio de Janeiro
Oct 6 Gregorio Gomez w pts 10 Buenos Aires
Nov 17 Celedonio Lima w ko 5 Buenos Aires
Dec 8 Antonio Aguilar w pts 10 Buenos Aires
Dec 29 Carlos Salinas w pts 10 Buenos Aires

1966

Feb 4 Ramon Rocha w pts 10 Santa Fe
Feb 17 Norberto Juncos w rsf 7 Santa Fe
Apr 29 Ismael Hamze w rsf 9 San Nicolas
Jun 3 Marcos Bustos drew 10 Rio Gallegos
Jul 8 Benito Sanchez w ko 4 San Pereyra
Sep 3 Jorge Fernandez w pts 12 Buenos Aires *(Argentine middleweight title)*
Oct 2 Angel Coria w pts 10 Mar del Plata
Nov 18 Luis Angel Pereyra w rsf 2 Santa Fe
Dec 2 Alberto Massi w rsf 8 Santa Fe
Dec 23 Marcelo Farias w ko 3 San Cristobal

1967

Jan 13 Carlos Salinas w ko 7 Santa Fe
Jan 27 Eudoro Robledo w ko 4 Charata
Feb 15 Alberto Massi w pts 10 San Francisco
Mar 9 Osvaldo Marino w rsf 7 Santa Fe
Mar 25 Angel Coria w ko 6 Mar del Plata
Apr 9 Benito Sanchez w rsf 3 Santa Elena
May 6 Bennie Briscoe drew 10 Buenos Aires
Jun 10 Jorge Fernandez w pts 12 Buenos Aires *(South American middleweight title)*
Jul 29 Antonio Aguilar w ko 9 Buenos Aires
Aug 16 Tito Marshall w pts 10 Buenos Aires
Sep 8 Ramon Rocha w pts 10 Rosario
Oct 6 Carlos Estrada w rsf 7 Trelew
Oct 20 Ramon Rocha w rsf 7 San Juan

Nov 18 Tito Marshall w pts 10 Buenos Aires

1968

Apr 5 Juan Aguilar drew 10 Mendoza
May 17 Alberto Massi w pts 10 Cordoba
Jun 19 Juan Aguilar w pts 10 Buenos Aires
Jul 5 Benito Sanchez w ko 4 Saenz Pena
Aug 14 Doug Huntley w ko 4 Buenos Aires
Oct 23 Charlie Austin w pts 10 Buenos Aires
Dec 7 Johnny Brooks w pts 10 Buenos Aires
Dec 20 Emilio Ale Ali w pts 10 Mendoza

1969

Jan 10 Ruben Orrico w ko 9 Santa Fe
(South American middleweight title)
Mar 14 Mario Taborda w ko 3 Saenz Pena
Apr 25 Carlos Salinas drew 10 Parana
Jun 6 Carlos Salinas w rsf 7 Parana
Jul 5 Harold Richardson w rsf 3 Buenos Aires
Aug 10 Tom Bethea w pts 10 Buenos Aires
Sep 10 Emilio Ale Ali w rsf 7 Tucuman
Oct 27 Manuel Severino w ko 6 Buenos Aires
(South American middleweight title)
Dec 12 Carlos Estrada w ko 2 Santa Fe

1970

Feb 11 Antonio Aguilar w ko 6 Mar del Plata
Mar 7 Juan Aguilar w rsf 9 Rosario
Apr 17 Adolfo Cardoza w rsf 3 Santa Fe
May 11 Ramon Rocha w ko 9 Tucuman
Jul 18 Eddie Pace w pts 10 Buenos Aires
Sep 19 Candy Rosa w ko 4 Buenos Aires
Nov 7 Nino Benvenuti w ko 12 Rome
(World middleweight title)
Dec 20 Charley Austin w ko 2 Buenos Aires

1971

Feb 19 Domingo Guerrero w rsf 2 Salta
Mar 5 Roy Lee w rsf 2 Santa Fe
May 8 Nino Benvenuti w rsf 3 Monte Carlo
(World middleweight title)
Sep 25 Emile Griffith w rsf 14 Buenos Aires
(World middleweight title)
Dec 5 Fraser Scott w rsf 3 Buenos Aires

1972

Mar 4 Denny Moyer w rsf 5 Rome
(World middleweight title)
Jun 17 Jean-Claude Bouttier w rsf 13 Paris
(World middleweight title)
Aug 19 Tom Bogs w rsf 5 Copenhagen
(World middleweight title)
Nov 11 Bennie Briscoe w pts 15 Buenos Aires
(World middleweight title)

1973

May 5 Roy Dale w ko 5 Rome
Jun 2 Emile Griffith w pts 15 Monte Carlo
(World middleweight title)
Sep 29 Jean-Claude Bouttier w pts 15 Paris
(World middleweight title)

1974

Feb 9 Jose Napoles w rtd 6 Paris
(World middleweight title)
Oct 5 Tony Mundine w ko 7 Buenos Aires
(World middleweight title)

1975

Jun 30 Tony Licata w rsf 10 New York
(World middleweight title)
Dec 13 Gratien Tonna w ko 5 Paris
(World middleweight title)

1976

Jun 26 Rodrigo Valdez w pts 15 Monte Carlo
(World middleweight title)

1977

Jul 30 Rodrigo Valdez w pts 15 Monte Carlo
(World middleweight title)

Fights 100 Won 88 Lost 3 Drawn 8 No Contests 1
Died January 1995, Aged 52

MUHAMMAD ALI

THE LOUISVILLE LIP

Muhammad Ali was more than the most famous boxer who ever lived. He transcended boxing, and for a while was possibly the most famous, certainly the most recognizable man in the world. As a boxer he was superb, lacking nothing in skill, strength, bravery and showmanship. His career was magnificent, yet he had to overcome the handicap of losing 3½ years of it when he was banned after his refusal to fight in Vietnam. And those 3½ years were when he would otherwise have been at his peak. His anti-war stand, his religion, his personal charisma and public speaking all combined to make him an idol to a whole generation in the 1970s. He called himself and his autobiography 'The Greatest', and he was.

Ali was born on 17 January 1942 in Louisville, Kentucky, with the name Cassius Marcellus Clay. According to Ali later, this name was a slave name, acquired from a 19th century plantation owner by his great, great grandfather. His father bore exactly the same name and his mother was Odessa Grady Clay. Two years after his birth, Cassius acquired a brother, Randolph Arnett Clay, who also was to change his name to Ali.

Cassius senior painted billboards and signs and the family were comfortably off. Young Cassius was well behaved and not particularly aggressive; in fact he didn't like playing American football because it was too rough. He preferred marbles, at which he was good. However, he did like a game in which his brother threw rocks and stones at him, as it allowed him to show off his agility and expertise at dodging, which became a hallmark of his boxing style.

Cassius became interested in boxing at 12, when his bicycle was stolen while he and a friend were at a bazaar in the Columbia Auditorium. He burst into tears, and was told to report the theft to a policeman who was working in the basement. This policeman was Joe Martin, who was teaching youngsters to box. He told Cassius that if he wanted to whip whoever stole his bike, he'd better learn to box too. From that day boxing was the passion of young Cassius.

The Columbia Gym presented a local television show called *Tomorrow's Champions* so some of Martin's boys enjoyed minor local celebrity status. Six weeks after joining, Cassius, weighing 89lb, had his first public contest, and won, and soon was on television himself. He loved the limelight, devoted his whole energy to boxing and dreamt of being a champion. His schoolwork suffered somewhat. He was never regarded as unintelligent, yet when he graduated from school in 1960 he was ranked 376th in a class of 391. By then, he was about to become an Olympic boxer.

Joe Martin said he was only average when he started boxing, but Cassius built a keen amateur record of 108 contests, winning two National Golden Gloves tournaments. He was selected for the 1960 Olympic Games and, despite a fear of flying which nearly persuaded him to decline the trip, he easily won the gold medal boxing at light-heavyweight. At 18 he was developing a magnificent physique, being already approaching 180lb and topping 6ft.

Popular and talkative, Cassius was soon one of the mostl-liked athletes at the Games, and was so proud of his medal that he didn't take if off for weeks. Interviewed by the press, he was forcible in defending his country against any suggestion by foreigners that he was discriminated against back home. But his views changed soon after he returned to the States.

After a big welcome home in Louisville, he signed a contract with a group of 11 white millionaires who called themselves the Louisville Sporting Group. They became his sponsors. Each put in $2,800, from which Cassius received a signing-on fee of $10,000 and a guaranteed $333 a month against earnings for two years, these earnings to be split 50-50 between Clay and themselves for four years, 60-40 in Clay's favour thereafter. The Group would pay expenses, including the salary of a trainer, who for his first fight was Fred Stones, a black coach who had trained him in his amateur days. There were options to renew the contract annually for six years.

With his professional debut already fixed, Cassius, still without taking his medal off, and a friend, Ronnie King, were refused service in a restaurant. Cassius pointed out who he was but to no avail. He was abused. Finally he and his friend had to flee from a group of white hooligans who chased them on their motorbikes, two of them catching the runaways by the Ohio River. In his autobiography *The Greatest*, written with Richard Durham, Clay/Ali describes dramatically the bloody fight and how afterwards he washed away the blood and then finally, in disgust at the standing of black people in his country, threw his gold medal in the river from the middle of the bridge. This story, however, is not in all the Ali biographies, and it is not mentioned in Thomas Hauser's *Muhammad Ali, His Life and Times*, written with Ali's co-operation. This book points out (not in relation to this story) that each page of *The Greatest* had to be approved and initialled by Herbert Muhammad, who had become Ali's religious teacher, and that the editor-in-chief of the publisher was not sure the book was a true story of Ali's life. Whatever the truth about the medal, the International Olympic Committee presented

Ali with a replacement medal when he took part in the opening ceremony at the 1996 Olympic Games.

Clay's first pro fight was before 6,000 fans at Louisville's Freedom Hall. His opponent was a tough part-time pro, Tunney Hunsaker, a police chief at Fayetteville, who had a record of 17 wins to eight defeats. He found Clay much too fast and skilful for him and was well beaten on points.

Clay's backers decided he needed a top-class trainer to realise his potential, and sent him to the great Archie Moore, then the light-heavyweight champion of the world. But it didn't work out. Moore insisted discipline and obedience were necessary attributes of an up-and-coming champion, and required Clay to do his share of the chores at training camp, but Clay thought he was above washing up, and that anyway Moore's tricks couldn't do much for him, and after a few weeks he went away. On advice the group next tried Angelo Dundee, who had been working in boxers' corners since becoming assistant to his brother, boxing promoter Chris. He had already been associated with three world champions, and had been impressed by Clay, whom he had met in his amateur days. He took on the job, and young Cassius went to live in Miami to further his boxing education in Dundee's Fifth Street gym. Clay's next four fights, all won by knockout or stoppage, were in Miami Beach.

Dundee tried to improve the power of Clay's punch, and the young man began scoring impressive wins. Lamar Clark, his sixth opponent, had won his previous 45 bouts inside the distance. Clay predicted he would stop his opponent in two rounds, and did.

Clay, by now 6ft 2in and 190lb, next outpointed a big Hawaiian, Duke Sabedong, 6ft 6in and 226lb, the first man to take him the distance. The contest was in Las Vegas, and Cassius put his relatively poor performance down to the enforced flight – he still feared flying. But on this trip he met – on a televised build-up programme – a wrestler also appearing in the town, George Zakarias. 'Gorgeous George' put on a display which included knocking over microphones and explaining how he would pull off his opponent's arm and beat him over the head with it. 'I am the Greatest', said George. Cassius realised how puny were his own pre-fight antics, especially when George drew 15,000 fans to his wrestling match. Cassius decided to go the whole hog himself and developed the sort of on-camera hysteria which made him so unpopular in his early career. He was called 'The Louisville Lip'.

Cassius developed his theme of predicting in which round he would beat his opponent by putting his predictions in verse, and upset even his own Louisville fans by extending his fight with outclassed Willie Besmanoff, whom he had called an 'unrated duck', until the seventh round, just so that he could stop him in the round predicted.

However, he delighted the New York boxing writers on his first fight at Madison Square Garden by his boasting, which made good copy. They called him 'Gaseous Cassius'. He was a late substitute against the useful Lucian 'Sonny' Banks, a big puncher. In the first round Banks caught Clay with a long left hook which put him down. All those who wanted to see the Lip buttoned rejoiced. But Cassius rose and beat Banks in the fourth, as he'd predicted. When in his next fight he stopped Don Warner in the fourth instead of the forecast fifth, he amused everybody by explaining he'd punished him a whole round for not shaking hands at the weigh-in.

Clay was now attracting attention even outside America, and after he beat Archie Moore, his fourth top-ten ranked victim, he was seen as a contender for the heavyweight championship. He already held ambitions to become the youngest ever champion, but was unimpressive against Doug Jones, ranked No. 2 by the WBA. Having correctly predicted that 'Archie Moore must fall in four', he now predicted round four for Jones. Nearly 19,000 saw the Madison Square Garden contest, in which Clay boxed exhibition-style with his arms at his sides. He was hurt in the first round, and was booed when the fourth round passed without him winning. He had a sticky eighth and ninth rounds, but won a close unanimous decision, though some angry fans called it a fix and threw things.

Clay's next fight was in London against British champion Henry Cooper, a boxer whose eyes were easily cut. Clay predicted a fifth-round win, but while messing about in the fourth was caught by Cooper's famed left hook, which put him down glassy-eyed. Luckily for him it was right at the end of the round and he was helped to his corner where smelling salts brought him round. Trainer Dundee tried to buy extra recovery time by enlarging a tear in Clay's glove and making a fuss to the referee, but there were no replacement gloves and the ruse won only a few extra seconds respite. Clay recovered well and savagely attacked the cuts around Cooper's eyes until the referee was forced to stop the bloodbath in the next round, the round predicted.

Clay returned to the States to take on Sonny Liston for the world title at the Miami Beach Convention Hall. Liston, the big, brooding ex-convict with the menacing stare was the most feared heavyweight champion for years, and Clay went almost out of control in his pre-fight psychological warfare against him. He caused disturbances at his home and training camp, fired a water-pistol at him in a casino and nearly came to blows with him at his arrival at Miami Airport, where he called Liston a chump and a big ugly bear. He seemed demented, and an attorney investigating boxing for the Governor of California said the degrading mismatch should be stopped to save Clay from grave injury.

Backed up by a new friend in hysteria, Bundini Brown, officially his assistant trainer, Clay went berserk at the weigh-in for the fight, screaming at Liston with crazed eyes. His pulse rate rose from 54 beats per minute to 120. The Miami Boxing Commissioner's doctor said Clay was scared to death. It was debated whether the fight should be called off. Yet Clay's own doctor, Ferdie Pacheco, claimed that soon afterwards he found Clay's pulse normal. He put it down to self-induced hysteria. In fact Clay was like a cat. He could produce bursts of fantastic activity and awareness, yet fall asleep next minute as if to replenish his store of energy.

At the time of the fight, the two protagonists were two of the most unpopular heavyweights for years. Clay was the more disliked, and the majority hoped the insufferable braggart would lose. All but three of the 46 pressmen polled at ringside thought 7–1 on favourite Liston was sure to win. It was an extraordinary fight, quiet enough for four rounds, with Liston's cheek cut in the third. As soon as the fourth round ended, Clay screamed out that he couldn't see. He demanded to be retired. Something from Liston's corner had somehow got into his eyes, possibly coagulant on Liston's cut had got onto Clay's glove and then into his eyes. In the interval Clay was screaming: 'Cut the gloves off'. Referee Barney Felix was about to stop the contest as the bell went for the fifth, but Angelo Dundee shoved a near-blind Clay out. For half the fifth round Clay danced around keeping his left arm extended, fiddling about to keep Liston at a distance. Suddenly his eyes cleared, and he lasted the round. In the sixth, he took charge, bemusing Liston with a stream of accurate jabs, and beginning to taunt him.

The interval before the seventh was as dramatic as that before the fifth. Liston was observed arguing with his corner and looking old, tired and discouraged. When the warning buzzer sounded, he spat out his gumshield. He wouldn't go on. He retired, claiming an injured shoulder. When he realised he was champion, Clay rushed round the ring out of control, mouth agape, shouting that he was king and screaming 'I told you' at the press. 'Eat your words'. He was 22, and world champion.

There had been rumours before the fight that Clay had joined what the press called the Black Muslim movement, and after the contest he announced he was a follower of Elijah Muhammad and the Nation of Islam, and that henceforth he was to be known as Muhammad Ali (the Praiseworthy One). At first the press almost universally ignored this name, but gradually it began to be used. Not by the WBA, who stripped him of his title. 'He is a detriment to the boxing world', said the president.

Ali had learned of the Lost-Found Nation of Islam in 1960 by reading a copy of their newspaper *Muhammad Speaks*. He went to meetings and made friends with Malcolm X, who at the time was suspended from the movement because of his extremist views, and in February 1965 was assassinated, in a plot believed to be inspired by supporters of Elijah Muhammad. Malcolm X delivered Ali to the Nation in an effort to regain favour. The Nation preached that the white man's civilisation would one day be destroyed to allow the black people revenge and salvation. Ali himself bore no ill-will towards white people. In fact, although a follower, he was also suspended from membership from the start since boxing was one of the activities the sect frowned upon. He did not mind overmuch because the suspension allowed him to maintain friendships with the young women who flocked around him as champion. Because Ali continued to support Elijah Muhammad after the assassination of Malcolm X, he was threatened with assassination himself and in his return fight with Liston was protected by 300 policemen. Elijah Muhammad died in 1975 leaving a movement with vast wealth. His son Herbert became Ali's manager.

Meanwhile, on 3 July 1964 Ali had met Sonji Roy, a 23-year-old night-club hostess and model with a young son, proposed marriage on the day he met her, and married her 41 days later, before the return with Liston. The marriage lasted only 16 months, Ali divorcing her because she failed to keep her promise to follow the beliefs of the Nation of Islam.

Ali's return with Liston, at Lewiston, Maine, was another extraordinary contest. Because he had embraced the Black Muslim movement Ali was even more unpopular than before. Most white Americans loathed him. The fight was banned in Boston, and took place in the Central Maine Youth Center, Lewiston, before the smallest crowd ever to watch a heavyweight title fight: 2,434 (plus the 300 policemen). Surprisingly, such was the mystique of big bad Liston, the ex-champ was 7–4 favourite. Ali caught Liston with a good right cross at the bell, then began taunting him, dropping his arms and inviting a punch, completely bamboozling Liston, to whom nobody had dared act like this before. Halfway through the round, another right, seemingly so soft it was called a 'phantom' punch, dropped Liston, who rolled over on to his back. Ali seemed surprised and stood over Liston yelling at him to get up. By the time an equally bemused referee, Jersey Joe Walcott, had taken Ali to a neutral corner and begun to count, the timekeeper had already counted Liston out and had begun again. Liston finally beat Walcott's count, and was ready to continue, but Walcott was persuaded by the timekeeper and the editor of *Ring*, Nat Fleischer, who was at ringside, that Liston had been knocked out. Walcott raised Ali's arm as winner. By now 2 minutes and 12 seconds had passed, but Liston had originally been counted out at 1 minute 42 seconds. The official time for the fight was later given as one minute. The fans shouted 'Fake'. Only Liston, who is dead, knows the real truth of this fight. Some say the Mob was behind his capitulation, others think that Liston, realising he couldn't beat Ali, was cocking a snook at boxing, which had treated him so badly, by making the contest a farce.

There was overwhelming support for former champion Floyd Patterson, who next challenged Ali, and claimed he would bring the title 'back to America'. Ali's response was to call Patterson a 'rabbit'. He systematically beat up Patterson, who injured his back in the third round. He called him 'Uncle Tom' and Patterson was in a sorry state when the fight was stopped in the 12th round.

Ali had failed the intelligence test for drafting into the army, being classified 1-Y, but in view of the needs of the Vietnam war, he was now reclassified as 1-A, and was inducted. He appealed, saying: 'I ain't got no quarrels with them Vietcongs', and quoting his status as a Minister of God and conscientious objector. He discovered he was being investigated by the FBI. Because of the antagonism against him, he was forced to continue his career abroad. In 1966 he defended his title in Toronto, London twice and Frankfurt, before returning to Houston to stop Cleveland Williams, 'The Big Cat', in the third round of what many believe to be his greatest exhibition of boxing. Williams was a good fighter who was thought to have a chance, but Ali's speed, skill and power was effortless as he dazzled with a bewildering display of punches. He introduced the footwork known as the 'Ali shuffle', more demoralising than functional. Williams was down four times before the seven minutes eight seconds of the masterclass ended. Respected boxing commentator Howard Cosell said that that night Ali was 'the most devastating fighter who ever lived'.

By now Ali was 6ft 3in and weighed around 212lb. He could hit and he could move. He was fast. His friend Bundini Brown famously described his method as to 'float like a butterfly and sting like a bee'. He was perfectly proportioned (his waist was a mere 34 inches). Somebody said he was a big heavyweight with a bantamweight's body.

Since the WBA had stripped Ali, Ernie Terrell had become their champion, and now the two men met to unify the division. Terrell had refused to call Ali by his new name, and in an infamous contest Ali proceeded to humiliate him, giving him an awful beating but refusing to knock him out. He punctuated his punches with the constant question: 'What's my name?' Terrell went to hospital after the fight and underwent operations to mend a bone beneath his left eyeball. This display, following the dismantling of Patterson, made Ali many enemies. Six weeks after his display against Terrell, he stopped challenger Zora Folley in the seventh round. Angelo Dundee thought that this was his best display, even better than the Williams encounter. 'There's no telling what he might have gone on to achieve,' he said.

What Ali wanted to achieve was the record number of successful championship defences, of which he had nine in less than two years – Joe Louis held the record of 25. He had signed for a return with Floyd Patterson when, on 25 April 1967, he was required to file a petition in the Federal Court stating his reasons for appealing against induction into the army. Next day, in the Armed Forces Induction Center in Houston, he refused to swear the oath of allegiance. Immediately the WBC and WBA withdrew recognition of him as champion.

Two months later Ali was fined $10,000 and sentenced to five years imprisonment for refusing induction. While he appealed, no state would give him a licence to box. He was a boxing outcast. During this time Ali built up a reputation on the campus lecture circuit, initially talking about his views on Vietnam and the draft, later introducing personal themes, like 'The Art of Personality'. On 17 August 1967 he married 17-year-old Belinda Boyd, whom he met in a Muslim bakery. They were to have four children: Maryum (born 1968), twins Rasheeda and Jamillah (1970) and Muhammad junior (1971). They were divorced in December 1976 after Ali became involved with another woman.

Gradually public opinion in the USA changed regarding the Vietnam war. A Peace Movement built up and gained huge support. Ali suddenly found that he was a hero and something of a spokesman for many Americans. In 1970 a Supreme Court ruling allowed religious beliefs as grounds for objecting to armed service and opened the door for Ali to be accepted back into boxing. His appeal against his sentence was finally upheld on 28 June 1971. He had escaped prison.

Meanwhile, although he and many others had thought during his exile that he would never fight again, he resumed his career in October 1970 in Atlanta, which had a black senator and no boxing commission. His opponent was 'white hope' Jerry Quarry, who had fought twice for the world title. Ali won when Quarry was badly cut over the eye in the third round. He then ambitiously tackled Oscar Bonavena, a tough Argentinian, who had never been stopped, but Ali managed to stop him in the last round on the three-knockdown rule.

Although Ali was only slightly heavier than before his 3½ year lay-off, he was much slower, and was forced to develop a new style whereby he rested on the ropes and even absorbed body punches rather than dance away in his old style. He was never to be again the boxer he had been in 1967, but to regain the level he did was a boxing miracle. In his third contest back he challenged Joe Frazier, the man who had assumed his crown, for the undisputed heavyweight championship.

Incredibly the previously loathed Ali was the popular favourite in this meeting with the highly respected Frazier. Both were unbeaten, Frazier with 26 wins, Ali with 30. The contest, at Madison Square Garden, was naturally billed as the 'Fight of the Century'. Each received record purses of $2.5 million. In the event Ali led early on, but then allowed Frazier to attack him on the ropes, where Frazier's body punches began to get the upper hand. He shook Ali with his favourite left hook in the 11th, and when he knocked Ali down in the 15th the result was assured. Frazier won a unanimous decision and both men went to hospital, Ali with a badly swollen cheek. Ali, the super-arrogant, who had possibly taken the fight too soon after his lay-off, was surprisingly graceful in defeat.

Ali beat Jimmy Ellis for the North American title, and defended it five times against good opponents before his second defeat, which came when Ken Norton, later to be proclaimed WBC champion, broke Ali's jaw with a first-round punch that caught Ali with his mouth open. A brave Ali fought on with a quarter-inch gap in the bone to lose a 12-round points decision and his NABF title. Less than six months later he regained this title by outpointing Norton, and in 1974 he avenged his only other defeat by outpointing Joe Frazier, who in the meantime had lost his world title to George Foreman.

Ali was now in line to challenge Foreman, and a flamboyant new promoter, Don King, ex-numbers racketeer and convicted killer, persuaded President Mobutu of Zaire to back the fight on the grounds of creating publicity and trade for the country. Ali was to receive over $5 million, an astonishing sum at the time, but he was now approaching 33, and many feared for his safety. Foreman was considered unbeatable, and he had destroyed Frazier in two rounds, one blow lifting Frazier off his feet.

Ali, now a super-hero in many parts of the world, soon had the local population so much on his side that wherever he went they chanted 'Ah-lee booma ya', meaning 'Ali, kill him'.

The fight, at Kinshasa in 1974, was called 'The Rumble in the Jungle' and was one of the greatest and most amazing in boxing history. Ali took his new tactics to extremes, retiring to the ropes and letting Foreman punch him to the body. He later called it his 'rope-a-dope' plan. Every critic beforehand would have called it suicidal. While Ali fielded and dodged many blows, some got through, and his corner-men, particularly Angelo Dundee, were panic-stricken. Dundee yelled at him between rounds: 'You're gonna get killed'. But as Foreman's blows failed to put Ali down, Ali began taunting him, and firing back bursts of blows to the head. Gradually, in the extreme heat, Foreman began to look tired and demoralised. In the eighth round, Foreman was punching away mechanically at Ali on the ropes when he missed, and Ali suddenly sprang into action, catching Foreman with two hard rights to the head as he leapt away from the ropes. Foreman turned, only to take a left hook, and then a chopping right to the head sent him stumbling past Ali to the canvas. He was so exhausted he couldn't beat the count, and Ali had pulled off possibly his greatest win. He was once more, incredibly, undisputed world champion after seven years.

Ali, the former vilified draft-dodger and upstart, was now an international celebrity upon whom sporting and other bodies showered awards. He was invited to the White House. He was as near to Superman as anybody could get, and he was happy, popular and accessible.

In 1975 Ali defended his crown three times before – nearly a year after beating Foreman – he met Joe Frazier for the third time. The fight was billed as 'The Thrilla in Manila'. Ali, who throughout their careers mocked and taunted Frazier, sometimes beyond Frazier's endurance, coined a jingle: 'It'll be a killa, a chilla and a thrilla when I beat the gorilla in Manila'. At press conferences he would produce a rubber gorilla and smash it around as a demonstration.

The contest was another great one, remarkable for the unconquerable spirit and will each brought to it. Ali led early but then had to conserve his energy whereupon Frazier came back strongly. On a humid, unbearably hot night, with the air conditioning having failed, it seemed after 11 rounds that neither man could take any more. Both were badly beaten and in a state of collapse. But for three more rounds they forced themselves on, with Ali getting the upper hand. Neither gave in, but after 14 rounds Frazier's trainer, Eddie Futch, wouldn't let his man take any more and retired him. Ali was still champion, but he sank to the canvas in a state of collapse, and said he'd been near death. His doctor, Ferdie Pacheco, said his brain did not recover for 24 hours because of his extreme exhaustion.

His personal life changed after events leading up to the Manila fight. He had fallen in love with Veronica Porche, who had attended the fight in Zaire as a prize for winning a beauty competition. They had an affair and Ali took her to Manila. At a reception President Marcos had complimented Ali on his 'wife's' beauty, and Ali responded by remarking on that of the President's wife. The exchange was reported, and immediately Ali's liaison, which many, including his wife Belinda, knew about, was all over the papers. Belinda took a plane to Manila where the two had a terrific

▲ **Randolph Turpin's** defeat of **Sugar Ray Robinson** on 10 July 1951 was one of the greatest of British fight nights. Middleweight champion Robinson (left) was unbeaten for 91 fights. No wonder the fans sang 'For he's a jolly good fellow'.

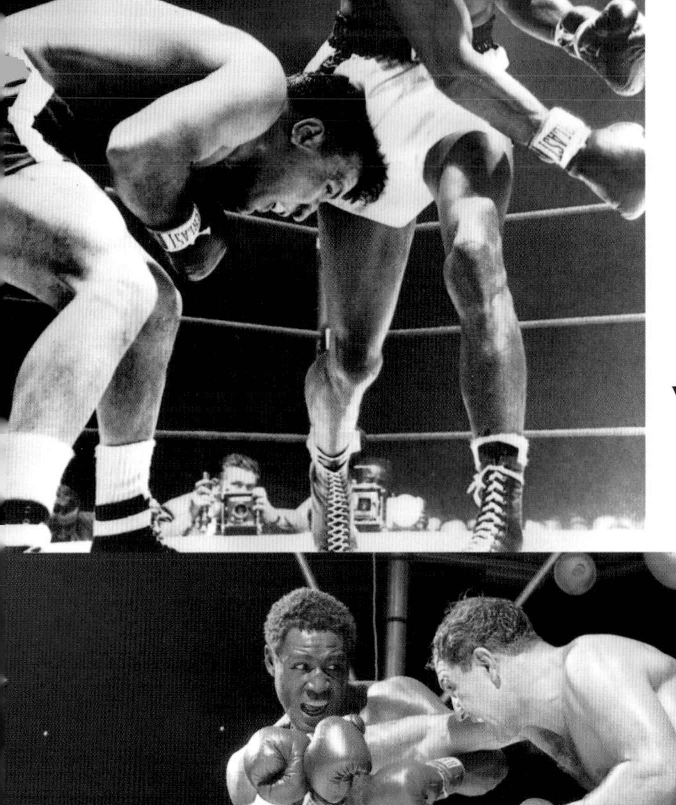

◀ Undefeated welterweight champion **Sugar Ray Robinson** (right) stepped up a division to take the middleweight crown on 14 February 1951 by stopping brave **Jake LaMotta**, whom he beat five times out of six.

▼ Unbeaten **Rocky Marciano** (right) defended his heavyweight crown in two great fights with **Ezzard Charles**. In this one, the second, a desperate Rocky was spouting blood from eye and nose when he got in the eighth-round punch which led to a knockout victory.

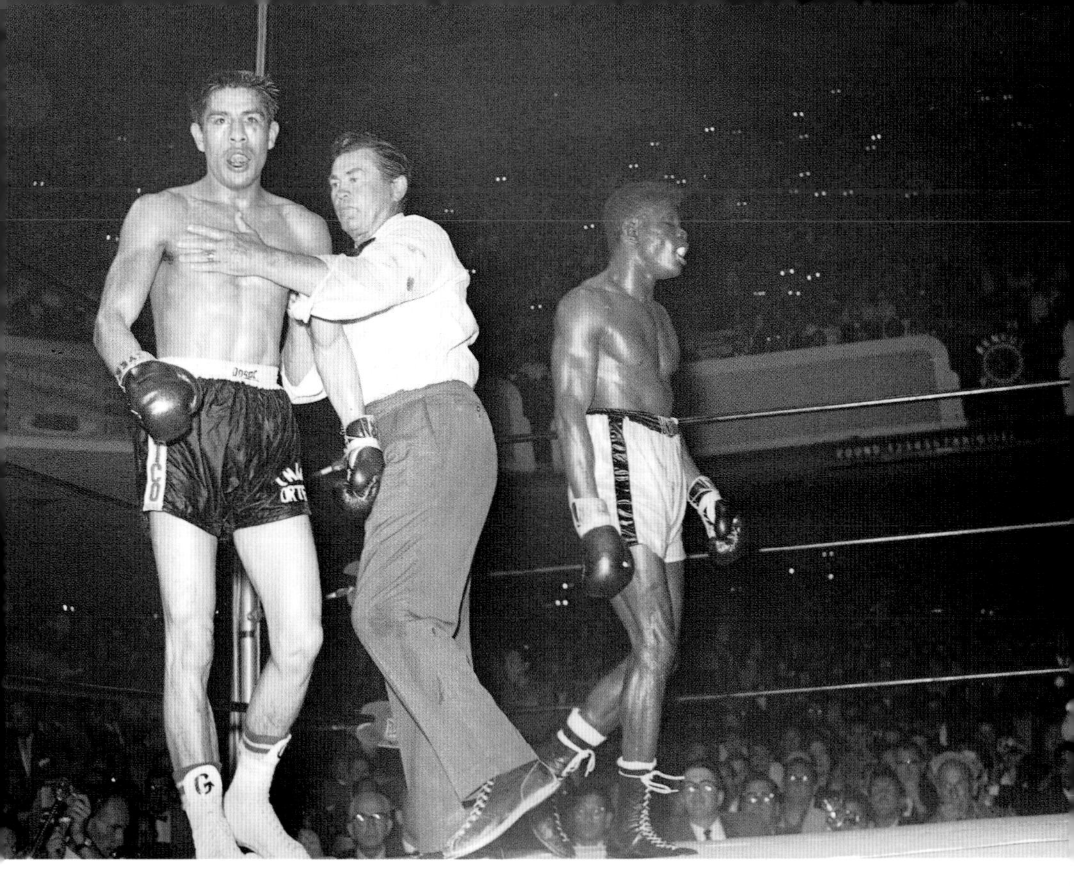

▲ The referee rescues **Gaspar Ortega** in the 12th round against **Emile Griffith** in June 1961 and Griffith completes a successful first defence of his world welterweight title.

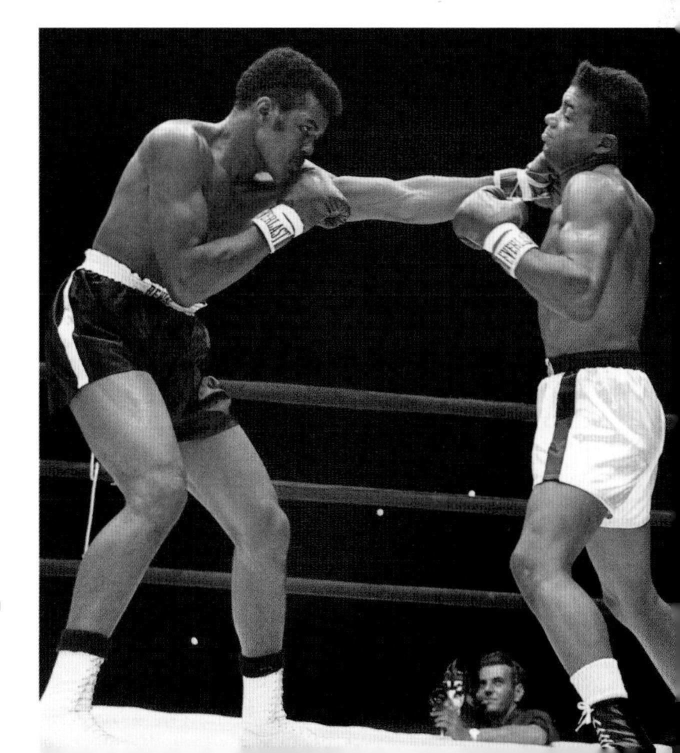

► **Tommy 'Hurricane' Jackson** connects with a left to heavyweight champion **Floyd Patterson's** chin in July 1957, but Patterson kept his crown with a tenth-round stoppage.

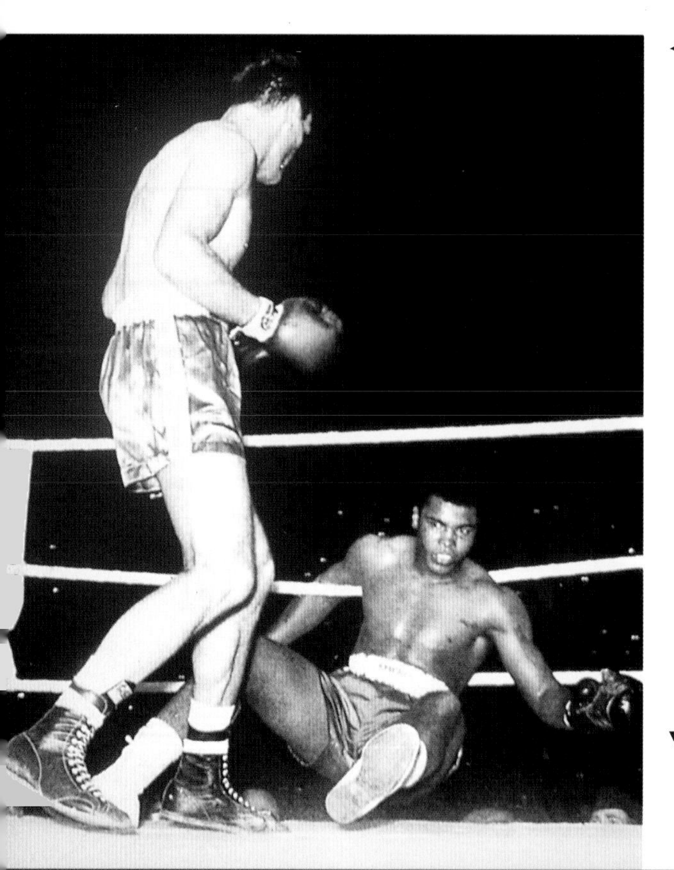

◀ A big surprise for the 'Louisville Lip'. **Cassius Clay** dumped on the canvas by **Henry Cooper's** left hook, June 1963. A bit of skulduggery with a torn glove helped Clay recover to win.

▼ Clay, now renamed **Muhammad Ali** and champion of the world, yells at **Sonny Liston** to get up after knocking him out with a 'phantom' punch in the first round of his first defence in May 1965.

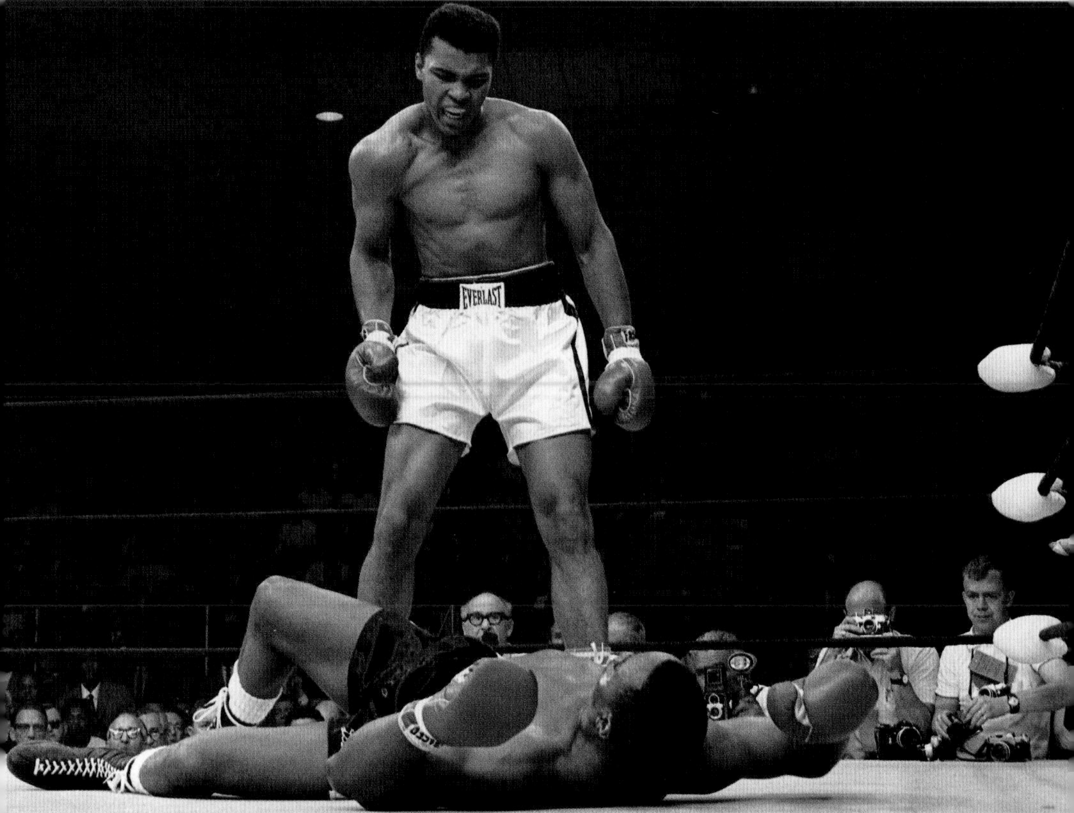

► **Nino Benvenuti** gets attention during his second meeting with **Emile Griffith**, New York, 1967. Griffith regained the middleweight title, but Benvenuti took it back in the rubber match five months later.

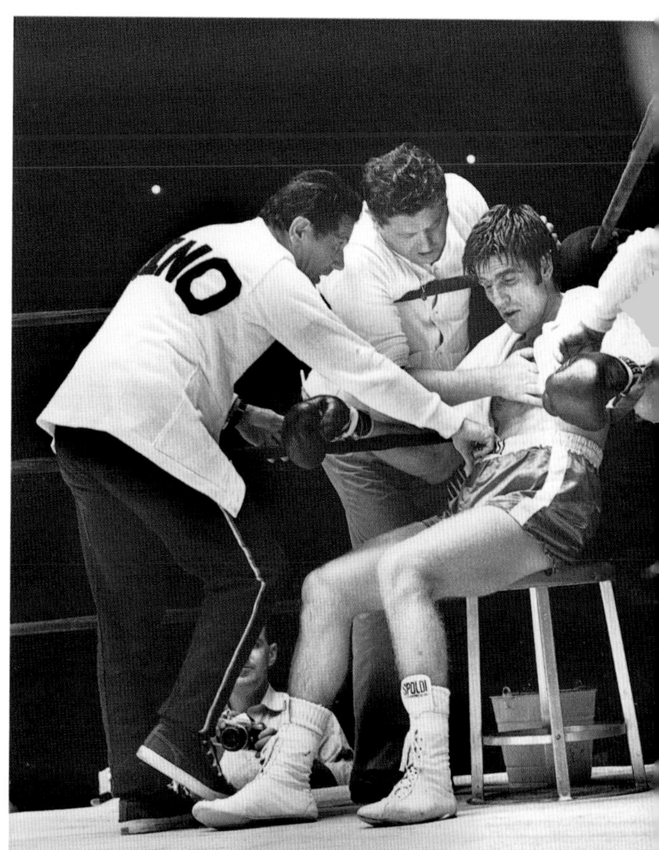

▼ 'Monzon, who are you?' asked the Italian press when Carlos went to Rome to challenge handsome idol **Nino Benvenuti** for the midleweight title. **Monzon** expresses a view with a fight poster and later won on a 12th-round knockout.

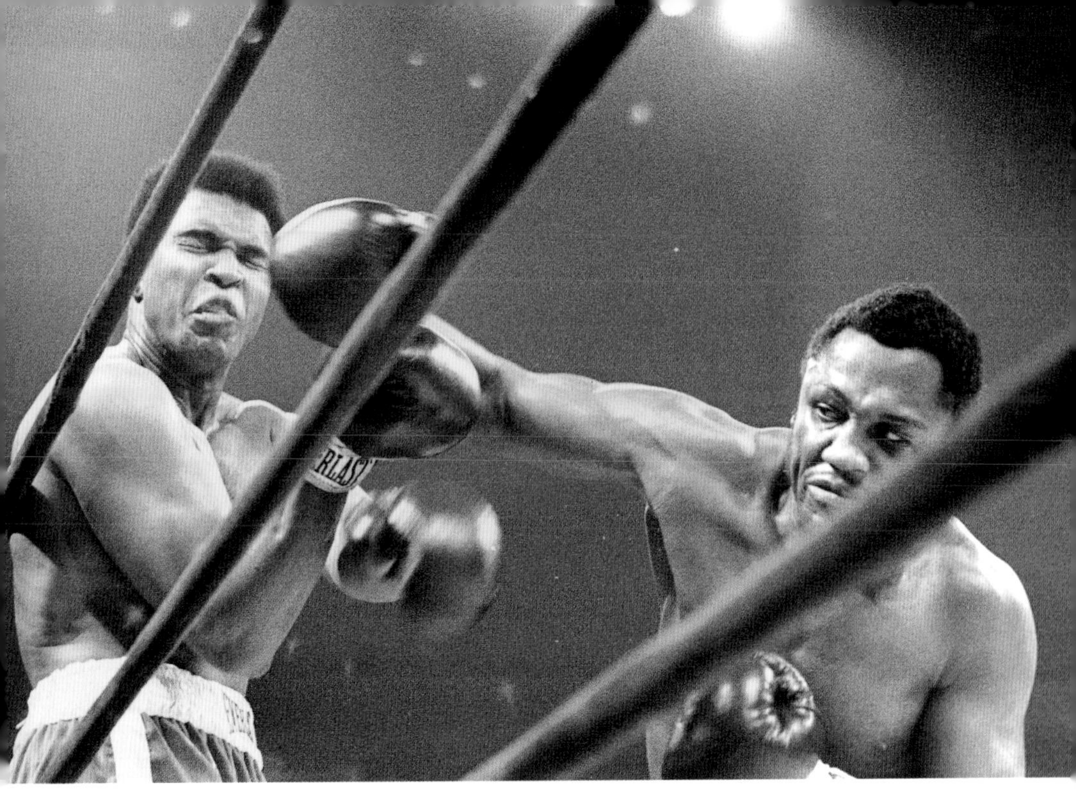

▲ 'The fight of the Century'. **Joe Frazier** (right) beats **Muhammad Ali** in the battle of the undefeated heavyweight champions in March 1971.

▼ The battle of weigh-in stares is close, but the fight wasn't. **George Foreman** (right) took the heavyweight title from **Joe Frazier** with six knockdowns in two rounds.

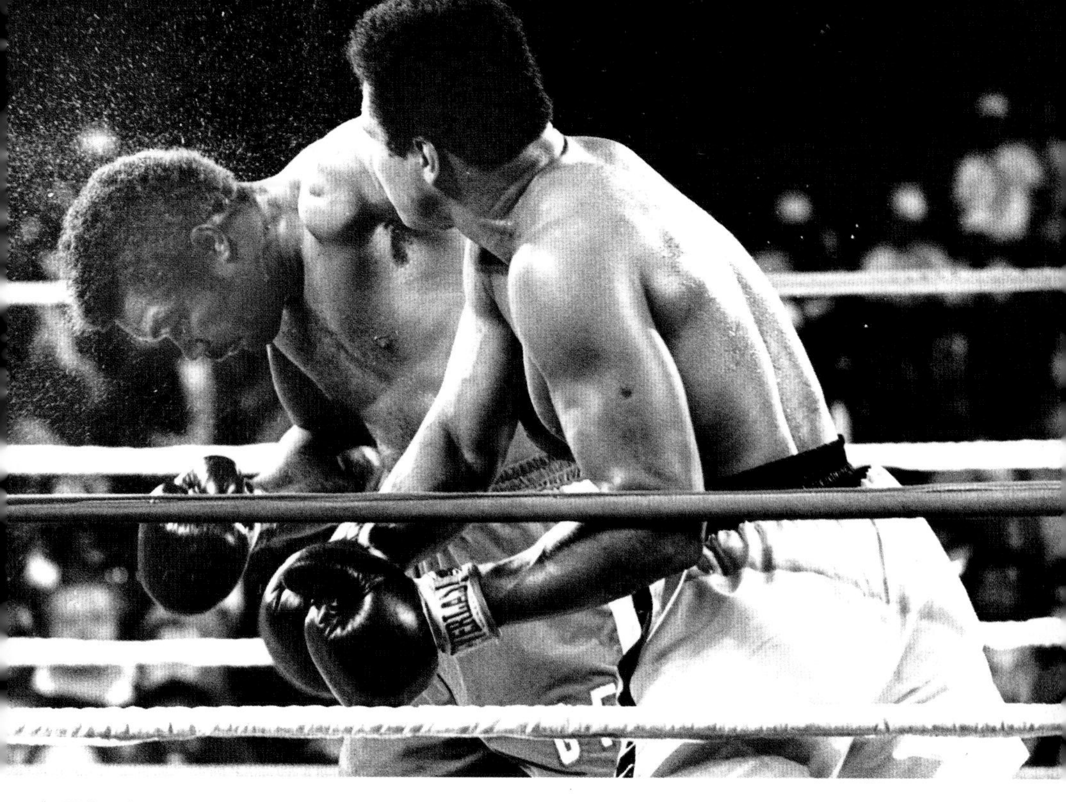

▲ **Ali** (right) knocks out **Foreman** to regain the world title in one of boxing's most amazing fights, 'The Rumble in the Jungle', Zaire, October 1974.

▼ **Ali** (right), by now champion again, makes his score 2–1 against **Frazier** by stopping him in the strength-sapping 'Thrilla in Manila' in October 1975.

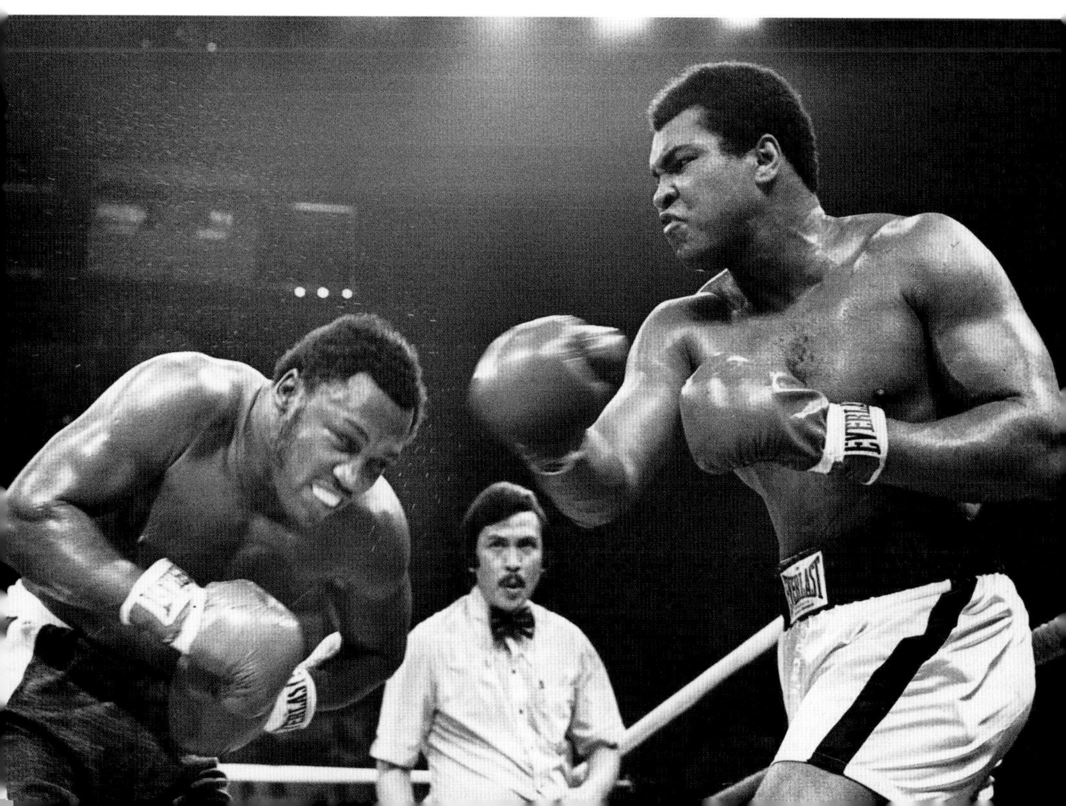

▲ **Ruben Olivares** (left) was a great champion but in November 1974 he was counted out in the 13th round and **Alexis Arguello** took his WBA featherweight title.

▼ **Ken Norton** (left) was awarded the WBC heavyweight title, but lost it on his first defence to long-reigning **Larry Holmes** in June 1978.

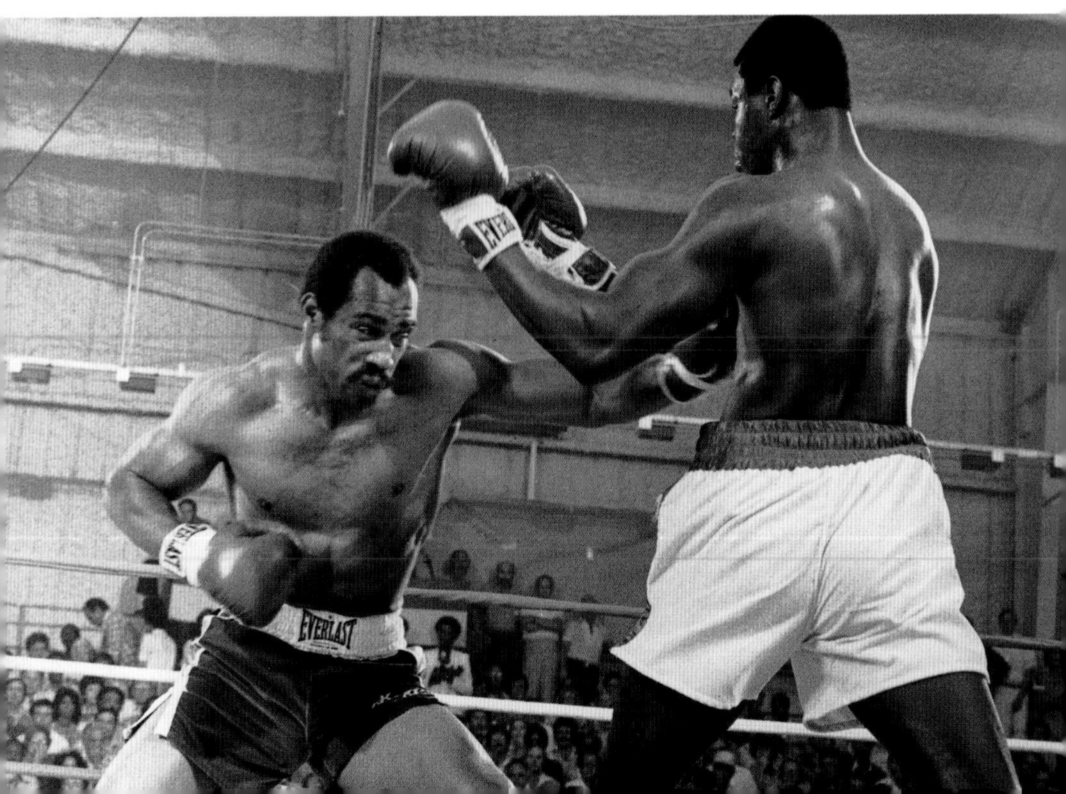

▲ Two all-time greats, **Roberto Duran** (facing) in his great win over **Sugar Ray Leonard** to take the WBC welterweight championship, June 1980.

▼ **Aaron Pryor** (left) lands a straight left on **Antonio Cervantes** in Cincinnati, 1980. Pryor took Cervantes' WBA light-welter title with a fourth-round knockout.

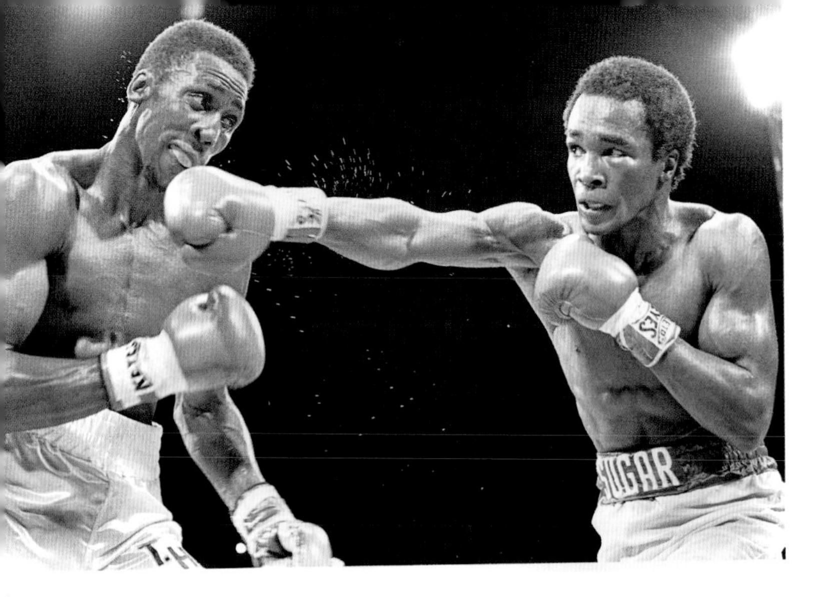

▲ Two bitter rivals, **Thomas Hearns** (left) and **Sugar Ray Leonard**. Leonard won this first meeting, at Caesars Palace, Las Vegas, in 1981, by a 14th-round stoppage for the undisputed welterweight title.

◀ 'Marvellous' **Marvin Hagler** celebrates his third-round knockout of **Thomas Hearns** in a thrilling, explosive battle in Las Vegas, April 1985.

▲ **Trevor Berbick** will rise and reel around the ring but still fail to beat the count, making **Mike Tyson** WBC Champion at 20, the youngest-ever heavyweight king.

▼ **Barry McGuigan** (left) had both Northern Ireland and the Republic, as well as Great Britain, behind him when he won the WBA featherwight title from long-reigning **Eusebio Pedroza** at the Queen's Park Rangers football ground in June 1985.

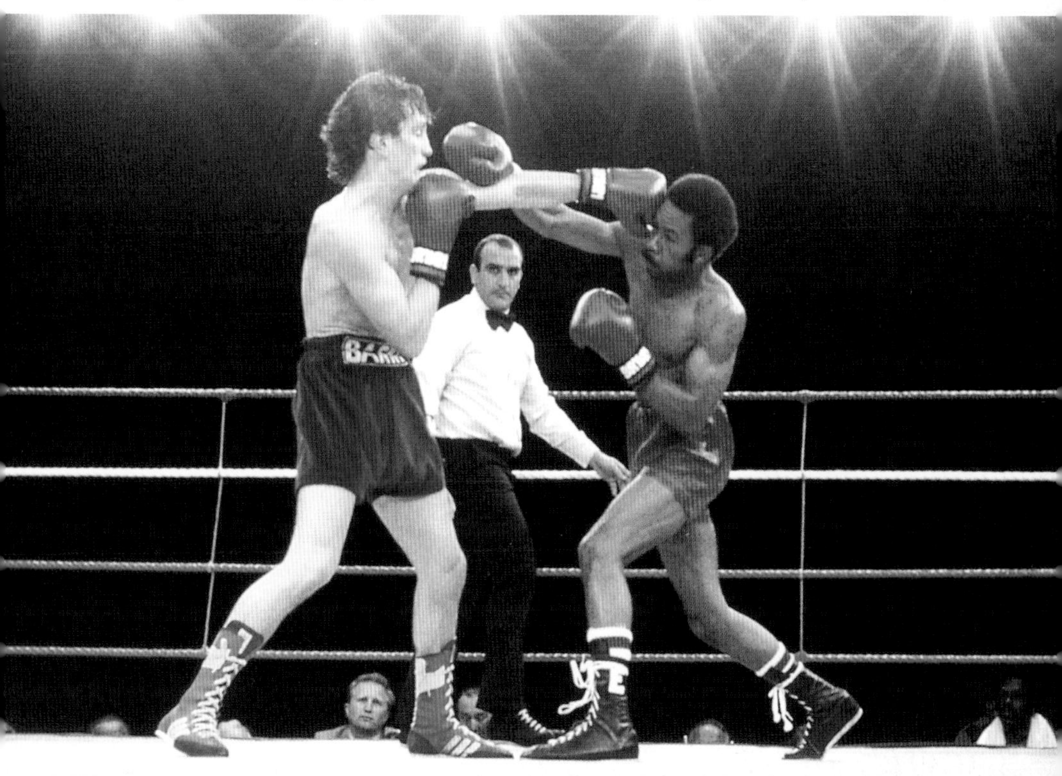

▲**Lloyd Honeyghan** and manager **Mickey Duff** after Honeyghan's surprise demolition of outstanding welterweight champion **Donald Curry** in Atlantic City, September 1986.

◀ **Sugar Ray Leonard** celebrates a keenly fought victory over **Marvin Hagler** to win the middleweight championship in April 1987 in Las Vegas.

▲ Powerful and controversial promoter **Don King** with his equally controversial heavyweight champion **Mike Tyson**, after Tyson's second-round stoppage of **Tony Tubbs** in Tokyo, 1988.

▼ Bitter rivals **Nigel Benn** (left) and **Chris Eubank** boxing a draw in Manchester in October 1993. It was an attempt to unify Benn's WBC super-middleweight title with Eubank's WBO title.

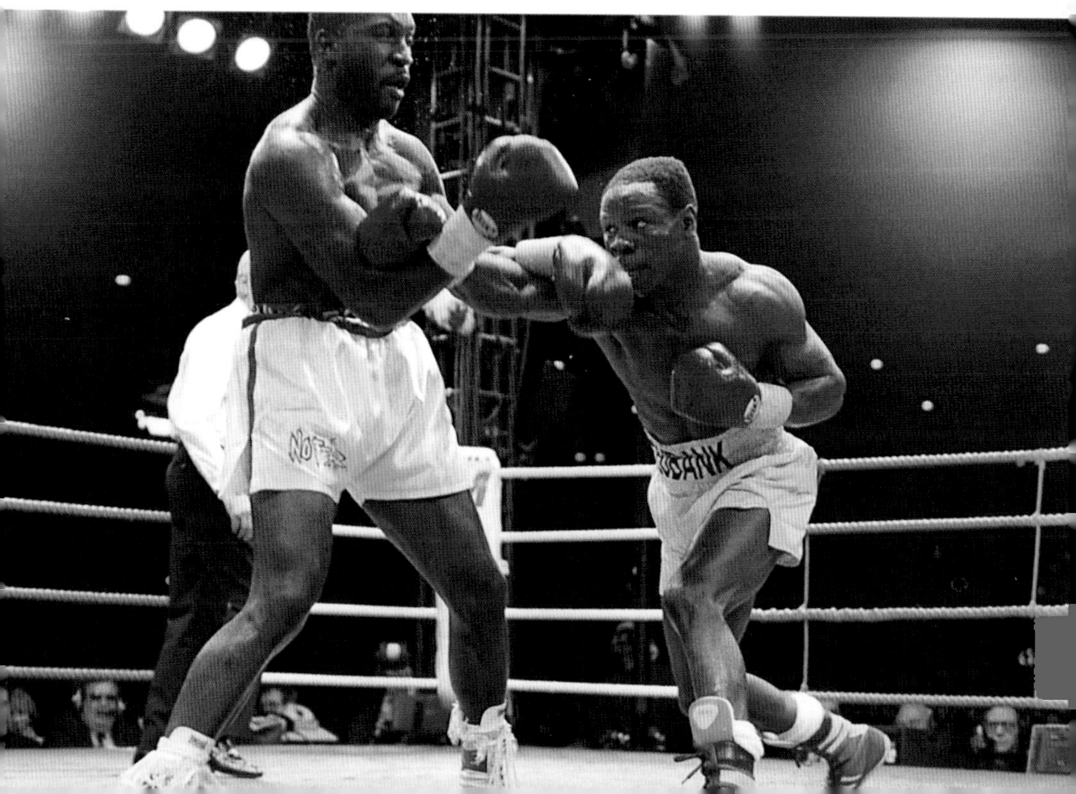

▲ **Lennox Lewis**, one of the top heavyweights of the late 1990s, has **Tony Tucker** down during a defence of his WBC title in May 1993 in Las Vegas. Lewis won on points.

▼ **Frank Bruno** celebrates at Wembley in September 1995. He had just won the WBC heavyweight title on points from **Oliver McCall**. It was his fourth attempt at a world title, nine years after his first.

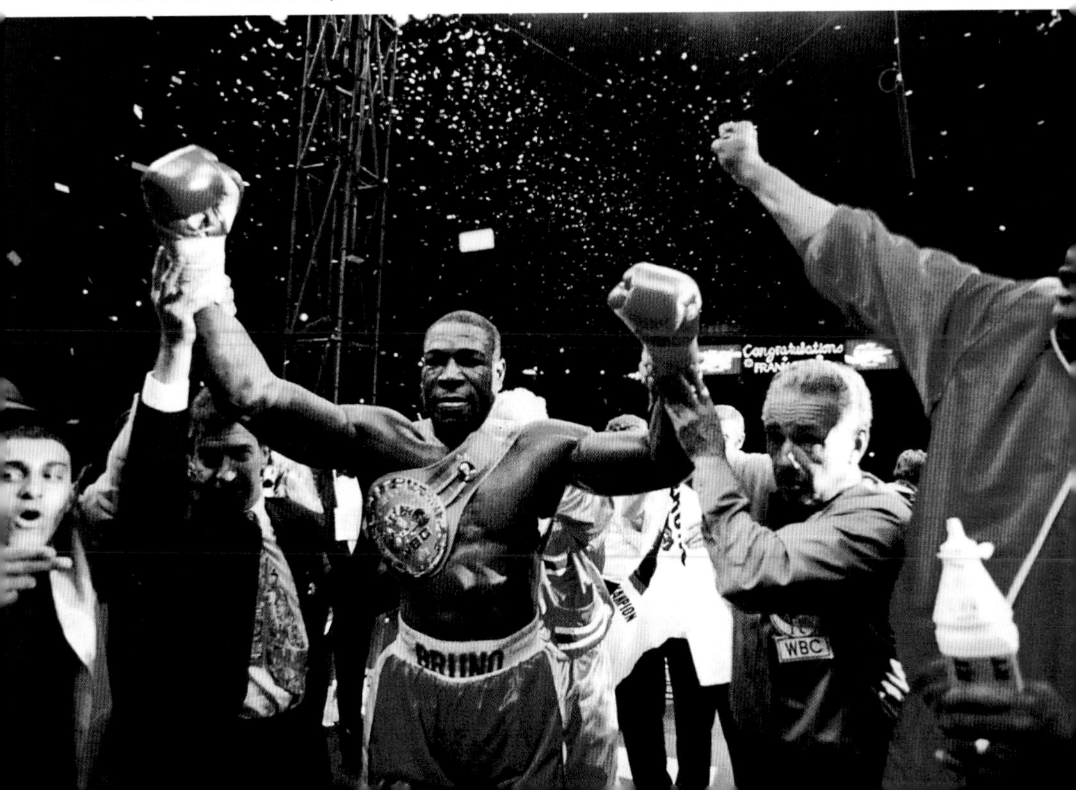

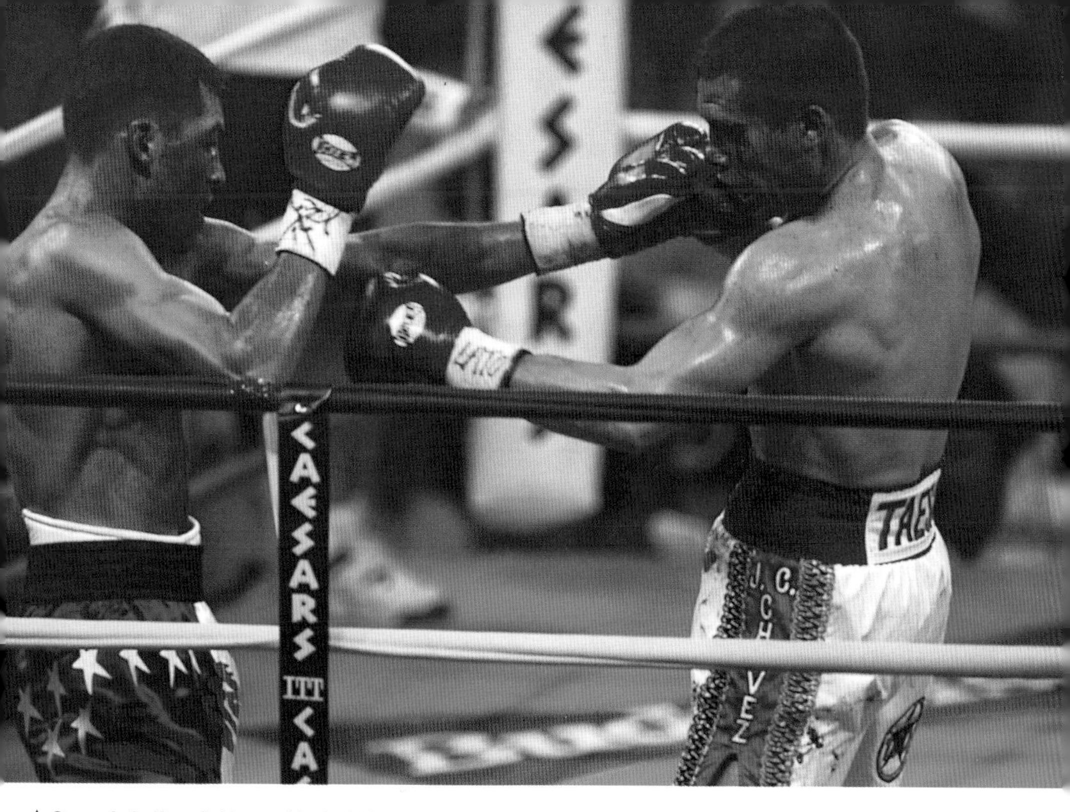

▲ **Oscar de la Hoya** (left), one of boxing's big stars of the late 1990s, stopping **Julio Cesar Chavez**, an outstanding boxer of the 1980s, for the WBC light-welterweight title, Las Vegas, June 1996.

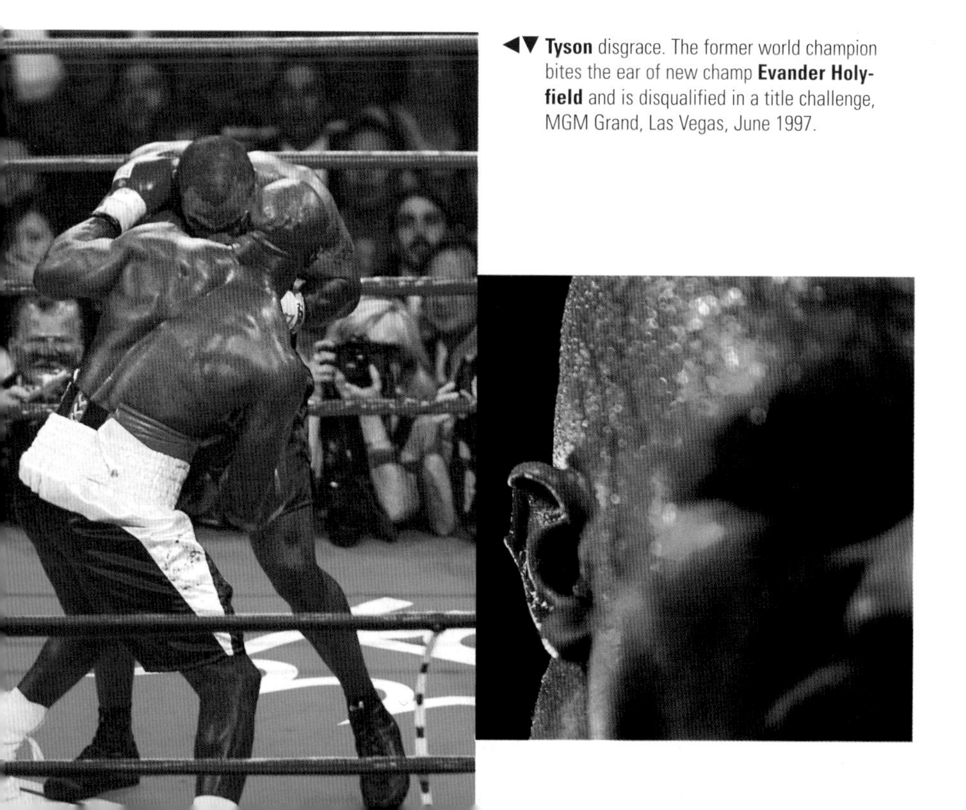

◀▼ **Tyson** disgrace. The former world champion bites the ear of new champ **Evander Holyfield** and is disqualified in a title challenge, MGM Grand, Las Vegas, June 1997.

▲ WBA heavyweight champion **Evander Holyfield** brings the IBF champion **Michael Moorer** to his Knees at Las Vegas on 8 November 1997 to unify the two titles. The doctor forced Moorer to retire at the end of the eighth round.

▼ **Prince Naseem Hamed** had been on the canvas four times himself before knocking out **Kevin Kelley** in a much-hyped explosive WBO featherweight title fight at Madison Square Garden in December 1997.

row. Ali, who had never drunk alcohol or smoked, had over the years accepted favours from many of the thousands of women who offered them. Ali has two daughters, Miya and Khaliah, born out of wedlock whom he doesn't see often but cares much for. The Nation of Islam just had to accept he liked women. Belinda divorced Ali over the affair in 1976, and Ali and Veronica were married in June 1977. She had two daughters by him, Hana (born 1976) and Laila (born 1978), making the total of his children seven daughters and a son.

If Ali was never the same after his layoff in 1967, he was also never the same after the battle with Frazier in 1975. In 1976 he defended his title four times. Against Jimmy Young, a 15–1 underdog, he fought, according to Angelo Dundee, the worst fight of his career to date, but won a unanimous decision. He fought a professional wrestler, Anthonio Inoki, in Tokyo, in a hybrid contest that ended in an arranged draw, but Ali took many dangerous kicks to his legs. Ken Norton should have beaten him again, being well ahead after eight rounds, but Ali sneaked it on the last round, when Norton was cautiously defending what he still thought was his lead.

Now the fans began to fear for their declining idol. Earnie Shavers might well have beaten him in 1977. Big puncher Shavers failed to press when Ali was exhausted, partly because Shavers, too, thought he was ahead when he wasn't. After this Dr Pacheco left Ali's entourage because Ali wouldn't take his advice to retire.

In 1978 Ali lost his crown. He was making an 11th defence since regaining it from Foreman. He lost it to a novice, Leon Spinks, an 8–1 underdog with only seven pro fights. Spinks was fast, energetic and 11 years younger, and took a split decision. Ali regained the WBA version of the crown from Spinks (the WBC stripped Spinks for giving Ali a return) seven months later by a wide unanimous margin. The 63,532 attendance at the New Orleans Superdome was a record for an indoor arena. Ali thus became the first man to win a heavyweight title three times.

Ali, with around $70 million earned from purses alone, now retired, but in October 1980, aged 38, he was moved to make a comeback to try to take Larry Holmes' WBC title. To medical men, it was clear his health was deteriorating, but he passed a Nevada Boxing Commission medical examination to get a licence. In the contest, Ali, now greying, retired after 10 rounds exhausted. Holmes could probably have knocked him out had he held him in less respect. It was discovered that Ali had taken pills before this fight that could have threatened Ali's life. Because he thought the pills had caused his defeat, Ali fought once more 14 months later, and was beaten on points by Trevor Berbick. He was pathetic by his own standards.

As soon as he had retired, rumours began circulating about Ali's health. His movements became slow, his speech soft, and his handsome face became puffy. In 1984 Parkinson's Syndrome was diagnosed. It is more a physical problem than an intellectual one and, despite his occasional vagueness, sleepiness and deliberate speech, doctors say his intelligence and sharpness of mind are intact. Medication controls his condition, which was undoubtedly caused by boxing, and by his willingness never to compromise and to give his profession all he had.

Veronica Porche divorced him in 1986, and four months later Ali married his fourth wife, Lonnie Williams, who has known him since she was five, being the daughter of his mother's best friend. They are devoted. Ali enjoys travelling and distributes religious pamphlets, obligingly autographed so that they won't be thrown away. The most lasting image of the 1996 Atlanta Olympic Games was the sight of Ali, his hand shaking uncontrollably, lighting the Olympic torch. He remains one of the best-known and best-loved people in the world.

CAREER STATISTICS

World heavyweight champion 1964-67, 1974-78, 1978-79
Louisville, Kentucky, born 17 January 1942
Name: Cassius Marcellus Clay jnr.
1960 Olympic light-heavyweight gold medal

1960
Oct 29 Tunney Hunsaker w pts 6 Louisville
Dec 27 Herb Siler w rsf 4 Miami
1961
Jan 17 Tony Esperti w rsf 3 Miami
Feb 7 Jim Robinson w rsf 1 Miami
Feb 21 Donnie Fleeman w rsf 7 Miami
Apr 19 Lamar Clark w ko 2 Louisville
Jun 26 Duke Sabedong w pts 10 Las Vegas
Jul 22 Alonzo Johnson w pts 10 Louisville
Oct 7 Alex Miteff w rsf 6 Louisville
Nov 29 Willi Besmanoff w rsf 7 Louisville
1962
Feb 10 Sonny Banks w rsf 4 New York
Feb 28 Don Warner w rsf 4 Miami
Apr 23 George Logan w rsf 4 Los Angeles
May 19 Billy Daniels w rsf 7 New York
Jul 20 Alejandro Lavorante w ko 5 Los Angeles
Nov 15 Archie Moore w ko 4 Los Angeles
1963
Jan 24 Charlie Powell w ko 3 Pittsburgh
Mar 13 Doug Jones w pts 10 New York
Jun 18 Henry Cooper w rsf 5 London
1964
Feb 25 Sonny Liston w rtd 6 Miami
(World heavyweight title)
1965
May 25 Sonny Liston w ko 1 Lewiston
(World heavyweight title)
Nov 22 Floyd Patterson w rsf 12 Las Vegas
(World heavyweight title)
1966
Mar 29 George Chuvalo w pts 15 Toronto
(World heavyweight title)
May 21 Henry Cooper w rsf 6 London
(World heavyweight title)
Aug 6 Brian London w ko 3 London
(World heavyweight title)
Sep 10 Karl Mildenberger w rsf 12 Frankfurt
(World heavyweight title)
Nov 14 Cleveland Williams w rsf 3 Houston
(World heavyweight title)
1967
Feb 6 Ernie Terrell w pts 15 Houston
(World heavyweight title)
Mar 22 Zora Folley w ko 7 New York
(World heavyweight title)
1968-69 inactive
1970
Oct 26 Jerry Quarry w rsf 3 Atlanta
Dec 7 Oscar Bonavena w rsf 15 New York
1971
Mar 8 Joe Frazier l pts 15 New York
(World heavyweight title)
Jul 26 Jimmy Ellis w rsf 12 Houston
(North American Boxing Federation heavyweight title)
Nov 17 Buster Mathis w pts 12 Houston
(NABF heavyweight title)
Dec 26 Jurgen Blin w ko 7 Zurich
1972
Apr 1 Mac Foster w pts 15 Tokyo
May 1 George Chuvalo w pts 12 Vancouver
(NABF heavyweight title)

Jun 27 Jerry Quarry w rsf 7 Las Vegas
(NABF heavyweight title)
Jul 19 Alvin Lewis w rsf 11 Dublin
Sep 20 Floyd Patterson w rsf 7 New York
(NABF heavyweight title)
Nov 21 Bob Foster w ko 8 Stateline
(NABF heavyweight title)

1973
Feb 14 Joe Bugner w pts 12 Las Vegas
Mar 31 Ken Norton l pts 12 San Diego
(NABF heavyweight title)
Sep 10 Ken Norton w pts 12 Los Angeles
(NABF heavyweight title)
Oct 20 Rudi Lubbers w pts 12 Jakarta

1974
Jan 28 Joe Frazier w pts 12 New York
(NABF heavyweight title)
Oct 30 George Foreman w ko 8 Kinshasa
(World heavyweight title)

1975
Mar 24 Chuck Wepner w rsf 15 Cleveland
(World heavyweight title)
May 16 Ron Lyle w rsf 11 Las Vegas
(World heavyweight title)
Jul 1 Joe Bugner w pts 15 Kuala Lumpur
(World heavyweight title)
Oct 1 Joe Frazier w rtd 14 Manila
(World heavyweight title)

1976
Feb 20 Jean Pierre Coopman w ko 5 San Juan
(World heavyweight title)
Apr 30 Jimmy Young w pts 15 Landover
(World heavyweight title)
May 24 Richard Dunn w rsf 5 Munich
(World heavyweight title)
Sep 28 Ken Norton w pts 15 New York
(World heavyweight title)

1977
May 16 Alfredo Evangelista w pts 15 Landover
(World heavyweight title)
Sep 29 Earnie Shavers w pts 15 New York
(World heavyweight title)

1978
Feb 15 Leon Spinks l pts 15 Las Vegas
(World heavyweight title)
Sep 15 Leon Spinks w pts 15 New Orleans
(WBA heavyweight title)

1979
Jun 27 Announced retirement, relinquished title.

1980
Oct 2 Larry Holmes l rtd 10 Las Vegas
(WBC heavyweight title)

1981
Dec 11 Trevor Berbick l pts 10 Nassau

Fights 61 Won 56 Lost 5

WILFRED BENITEZ

THE YOUNGEST CHAMP

Wilfred Benitez fought with the joy and exhilaration of youth. He had brilliant reflexes, speed, smooth skills and could time his punches to knock out the best. But youth never lasts. And it left Benitez so soon. Watching him, even as a comparatively young man of 25, was to see a man struggling to believe what was happening to him. Although he boxed on until 1990, when he was 32, it is the Benitez of the second half of the 1970s who should be remembered and celebrated.

Wilfred was the son of Puerto Rican immigrants to New York, Gregorio and Clara Benitez, and was born in the Bronx on 12 September 1958. Gregorio was a boxing man, who believed in teaching his sons with an iron fist. By the age of four, Wilfred was in the gym with his elder brothers Frankie, Alphonso and Gregorio jnr, all of whom would become good class professionals. Three years later, the family returned to San Juan, where Wilfred's precocious talents were allowed to flourish.

In 1973, when he was still only 14 but as he would do for some time, claiming to be a couple of years older, he boxed for Puerto Rico in the Caribbean Games in Costa Rica, and lost a split decision to the previous year's Olympic bantamweight gold medallist, Orlando Martinez of Cuba. It was one of only six defeats in more than 100 amateur contests.

As the authorities believed he was 17, he was allowed to make his professional debut in San Juan in November 1973. He knocked out Hiram Santiago in one round. After 11 wins in nine months, Gregorio Benitez took his boys back to New York where they could find better class fights. Wilfred won his American debut at the Felt Forum, the smaller arena in Madison Square Garden, in September 1974, when, unknown to the authorities, he was still only four days past his 16th birthday. He stopped Bronx light-welterweight Albert Hughes in the fifth round.

A month later he stopped Terry Summerhays, and he rounded off a wonderful year with a landslide eight-round points win over Canadian Lawrence Hafey. Sam Taub wrote in *Ring*: 'Benitez was like a well-oiled piece of machinery as, time and again, he bombarded Hafey with both hands.'

However, Gregorio Benitez did not want his sons working the smaller arena. Even though Wilfred was still only 16, Gregorio felt he was good enough to star in the Garden itself. Feeling that things were not working out, he took them all back to San Juan for the start of 1975. 'Wilfred is smart and will be smarter,' said Gregorio. 'He doesn't worry about an opponent. That is the thing I teach him, to have knowledge and use it.'

Most of the year was spent beating hopelessly inferior opposition, but there were a few tough old pros tossed into the pot. And the year ended with his most prestigious victory so far, a decision over Chris Fernandez, a 32-year-old veteran from the Dominican Republic, who had outpointed Frankie Benitez in New York in October 1975. Fernandez had boxed a string of world champions over the previous seven or eight years, including Ken Buchanan, the late Carlos Teo Cruz, Angel Espada, Saoul Mamby and Bruno Arcari.

Benitez was now unbeaten in 25 fights, but was still only 17, and it raised a few knowing eyebrows when Gregorio accepted an offer for Wilfred to challenge the great WBA light-welterweight champion Antonio 'Kid Pambele' Cervantes of Colombia. On paper, the fight should not have happened, but boxing sometimes defies logic.

Cervantes, hardly over the hill at 30, was nevertheless a veteran of 59 professional fights and had held the WBA 140lb belt since 1972. Benitez was his 11th challenger ... and the youngest world title contestant on record.

They met in the Hiram Bithorn stadium in San Juan in March 1976, before an official crowd of 17,200. However, it was widely believed that more than 20,000 were in the ground, around 3,000 with fake tickets! Fairly early on it was clear that the champion had seriously underestimated the young man in front of him. Cervantes, who was being paid $100,000 to the $7,500 of his challenger, was lethargic, almost lazy at times, as if he believed he could finish the fight whenever he pleased. Benitez boxed his way into the lead by the halfway stage, and survived a torrid 11th round when he was shaken by a right hand. By the end he had outboxed, outfought and outlasted the champion. Referee Isaac Herrera agreed with a 148–144 scoreline, but Panamanian judge Jesus Celis surprisingly had Cervantes in front by 147–145. The deciding card from judge Roberto Ramirez was 147–142 for Benitez. Wilfred Benitez had created history.

'Cervantes took him too lightly,' suggested referee Herrera, while a jubilant Gregorio Benitez was ready to celebrate in style. 'Everybody thought I was crazy when I accepted this fight for my son, but I proved that Cervantes is on the way down.'

Benitez snr had given his son a hard time in the corner, but said it was because he was worried. 'You don't think I was afraid? I sure was. I know that if he fails, I fail. So I pretend ... Maybe I bully him a little in the corner, just to make him feel I don't have doubts.'

Two months later in the Roberto Clemente Stadium in San Juan, Benitez turned back the challenge of Emiliano Villa of Colombia on a unanimous decision. The taller Villa tried to make a fight of it, but Benitez edged the early rounds and then took over completely from round seven, when he hurt Villa with a right hand. Villa was staggered again in the 11th and cut by round 13.

Benitez said afterwards: 'I want to dedicate this victory to the eternal love of Christ, who is my guiding force. May it be symbolic to the youth of Puerto Rico of what faith in God can accomplish.'

Cervantes was thumping the tub for a return – 'I am going to slaughter that boy the next time we get in a ring' – but Benitez ignored him. He closed the year in October with an easy third-round stoppage of Tony Petronelli, who was floored four times. Petronelli was handled by his father Pat and uncle Goody, who went on to greater things with Marvin Hagler in the 1980s.

Benitez's backers wanted to continue with more routine defences, but the WBA ordered the champion to give Cervantes a return next. Gregorio stalled for time, claiming Wilfred had been injured in a car crash, but the WBA sent their own doctor to Puerto Rico and he passed him fit to box. Gregorio then said they were not prepared to box Cervantes, and the WBA took away the title.

Wilfred was still recognised by the New York Commission, but his 15th round stoppage of Jose Guerrero Chavez in Madison Square Garden in August 1977 was a relatively low-key affair. By then Benitez, filling out at 18 and just beginning to live less like a champion than he should, was having terrible trouble making 140lb. He admitted that he took off more than 20lb, the last seven on the day of the fight, and decided never to put himself through that kind of nightmare again.

Earlier in the year, in February, he had been held to a 10 round draw by a crafty welterweight, Harold Weston, in the Garden, drawing a good sized crowd of almost 11,000.

After he beat Chavez, Benitez boxed Bruce Curry and found himself on the floor for the first time in his career. Down twice in round five and on the brink of a stoppage defeat, he was saved by the bell. He won on points, but it was a controversial, split verdict. They were matched again for February 1978, and this time Benitez dominated, only to be given a majority decision. Referee Tony Perez gave him nine of the 10 rounds, with a seven-three vote from judge Artie Aidala. Surprisingly, the other judge, Al Reid, had the fight level. It didn't really matter. The 16,000 fans in the Garden knew who had won.

A sixth-round stoppage of welterweight contender Randy Shields put him into contention at 147lb, on the night of the infamous riot at the Garden which followed a controversial contest between Vito Antuofermo and Willie Classen, and his opportunity arrived in January 1979 against reigning champion Carlos Palomino.

Palomino had held the WBC belt since 1976 when he had knocked out John H. Stracey in the 12th round at Wembley. When he fought Benitez, he was 29, with seven successful defences behind him, a highly respected if unspectacular champion. Benitez was still only 20 years old, but outboxed Palomino – who had been sidelined by a broken hand for eight months – most of the way. Wilfred won, but the scoring was strange. English judge Harry Gibbs had 146–143, or seven rounds to four, with four even. Referee Jay Edson's 148–143 card translated at seven to two, with a surprising six even. But the tally of veteran Zach Clayton was bizarre: 145–142 for Palomino, eight to five with two shared.

Promoter Bob Arum was beside himself. 'Nobody in their right mind could have scored that fight for Palomino.' Even Carlos agreed. 'Benitez was the best man today,' he said, explaining that it was the speed of the youngster that was too much for him. A chastened Clayton claimed he had been unable to see properly because the sun was in his eyes.

Benitez, by now living on the outskirts of San Juan, said afterwards he planned no serious celebrations. 'I will keep on training. I have a job to do ...'

He certainly had a tough task ahead against Harold Weston, the slippery New Yorker who had held him to a draw two years before. They fought for Benitez's WBC welterweight belt in blistering heat in San Juan in March 1979 ... and suddenly the cracks were showing. Wilfred's weight-making at 140lb was understandable, but at 147lb he should not have had difficulty. In fact, he lost 18lb in the last five days before the fight, and admitted he was physically drained after 11 rounds. Only the urging of Gregorio, who slapped him in the face in the corner, kept him going to win a unanimous decision. Again, the scoring was odd: the two ringside judges saw it close with one and two round margins, while referee Richard Steele had Benitez in a huge 11 point lead at the final bell. The young champion grossed a career highest $140,000.

If he had lived correctly, then Benitez might have gone on to even greater things. As it was, he was struggling to keep his mind on his work. Gregorio, who could probably see what was happening to his son but was also ready to make his own money while he could, sold the managerial contract to Jim Jacobs for $70,000 and then decided to train him anyway. When he found Wilfred unwilling to work hard, he condemned him publicly. The youngster was probably an emotional wreck by the time he defended his WBC welterweight belt against Ray Leonard in November 1979 for a gross purse of $1.2 million. Not surprisingly, a look of relief seemed to cross his face when the fight was stopped just six seconds from the final bell, as if a weight had been lifted from him. Before the 15th, it was very close, but when Leonard lifted the pace, Benitez lacked the inner resolve to go with him.

Although he won three out of three in 1980, and won the WBC light-middleweight title with a crushing 12th-round knockout of British-based Antiguan Maurice Hope in Las Vegas in May 1981, he would not be at the top for much longer.

He was involved in a boring 15-round points win over fellow Puerto Rican Carlos Santos, and then grossed another $1 million by outboxing a discredited Roberto Duran in a second WBC 154lb defence in January 1982. Behind the scenes, he was involved in more financial wrangling, and was out of the ring for 11 months. When he returned it was against Thomas Hearns, who was too sharp for him in a dull, methodical 15-round fight that, incredibly, was only a majority vote. One judge scored it level. 'He must have been asleep,' grunted Hearns.

Although he was a three-weight champion and still only 24, Benitez never fought for a world title again. He lost a decision to brawling southpaw Mustafa Hamsho, was hammered in two rounds by Davey Moore, and stopped twice in four fights in 1986, by Matthew Hilton and Carlos Herrera. He retired, and a comeback in 1990 brought nothing but faded memories of what he once was.

By the mid-1990s he was a shell of his old self. Before his 40th birthday, he was looked after by his mother, living on a government pension of $150 a week, and officially recognised as unable to handle his own affairs. But oh, how good he once was, and how young!

CAREER STATISTICS

WBA light-welterweight champion 1976–77
WBC welterweight champion 1979
WBC light-middleweight champion 1981–82
San Juan, Puerto Rico, born Bronx, New York, 12 September 1958

1973
Nov 22 Hiram Santiago w ko 1 San Juan
Nov 30 Jesse Torres w ko 2 St Martin
1974
Jan 7 Hector Amadis w ko 4 San Juan
Jan 26 Joe York w ko 2 St Martin
Feb 18 Roberto Flanders w rsf 4 San Juan
Apr 1 Victor Mangual w pts 8 San Juan
Apr 30 Juan Disla w rsf 3 San Juan
May 11 Sonny Lake w ko 1 St Martin
Jun 21 Ives St. Jean w ko 1 St Martin
Jun 26 Carlos Crispin w rsf 3 San Juan
Aug 31 Sonny Lake w rsf 5 St Martin
Sep 16 Al Hughes w rsf 5 New York
Oct 25 Terry Summerhays w rsf 6 New York
Dec 2 Lawrence Hafey w pts 8 New York
1975
Jan 4 Francisco Rodriguez w ko 7 San Juan
Feb 8 Santiago Rosa w ko 4 San Juan
Mar 31 Wilbur Seales w rsf 4 San Juan
May 5 Santos Solis w pts 10 San Juan
Jun 9 Angel Garcia w pts 10 San Juan
Jun 28 Joe Henry w rsf 8 San Juan
Aug 1 Eyue Jeudy w ko 4 St Martin
Aug 19 Young Woodall w ko 4 St Martin
Sep 1 Marcelino Alicia w rsf 2 San Juan
Oct 20 Omar Piton w rsf 6 New York
Dec 13 Chris Fernandez w pts 10 San Juan
1976
Mar 6 Antonio Cervantes w pts 15 San Juan *(WBA light-welterweight title)*
May 31 Emiliano Villa w pts 15 San Juan *(WBA light-welterweight title)*
Oct 16 Tony Petronelli w rsf 3 San Juan *(WBA light-welterweight title)*
1977
Feb 2 Harold Weston drew 10 New York
Mar 6 Mel Dennis w pts 8 Marion, Ohio
Jun 2 Roberto Gonzalez w ko 1 St Thomas
Jul 1 Easy Boy Lake w ko 1 St Thomas
Aug 3 Guerrero Chavez w rsf 15 New York *(WBA light-welterweight title)*
Nov 18 Bruce Curry w pts 10 New York
1978
Feb 4 Bruce Curry w pts 10 New York
Aug 25 Randy Shields w rsf 6 New York
Dec 5 Vernon Lewis w pts 10 New York
1979
Jan 14 Carlos Palomino w pts 15 San Juan *(WBC welterweight title)*
Mar 25 Harold Weston w pts 15 San Juan *(WBC welterweight title)*
Nov 30 Ray Leonard l rsf 15 Las Vegas *(WBC welterweight title)*
1980
Mar 9 Johnny Turner w rsf 9 Miami
Aug 1 Tony Chiaverini w rsf 8 Las Vegas
Dec 12 Pete Ranzany w pts 10 Sacramento
1981
May 23 Maurice Hope w ko 12 Las Vegas *(WBC light-middleweight title)*
Nov 13 Carlos Santos w pts 15 Las Vegas *(WBC light-middleweight title)*
1982
Jan 30 Roberto Duran w pts 15 Las Vegas *(WBC light-middleweight title)*
Dec 3 Thomas Hearns l pts 15 New Orleans *(WBC light-middleweight title)*
1983
May 18 Tony Cerda w pts 10 Las Vegas
Jul 16 Mustafa Hamsho l pts 12 Las Vegas
1984
Feb 11 Stacy McSwain w pts 10 Detroit
Jul 14 Davey Moore l rsf 2 Monte Carlo
1985
Mar 30 Mauricio Bravo w rsf 2 Oranjestad
Jul 7 Danny Chapman w rsf 7 Washington DC
Aug 21 Kevin Moley w pts 10 New York
1986
Feb 15 Matthew Hilton l ko 9 Montreal
Jul 1 Paul Whittaker w pts 10 New Orleans
Sep 17 Harry Daniels w pts 10 Baltimore
Nov 28 Carlos Herrera l rsf 7 Salta
1987-89 inactive
1990
Mar 8 Ariel Conde w ko 7 Phoenix
May 23 Pat Lawlor l pts 10 Tucson
Aug 24 Sam Wilson w pts 10 Denver
Sep 18 Scott Papsadora l pts 10 Winnipeg

Fights 62 Won 53 Lost 8 Drawn 1

ALEXIS ARGUELLO

HAVE TITLE WILL TRAVEL

They called him 'El Flaco Explosive', or 'The Explosive Thin Man', and for 10 years, Alexis Arguello was a pleasure to watch, one moment methodical, organised and systematic; the next dramatically exciting. He had a solid jaw, and hit hard and fast. He also held world titles at three separate weights, from featherweight to lightweight. It took a fighter as distinguished as Aaron Pryor to prevent him turning three into four.

Arguello was born in the Managua slums on 19 April 1952, one of nine children. From the 1930s until the 1970s, Nicaragua was ruled by the Somoza family. It was a cruel, army-backed dictatorship, under which while most of the people struggled under serious hardship, the Somozas amassed a fortune of almost $1 billion.

From the 1960s, the Sandinista National Liberation Front established themselves as a guerilla opposition and the country Alexis grew up in was a dangerous hotbed of suppressed political unrest.

Under the Somozas, there was a considerable amount of professional boxing, but the lack of major financial input prevented almost all Nicaraguan sportsmen and women from fulfilling their potential. Arguello's brother-in-law Eduardo 'Raton' Mojica was one of his country's best. He beat world flyweight champion Chartchai Chionoi in a non-title fight in Managua in 1968, but not enough money could be found to tempt Chionoi back for a championship rematch. Mojica, 13 years Alexis's senior, fought professionally from 1958 until 1973. He boxed another world flyweight champion, Efren 'Alacran' Torres of Mexico, four times.

Mojica was an inspiration for Alexis, buying him his first pair of gloves and then his kit when he showed some ability and dedication. There was no point in boxing as an amateur because any amount of cash was useful for the family, and so as a 16-year-old flyweight he turned professional. He worked the four- and six-round class until it was discovered that he was under the legal minimum age of 18, and so his licence was suspended until he was old enough. The wait did him no harm, for he may easily have burned out if he had taken too many fights too soon.

By 1970, when he returned, he was bigger, stronger and more able to cope with a professional ring. He was quickly operating at 10-round level, and winning most of his fights inside the distance. He broke a hand when stopped by Jorge Reyes, and had it permanently wired. Soon afterwards he received a state handout on the direct orders of dictator Anastasio Somoza, which enabled him to give up his job in a car body shop. However, almost all of his contests were in Managua, and although he earned a world rating with knockouts of world class opponents like Octavio Gomez of Mexico, and the former world featherweight champion Jose Legra, international critics remained somewhat sceptical, largely because they had never seen him.

The Gomez fight, in Managua in June 1973, was especially welcome. He used his entire purse to rebuild the family home, which had been wrecked in a terrible earthquake the previous year when thousands died.

In February 1974, the 21-year-old Nicaraguan travelled to Panama City to challenge for the WBA title held by the talented, stylish Ernesto Marcel. He fought well but Marcel's experience saw him draw clear over the final five rounds. 'I had so much to learn,' said Arguello. 'But he taught me that I must work even harder to succeed.'

At least, he had confirmed that he belonged in world class. Three months later Marcel honoured a promise to his mother and retired, leaving the title vacant. Alexis confirmed his right to occupy one corner in the fight that would decide Marcel's successor by taking care of four opponents, three inside the distance. Only Oscar Aparicio, in a Central American title fight in Masaya, Nicaragua, in August, managed to stay the required distance, in this case 12 rounds.

And in November 1974, Arguello disputed the WBA featherweight championship with the great Mexican, Ruben Olivares, at the Inglewood Forum in Los Angeles. Roared on by more than 11,000 fans, Olivares rocked him several times between rounds eight and 10, and Arguello had to show great character to come through the prolonged crisis.

In round 13, when behind on points, he found what he was looking for, a perfect left hook. Olivares went down, hauled himself up, only to be knocked out. At 22, Arguello was the first world boxing champion produced by Nicaragua, and a national hero. He could already speak English, which helped his market status, because General Somoza had seen his potential as a sporting ambassador and sent him to an army school to learn the language.

In his first defence Alexis stopped Leonel Hernandez in eight rounds in Caracas, and then honoured his own fans by defending at home against Rigoberto Riasco of Panama. It was all over in round two, with Riasco sagging helplessly on the ropes.

Arguello travelled to Tokyo in October 1975 to meet the unbeaten Japanese star Royal Kobayashi, who had boxed in the Munich Olympics. On paper, it was a calculated risk. But fights are not won on paper. Arguello knocked him out in the fifth with a cruel left hook to the ribs.

His final 126lb defence was in Los Angeles in June 1976, a three-round blastout of Salvador Torres of Mexico, which grossed him $50,000. By now he had amassed considerable property in Nicaragua, and other trappings of fame, but his second marriage was also over and he twice announced his retirement because of personal problems. His overheads were high.

In January 1978, he won the WBC super-featherweight crown by stopping the clever Puerto Rican Alfredo Escalera at the end of the 13th round away from home in Bayamon. Escalera said he planned to smother Arguello and outwork him on the inside, but in getting close he absorbed pounding hooks, was floored in round two and badly cut. Escalera fought his heart out, but was pulled out by referee Arthur Mercante in the 13th. The beaten champ needed 30 stitches in his face. Arguello was a star, as popular in Madison Square Garden as he was in Los Angeles, and as welcome in the USA as he was in Managua.

At the Inglewood Forum, he outclassed Rey Tam from the Philippines in three rounds and in San Juan he blew away Diego Alcala in one. A showdown with lightweight champion Roberto Duran was in the offing, but he missed out on that when he was surprisingly outscored by New York cab driver Vilomar Fernandez in the Garden in July 1978.

The next month the Sandinista guerillas, led by Eden Pastora Gomez, otherwise known as Commander Zero, stormed Somoza's palace in Managua and held the national congress hostage for two days. Eventually, after being paid a substantial ransom and freeing political prisoners, they withdrew, but the country was in turmoil. And the following year, the Sandinistas forced Somoza out of power and set up their own Marxist–Socialist state. One of Arguello's brothers had died fighting for the Sandinistas, and in July 1979 when he stopped Rafael 'Bazooka' Limon in Madison Square Garden, Alexis caused a stir by carrying the Sandinista flag into the ring. The new leaders were unimpressed, however, and saw him as a protégé of the Somoza years. They confiscated his land, property and around $300,000 of his money. He immediately emigrated to Miami with his third wife and small son.

Earlier that year he had beaten Escalera in a thrilling rematch in Italy, and in November 1979 he stopped the popular Californian Bobby Chacon in seven rounds. The following January he overcame Ruben Castillo in round 11 in Tucson, Arizona. Castillo, who had not lost in 45 previous fights, said he could handle Arguello in terms of technique, but was astonished by his sheer strength.

His final defence at super-featherweight was a fifth-round stoppage of Filipino southpaw Rolando Navarette in San Juan in April 1980. He had not relinquished the WBC 130lb belt when he fought a non-title bout against British based Ugandan Cornelius Boza-Edwards, but had admitted he would have to move up to lightweight. Boza gave him a test before retiring after eight rounds.

Two months later he officially gave back the super-featherweight title and announced his intention to win a third championship. After he outpointed Mexican southpaw Jose Luis Ramirez and stopped Texan Robert Vasquez in three rounds, he travelled to London to challenge WBC lightweight champion Jim Watt at Wembley in June 1981. Watt had been a fine champion, but had lost the edge of hunger that made him into a world champ when past his 30th birthday. Arguello was too much for him, and the Scottish southpaw was soundly outpointed after being floored in round seven. But he finished the fight on his feet and fought proudly. It was a good fight, and surprisingly only the third time in his career Arguello had been forced to go the full 15 rounds.

'I have no complaints,' said Watt. 'I went out like a man, I didn't quit. He was a hard puncher, but I thought I could outsmart him ... my title's in good hands. I lost my crown to a great fighter and a gentleman.'

Arguello was to make four defences of the lightweight crown: Ray Mancini, himself a future champion, was stopped in round 14, Robert Elizondo knocked out in seven, James Busceme halted in eight and Andy Ganigan in five. Ganigan, however, had the rare satisfaction of putting Arguello down before he himself was knocked out.

By this time Arguello was trained by the great Eddie Futch, who said after the classy victory over Elizondo in Las Vegas in November 1981: 'Arguello is a consummate ring technician. No matter what style his opponent employs, Alexis can come up with an effective strategy to counter and win.'

The champion agreed. 'I have different styles for different fighters, and I always keep myself in top condition.'

Arguello wanted a fourth belt at 140lb, but it was not to be. He reached too high in Miami in November 1982 when he was worn down in the 14th round of a tremendous battle against Aaron Pryor, the wonderful 'Cincinnati Hawk'. He was exhausted and hurt and when South African referee Stanley Christodoulou stopped it, he slumped unconscious to the canvas. It was one of the fights of the decade, witnessed live by a crowd of 23,800 and by millions on television around the world.

In his poignant autobiography *The Flight Of The Hawk*, Pryor recalled how much beating Arguello meant to him. 'I stopped history from being made. Everybody wanted to witness and be a part of Alexis Arguello winning his fourth title ... What people didn't realise was that if Alexis Arguello lost that fight, he was still a three-time world champion. If I lost that fight, it would have been back to the ghetto, armed with a hair-net, plastic see-through gloves cooking up greasy fries and serving Big Macs.'

However, the HBO tape picked up a corner conversation in which Pryor's notorious trainer Panama Lewis was heard to ask for a black bottle containing his 'special mix'. Nobody found out what was in it, but during a fight, a man can only take plain water. Enough doubt was cast on the nature of Pryor's win for a rematch to become viable.

Arguello's 22nd and final world title bout was the return with Pryor in Las Vegas in September 1983. This time he was overpowered in 10 rounds. At the end he sat on the canvas, hurt and demoralised, almost accepting that he had reached too high. 'I've got nothing to prove,' he said. 'I didn't get up because I didn't want to risk my life.'

He retired, but then returned under manager Bill Miller in 1985. Sadly, he still needed the money, and he found he was also bored without boxing. Miller said: 'Since he was 15, he has always had somebody to tell him what to do, has had to train and fight. Now he doesn't know what to do. You can only go fishing so much ...'

But after a fourth-round win over Bill Costello in Reno in 1986, he was diagnosed as suffering from a heart problem. He retired, returned for a couple of fights in 1994, and then retired for good, accepting finally that he would only embarrass himself if he went on. By this time, he was financially sound. The Sandinistas had fallen, and much of his land had been returned to him by the new government.

CAREER STATISTICS

WBA featherweight champion 1974–77
WBC super-featherweight champion 1978–80
WBC lightweight champion 1981–83
Managua, Nicaragua, born 19 April 1952

1968
Nov 18 Israel Medina w ko 1 Managua
Dec 14 Alacran Espinosa w pts 4 Managua

1969
Jan 23 Burrito Martinez w ko 3 Managua
Apr 16 Alacran Espinosa l pts 6 Managua

1970
Jul 29 Carlos Huete w pts 8 Managua
Aug 12 Ricardo Donoso w ko 2 Managua
Sep 7 Marcelino Beckles w rsf 8 Managua
Oct 17 Mario Bojorge w ko 3 Managua
Nov 14 Jose Urbina w ko 1 Managua
Dec 5 Julio Morales w ko 3 Managua
Dec 19 Armando Figueroa w rsf 1 Managua

1971
Feb 12 Tony Quiroz w ko 6 Managua
Mar 13 Raton Hernandez w pts 10 Managua
Apr 17 Raton Hernandez w pts 10 Managua
May 1 Halcon Buitrago w ko 7 Managua
Jun 5 Kid Chapula w ko 1 Managua
Jun 26 Marcial Loyola w rsf 2 Managua
Jul 17 Hurricane Clay w rsf 5 Managua
Aug 14 Catalino Alvarado w ko 1 Managua
Sep 4 Rey Mendoza w ko 1 Managua
Oct 2 Hurricane Clay w pts 10 Managua
Nov 18 Vicente Worrel w ko 2 Managua

1972
Feb 8 Guillermo Barrera w ko 1 Managua
Apr 11 Tanguecito Gonzalez w ko 2 Managua
Jun 22 Jorge Reyes l rsf 6 Managua
Aug 16 Fernando Fernandez w ko 1 Managua
Sep 23 Jorge Benitez w ko 1 Managua
Nov 17 Memo Ortiz w ko 2 Managua
Dec 12 Rafael Gonzalez w rsf 7 Managua

1973
Mar 30 Fernando Fernandez w rsf 2 Managua
Apr 22 Magallo Lozado w pts 10 Managua
May 26 Kid Pascualito w ko 3 Managua
Jun 30 Octavio Gomez w ko 2 Managua
Aug 25 Nacho Lomeli w ko 1 Masaya
Oct 17 Sigfrido Rodriguez w rsf 9 Managua
Nov 27 Jose Legra w ko 1 Masaya

1974
Jan 8 Raul Martinez w ko 1 Managua
Feb 16 Ernesto Marcel l pts 15 Panama City
(WBA featherweight title)
Apr 27 Enrique Garcia w ko 3 Masaya
May 20 Art Hafey w ko 5 Masaya
Aug 29 Oscar Aparicio w pts 12 Masaya
(Central American featherweight title)
Sep 21 Otoniel Martinez w ko 1 Masaya
Nov 23 Ruben Olivares w ko 13 Los Angeles
(WBA featherweight title)

1975
Feb 8 Oscar Aparicio w pts 10 San Salvador
Mar 15 Leonel Hernandez w rsf 8 Caracas
(WBA featherweight title)
May 31 Rigoberto Riasco w rsf 2 Granada
(WBA featherweight title)
Jul 18 Rosalio Muro w rsf 2 San Francisco
Oct 12 Royal Kobayashi w ko 5 Tokyo
(WBA featherweight title)
Dec 20 Saul Montano w ko 3 Managua

1976
Feb 1 Jose Torres w pts 10 Mexicali
Apr 10 Modesto Concepcion w ko 2 Managua

Jun 19 Salvador Torres w ko 3 Los Angeles
(WBA featherweight title)

1977

Feb 19 Godfrey Stevens w ko 2 Managua
May 14 Alberto Herrera w ko 1 Managua
Jun 20: Relinquished WBA featherweight title.
Jun 22 Cocoa Sanchez w rsf 4 New York
Aug 3 Jose Fernandez w rsf 1 New York
Aug 27 Ben Ortiz w pts 10 San Juan
Sep 29 Jerome Artis w rsf 2 New York
Dec 18 Enrique Solis w ko 5 Managua

1978

Jan 28 Alfredo Escalera w rsf 13 Bayamon
(WBC super-featherweight title)
Mar 25 Mario Mendez w rsf 3 Las Vegas
Apr 29 Rey Tam w rsf 5 Los Angeles
(WBC super-featherweight title)
Jun 3 Diego Alcala w ko 1 San Juan
(WBC super-featherweight title)
Jul 26 Vilomar Fernandez l pts 10 New York
Nov 10 Arturo Leon w pts 15 Las Vegas
(WBC super-featherweight title)

1979

Feb 4 Alfredo Escalera w ko 13 Rimini
(WBC super-featherweight title)
Jul 8 Rafael Limon w rsf 11 New York
(WBC super-featherweight title)
Nov 16 Bobby Chacon w rsf 7 Los Angeles
(WBC super-featherweight title)

1980

Jan 20 Ruben Castillo w rsf 11 Tucson
(WBC super-featherweight title)
Mar 31 Gerald Hayes w pts 10 Las Vegas
Apr 27 Rolando Navarette w rsf 5 San Juan
(WBC super-featherweight title)
Aug 9 Cornelius Boza-Edwards w rsf 8 Atlantic City
Oct: Relinquished WBC super-featherweight title.
Nov 14 Jose Luis Ramirez w pts 10 Miami

1981

Feb 7 Robert Vasquez w rsf 3 Miami
Jun 20 Jim Watt w pts 15 London
(WBC lightweight title)
Oct 3 Ray Mancini w rsf 14 Atlantic City
(WBC lightweight title)
Nov 21 Roberto Elizondo w ko 7 Las Vegas
(WBC lightweight title)

1982

Feb 13 James Busceme w rsf 6 Beaumont
(WBC lightweight title)
May 22 Andrew Ganigan w ko 5 Las Vegas
(WBC lightweight title)
Jul 31 Kevin Rooney w ko 2 Atlantic City
Nov 12 Aaron Pryor l rsf 14 Miami
(WBA light-welterweight title)

1983

Feb: Relinquished WBC lightweight title.
Feb 26 Vicente Fernandez w pts 10 San Antonio
Apr 24 Claude Noel w rsf 3 Atlantic City
Sep 9 Aaron Pryor l ko 10 Las Vegas
(WBA light-welterweight title)

1984 inactive

1985

Oct 25 Pat Jefferson w rsf 5 Anchorage

1986

Feb 9 Bill Costello w rsf 4 Reno

1987-93 inactive

1994

Aug 27 Jorge Palomares w pts 10 Miami

1995

Jan 21 Scott Walker l pts 10 Las Vegas

Fights 88 Won 80 Lost 8

AARON PRYOR

THE HAWK

While the most casual boxing fans will know of the deeds of multi-millionaire genius Sugar Ray Leonard, many will have forgotten his friend and contemporary Aaron Pryor. But Pryor had an equally impressive boxing record, and it would be difficult to show that one was a greater boxer than the other. Coincidentally both fought after retiring with detached retinas, but in Pryor's case drugs cut short his career and for a while threatened to destroy or even end his life.

Tragedy surrounded Aaron Pryor from the day of his birth on 20 October 1955, in the Avondale district of Cincinnati, Ohio. His mother, Sara Shelery, gave birth to seven children, five of whom had different fathers. She was a beautiful, slim, half-black, half-Japanese woman, who had had a tough life herself. Her own mother had been shot and killed by a boyfriend when she was seven. In adult life she was an alcoholic. According to Aaron, she was the one from whom he obtained his fighting ability. Only 135lb, she readily laid out boyfriends who upset her with a single punch.

When Aaron was born, Ted Pryor was the man of the household, hence Aaron's name, but his real father was Ike Graves, the husband of Sara's best friend. Graves did not know of his relationship to Aaron until it was revealed to him when Aaron was 16. This caused an argument between him and his wife during which Ike Graves pulled a pistol and accidentally shot in the back his son Ronnie (thus Aaron's half-brother) who was trying to protect his mother. Ronnie was paralysed for life. Ike was imprisoned for three years.

Aaron was the fifth of the seven children. The family lived on welfare, and did comparatively well, because there was always a man in the house who was earning. None of the children, except Aaron, made much of themselves, and Aaron said in his autobiography that they were always a source of anger and resentment to him. He described their future occupations as 'drinking, drugging, stealing, robbing and killing'.

Aaron himself was sexually assaulted by a Baptist minister when he was seven, which made him an object of ridicule by his schoolmates. He was a slow learner, and put into a class for the handicapped. He traces his fighting career from the day he was beaten up by a bigger boy and his mother sent him and Lorenzo back out to beat up the other boy, which they did.

Aaron was too small, light and slow to get on basketball, football or athletics teams at school, but one day saw some boys out running and discovered that they were training for boxing. He went to the Emanuel Community Center gym and was immediately hooked on the sport. He was 13. Soon he was practically living at the gym. He found he was a natural boxer from the start. After three months he was entering competitions. By 15 he was a Cincinnati Golden Gloves champion.

His mother then decided to marry a man who earned enough to allow the family to move to a better district. Aaron cried because he would have to leave his gym. Eventually, he was left behind to stay with a boxing friend, Roosevelt Green, on the promise that he would attend school. Soon, he was so much around the gym that the resident trainer, Phil Smith, a former pro boxer, gave him a key. He set a bed in the back, and was in his element.

Aaron did not renege on his promise to go to school, and he also earned some cash working on a fruit stand owned by another ex-boxer, Tony La Rosa. La Rosa's brother, Buddy, who built up an empire of pizza houses, would later become Pryor's manager. At the fruit stall, Aaron found a girl friend, Debbie Harris, who lived with her schoolteacher mother. Soon Aaron was sleeping occasionally at their house. They were both still at school when their son, Antoine, was born on 18 February 1973. Soon afterwards they were engaged and lived together openly.

At 16, Pryor entered the National Golden Gloves competition, but lost to the national champion, Norman Goins, who represented the USA in the 1972 Olympics. When the Olympics team turned pro, Pryor found himself a leading amateur, representing his country 21 times (with only one defeat) in many parts of the world, including the USSR. Returning from this trip he found his fiancée, Debbie, at his sister's house with another man. He snatched back his engagement ring and fled, crying.

Soon Aaron had a new regular girl friend in 16-year-old Carol Clarke, whom he met at school. They were steady friends till 1976, when they married on 18 December. By then Aaron had become the first in his family to get his high school degree (sister Barbara was to follow). He had also failed again to get into the Olympic team, losing twice in the trials finals to Howard Davis, decisions which he and Rollie Schwarz, the Olympic coach, thought politically motivated, Davis being a clean-cut all-American kid. Meanwhile Aaron's mother had emptied a pistol of six bullets at her new provider, who lived but was partially paralysed.

With a superb amateur record of 204 wins in 220 fights, it was time for Aaron to think about turning pro. Pryor made his debut as a lightweight at Cincinnati Convention Center on 12 November 1976, knocking out Larry Smith in the second round. He was paid $200, and on the strength of being a professional married Carol. On 16 June 1978

Carol gave birth to Aaron junior, Pryor's second son. But she confessed the marriage was becoming strained.

Early in 1979 Aaron became dissatisfied with trainer Jimmy Brown, who was old and infirm, and persuaded La Rosa that he should 'let him go'. Assistant trainer Frankie Sims claimed this was a big mistake, as Brown's wisdom had helped Pryor considerably, but he went, and was replaced by Carlos 'Panama' Lewis, who had been in Roberto Duran's corner. Aaron beat Norman Goins, his first conqueror as an amateur, and followed up with several other impressive wins which marched him up to No. 5 in the rankings by the end of 1979.

By now Aaron was also working in a men's clothing store, and one day in walked Theresa Adams with her mother. Theresa was black, but pale, a beauty who had been a bunny girl at the Cincinnati Playboy Club, and was at the time comfortably off working for a cosmetics company. Aaron was immediately smitten, and she apparently reciprocated. Six years older, much more intelligent and worldly-wise, she allegedly manipulated Pryor and according to Buddy La Rosa played a big part in his downfall.

Having won 24 contests, 22 inside the distance, Pryor contacted Harold Smith, a promoter at one time connected with Ali. He wanted a title fight. Smith offered a title challenge against Antonio Cervantes of Colombia, the WBA light-welterweight champion at the Cincinnati Riverfront Coliseum. Pryor says he was paid $50,000 in cash in a briefcase, and the purse offer was also $50,000. Pryor jumped at the chance, even though it meant stepping up a division. He was determined to win. When the fight arrived on 2 August 1980, his non-stop attack paid off with a fourth round knockout.

Pryor was now world champion, and rich. But he couldn't handle either situation. At the celebration afterwards he took no trouble to conceal his relationship with Theresa, which was the last straw for his wife Carol, who left him. Suddenly, too, Pryor acquired an entourage of hangers-on. Unfortunately his new friends were not the best people for him. His two new bodyguards were leading drug dealers, both of whom were eventually to pick up long jail sentences.

As a fighter at this time Pryor was unbeatable. He was strong, fast, aggressive and an awesome puncher. He also had an iron chin. He was called 'The Hawk'. When he became champion he called his entourage 'The Hawk Troopers'. They wore a cap with a hawk on it and he swore them in while they raised their right hands.

One person who surprisingly failed to manipulate him, at least not totally, was Don King. When promoter Harold Smith was sent to prison for a spectacular embezzlement of $21 million from the Wells Fargo Bank, Pryor signed a contract with Don King to promote four title defences. Pryor received $100,000 plus his purses, of about $150,000 each. King's chosen opponents were all his own fighters, and good ones. It was clear that King really wanted to take Pryor's title into his stable. When King tried to renew the contract, Pryor resisted all King's legal manoeuvrings and threats, and managed to free himself of the entanglement.

Before that there'd been another shooting. Theresa had disagreed with his going out one night, and fired at him, the bullet going through his left forearm, with which he was trying to protect himself, and into his chest, where it lodged only an inch from his heart. While recovering he declined to press charges against Theresa, who smartly checked into a mental institution for a while until things quietened down. She then began secretly phoning Pryor, who was so besotted that he took her back. Pryor tried to get out of his contract with La Rosa and, after legal battles, the contract was renegotiated but there was now constant bitterness from Pryor. He also forced trainer Frankie Sims to cut his percentage by half, but still made things so unpleasant for Sims that he walked out altogether.

Theresa Adams gradually assumed control of Pryor's affairs. She helped form his companies, Aaron Pryor Inc. and Hawk Productions. All was building up for 'The Battle of the Champions', a challenge from Alexis Arguello of Nicaragua. Arguello was a master boxer, three years older than Pryor, who had won world titles at three different weights: feather, super-feather and lightweight. He was now moving up to light-welter in a bid to become the first man to win a world title at four weights. He was an intelligent, soft-spoken, well-mannered boxer, an image the press contrasted with the wild life of Pryor and his family. Arguello was the 11–5 favourite.

The contest, at the Miami Orange Bowl before 23,800 spectators and millions of TV viewers worldwide, was a classic. It was fought at a whirlwind pace, with Pryor throwing 130 punches in the first round alone. Arguello landed two huge punches in the second round which would have knocked out anybody else, but he was himself cut over the eye in the sixth. Although Arguello slowed, he shook Pryor again in the 13th. Before the 14th Panama Lewis gave Pryor something from a black bottle that later was to cause much controversy. Pryor launched a terrific assault in the 14th which left Arguello helpless on the ropes and the referee, Stanley Christodoulou, stopped it. Later Arguello was unconscious for several minutes. Pryor was still champion after an outstanding fight.

When it became known that for some reason Pryor escaped giving a urine sample after the fight, there was much press speculation about the contents of the black bottle. Peppermint Schnapps, which cools the throat, was the corner's answer, but many wondered. Pryor's purse was $1.6 million, and he and Theresa got married and bought a big house in fashionable Clifton, Cincinnati, but very soon moved to Miami. Pryor amicably bought legal custody of his two sons from their mothers and signed a new promotional contract with actor Sylvester Stallone's company.

Dan Duva won the right to promote Pryor's return with Arguello, which was set for 10 September 1983 at Las Vegas. Pryor went to training camp at Lake Tahoe and wouldn't allow Theresa to go with him. She stormed from the apartment and went to drown her sorrows with Sylvester Stallone in Malibu for a fortnight. Pryor believed the rumours circulating that they were having an affair. A couple of weeks before the fight, Pryor was served divorce papers, and a restraining order preventing him from approaching Theresa. She eventually got a divorce with a $500,000 settlement.

Pryor suffered eye trouble in training; a detached retina was diagnosed. The problem was concealed and the return contest with Arguello was another classic, with severe blows exchanged for 10 rounds. It was a question of who would yield, and the answer was Arguello. In December, without fighting again, Pryor announced his retirement because of his eye trouble. He had won all his 34 contests, nine for the world title, and all but two inside the distance.

After beating Arguello, Pryor went back to Miami to try to make it up with Theresa, despite the restraining order. He found her and a woman friend smoking crack cocaine, and was invited to join in. Within weeks he was an addict, spending hundreds of dollars a day on cocaine. After six months he was caught in possession of drugs, but lawyers got him off the charge.

Pryor, at 28, with a suspect eye and a serious drug problem, was now washed-up as a fighter but, because he was using money so fast, he made a comeback. He had given up the WBA title, of course, but was now proclaimed IBF champion, outpointing his first challenger, Nicky Furlano of Canada, in Toronto.

Buddy La Rosa arranged another defence, hoping he would pull himself together. It was at the Sands Hotel, Atlantic City, which was part-owned by Sylvester Stallone, who still had Pryor under contract. Challenger Gary Hinton was not in Pryor's class, but such was Pryor's physical condition that he took a lot of punishment and won only by a split decision. Pryor wept at the knowledge he was finished and bought his contract back from Stallone. Then *Sports Illustrated* interviewed him, and the whole world knew he was a hopeless drug addict. He retired again.

Aaron made another boxing comeback nearly two-and-a-half years after the travesty of the match with Hinton. Buddy La Rosa refused to have anything to do with the project but Pryor nevertheless fought Bobby Joe Young, a journeyman welterweight with 29 wins and five defeats. Aaron was counted out in the seventh while on his feet but inexplicably making the sign of the cross. He claimed it was a manifestation of the influence of the drugs he was taking. He fought again 15 months later and won, for a purse of $2,000.

In 1990 Aaron took a third wife, Jeannie Ellis, who already had three girls and a nice home, but she couldn't keep him off the drugs, and the marriage lasted less than a year. A month after the wedding he fought a friend, Darryl Jones, and won, admitting that he 'used' immediately afterwards, and he had his last contest, another win, in December 1990. In 1991 he was arrested for drug trafficking and sentenced to six months in prison. He served nearly four. A white girl friend from rehabilitation classes, Frankie Wagner, moved in with him. Soon, much to Aaron's despair, she was on crack cocaine too. Before long Aaron was begging from acquaintances and singing in the street for money for drugs.

In April 1993 Aaron was smoking crack in the doorway of an old abandoned crack house in Cincinnati when he collapsed with severe stomach pains. He was incoherent when they got him to Bethesda Hospital, where they operated for bleeding ulcers. He was so ill his weight dropped to 100lb, and he nearly died. On his release, Aaron turned to the Church. He got jobs training kids how to box, and currently makes $150 or so per week from this. In 1994 he was ordained as a deacon in the New Friendship Church in Avondale. He lectures in schools about the horrors of drugs and talks to addicts. He is a member of Narcotics Anonymous. He lives with his sister, and is earning the respect he is due as one of the greatest boxers ever. He was inducted into the International Boxing Hall of Fame in 1996. In 1997 he said: 'I lost everything but the most important thing – my life'.

CAREER STATISTICS

WBA light-welterweight champion 1980-83
IBF light-welterweight champion 1984-85
Cincinnati, Ohio, born 20 October 1955

1976
Nov 12 Larry Smith w rsf 2 Cincinnati
1977
Feb 1 Larry Moore w rsf 4 Cincinnati
Feb 24 Harvey Wilson w ko 1 Cincinnati
Mar 12 Nicky Wills w ko 1 Lincoln Hts.
Mar 26 Isaac Vega w ko 2 Cincinnati
May 7 Jose Resto w pts 8 Cincinnati
Sep 3 Melvin Young w ko 4 Covington
Oct 7 Johnny Summerhays w pts 8 Cincinnati
Nov 4 Angel Citron w ko 3 Cincinnati
1978
Jan 16 Robert Tijernia w ko 2 Cincinnati
Mar 1 Ron Pettigrew w rsf 5 Dayton
Mar 10 Alfred Franklin w rsf 3 Cincinnati
May 3 Scotty Foreman w rsf 6 Miami
Jul 18 Marion Thomas w ko 8 Dayton
1979
Mar 16 Johnny Copeland w ko 7 Cincinnati
Apr 13 Norman Goins w ko 9 Cincinnati
Apr 27 Freddie Harris w ko 3 Dayton
May 11 Al Ford w rsf 4 Cincinnati
Jun 23 Jose Fernandez w ko 1 Cincinnati
Oct 20 Alfonso Frazer w rsf 5 Cincinnati
1980
Feb 24 Juan Garcia w ko 1 Las Vegas
Mar 16 Julio Valdez w rsf 4 Miami
Apr 13 Leonidas Asprilla w rsf 10 Kansas City
Jun 20 Carl Crowley w ko 1 Cincinnati
Aug 2 Antonio Cervantes w ko 4 Cincinnati (WBA light-welterweight title)
Nov 1 Danny Myers w rsf 3 Dayton
Nov 22 Gaetan Hart w rsf 6 Cincinnati (WBA light-welterweight title)
1981
Jun 27 Lennox Blackmoore w rsf 2 Las Vegas (WBA light-welterweight title)
Nov 14 Dujuan Johnson w rsf 7 Cleveland (WBA light-welterweight title)
1982
Mar 21 Miguel Montilla w rsf 12 Atlantic City (WBA light-welterweight title)
Jul 4 Akio Kameda w rsf 6 Cincinnati (WBA light-welterweight title)
Nov 12 Alexis Arguello w rsf 14 Miami (WBA light-welterweight title)
1983
Apr 2 Sang-hyun Kim w rsf 3 Atlantic City (WBA light-welterweight title)
Sep 9 Alexis Arguello w ko 10 Las Vegas (WBA light-welterweight title)
Dec: Relinquished WBA title.
1984
Jan: Proclaimed IBF champion.
Jun 22 Nicky Furlano w pts 15 Toronto (IBF light-welterweight title)
1985
Mar 2 Gary Hinton w pts 15 Atlantic City (IBF light-welterweight title)
Dec: Stripped of IBF title.
1986 inactive
1987
Aug 8 Bobby Young l ko 7 Sunrise, Florida
1988
Dec 15 Herminio Morales w ko 3 Rochester
1989 inactive
1990
May 16 Daryl Jones w ko 3 Madison, Wisconsin
Dec 4 Roger Choate w rsf 7 Oklahoma

Fights 40 Won 39 Lost 1

LARRY HOLMES

THE BLACK CLOUD

Larry Holmes was a throwback to the craftsmen of the 1920s and 1930s, a ring general who saw boxing as a job as well as an art form. He was proud – when he felt he had been badly treated, he could be fiercely indignant – but was pragmatic enough to see boxing for what it was: a way of making a good life for those who depended on him. He said once: 'Why do you think I'm fighting? The glory? You show me a man says he ain't fighting for money, I'll show you a fool ...'

At the end of his 25-year career, he accepted what seemed to some a pointless exercise in Denmark against a lumbering, but unbeaten local ticket seller, Brian Nielsen. 'It's another half a million dollars to feather the nest,' he explained.

Holmes was born in Cuthbert, Georgia, a small town close to the Alabama border, on 3 November 1949. One of 12 children of a cotton picker, he was six when the family moved north to Easton, Pennsylvania. At 13 he was shining shoes for a living. He washed cars, swept floors, took whatever manual jobs were going, and at 21, already a father of two, he walked into a boxing gym for the first time. His life changed forever.

His natural ability was quickly discovered, but he was still woefully inexperienced when he reached the 1972 Olympic trials finals. Overawed by the occasion, he was disqualified for not trying against hot favourite Duane Bobick, and subsequently ignored by the top professional promoters. After 19 wins in 22 amateur bouts, he decided there was no further point in playing the circuit – he signed pro terms with his old trainer and friend, Ernie Butler. By then a lorry driver, a four-round points win over Rodell Dupree at Scranton brought him $63. Of that, $10 went into a newly opened bank account. The die was cast.

Eventually, Don King signed him on the recommendation of trainer Richie Giachetti, and by 1974 he was working as Muhammad Ali's sparring partner. Although he gained some exposure by fighting on Ali undercards, his relationship with King was often forthright. At one point he almost retired, but they stayed together and in June 1978 he was matched with Ken Norton for the World Boxing Council heavyweight title.

Norton had been awarded the championship when Leon Spinks refused to defend against him and instead signed for a rematch with Ali. Boxing tradition says a title can only be won and lost in the ring, and Norton's was considered a cardboard crown. Nevertheless, before a sellout crowd at Caesars Palace, Las Vegas, Norton and Holmes staged one of the finest title fights in heavyweight history. Holmes, known as 'Black Cloud' and then 'The Easton Assassin', won by the closest of split decisions.

Ali beat Spinks but then retired, which left the way open for Holmes to be regarded as the best heavyweight in the world. He knocked out Alfredo Evangelista, Uruguayan born and based in Spain, in seven one-sided rounds. While the result was predictable, Holmes was impressive. By now, he had learned his trade. Like all the great heavyweight champions, he had a wonderful jab, upon which everything else was built.

Next he demolished Puerto Rican outsider Osvaldo 'Jaws' Ocasio in seven rounds, knocking him down four times, and then came through a surprisingly hard test against a muscular but unproven Texan named Mike Weaver, who had lost eight of his 27 fights. Weaver shook and floored Holmes in the 10th round, but the champion responded magnificently. He scored a knockdown in round 11, and finished the fight with an unanswered barrage of blows in the 12th.

Earnie Shavers was one of the biggest single-punch hitters the world has ever seen. He wasn't quick, and his skills were ordinary, but he could hurt with every shot. Fighting him took something out of a man. Holmes had outpointed him in a good fight over 12 rounds to earn his chance with Norton, and gave him a rematch for the WBC title in Las Vegas in September 1979.

Holmes built up a big points lead, but was floored heavily by Shavers' right hand in round seven. His legs betrayed him, his senses were foggy, but somehow he managed to cling on and fiddle his way through to the bell. He recovered, and took over. Shavers wouldn't quit, but could not land cleanly again. By the 11th round he had nothing left and referee Davey Pearl stopped it.

By now everyone knew Holmes was the best heavyweight in the world. John Tate had won the WBA belt when Ali retired, but lost it to Weaver, whom Holmes had already beaten.

In February 1980, and by now 30 years old, Holmes brushed aside a mediocre, uncertain Italian named Lorenzo Zanon in six rounds without moving into top gear. Then Leroy Jones, a skilful but fat contender from Denver, was outclassed in eight. Scott LeDoux, a game but modestly skilled slugger from Minnesota, was stopped in pain in round seven. His eyelid had folded under his eyeball, but he was still on his feet, taking the punches, when it was called off.

And then the unthinkable happened: Muhammad Ali returned to the ring and demanded to fight Holmes. Inevitably, for all the misgivings about Ali's age and the increasing rumours about his health, the match was made for Caesars Palace in October 1980. It was one of the most depressing episodes in boxing's chequered history, and Holmes, although he had to take the fight, knew he could gain nothing from it beyond the payday. The great man was 38 years old and using dye to hide the grey in his hair. Unknown to everyone outside his closest aides, he was also being prescribed weight-reducing drugs. Ali talked of conjuring a miracle, but that's what a win for him would have been. He had no more chance, probably less, than Evangelista, Zanon, Jones and LeDoux had of taking Larry's title belt.

From the start Holmes thudded his jabs into Ali's face. He barely took a worthwhile punch in reply, holding back when he could have opened up, attempting to spare his old employer humiliation. After 10 rounds, Ali was pulled out by trainer Angelo Dundee. It was a sad, almost pointless night.

Thirty years earlier, Ezzard Charles had given Joe Louis a similar pounding, and had never been given proper respect because he followed a legend. And Holmes had similar problems because he not only followed Ali, but Joe Frazier and George Foreman. These were all exceptional heavyweights, and for long spells it seemed Holmes was king of a second rate division. His challengers seemed poor imitations of the giants of such a short time ago.

What could he do but go on earning, accumulating defences against whoever he was asked to fight? In April 1981, he outboxed a tough Jamaican, Trevor Berbick, who was to have the dubious honour of becoming the man to end Ali's career in the Bahamas late that year. Berbick was solid, but unexceptional.

By 1981, Leon Spinks was in freefall. The former Olympic light-heavyweight gold medallist had beaten Ali in his eighth professional fight, an achievement that was scarcely believable at the time. But he had been utterly unable to cope with his sudden elevation, lost to Ali in the return, and had been knocked out in one by Gerrie Coetzee from South Africa. He did go through four fights unbeaten in 1980, and that was enough for him to be given a shot at Holmes. Obviously, he claimed to have put the bad times behind him, and at 27 was certainly young enough to have a few more years at the top.

However, poor Spinks met a Holmes who was at his most ruthless. It was all over by round three, and Spinks drifted back into No Man's Land.

Holmes' vulnerability to a right hand over the top surfaced again in his next defence, his eleventh, when unheralded Renaldo Snipes connected with his chin in the seventh. The champion went down heavily, and looked a beaten man. He got up, tottered away from referee Rudy Ortega and bought himself a few seconds. Some officials would have stopped it, but Ortega held Snipes back until the champion was facing the right way. At the bell, Holmes was still on his feet, but wobbling.

His fitness brought him round, and Snipes, like Weaver and Shavers before him, had missed his chance. When Holmes hurt Snipes in round 11, the fight was stopped to the anguish of the challenger and his corner, who rightly pointed out that the champion had been given every chance to recover from a far worse plight four rounds earlier. They had a point.

Gerry Cooney was a big, heavy-handed, exciting New Yorker with a dangerous left hook. He was also white, which made him a marketing dream. A one-round demolition of Ken Norton had shoved him into the limelight, and there were those who believed he was good enough to take out a champion who was by now living in a luxury, 11-bed-roomed house in Easton with his wife Diane and their children. Some speculated that he might be losing the hunger.

However, behind the scenes Cooney's life was in turmoil and mentally he was uncertain. Holmes, far prouder and more professional than his critics suspected, was in top shape. 'If I was ninety years old, Cooney couldn't beat me,' he said. And he was right. Cooney fought well, but by the 13th had nothing left. His trainer, Victor Valle, ran into the ring too soon, and officially it was announced as a disqualification, although Mills Lane was stopping it anyway. Record books regard it as a stoppage.

That was Holmes' last great performance as heavyweight champion, although he stayed on top for three more years. He outpointed the absorbent, eccentric Randall 'Tex' Cobb over 15 horribly one-sided rounds, after which commentator Howard Cosell quit in disgust. Cobb said: 'I can do my sport no greater service than this!' At the final bell, he had also laughed at Holmes: 'Let's party!'

Lucien Rodriguez of France and the young Tim Witherspoon also lasted the distance – by now cut to 12 rounds – and hopelessly outclassed Scott Frank was beaten in five. The WBC, however, refused to sanction a defence against Marvis Frazier, Joe's son, in Las Vegas in November 1983. Holmes took the fight anyway, split from the WBC and after demolishing Frazier in the first round, linked up with the International Boxing Federation, which had been formed the previous year by American administrator Bobby Lee, who had walked out on the WBA.

Without Holmes, the IBF might well have failed. But the heavyweight champion brought TV interest, and established them. In the spring of 1984, Gerrie Coetzee was WBA champ, and Witherspoon beat Greg Page for the vacant WBC belt.

Holmes stopped new generation contenders James 'Bonecrusher' Smith and David Bey, in 12 and 10 rounds respectively, but had unexpected trouble when he had to go the full 15 to outpoint Carl 'The Truth' Williams in Reno, Nevada. Holmes finished with one eye shut. 'The Truth Hurts' was the verdict British trade paper *Boxing News*.

By now he was on 48 consecutive wins. One more would equal Rocky Marciano's record for a heavyweight champion. But on 22 September 1985, he lost a disputed points verdict to light-heavyweight champion Michael Spinks. Marciano's family had attended the fight to respect Holmes' achievement, but were then insulted at the post-fight press conference when the deposed champ said bitterly: 'Rocky Marciano couldn't have carried my jockstrap ...' It was a bad mistake, for which he apologised within 24 hours, but the damage was done.

A rematch with Spinks seven months later ended similarly, and this time Holmes grumbled: 'The judges can kiss me where the sun don't shine ...'

By then he had almost $100 million in the bank, and owned a hotel, restaurants, and other properties in Easton. However, he felt the fortune needed a little more replenishment, and when offered a payday of almost $3 million to meet the new, rampaging star, Mike Tyson, in Atlantic City in January 1988, he took it. It made sense financially, but in no other way. Tyson knocked him out brutally in the fourth.

The financial crash which ushered in the 1990s diminished his bank balance to the point where he felt it prudent to bolster it by boxing again. George Foreman had proved there was still a market for senior citizens, and Holmes also enjoyed himself against men who were babies when he began his career.

It was a success, too. Tyson's star had already faded, and Evander Holyfield was only just establishing his heavyweight reputation. Holmes proved he still had class when he outpointed Ray Mercer, and then picked up an extraordinary $7 million to challenge Holyfield in Las Vegas in June 1992. At the end the 42-year-old grandfather was still on his feet, and although outpointed, far from disgraced.

He had enjoyed it enough to go on, and in April 1995 had one last title fling when he took WBC champion Oliver McCall to a points decision. He lost, but it was close.

He continued to pick up paydays here and there into 1997, always ready to teach a youngster a trick or two. Even when he said he had finally retired, nobody could be sure he wouldn't turn out to feather his nest just one more time.

CAREER STATISTICS

WBC heavyweight champion 1978-84
IBF heavyweight champion 1984-85
Easton, Pennsylvania, born Cuthbert, Georgia, 3 November 1949

1973

Mar 21 Rodell Dupree w pts 4 Scranton
May 2 Art Savage w rsf 3 Scranton
Jun 20 Curtis Whitner w ko 1 Scranton
Aug 22 Don Branch w pts 6 Scranton
Sep 10 Bob Bozic w pts 6 New York
Nov 14 Jerry Judge w pts 6 Scranton
Nov 28 Kevin Isaac w rsf 3 Cleveland

1974

Apr 24 Howard Darlington w rsf 4 Scranton
May 29 Bob Mashburn w rsf 7 Scranton
Dec 11 Joe Hathaway w rsf 1 Scranton

1975

Mar 24 Charley Green w ko 2 Cleveland
Apr 10 Oliver Wright w rsf 3 Honolulu
Apr 26 Robert Yarborough w ko 3 Toronto
May 16 Ernie Smith w ko 3 Las Vegas
Aug 16 Obie English w rsf 7 Scranton
Aug 26 Charlie James w pts 10 Honolulu
Oct 1 Rodney Bobick w rsf 6 Manila
Dec 9 Leon Shaw w ko 1 Washington DC
Dec 20 Billy Joiner w rsf 3 San Juan

1976

Jan 29 Joe Gholston w rsf 8 Easton
Apr 5 Fred Askew w rsf 2 Landover
Apr 30 Roy Williams w pts 10 Landover

1977

Jan 16 Tom Prater w pts 8 Pensacola
Mar 17 Horacio Robinson w rsf 5 San Juan
Sep 14 Sanford Houpe w rsf 7 Las Vegas
Nov 5 Ibar Arrington w rsf 10 Las Vegas

1978

Mar 25 Earnie Shavers w pts 12 Las Vegas
Jun 9 Ken Norton w pts 15 Las Vegas *(WBC heavyweight title)*
Nov 10 Alfredo Evangelista w ko 7 Las Vegas *(WBC heavyweight title)*

1979

Mar 23 Osvaldo Ocasio w rsf 7 Las Vegas *(WBC heavyweight title)*
Jun 22 Mike Weaver w rsf 12 New York

(*WBC heavyweight title)*
Sep 28 Earnie Shavers w rsf 11 Las Vegas
(*WBC heavyweight title)*
1980
Feb 3 Lorenzo Zanon w ko 6 Las Vegas
(*WBC heavyweight title)*
Mar 31 Leroy Jones w rsf 8 Las Vegas
(*WBC heavyweight title)*
Jul 7 Scott LeDoux w rsf 7 Bloomington
(*WBC heavyweight title)*
Oct 2 Muhammad Ali w rtd 10 Las Vegas
(*WBC heavyweight title)*
1981
Apr 11 Trevor Berbick w pts 15 Las Vegas
(*WBC heavyweight title)*
Jun 12 Leon Spinks w rsf 3 Detroit
(*WBC heavyweight title)*
Nov 6 Renaldo Snipes w rsf 11 Pittsburgh
(*WBC heavyweight title)*
1982
Jun 11 Gerry Cooney w rsf 13 Las Vegas
(*WBC heavyweight title)*
Nov 26 Randall Cobb w pts 15 Houston
(*WBC heavyweight title)*
1983
Mar 27 Lucien Rodriguez w pts 12 Scranton
(*WBC heavyweight title)*
May 20 Tim Witherspoon w pts 12 Las Vegas
(*WBC heavyweight title)*
Sep 10 Scott Frank w rsf 5 Atlantic City
(*WBC heavyweight title)*
Nov 25 Marvis Frazier w rsf 1 Las Vegas
Relinquished WBC heavyweight title.
1984
Proclaimed IBF heavyweight champion.
Nov 9 James Smith w rsf 12 Las Vegas
(*IBF heavyweight title)*
1985
Mar 15 David Bey w rsf 10 Las Vegas
(*IBF heavyweight title)*
May 20 Carl Williams w pts 15 Reno
(*IBF heavyweight title)*
Sep 22 Michael Spinks l pts 15 Las Vegas
(*IBF heavyweight title)*
1986
Apr 19 Michael Spinks l pts 15 Las Vegas
(*IBF heavyweight title)*
1987 Inactive
1988
Jan 22 Mike Tyson l rsf 4 Atlantic City
(*World heavyweight title)*
1989-90 inactive
1991
Apr 7 Tim Anderson w rsf 1 Miami
Aug 13 Eddie Gonzales w pts 10 Tampa
Aug 24 Michael Greer w ko 4 Honolulu
Sep 17 Art Card w pts 10 Orlando
Nov 12 Jamie Howe w rsf 1 Jacksonville
1992
Feb 7 Ray Mercer w pts 12 Atlantic City
Jun 19 Evander Holyfield l pts 12 Las Vegas
(*World heavyweight title)*
1993
Jan 5 Everett Martin w pts 10 Biloxi
Mar 9 Rocky Pepeli w rsf 5 Bay St Louis
Apr 13 Ken Lakusta w rsf 7 Bay St Louis
May 18 Paul Poirier w rsf 6 Bay St Louis
Sep 28 Jose Ribalta w pts 10 Bay St Louis
1994
Mar 8 Garing Lane w pts 10 Mashantucket, Ct.
Aug 9 Jesse Ferguson w pts 10 Prior Lake, Mn
1995
Apr 8 Oliver McCall l pts 12 Las Vegas
(*WBC heavyweight title)*
Sep 19 Ed Donaldson w pts 10 Bay St Louis
1996
Jan 9 Curt Shepard w ko 4 Galveston, Tx.
Apr 16 Quinn Navare w pts 10 Bay St Louis
Jun 16 Anthony Willis w ko 8 Bay St Louis
1997
Jan 24 Brian Nielsen l pts 12 Copenhagen
Jul 29 Maurice Harris w pts 10 New York

Fights 72 Won 66 Lost 6

BARRY McGUIGAN

THE CLONES CYCLONE

For three exciting years Barry McGuigan provided boxing fans of Great Britain and both halves of Ireland with some of the greatest thrills of their lives. He seemed to march from one dazzling win to the next in an unstoppable surge towards the world featherweight championship. A series of exciting nights in the electric atmosphere of the King's Hall, Belfast, led to the great title-winning victory over Eusebio Pedroza at Queen's Park Rangers football stadium in London. For a while McGuigan made the warring factions in Ireland forget their despairs as universal support swept him to the top. It all ended prematurely with a venture into the suffocating heat of Las Vegas, but it was stupendous while it lasted.

Barry McGuigan (the 'Barry' is short for Finbar) was born in Clones, Co Monaghan, on the southern side of the border which separates the Republic of Ireland from Northern Ireland. Both his parents were born in Northern Ireland. His father, Pat, had worked as a stoker on the railway, which was the main industry of Clones, and after the railway died in the mid-1950s had worked as a bus conductor for a spell in Glasgow, but he returned to Clones to pursue a career as a professional singer.

A few years after Barry's birth on 28 February 1961 Pat formed his own band, Pat McGeegan and the Big Four. He called himself McGeegan because it was reckoned easier to pronounce than McGuigan, as his son was to discover was true when he achieved much greater fame. Pat McGuigan's big moment came when he represented Ireland in the 1967 Eurovision Song Contest and came third with a song called 'Chance of a Lifetime'.

Father Pat had been an amateur boxer and was keen on the sport (he was often to be seen in the ring at Barry's fights singing 'Danny Boy') and Barry and his brother Dermot, who was a year older, became interested, too, particularly when with three pals they found an old pair of boxing gloves in a derelict house. They scrapped among themselves, wearing one glove each. Later a bandsman loaned Barry's dad a set of two pairs of gloves which Barry and Dermot used. Barry reckons that he was so strong he could knock out his contemporaries with one punch when he was six years old.

When Barry was 12 he crossed the border to join the Wattlebridge amateur club, and thought the gym was the greatest thing he'd ever seen. Soon he represented the club in a tournament in Clones and was reprimanded for walloping his opponent as soon as the referee's instructions were over. Barry didn't realise he had to go back to his corner and await the bell. Barry won a trophy for this first fight which was the only one to survive a fire in his mother's house the night Barry won the world title.

One night Barry and his pal were cycling home along the unapproved border roads from Wattlebridge when they passed police recovering two bodies from a hedge, victims of the 'troubles', and Barry was banned by his parents from going there again. So he joined The Smithboro club eight miles from his home, and Frank Mulligan, who ran it, soon recognised Barry's potential. Barry won the national under-14 championship and he embarked on a successful amateur career, which saw him win the Irish senior championship and become an international at 17. In the same year, 1978, came the highlight of his amateur days when he won the Commonwealth Games bantamweight title for Northern Ireland (on the strength of his parents' nationalities) at Edmonton, Canada, although truthfully he was a little lucky to get the decision in the final. Nevertheless the pictures of the pale and personable McGuigan crying on the winners' rostrum captured the imagination of Irish people on both sides of the border.

Barry failed in the 1980 Olympics, when outpointed by a much taller man from Zambia and, after receiving a couple of bad decisions in other important tournaments, decided to turn pro.

There were plenty of well-known names willing to manage the young McGuigan, some of whom, like Terry Lawless and Mickey Duff, approached him. But Barry's choice fell on a local man Barney Eastwood, who had built up a huge personal fortune which started when accepting bets over the bar of a public house and developed into the ownership of a chain of bookmaking shops and big assets in property. He had promoted boxing some years before. Barry was influenced in his choice by his father, who always had a big say in Barry's decisions, and by the fact that he was by now engaged to his childhood sweetheart, Sandra Mealiff, and didn't want to move too far away. Sandra and Barry had known each other since they were three years old, and had begun courting when they were 17.

In Barry's corner when he turned pro, apart from Eastwood, were trainer Eddie Shaw and matchmaker Paddy Byrne, who was a cuts man. Shaw had briefly been a professional boxer, and McGuigan was the first pro he'd trained. Paddy, another ex-pro, was the life and soul of the party. Barry's brother Dermot was also important in his training, helping Barry especially in the routine business of maintaining basic fitness. Eastwood built a gym in Belfast where Barry finished off the training for each fight.

Barry and Dermot had studied the best boxers and their methods, watching old fight films, and Barry had already evolved the basic style which made him successful. He was a particularly good body puncher, especially with a left hook, but found early in his career that many of his body shots would catch the elbows of the opponent and not get through cleanly. Then he discovered from watching Alexis Arguello how to turn his elbow to deliver the punch with maximum effect. And he learned how to catch opponents off guard by going for the head first, and then switching to the debilitating body attack. The method had its drawbacks in that he was often accused of being near the borderline with his body shots, but when he powered forward in his non-stop style few could stand up to his punches for long.

McGuigan's professional debut came on 10 March 1981 at Dalymount Park soccer ground, Dublin. His opponent, Selvin Bell, was a Jamaican journeyman with 42 defeats in 58 contests. It was no surprise when Barry stopped him in the second round with some well-placed punches, but Barry's family and friends leapt into the ring to celebrate anyway. His second fight was on the undercard at Wembley when Jim Watt fought gallantly but was well beaten by Alexis Arguello, who took his world title. But Barry himself won impressively with another stoppage.

If Barry thought everything was going to be easy, his third contest was a rude shock. He was fighting Peter Eubanks at Brighton. Eubanks was a year younger than Barry and had been a pro six months longer, but had lost four of his seven fights. He was expected to be an easy victim, but after eight two-minute rounds he was given the decision by referee Roland Dakin by half a point, or one round. Barry was convinced he'd won (he put Eubanks down) and cried in disappointment.

Barry himself hit the canvas in his next contest, against a good Belgian, Jean-Marc Renard, a future European champion, but he got up to win. This contest marked a return to promoting for Barney Eastwood, who saw the potential of an exciting young 'local' boxer performing in Belfast. The compact Ulster Hall was the venue, and the show was the first great McGuigan success there. Barry avenged his defeat by Peter Eubanks by stopping him in a good match, and six days later married Sandra. Sandra set up a hairdressing business with Barry's sister, Sharon, which she left when their first child, Blain, arrived.

Barry continued to stop opponents impressively, and Eastwood advised him to take out British citizenship in order to challenge for a British title, a step which caused a minor hiccup in his fast-growing Irish support. A bigger setback to his ambitions occurred in his 12th contest, a World Sporting Club dinner-boxing show at the Grosvenor House Hotel, London. Barry had to face a late substitute, the West African bantamweight champion, Young Ali, making his British debut. Ali was knocked out, and collapsed between the tables when leaving the ring. He was operated on but remained in a coma, and was still in a coma when taken back to Nigeria some months later. During that time Barry was devastated. Young Ali's wife was pregnant and the tragedy removed Barry's desire to fight. It was four months before he returned to the ring with two Belfast wins which set him up for a British featherweight title challenge. Then, in December 1982, Young Ali died and Barry's emotional turmoil was stirred up again.

However, Barry decided his career had to go on, and in April 1983 he faced Vernon Penprase at the Ulster Hall for the vacant British featherweight title. Barry was at his best and stopped Penprase in the second round. There was now no stopping McGuigan's upward progress. He won his first contest in America with a first-round knockout, and took the European title with a knockout of the Italian Valerio Nati. This was Barry's first appearance at the King's Hall, Belfast, which held 7,000 spectators and which Eastwood reopened in anticipation of the great McGuigan nights which were to follow. In 1984 Barry stopped Charm Chiteule of Zambia in a final eliminator for the Commonwealth title (Barry never did get around to an actual Commonwealth title fight), stopped Jose Caba of Colombia in an eliminator for the WBC world title and defended his European crown against Esteban Eguia of Spain.

McGuigan's first big fight of 1985 was a frantically exciting King's Hall battle with the recent WBC champion Juan Laporte, a New York-based Puerto Rican. Barry was having the best of a great scrap but was badly shaken by a right cross in the ninth round, only to come back with a terrific hook of his own in the tenth and last. He took the decision. The fight was televised live in the USA, and Barry was now a desirable property on both sides of the Atlantic. Less then four months later Barry was fighting for the WBA world title against one of the best champions of the day: Eusebio Pedroza of Panama, who had won the title in 1978 and defended it no fewer than 19 times.

Pedroza's connections would not allow the contest to be held in Ireland, so it took place at the Queen's Park Rangers football ground in Loftus Road, London, with 26,000 fans present, many having made the trip from Ireland. Pedroza was 32, a wily, experienced boxer. But on another wildly exciting night Barry proved too young and strong for him. The fight was more or less decided in the seventh round, when Barry scored a knockdown. He hurt Pedroza again in the ninth and 13th and won the title with a unanimous and wide decision.

McGuigan received the most fantastic welcome back in Ireland – in Belfast, in Clones and in Dublin, where there was a civic reception and it was said that more people turned out to see him than had welcomed the Pope a few years before. For a while he was even seen as a 'peacemaker' who drew both communities of Northern Ireland, Catholic and Protestant, together. It was an exaggerated claim, but certainly McGuigan was a hero to all the Irish people.

McGuigan was brilliant in winning the title, but struggled a little in the two successful defences he made in the next eight months. He lost the first five rounds against the very fast Bernard Taylor in Belfast, but caught him with such a good body punch in the eighth that Taylor couldn't come out for the ninth. His next defence, in Dublin, should have been against an Argentinian, Fernando Sosa, but Sosa pulled out with a broken finger and with 17 days to go a boxer from the Dominican Republic, Danilo Cabrera, stepped in as substitute. He gave Barry a very hard fight and cut him a few times before Barry hurt him enough for the referee to step in in the 14th round.

By now the relationship between Barry and manager/promoter Barney Eastwood was very strained. Barry was concerned about what he saw as lack of information about the possible deals and purses which Eastwood was negotiating and accepting or declining. Barry was keen next to challenge Wilfredo Gomez for his WBA super-featherweight title in Madison Square Garden, New York. Eastwood proposed a Las Vegas defence of Barry's featherweight title against Fernando Sosa.

Eventually the Las Vegas contest was arranged, allied to a prefight publicity tour which took in several US cities. No sooner was McGuigan in training for the fight than Sosa withdrew with severe eye problems. Barry was unhappy in training camp and saw this as an excuse to pull out, but Steve Cruz of Texas was signed as a substitute and Eastwood allayed Barry's unhappiness with a promise to pay him $250,000 should he lose.

In the contest itself Barry had great trouble with the 110 degree F heat at Caesars Palace, and after being in control faded badly in the middle rounds. He was down in the tenth round, fought back but, becoming increasingly dehydrated, was down twice more in the 15th, which decided the fight. Barry lost unanimously, but by a single point only on two cards. The last round was decisive. His title was gone and he was wrapped in foil and taken to hospital where he spent the night on a drip.

After the Cruz fight, many of the important matters, especially financial (including the $250,000 promise), between McGuigan and Eastwood were conducted by letters through lawyers, and the final severance of the partnership involved dealings through the courts.

While this was going on McGuigan was out of the ring for nearly two years, during which time he tried to establish himself in the car racing business. He suffered a great blow when his father died in June 1987, aged 52. It left Barry with no appetite to resume a boxing career, but eventually the craving to give it another try came, and in April 1988, nearly two years after his previous fight, Barry returned to the ring. He moved to England and signed a contract with promoter/manager Frank Warren. Jimmy Tibbs was his trainer, and Barry fought as a super-featherweight. He stopped the American champion, Nicky Perez, in the fourth. The same result against Tomas Da Cruz lifted Barry to third place in the WBC rankings, and he was approaching his objective, another world title fight. But Barry was cut over the eyes in his next contest, when he took eight rounds to stop Julio Miranda, and his career ended for good in his fourth comeback fight. Promoter Barry Hearn offered £250,000 to McGuigan to fight Jim McDonnell, and Barry got a bad cut over his eye in the second round, which led the referee to stop it in the fourth. Barry retired.

Sandra who, two years earlier, had prayed by Barry's bed in Las Vegas, had supported her husband's comeback, even though she was pregnant with their fourth child (three boys and a girl). His family has always played a big part in Barry's life. He has remained a prominent figure in boxing. In his book *The Untold Story*, Barry said: 'I am fed up with the way the game is being run, with the hypocrisy of professional boxing in Britain'. One of his first achievements after retiring was to be instrumental in forming the Professional Boxers Association. He is now a regular summariser and presenter on Sky Sports television and writes a boxing column for a national newspaper.

CAREER STATISTICS

WBA featherweight champion 1985-86
Clones, Ireland, born 28 February 1961

1981
Mar 10 Selvin Bell w rsf 2 Dublin
Jun 20 Gary Lucas w rsf 4 London
Aug 3 Peter Eubanks l pts 8 Brighton
Sep 22 Jean-Marc Renard w pts 8 Belfast
Oct 27 Terry Pizzaro w rsf 4 Belfast
Dec 8 Peter Eubanks w rsf 8 Belfast
1982
Jan 27 Luis de la Sagra w pts 8 Belfast
Feb 8 Ian Murray w rsf 3 London
Feb 23 Angel Oliver w rsf 3 Belfast
Mar 23 Angel Licata w rsf 2 Belfast
Apr 22 Gary Lucas w ko 1 Enniskillen
Jun 14 Young Ali w ko 6 London
Jul 5 Jimmy Duncan w rtd 4 Belfast
Nov 9 Paul Huggins w rsf 5 Belfast
1983
Apr 12 Vernon Penprase w rsf 2 Belfast
(vacant British featherweight title)
May 22 Sammy Meck w rsf 6 Navan
Jul 9 Lavon McGowan w ko 1 Chicago
Oct 5 Ruben Herasme w ko 2 Belfast
Nov 16 Valerio Nati w ko 6 Belfast
(vacant European featherweight title)
1984
Jan 25 Charm Chiteule w rsf 10 Belfast
Apr 4 Jose Caba w rsf 7 Belfast
Jun 5 Esteban Eguia w ko 3 London
(European featherweight title)
Jun 30 Paul DeVorce w rsf 5 Belfast
Oct 16 Felipe Orozco w ko 2 Belfast
Dec 19 Clyde Ruan w ko 4 Belfast
(British & European featherweight titles)
1985
Feb 23 Juan LaPorte w pts 10 Belfast
Mar 27 Farid Gallouze w rtd 2 London
(European featherweight title)
Jun 8 Eusebio Pedroza w pts 15 London
(WBA featherweight title)
Sep 28 Bernard Taylor w rtd 8 Belfast
(WBA featherweight title)
1986
Feb 15 Danilo Cabrera w rsf 14 Dublin
(WBA featherweight title)
Jun 23 Steve Cruz l pts 15 Las Vegas
(WBA featherweight title)
1987 inactive
1988
Apr 20 Nicky Perez w rsf 4 London
Jun 25 Tomas Da Cruz w rsf 4 Luton
Dec 1 Julio Miranda w rsf 8 London
1989
May 31 Jim McDonnell l rsf 4 Manchester

Fights 35 Won 32 Lost 3

MICHAEL SPINKS

THE SPINX JINX

Michael Spinks, a fine, thoughtful fighter, lasted longer than his wild-child brother Leon, made his fortune over 15 world title fights at light-heavy and heavyweight, and kept it. Michael was three years younger than Leon, born one of seven children in St Louis, Missouri, on 13 July 1956. Their father was rarely home, and their mother Kay raised them on welfare on a notorious housing project named Pruitt-Igoe. A den of iniquity which housed prostitutes, pimps, drug dealers and general criminals, it was demolished 12 years after it was built. 'In its own way, it was like a prison,' he said. His mother tried to teach them right from wrong by reading the Bible to them every day, and that, coupled with his own inner discipline, kept Michael clear of trouble. As a boy with a nervous stutter, he sold newspapers, attended high school and learned how to box at the Capri Recreation Center.

He was exceptional, winning 88 of 93 amateur bouts, including two National Golden Gloves titles and then the Olympic middleweight gold medal in the magnificent Montreal Games when Leon won the light-heavyweight gold, and the US team won in five weight divisions. People in the St Louis project imagined already he was a rich man. In fact, he was working night shifts in a chemicals factory.

At 6ft 2in, Michael was very tall for a middleweight, and by the time he turned pro in April 1977 he was already filling out into a light-heavy. Keen to make the whole thing an entirely new enterprise, he left St Louis for Philadelphia, while still forming an integral part of the team behind Leon. 'He was my main man,' he was to say. On the night Leon beat Muhammad Ali in Las Vegas in February 1978, Michael appeared on the undercard, outpointing veteran contender Tom Bethea.

Brother Leon couldn't cope with the fame and adulation that followed such an unexpected and memorable victory, so Michael took a back seat for a while and attempted to keep his brother thinking straight. It was an impossible task, and eventually he had no choice but to concentrate on his own career. Knee injuries ruled him out for most of 1979, and continued to plague him from time to time throughout his career.

Promoted and managed by the maverick Butch Lewis, he picked up national television exposure and moved into world class in 1980 when he outpointed Murray Sutherland and stopped veteran Alvaro 'Yaqui' Lopez in seven rounds. A fourth-round knockout of former light-heavyweight champ Marvin Johnson set him up for a WBA title shot against Eddie Mustafa Muhammad in Las Vegas in July 1981. The last of the 1976 Olympic gold medallists to fight for a world title, he won on points. 'It feels so good,' he said. 'This is what I've always wanted. I owe St Louis a visit. I said I wouldn't go back until I accomplished my mission.'

His first challenger was the stringbean Vonzell Johnson, who was 6ft 4in tall. Spinks outboxed him and then stopped him in round seven. Four solidly impressive defences followed in 1982, all inside the distance against Mustapha Wasajja (six rounds), Murray Sutherland (eight) Jerry Celestine (eight) and Johnny Davis (nine).

Already Butch Lewis was talking of a future at heavyweight – a $1 million offer was made to WBA champion Mike Weaver in 1982 – but that was still some way ahead. Meanwhile, in March 1983 in Atlantic City, Spinks put aside personal tragedy to outpoint Dwight Muhammad Qawi to unify the light-heavyweight division. Qawi had held the WBC belt, and scored a controversial, disputed knockdown when he appeared to tread on Michael's foot in round eight, but Spinks dictated from a distance to win decisively on points. Two months earlier, his common-law wife Sandra died in a car accident. As their two-year-old daughter Michelle sat on his knee in the dressing room after the win over Qawi, she asked: 'Where's mummy?' The new champion broke down.

He stopped an unbeaten, troublesome Peruvian, Oscar Rivadeneyra, in 10 rounds in Vancouver in November 1983, and then outpointed Eddie Davis, a crafty old pro from Freeport, New York, in Atlantic City in his only fight in 1984.

By now the move up to heavyweight was being seriously plotted. Larry Holmes was in his mid-thirties, and the division was opening out. Holmes had fallen out with the WBC, and was now IBF champion. At the end of 1984 Greg Page knocked out Gerrie Coetzee to become WBA champion, and Pinklon Thomas had beaten Tim Witherspoon for the WBC version. Don King had bought almost every heavyweight around ... but Spinks would not go with the flow, which slowed up his switch from light-heavy. 'I don't like Don King, I don't want to have anything to do with Don King,' he said, emphatically.

At the time the cruiserweight division was unattractive, and so Spinks could only wait. He stopped David Sears and Jim MacDonald, neither of whom broke much ice with boxing fans. Finally, it happened: Lewis negotiated a shot at Larry Holmes, who was hoping to equal the 49-fight unbeaten run set by Rocky Marciano.

And on 22 September 1985, at the Riviera Hotel, Las Vegas, Spinks became the latest name on the roll-call of heavyweight champions. It was close, Holmes didn't like it, but at the end of 15 rounds, the judges were unanimous: Spinks had done enough. 'I think I might have dreamed it once, but I never really saw myself winning this fight,' said the modest, one-time ghetto kid from St Louis.

Inevitably, there was a return, at the Las Vegas Hilton in April 1986. Again, Holmes was sure he had won. So, to be fair to him, were many writers. The judges were not: Spinks won a split decision, outwitting and outhustling the ageing champion in spite of being hurt two or three times.

He had relinquished the light-heavyweight title – he was weighing more than 200lb now anyway – and set about taking on contenders who were not tied to King. There weren't many around, but he did stop Norwegian outsider Steffan Tangstad in four in Las Vegas in September 1986. Tangstad, a brave man who went on to be a high-power television executive in Scandinavia, felt he could have gone on, as fighters will.

By 1987, Spinks owned a country estate near Wilmington, Delaware, and still trained in Philadelphia. American TV giants HBO wanted to clean up the heavyweight situation with what amounted to an elimination tournament, but Spinks and Lewis wanted to play by their own rules. A fall-out followed with the IBF, who were happy to go along with the HBO deal.

In the wake of that, Spinks took a payday of around $7 million to fight Gerry Cooney, who had re-established himself after his defeat by Holmes five years earlier. Cooney had lost only that solitary fight against 28 wins, was bigger, stronger, heavier and harder hitting. But at the Atlantic City Convention Center, with nothing more than what they described as the 'people's championship' on the line, Spinks outboxed, outfought and outwilled him. It was all over in five rounds. The drums began beating for a fight with Mike Tyson, who unified the division the following month by defeating Spinks' successor as IBF champion, Tony Tucker.

It took a year to put the fight together, with King and Lewis taking promotional billing alongside Donald Trump through the Trump Plaza hotel and casino. They called it 'Once And For All', and at the 21,000-capacity Atlantic City Convention Center, Spinks' 11-year, 31 fight, unbeaten spell was snapped by Tyson at his absolute pinnacle. The whole thing was over in 91 seconds, when Spinks, down for the second time, failed to beat the count.

He took defeat with dignity, without excuse, and then produced an analysis of his own fate, and perhaps a prophecy of that which was to befall the supposedly unbeatable Tyson.

'There is always somebody on earth that can beat someone else. Nobody is invincible,' he said.

Spinks, whose money was wisely invested, retired and resisted the urge to come back, in spite of rumours that he was contemplating it in the early 1990s when Holmes and George Foreman were earning well in their middle 40s. In fact, he had simply been spotted working out in a gym.

He did not stay in boxing, but visited social functions like the Boxing Writers of America dinner and Hall of Fame convention, always cutting the same calm, quietly dignified figure that he was during his days as a champion.

CAREER STATISTICS

IBF heavyweight champion 1985-87
World light-heavyweight champion 1981-85
(WBA light-heavyweight champion only 1981-83)
St Louis, Missouri, born 13 July 1956
1976 Olympic middleweight gold medal

1977

Apr 17 Eddie Benson w ko 1 Las Vegas
May 9 Luis Rodriguez w pts 6 St Louis
Jun 1 Joe Borden w ko 2 Montreal
Aug 23 Jasper Brisbane w ko 1 Philadelphia
Sep 13 Ray Elson w ko 1 Los Angeles
Oct 21 Gary Summerhays w pts 8 Las Vegas

1978

Feb 15 Tom Bethea w pts 8 Las Vegas
Dec 15 Eddie Phillips w ko 4 White Plains

1979

Nov 24 Mark Hans w ko 1 Bloomington

1980

Feb 1 Johnny Wilburn w pts 8 Louisville
Feb 24 Ramon Ronquillo w rsf 6 Atlantic City
May 4 Murray Sutherland w pts 10 Kiamesha Lake
Aug 2 David Conteh w ko 9 Baton Rouge
Oct 18 Alvaro Lopez w ko 7 Atlantic City

1981

Jan 24 Willie Taylor w ko 8 Philadelphia
Mar 28 Marvin Johnson w ko 4 Atlantic City
Jul 18 Eddie Mustafa Muhammmad w pts 15 Las Vegas *(WBA light-heavyweight title)*
Nov 7 Vonzell Johnson w rsf 7 Atlantic City *(WBA light-heavyweight title)*

1982

Feb 13 Mustapha Wasajja w rsf 6 Atlantic City *(WBA light-heavyweight title)*
Apr 11 Murray Sutherland w rsf 8 Atlantic City *(WBA light-heavyweight title)*
Jun 12 Jerry Celestine w rsf 8 Atlantic City *(WBA light-heavyweight title)*
Sep 18 Johnny Davis w rsf 9 Atlantic City *(WBA light-heavyweight title)*

1983

Mar 18 Dwight Muhammad Qawi w pts 15 Atlantic City *(World light-heavyweight title)*
Nov 25 Oscar Rivadeneyra w rsf 10 Vancouver *(World light-heayvweight title)*

1984

Feb 25 Eddie Davis w pts 12 Atlantic City *(World light-heavyweight title)*

1985

Feb 23 David Sears w rsf 3 Atlantic City *(World light-heavyweight title)*
Jun 6 Jim MacDonald w rsf 8 Las Vegas *(World light-heavyweight title)*
Sep 22 Larry Holmes w pts 15 Las Vegas *(IBF heavyweight title)*

1986

Apr 19 Larry Holmes w pts 15 Las Vegas *(IBF heavyweight title)*
Sep 6 Steffen Tangstad w rsf 4 Las Vegas *(IBF heavyweight title)*

1987

Stripped of IBF heavyweight title
Jun 15 Gerry Cooney w rsf 5 Atlantic City

1988

Jun 27 Mike Tyson l ko 1 Atlantic City *(World heavyweight title)*

Fights 32 Won 31 Lost 1

MARVIN HAGLER

MARVELOUS MARVIN

Marvin Hagler's was a career carved out of discipline and dedication. When he was at his menacing peak as undisputed world middleweight champion, he trained in a remote beach hotel near Cape Cod. When his workouts were over, and it wasn't time to eat, sleep or study a video of himself in training or his opponent in a fight, it was said he sat for hours at his window, relentlessly contemplating the ocean.

Hagler knew the value of solitude and inner calm, and knew how best to fuel his own need for recognition. During the last week of training, he routinely locked himself away, refusing all requests for last-minute interviews, resenting any interference in his routine. This man from the mean streets understood fighters and fighting, and this alongside his own natural toughness and skill, made him one of the most able ring craftsmen of them all. His chin never let him down; although he was a southpaw, he could fight orthodox; he had a long reach, and could punch viciously and accurately with either hand.

'The man was an artist, a master,' said 1983 victim Tony Sibson. 'He put me in a cage, locked the door and tossed away the key.'

Hagler was undisputed world middleweight champion for seven years. It should have been longer because most accepted he was the best middleweight in the world for two years before he won the title on a bitter, depressing night in London in 1980 when British fans erupted in a shameful riot following Hagler's short, emphatic win over Alan Minter.

Hagler was born in Newark, New Jersey, the eldest child of Robert Sims and Ida Mae Hagler. He took his mother's name; his younger brother Robert was given the name Sims after his father. (Robert fought unsuccessfully for the WBA and WBO middleweight titles in the late 1980s.)

After his father left home, and following race riots in Newark, Marvin's mother moved them all to Brockton, Massachusetts, where he eventually began boxing at the gym run by brothers Pat and Goody Petronelli. They helped him overcome an early distrust of white people and he made remarkable progress, winning the 1973 National AAU middleweight title. Officially he was 20, with a birthdate of 23 May 1952, but later Marvin produced a birth certificate which showed he was two years younger, and therefore only 18 when he reached the top in the amateur game.

He didn't want to wait around for the 1976 Olympics. 'Trophies don't buy groceries,' he said, and made his professional debut in Brockton in May 1973, still a week short of his 19th birthday. He scaled 160lb, and 14 years later when he retired, he was still at the same weight – evidence of his remarkable dedication.

He moved into world class in August 1974, only 15 months after his debut, when he outpointed 1972 Olympic gold medallist Ray Seales over 10 rounds in Boston. A rematch three months later in Seattle finished in a draw, the first minor blemish on his 18-fight record.

His first defeat was an outrageous decision handed to local favourite Bobby 'Boogaloo' Watts in Philadelphia in January 1976, but two months later when he returned to the so-called 'City of Brotherly Love' he was outpointed by Willie 'The Worm' Monroe. This time he had no complaints. Monroe, tricky and awkward, won clearly. However, a third trip that year to Philadelphia saw him batter the resistance out of another local prospect Eugene 'Cyclone' Hart in eight rounds. Hart was booed from the ring.

A rematch with Monroe was set up in Boston in February 1977 and again Hagler had trouble early on, before grinding 'The Worm' to a 12th-round stoppage defeat. Six months later, they had the decider in front of more than 8,000 fans at the Philadelphia Spectrum, and this time Hagler outclassed Monroe in two rounds, literally lifting him off the floor and stretching him on his back with a left and right hand.

Mike Colbert was a clever boxer from Portland, Oregon, who was in the world title frame following the retirement of Carlos Monzon. He had won 19 in a row, including a decision over former Monzon challenger Tony Licata, but only four of those victories had come inside the distance. Lack of power was his major problem. He was quick, and his perpetual movement gave Hagler some problems when they met in Boston in November 1977, but Marvin suddenly got to him in the 11th and in the 12th Colbert was badly knocked out, his jaw broken in several places.

That fight established Hagler as the most dangerous middleweight in the world, although the advice given him by Joe Frazier years before must have run through his mind time and again. 'You've got three strikes against you: you're black, you're a southpaw, and you're good,' he said. In other words, no world champion in their right minds would be overjoyed to defend the title against him.

So it proved. Rodrigo Valdez of Colombia had outpointed Bennie Briscoe for the title left vacant by Monzon. Valdez lost it to Hugo Corro of Argentina in April 1978, and he stayed well clear of Hagler until he in turn lost it to Vito Antuofermo in 1979.

All through this period, Hagler kept winning. He twice cut up Britain's Kevin Finnegan, turned boxer to outpoint Briscoe, and stopped a string of competent opponents. He also blasted out Sugar Ray Seales in one round, erasing the blot on his record from five years before. Eventually, however, he could be avoided no more. And Antuofermo, the rugged Italian-born slugger who made up in workrate and pressure for what he lacked in technical skills, gave him a chance in November 1979. When Antuofermo won the title by outpointing Corro in Monte Carlo five months earlier, Hagler stopped Argentine brawler Norberto Cabrera in eight rounds.

He outfought Antuofermo at Caesars Palace, Las Vegas, appearing to dominate the fight, even if he did fade a little in the late rounds. The defending champion chugged along at the same pace, but seemed some way adrift at the final bell. One judge, Duane Ford, agreed. He gave the fight to Hagler by a decisive 145–141. Hal Miller sat on the fence at 143–143, but amazingly Dalby Shirley saw it 144–142 for Antuofermo. There were howls of dismay, and Hagler bitterly blamed boxing politics. 'In my heart I believe I am the middleweight champion,' he said, and then went off to marry his fiancée Bertha Washington.

Antuofermo lost the title on a split decision to Alan Minter (who seemed to win by some distance), and Hagler had to wait until September 1980 before his second chance arrived in Wembley Arena. The atmosphere was fired up before the start, almost boiling over with misplaced jingoism. Minter had also been quoted as saying: 'I'll never lose my title to a black man,' an appalling error of judgement that fuelled the racist element which at the time was enjoying a high presence in Britain. Consequently, when Minter was outpunched and badly cut over both eyes inside three rounds, the reaction was hostile in the extreme. Bottles rained down on the ring as Hagler was shielded by his cornermen. Police rushed him down the ring steps and back to the dressing room. The moment of receiving his world title belt in the ring was denied him, but he had what he had come looking for: after seven long years, he was the undisputed middleweight champion of the world.

Anyone who suspected this might be enough for him must have realised fairly quickly this was not the case. 'The anger is still there,' he said. 'I'm still a hungry fighter.'

Now he was world champion, he wanted to be acknowledged as one of the all-time greats. Nothing less would do. Whereas the welterweight division had thrown together Ray Leonard, Roberto Duran, Thomas Hearns, Pipino Cuevas, Wilfred Benitez and Carlos Palomino, the middleweights seemed a far less impressive bunch. There was no immediate dream fight to give Hagler recognition. The respect he had earned from the trade could only become worldwide by a cumulative process, by longevity, reliability; by proving repeatedly that he was the best 160lb fighter in the world.

Fulgencio Obelmejias of Venezuela tried to beat him twice. He lasted eight rounds the first time, and five in the rematch. Hagler set the record straight by butchering Antuofermo into a four rounds retirement. He stopped the aggressive Syrian Mustafa Hamsho in round 11 and in a rematch three years later knocked him out in the third.

William 'Caveman' Lee from Detroit was blasted out in 67 seconds, a chilling burst of 17 unanswered head blows connecting to force the stoppage. In February 1983 he dismissed mandatory challenger Tony Sibson with a brilliant performance in six rounds in Worcester, Massachusetts. Wilford Scypion, another good fighter, was outclassed in four.

In Las Vegas in November 1983 Roberto Duran, by then the reigning WBA light-middleweight champion, attempted to beat him to win a world title at a fourth weight. It was a dull fight, with Hagler working mechanically and Duran defiant. At the end it was surprisingly close, but the decision was unanimous: Marvelous Marvin, as he was now legally known, having changed his name by deed poll, was still champion.

A brawling Argentine, Juan Domingo Roldan, scored an official knockdown against him in Las Vegas in March 1984, but the film shows it was a slip, which Hagler claimed indignantly at the time. He eventually stopped Roldan in the tenth.

The defining fight of his career came at Caesars Palace on 15 April 1985 when he broke the resistance of Thomas Hearns in three magnificent rounds. It was right up there with the greatest fights of the modern era. Hagler had trained for this one with a degree of enthusiasm and intensity that was extreme even for him. He had held the world middleweight title for nearly five years with 10 successful, and generally impressive, defences, only one of which had gone the distance, that against Roberto Duran.

Coincidentally, Duran's next fight had been against Hearns, who had beaten him by a knockout in the second round, the only knockout ever inflicted on him. With this psychological advantage and the benefits of height and reach, Hearns threw in a few insults for good measure in the publicity build-up to the fight, which incensed Hagler and no doubt made him even more determined to settle the score against the popular Hearns.

Marvin had anticipated a boxing match but Hearns attacked from the first bell. Hagler was surprised by this unexpected start, but after the initial onslaught he switched to the attacking mode and the two of them stood there, toe to toe, trading punches. The pace was intense, the experience compelling and exhausting. Three minutes of mayhem – and the crowd loved it. They came out for round two and the change in tempo was hardly discernible. The challenger had caught the champion on one of his best days, but even so he was still giving a good account of himself.

A cut in the centre of Hagler's forehead bled so profusely that after round two, referee Richard Steele asked him if he could see. The reply has gone down in boxing lore: 'I ain't missing him, am I?' In the third, following a medical inspection of the damage, Hagler took away Hearns' legs with a series of pulverising right hands. He got up, but tottered, and Steele stopped it after seven minutes and 52 seconds of fighting.

Caesars Palace erupted! The crowd didn't have to come to their feet – most of them were already there. Nothing endears a boxer to the crowd more than a sensational blood-and-guts display of two-fisted attacking – and that is what Hagler gave them. Suddenly he was acknowledged as one of the greatest middleweight champions in history, but still he wanted more. There was Carlos Monzon's record of 14 defences to match, or beat. Hearns was his 11th challenger. Although he and his family were secure financially, there was more to be done.

He took almost a year off after Hearns, but then defended against the thunderous punching Ugandan John Mugabi in Las Vegas in March 1986. Mugabi's trainer George Francis said when the African landed solidly, he had seen the colour drain from the opponent's face. Mugabi's manager Mickey Duff backed his man with confidence. By now, Hagler was approaching either 32 or 34, depending on whom you believed, and in the fight there did seem to be some evidence of his slowing down. Nevertheless, he absorbed Mugabi's blows, kept him under control and knocked him out in round 11.

By now he had come through 66 professional fights, with only two defeats, both of which he had avenged. He had everything he needed.

And then came an offer that must have sounded so sweet for him – a guarantee of somewhere around $12 million to defend against Sugar Ray Leonard. It was a controversial match, with many believing it should not have been made. Leonard had boxed only once in the previous five years, retiring because of an eye injury in 1982, and then again after a mediocre performance in a comeback fight in 1984 against Kevin Howard, who had floored him. Leonard won in the ninth, but was embarrassingly poor.

Yet he had the audacity to step up to middleweight and fight Hagler. Logic suggested it was crazy, stupid, masochistic, yet he promised to play mind games with the champion. 'I'm going to mess up his life,' he said. Hagler made a crucial error in judgement when he allowed the fight to be made over 12 rounds instead of 15, but at the time it did not seem important.

Before a full house of 15,000 at Caesars Palace, Leonard danced and sniped his way into an early lead. He said all along that he planned to steal the fight on the move, and for the first half it seemed that he was doing just that. Then gradually Hagler began to hurt him, Leonard's blows lost their snap and he ran, twisting and turning to find an edge for a few seconds, when he would launch flashy combinations of little substance. At the end it seemed close. Both thought they had won. Leonard had, by a split vote from the judges.

Hagler was furious. 'Leonard fought like a girl,' he sneered. 'His punches meant nothing ... I can't believe they took it away from me.'

The hurt was enormous and Hagler, for so many years a man of iron will and discipline, lost the plot. He was completely devastated by the decision and the apparent unfairness of it obviously rankled sufficiently for him to depart the fight game. His behaviour was bad enough to wear out the patience and loyalty of his wife. They divorced. He eventually straightened himself out, and emigrated to Milan where he learned a new job ... acting. He was still there almost 10 years on, looking in marvellous shape, only a few pounds over his old fighting weight and celebrated whenever he chose to return to be among boxing folk for a short time. The man had class.

CAREER STATISTICS

World middleweight champion 1980-87
Brockton, Massachusetts, born Newark, New Jersey, 23 May 1954

1973
May 18 Terry Ryan w ko 2 Brockton
Jul 25 Sonny Williams w pts 6 Boston
Aug 8 Muhammad Smith w ko 2 Boston
Oct 6 Don Wigfall w pts 8 Brockton
Oct 26 Cove Green w ko 4 Brockton
Nov 18 Cocoa Kid w ko 2 Brockton
Dec 7 Manny Freitas w ko 1 Portland
Dec 18 James Redford w ko 4 Boston
1974
Feb 5 Bob Harrington w ko 5 Boston
Apr 5 Tracy Morrison w rsf 8 Boston
May 4 James Redford w rsf 2 Brockton
May 30 Curtis Phillips w ko 5 Portland
Jul 16 Robert Williams w rsf 3 Boston
Aug 13 Peachy Davis w ko 1 New Bedford
Aug 30 Ray Seales w pts 10 Boston
Oct 29 Morris Jordan w rsf 4 New Bedford
Nov 16 George Green w ko 1 Brockton
Nov 26 Ray Seales drew 10 Seattle
Dec 20 D.C.Walker w ko 2 Boston
1975
Feb 15 Don Wigfall w ko 5 Brockton
Mar 31 Joey Blair w ko 2 Boston
Apr 14 Jimmy Owens w pts 10 Boston
May 24 Jimmy Owens w dis 6 Brockton
Aug 7 Jesse Bender w ko 1 Portland
Sep 30 Lamont Lovelady w rsf 7 Boston
Dec 20 Johnny Baldwin w pts 10 Boston
1976
Jan 13 Bobby Watts l pts 10 Philadelphia
Feb 7 Matt Donovan w rsf 2 Boston
Mar 9 Willie Monroe l pts 10 Philadelphia
Jun 2 Bob Smith w rsf 5 Taunton
Aug 3 D.C.Walker w rsf 6 Providence
Sep 14 Eugene Hart w rsf 8 Philadelphia
Dec 21 George Davis w rsf 6 Boston
1977
Feb 15 Willie Monroe w rsf 12 Boston
Mar 16 Reginald Ford w ko 3 Boston
Jun 10 Roy Jones w ko 3 Hartford
Aug 23 Willie Monroe w rsf 2 Philadelphia
Sep 24 Ray Phillips w rsf 7 Boston
Oct 15 Jim Henry w pts 10 Providence
Nov 26 Mike Colbert w ko 12 Boston
1978
Mar 4 Kevin Finnegan w rtd 8 Boston
Apr 7 Doug Demmings w rsf 8 Los Angeles
May 13 Kevin Finnegan w rtd 6 Boston
Aug 24 Bennie Briscoe w pts 10 Philadelphia
Nov 11 Willie Warren w rsf 7 Boston
1979
Feb 3 Ray Seales w rsf 1 Boston
Mar 12 Bob Patterson w rsf 3 Providence
May 26 Jaime Thomas w ko 3 Portland
Jun 30 Norberto Cabrera w rsf 8 Monte Carlo
Nov 30 Vito Antuofermo drew 15 Las Vegas
(World middleweight title)
1980
Feb 16 Loucif Hamani w ko 2 Portland
Apr 19 Bobby Watts w rsf 2 Portland
May 17 Marcos Geraldo w pts 10 Las Vegas
Sep 27 Alan Minter w rsf 3 London
(World middleweight title)
1981
Jan 17 Fulgencio Obelmejias w rsf 8 Boston
(World middleweight title)
Jun 13 Vito Antuofermo w rsf 5 Boston
(World middleweight title)
Oct 3 Mustafa Hamsho w rsf 11 Rosemont
(World middleweight title)
1982
Mar 7 William Lee w rsf 1 Atlantic City
(World middleweight title)
Oct 30 Fulgencio Obelmejias w ko 5 San Remo
(World middleweight title)
1983
Feb 11 Tony Sibson w rsf 6 Worcester
(World middleweight title)
May 27 Wilford Scypion w ko 4 Providence
(World middleweight title)
Nov 10 Roberto Duran w pts 15 Las Vegas
(World middleweight title)
1984
Mar 30 Juan Domingo Roldan w rsf 10 Las Vegas
(World middleweight title)
Oct 19 Mustafa Hamsho w ko 3 New York
(World middleweight title)
1985
Apr 15 Thomas Hearns w rsf 3 Las Vegas
(World middleweight title)
1986
Mar 10 John Mugabi w ko 11 Las Vegas
(World middleweight title)
1987
Apr 6 Ray Leonard l pts 12 Las Vegas
(World middleweight title)

Fight 67 Won 62 Lost 3 Drawn 2

LLOYD HONEYGHAN

HONEY

For two years Lloyd Honeyghan, otherwise known as 'Ragamuffin Man', was king of the welterweight walk. He rose out of the pack with a triumphant sneer to tear the title away from the supposedly invincible Donald Curry on an unforgettable night in Atlantic City in 1986. It was the performance of the decade from a British boxer, and established Honeyghan's place in world championship history.

Honeyghan was born in St Elizabeth, Jamaica, on 22 April 1960, and lived in the Bermondsey area of south-east London from boyhood. He had a promising but not outstanding amateur career with two London clubs, Fitzroy Lodge and Downside. He won a National Boys Clubs championship and boxed for England at youth and senior levels, but in three attempts never progressed further than the quarter-finals of the ABA championships. Nobody could have guessed what lay ahead.

He turned professional at 20 in December 1980, outpointing Mike Sullivan from Plymouth. His first manager, Terry Lawless, nurtured him in typically steady fashion, but in April 1983 he won the vacant British welterweight title by outpointing Cliff Gilpin from Telford over 12 hard rounds, during which both were knocked down.

Eventually, he switched from Lawless to be managed by Mickey Duff, a relationship that was often prickly but ultimately extremely successful. Duff assessed it memorably: 'There is nothing in our contract that says we have to like each other'. Honeyghan was still with Duff at the tail-end of his career in 1991, when he said: 'We don't mix outside. Mickey looks at me as a pawn, a commodity.'

Nevertheless, Honeyghan won the European welterweight title with a surprise third round knockout of Italian Gianfranco Rosi in Perugia in January 1985. Rosi went on to hold two versions of the world light-middleweight title, but a big right hand from Honeyghan, who fought with a fractured rib, put him away. It was an eye-catching win. That year saw him close in on the undisputed world champion Donald Curry, with five more wins, the last of them a British, Commonwealth and European title fight against Sylvester Mittee, who was stopped in eight rounds at Alexandra Palace in north London.

Duff then negotiated a WBC title final eliminator with a competent but unspectacular American named Horace Shufford at Wembley in May 1986. Honeyghan stopped him in the eighth round to clinch the title fight with Curry, which many saw as a dubious privilege. Curry was considered the next logical contender for Marvin Hagler's middleweight crown. Honeyghan did not share the critics' fears. 'I ain't scared of nobody, I'm going out there to bash him up,' he said. In the opening round at Caesars in Atlantic City in September 1986, he announced his intentions in a far more relevant way when he landed a thumping right hand to the jaw. Even more important, he outfought Curry on the inside. Curry was weight-drained, Honeyghan inspired. Curry tried to turn things round with a big assault in round three, but Honeyghan took the shots and gradually regained control. At the end of the sixth, the Texan was pulled out. His bottom lip was torn, a gash over his left eye was so severe it would need 20 stitches to close it, his nose was broken ... and a $10 million payday with Hagler had just disappeared. Honeyghan, on the other hand, collected a bonus of $25,000 from a $5,000 bet on himself at 5–1. His gross purse also came to $162,750, way above anything he had earned before.

Although he won the undisputed title, he gave up the World Boxing Association belt three months later because they ordered him to defend against a South African, Harold Volbrecht. Although the fight would probably have been relatively straightforward, Honeyghan took an anti-apartheid stance and handed back the belt in protest.

His first defence in February 1987 was sanctioned only by the IBF. The WBC did not rate Johnny Bumphus, a southpaw from Tacoma, Washington, worthy of a place in their top ten and refused to recognise it as a title fight. That was not viewed with any great significance by Honeyghan – it was one less fee to pay – although the WBC decision was reinforced by what happened in the fight: Bumphus looked shot to pieces and Honeyghan bulldozed him to defeat early in round two.

The WBC did, however, ratify defence number two against the tall, angular Maurice Blocker, a 23-year-old stylist from Washington DC. Blocker was unbeaten and tough, but Honeyghan's pressure and workrate earned him a unanimous decision in a hard fight at the Albert Hall, the venue where he had made his professional debut six-and-a-half years earlier. In the Spanish resort of Marbella in August 1987, Honeyghan defended against another former light-welterweight champion, Gene 'Mad Dog' Hatcher, from Fort Worth, Texas, the same town as Don Curry. He was 28, had been 140lb champion for 18 months in 1984–85 ... and didn't stand a chance.

After heavy rain had delayed the fight in the open air bullring for 24 hours, Honeyghan blazed out from the start, landed a right that dropped Hatcher and never let up. The American was rescued, helpless under a savage pounding on the ropes. Officially, it was timed at 40 seconds, but the tape shows it was 45 seconds from first bell to the intervention of the referee. It remains one of the quickest wins in world title history. Duff said afterwards: 'I've been involved with 17 world champions. The best was John Conteh, even though he never reached his full potential. Lloyd is catching him up fast. I've never known a more dedicated fighter. He's a dream.'

When the WBC held its convention in London, a show was arranged to coincide with it. Honeyghan was an obvious choice for a showcase defence, and Jorge Vaca of Mexico seemed to present a relatively safe opponent. Vaca was tough but slow, capable but lacking in flair. The IBF, knowing it was the WBC's show, opted out and left them to it.

Sadly for Honeyghan, and embarrassingly for the WBC, the title changed hands on a bizarre, new-fangled rule. A head clash left Vaca with an S-shaped cut snaking through his eyebrow in round eight. He could not go on. Under the complicated WBC rules, Honeyghan was penalised a point for an accidental head butt; in other words, for not getting cut in an accidental collision! Although he was penalised for this 'offence' in round eight, the session itself was not scored. The judges' totals at the end of round seven were tallied, then Honeyghan's penalty taken off, with the result that he lost his championship on something called a split technical decision. The IBF then increased Honeyghan's frustration by withdrawing recognition of him on the grounds that he had lost under championship conditions. Vaca was persuaded to return to London for a fight at Wembley the following March, and Honeyghan launched a furious, all-out assault from the opening bell. By the third, Vaca was down for the count.

Lloyd's first defence of this second WBC championship reign was another strange one. In Atlantic City he hit Young-kil Chung of Korea accidentally low in round five. Under WBC rules, Chung was given five minutes to recover, at the end of which he had to go on. When he refused, the fight was stopped in Honeyghan's favour.

By February 1989, Honeyghan was suffering serious hand trouble. In Las Vegas he also faced his sternest challenge from the former WBA champion Marlon Starling, who was an accomplished technician with a cool head. Starling proved too much for the Englishman, who had to take pain-killing injections in his hands before the fight (for which he was later fined by the Nevada Commission). Starling stopped Honeyghan in the ninth round, outboxing him and leaving him with a horribly swollen face, thanks to a left hook which landed on a nerve in the third round. 'The pain was so terrible, you just can't imagine. It was like someone just drilling my head all the time ... After that I didn't try to win, I was just trying to avoid getting hit in the face.' Having said that, Honeyghan described his performance as stupid because he lost his cool.

A comeback win over Delfino Marin in Miami paved the way for a shot at WBA champion Mark Breland in 1990, but he was weight-drained, ill-prepared and looked worryingly vulnerable as the stringbean American floored him six times for a third round win.

It seemed as if he must finish, but instead the following year he moved up to light-middleweight. He didn't win the world title he wanted – a defeat by Vinny Pazienza ended that dream – but he did become Commonwealth champion with a fifth-round stoppage of Mickey Hughes at Brentwood in 1993.

He retired in 1995 following a stoppage defeat by rising hopeful Adrian Dodson at the London Arena.

CAREER STATISTICS

World welterweight champion 1986-87
WBC welterweight champion 1988-89
London, born Jamaica 22 April 1960

1980
Dec 8 Mike Sullivan w pts 6 London
1981
Jan 20 Dai Davies w rsf 5 London
Feb 10 Dave Sullivan w pts 6 London
Nov 16 Dave Finigan w rsf 1 London
Nov 24 Alan Cooper w rsf 4 London
1982
Jan 25 Dave Finigan w ko 2 London
Feb 9 Granville Allen w rsf 5 London
Mar 2 Tommy McCallum w pts 6 London
Mar 15 Derek McKenzie w rsf 6 London
Mar 23 Dave Sullivan w rsf 3 London
May 18 Kostas Petrou w pts 8 London
Sep 22 Ian Murray w rsf 3 London
Nov 22 Frank McCord w ko 1 London
1983
Jan 18 Lloyd Hibbert w pts 10 London
Mar 1 Sid Smith w ko 5 London
Apr 5 Cliff Gilpin w pts 12 London
(vacant British welterweight title)
Jul 9 Kevin Austin w rsf 10 Chicago
Oct 24 Harold Brazier w pts 10 London
Dec 6 Cliff Gilpin w pts 12 London
(British welterweight title)
1984
Jun 5 Roberto Mendez w pts 8 London
1985
Jan 5 Gianfranco Rosi w ko 3 Perugia
(European welterweight title)
Feb 12 R.W.Smith w rtd 6 London
Mar 6 Roger Stafford w rsf 9 London
Aug 30 Danny Paul w pts 10 Atlantic City
Oct 1 Ralph Twinning w rsf 4 London
Nov 27 Sylvester Mittee w rsf 8 London
(British, Commonwealth & European welterweight titles)
1986
May 20 Horace Shufford w rsf 8 London
Sep 27 Donald Curry w rsf 6 Atlantic City
(World welterweight title)
Dec; Relinquished WBA title.
1987
Feb 22 Johnny Bumphus w rsf 2 London
(IBF welterweight title)
Apr 18 Maurice Blocker w pts 12 London
(WBC, IBF welterweight titles)
Aug 30 Gene Hatcher w rsf 1 Marbella
(WBC welterweight title)
Oct 28 Jorge Vaca l tdec 8 London
(WBC welterweight title)
Oct: Stripped of IBF title.
1988
Mar 29 Jorge Vaca w ko 3 London
(WBC welterweight title)
Jul 29 Yung-kil Chung w rtd 5 Atlantic City
(WBC welterweight title)
1989
Feb 4 Marlon Starling l rsf 9 Las Vegas
(WBC welterweight title)
Aug 25 Delfino Marin w pts 10 Miami
1990
Mar 3 Mark Breland l rsf 3 London
(WBA welterweight title)
1991
Jan 10 Mario Olmedo w rsf 4 London
Feb 12 John Welters w rsf 1 Basildon
May 8 Darryl Anthony w ko 2 London
1992
Apr 22 Alfredo Ramirez w pts 8 London
May 13 Mickey Duncan w rsf 2 London
Oct 28 Carlo Colarusso w rsf 6 London
1993
Jan 30 Mickey Hughes w rsf 5 Brentwood
(Commonwealth light-middleweight title)
Jun 26 Vinny Pazienza l rtd 10 Atlantic City
Nov 2 Steve Goodwin w rsf 6 London
1994
Feb 26 Kevin Adamson w rsf 6 London
(Commonwealth light-middleweight title)
Stripped of Commonwealth title.
1995
Feb 25 Adrian Dodson l rsf 3 London

Fights 48 Won 43 Lost 5

JEFF FENECH

THE THUNDER FROM DOWN UNDER

A Truculent terrier of a fighting machine, Jeff Fenech was the most successful of all Australian boxers. He held world titles at bantamweight, super-bantam and featherweight. His success was all the more remarkable for his brittle hands and a breathing problem caused by a childhood accident – a friend hit him on the nose with a plastic spade!

Born in Sydney, on 28 May 1964, Jeff was the sixth child of Maltese immigrants, Mary and Paul Fenech. His father suffered a heart attack which left him an invalid and his mother worked as a cleaner to keep them above the breadline. He was a street kid who got into his share of scrapes, and was sent to a boys home for a couple of months at the age of 12, but in spite of an explosive temper and a willingness to fight anybody, no matter how big, his teenaged antics fell some way short of hardened villainy.

At 15 he walked into a boxing gym and met Johnny Lewis, the trainer who would teach him and be with him all the way to the top. By the age of 17 he was working as an apprentice bricklayer, and out of the ring had befriended a handicapped youth from the same area, Con Spyropoulos, who was still a part of his team when he was world champion. 'I have to look after him,' he said later. 'But it's more a pleasure than a job. If I can help somebody who needs it, why not?'

He boxed for Lewis's Newtown Police Youth Club and trained like a professional from his teens. He fought ferociously every time they let him loose. He won a bronze medal at the 1983 Commonwealth Federation Championships and by the age of 20 was the Australian boxing team captain for the Los Angeles Olympics of 1984. In the flyweight quarter-final, he was given a 3–2 verdict by the judges over Redzep Redzepowski of Yugoslavia, only for the result to be reversed by an overseeing jury. Fenech was heartbroken and indignant: 'I've worked so hard for the chance to win Australia's first boxing gold medal only to have the chance taken away by a bunch of senile old men.'

As soon as he returned from the Games, he and Lewis turned professional. He made his debut in Marrickville, but surprisingly his early fights failed to draw. Although he won the Australian super-flyweight title in his third bout, it was only when he linked up with Bill Mordey – a would-be promoter who earned a living in gambling and publishing – the following year his career took off.

When Mordey suggested to Lewis that Fenech, who was nicknamed the 'Marrickville Mauler' and tried to model himself on Roberto Duran, might fight the IBF bantamweight champion Satoshi Shingaki of Japan for the world title, the trainer dismissed the idea. After all, Jeff had only six fights behind him. Then he saw tapes of Shingaki, a 21-year-old southpaw from Okinawa, and changed his mind. 'He was probably the worst world champion of all time,' he said, and they set about luring him out of Japan.

Sure enough, in Hordren Pavilion, Moore Park, Sydney, in April 1985, only six months after his professional debut, Fenech mauled Shingaki to a ninth-round defeat. He was a world champ ... but Lewis knew there was still so much learning to be done, and so little time to be bought. They fitted in two non-title fights and somehow persuaded the IBF to offer Shingaki a rematch. Fenech knocked him out in four.

But after another non-title win, the IBF could not be staved off any more. Jerome 'Kid' Coffee, an elegant, slick boxer from Nashville, Tennessee, had won all 26 fights. He arrived in Australia promising to take the inexperienced champion to school, but when they fought at the Sydney Entertainment Centre in December 1985, Coffee's skills won him rounds, Fenech's aggression, persistence and harder punching won him a unanimous decision.

He was beginning to earn worldwide attention. His 10-round points win over the enduring Mexican southpaw Daniel Zaragoza in Perth in April 1986 was shown on television in Britain. Three months later, he faced another severe test against Steve McCrory of Detroit, the flyweight gold medallist from the Los Angeles Olympics. It was set up as a fight to put the record straight.

Like Coffee, McCrory scoffed at Fenech's lack of technical knowledge. Known as the 'Bluesman', McCrory was trained by the great Emanuel Steward and was a product of the Kronk gym which had produced Thomas Hearns. Fenech had terrible trouble making the 118lb weight limit. He lost nine pounds in the last three days, weighed in four pounds too heavy and Lewis wanted to cancel the fight and give up the title. Today's medical advice would say to risk boxing was madness, but somehow Fenech made the weight overnight. He was gaunt and tired, and admitted to being in pain, but somehow perked up when the bell went. He was hurt in rounds six and seven, and his hands caused him pain, but he kept pounding away and miraculously managed to outstay the American. By the 14th McCrory had nothing left and it was stopped. The American's manager Prentiss Byrd shook his head and described Fenech as awesome.

His hand trouble kept him sidelined, but Mordey negotiated him a shot at WBC super-bantamweight champion Samart Payakarun of Thailand. Payakarun was the handsome, glamour boy of Thai boxing, whose short professional career did not tell the whole story. Before he turned to 'international style' fighting, he was a top class kick boxer. A tall, elegant southpaw, he had knocked out Mexican Lupe Pintor the previous year to win the title. Now Thais gambled enormous sums of money on him beating Fenech, ignoring the danger sign that his Liverpudlian trainer Charles Atkinson had quit the camp in disgust. Payakarun had lost his discipline.

Fenech could not match the Thai for skill and was put down early on, but then went into overdrive and Payakarun was knocked out in round four. When he returned to Bangkok, the former champion was threatened by angry fans who had lost money and took refuge in a monastery, wearing the robes of a Buddhist penitent.

Fenech was at his peak in these years, although he was sorry that his father died during that time. 'I'm sure my career kept my dad alive for a couple more years,' he said proudly. He overpowered Greg 'The Flea' Richardson, a darting, sniping puncher from Ohio, in five. Richardson said: 'He cuts the ring off better than anyone I've seen or fought. And physically, he's the strongest I've fought.'

In October 1987 Carlos Zarate, the Mexican veteran, challenged Fenech for his super-bantamweight title. Zarate had held the WBC bantamweight title during the late 1970s and was considered to be one of the hardest punching bantamweights in history. Unfortunately, his ventures into the super-bantamweight class resulted in three of his four defeats, Fenech inflicting one of them with a fourth-round technical decision.

Then in 1988 he moved up to featherweight and became the first three-weight world champion in Australian history when he stopped clever Puerto Rican Victor Callejas in the 10th, in spite of a broken hand. By now he had cortisone injections even to spar.

From his first world title success at bantamweight in April 1985 he had now won his third world title at three different weights in the space of three years: a remarkable achievement considering that in the opinion of many so-called experts he suffered from a lack of technical knowledge. Not only did he achieve this success in just three years, but that first title had come only six months after his first professional fight. Many recognised boxers wait longer than that for a crack at a title.

He battered Tyrone Downes from Trinidad and Georgie 'Go-Go' Navarro from New Jersey into defeat in five rounds apiece, and then faced the notoriously durable Marcos Villasana, a maize farmer from Mexico, all in Melbourne. The crowd response was incredible. Fenech had inspired an amazing revival in boxing as a spectator sport in Australia. Lewis said before he came along, fight cards would draw maybe 1,000 people. Fenech sold out major arenas. There weren't enough tickets to satisfy the need.

'When the people get behind you like that you just can't lose,' said Fenech. 'I just couldn't let them down. I have to win for them.'

In the Downes fight, he drew around 14,000 fans, in spite of a major concert and an Australian Rules Football game in town on the same night. He was badly cut on the left eyebrow in round one, but his corner stopped the bleeding and he came through well enough, flooring Downes four times.

'I'll watch the video – probably about 200 times!' he said. 'I want to improve in every fight. If I don't, I think I should probably get out ...'

Before the Villasana fight, there were plans for him to unify the featherweight division. 'Any boxer wants to say "I am the world champion",' said Lewis. Mordey was hoping to lure the WBA champion, Antonio Esparragoza of Venezuela, to fight Fenech in Melbourne.

Jeff said he had been warned how tough Villasana was from Julio Cesar Chavez when he was staying in Las Vegas, and told his fans: 'It's Jeff Fenech, but more importantly Australia who is on the line.' In spite of more weight troubles – he was 11 pounds over the 126lb limit with ten days to go – he lived up to his billing, pounding out a points win over a man who refused to buckle. But there was to be no unification fight. Fenech's hands gave way again and this time he announced his retirement. He talked of playing rugby and of raising a family.

After enjoying himself for a few months, he decided to box again, broke both hands on the head of Mexican Mario Martinez, and for a long time seemed as if he could not, whether he liked it or not, box again. By 1991, however, he had worked himself into a position to challenge WBC super-featherweight champion Azumah Nelson of Ghana. Nelson is one of boxing's greatest legends, and the finest fighter ever produced in Africa. Fenech had signed a four-fight deal with Don King designed to bring him a total of $5 million. It was conditional, of course, on his beating Nelson, but King said: 'Fenech's a fighter's fighter. What you see is what you get. He gives his all in a ring. That's all you can ask of a man. The American people are going to love this guy.'

Fenech told the Las Vegas media: 'Americans don't really know me. But after this fight, maybe they'll sit up and take notice.'

Fenech and Nelson met at the Mirage on a searingly hot Las Vegas afternoon in June 1991, as a double header with the Mike Tyson-Razor Ruddock rematch. For the full 12 rounds Fenech, whom Americans labelled 'Thunder from Down Under', piled on pressure, energetic and intense as ever, finishing like an express train. Nelson waited, countered, moved and sometimes simply covered up on the ropes, blocking and smothering the punches. Later he said he was suffering from malaria. There were those who said two of the three judges were suffering from myopia. One saw it 116–112 for Nelson, another scored 115–113 Fenech, and the third had it even at 114–114. The result, a draw.

The deal with King blown, Fenech returned home, grumbling bitterly about being robbed. Australia remembered 1984 when he came back from the Olympic Games after receiving similar treatment. King was blamed.

Nelson was persuaded to give him a return at the Tennis Centre, Melbourne, in March 1992, where in spite of the rain, a 35,000 crowd turned out to witness Fenech's crowning as one of boxing's elite: a four-weight world champion. It didn't happen. Nelson was at his most brilliant. He dropped Fenech in the opening round with a sharp right hand, and then repeated the point in round two. Fenech fought back with surging, rolling attacks but Nelson controlled him with a tight defence and smart countering, and then opened up to rock him again at the end of round seven. It was all over, with another knockdown, in the eighth.

Fenech took his first defeat with dignity, although like so many beaten fighters, he was concerned at having let his fans down. 'I was a champion fighter,' he said. 'Now I want to show that I am a champion person.'

He tried again, but was knocked out in seven rounds by former IBF featherweight champion Calvin Grove in June 1993.

There was one more comeback, which led to a final title bid as a lightweight in 1996. Ten days before his 32nd birthday, he was overpowered in two rounds by a rugged, powerful South African named Philip Holiday, who was defending his IBF 135lb title. It was sad and painful to watch for anyone who had seen Fenech in his rampaging, bright-eyed prime.

Australia has had its share of great fighters during the last 100 years: Young Griffo, Les Darcy, Dave Sands, Jimmy Carruthers, Lionel Rose, Johnny Famechon and others. But few could match the popular appeal of the little mauler from Marrickville, Jeff Fenech, considered by many to be the finest boxer Australia has ever produced.

CAREER STATISTICS

IBF bantamweight champion 1985-86
WBC super-bantamweight champion 1987-88
WBC featherweight champion 1988-89
Sydney, Australia, born 28 May 1964

1984
Oct 22 Bobby Williams w rsf 2 Marrickville
Oct 26 Percy Israel w rsf 7 Marrickville
Nov 30 Junior Thompson w rsf 3 Marrickville
(vacant Australian super-flyweight title)
Dec 15 Ilesia Manila w rsf 2 Suva, Fiji
1985
Feb 1 Wayne Mulholland w rsf 5 Dapto
Mar 4 Rolando Navarro w rsf 4 Sydney
Apr 26 Satoshi Shingaki w rsf 9 Sydney
(IBF bantamweight title)
Jun 14 John Matienza w rsf 6 Sydney
Jul 26 John Farrell w ko 9 Brisbane
Aug 23 Satoshi Shingaki w rsf 3 Sydney
(IBF bantamweight title)
Nov 4 Kenny Butts w rtd 2 Brisbane
Dec 2 Jerome Coffee w pts 15 Sydney
(IBF bantamweight title)
1986
Apr 11 Daniel Zaragoza w pts 10 Perth
Jul 18 Steve McCrory w rsf 14 Sydney
(IBF bantamweight title)
1987
Mar 4 Tony Miller w pts 12 Melbourne
(Australian featherweight title)
May 8 Samart Payakarun w rsf 4 Sydney
(WBC super-bantamweight title)
Jul 10 Greg Richardson w rsf 5 Sydney
(WBC super-bantamweight title)
Oct 16 Carlos Zarate w tdec 4 Sydney
(WBC super-bantamweight title)
Dec 11 Osmar Avila w ko 1 Sydney
1988
Mar 7 Victor Callejas w rsf 10 Sydney
(WBC featherweight title)
Aug 12 Tyrone Downes w rsf 5 Melbourne
(WBC featherweight title)
Nov 30 Georgie Navarro w rsf 5 Melbourne
(WBC featherweight title)
1989
Apr 8 Marcos Villasana w pts 12 Melbourne
(WBC featherweight title)
Nov 24 Mario Martinez w pts 12 Melbourne
1990 inactive
1991
Jan 19 John Kalbhenn w rsf 4 Adelaide
Jun 28 Azumah Nelson drew 12 Las Vegas
(WBC super-featherweight title)
Sep 13 Miguel Franca w pts 10 Melbourne
1992
Mar 1 Azumah Nelson l rsf 8 Melbourne
(WBC super-featherweight title)
1993
Jun 7 Calvin Grove l ko 7 Melbourne
1994 inactive
1995
Nov 18 Tialano Tovar w rsf 8 Atlantic City
1996
Mar 9 Mike Juarez w rsf 2 Melbourne
May 18 Philip Holiday l rsf 2 Melbourne
(IBF lightweight title)

Fights 32 Won 28 Lost 3 Drawn 1

ROBERTO DURAN

MANOS DE PIEDRA

From June 1980 to January 1990, Roberto Duran was a world champion, off and on, at welter, light-middle and middleweight, and a challenger at super-middleweight. An exceptional career. Yet nobody who saw him in those years only, or continues to watch him in the 1990s, can have a notion of just how great he was. Throughout the 1970s he was arguably the very best and certainly one of the most destructive and colourful lightweights the boxing world has ever seen. From winning the title in 1972 to relinquishing it in 1979, after 12 successful defences, Duran was a legendary champion. His fanatical singleness of purpose meant he fought with unequalled savagery, showing no mercy, consideration or even ordinary courtesy to opponents. In fact, if he could disconcert them with an insult about their wives, or cripple them with a knee to the groin, as was alleged, he regarded it as all part of the business. To his Panamanian countrymen he was a macho idol. The fists with which he dealt destruction they called 'Manos de Piedra', Hands of Stone.

Duran's birth and early years still have some mystery about them. He was the second of nine children, and was born on 16 June 1951. Duran's mother, Clara Samariego, lived in Los Chorrillos, a district on the outskirts of Panama City but, for a short while, around the time of Roberto's birth, lived at Guarare, about 150 miles away. An American investigative journalist has claimed to have identified Duran's real father, a serving GI from Arizona of Mexican and Indian blood, who left Panama before Duran was born.

The family was almost inevitably very poor, and Duran provided his own entertainment as a child, running wild on the beaches, stealing mangoes and coconuts from the plantations around, and getting into endless scrapes, fighting with other boys, usually bigger and older.

He rarely attended school, so acquired little learning, and at 13 he was expelled anyway when one of his opponents in a scrap was knocked downstairs. Duran now became more unruly than ever, and established one part of the local beach as his 'territory' by seeing off rivals, much as animals do, and was later honoured by the stretch being named after him. He fished the waters which, with his raids on the plantations, helped keep him and his family fed. Duran also earned some small change by shining shoes. He was a man of the streets and it was street-fighting methods that he refined (but not too much) into his successful ring technique.

Such a notorious character was soon persuaded into amateur boxing, but the niceties of the amateur game did not appeal to Roberto. He would have been happier fighting without gloves, let alone vests and over-solicitous referees. After 16 amateur contests (13 wins), he turned professional. His first manager was Alfredo Vasquez, and he obtained Duran his first professional bout on 8 March 1967. Duran was 15 years old. The contest was in Colón, and Duran won on points over four rounds.

After two further contests in Colón, Duran had a dozen bouts in Panama City, where he trained at the Marañon Gymnasium. One of Duran's finest performances in the ring came on his 19th birthday when he stopped fellow Panamanian Ernesto Marcel, becoming the only boxer ever to stop Marcel in his career. Marcel was later to become the WBA featherweight champion.

In 1971 Roberto Duran's contract was bought by local industrialist and land-owner Carlos Eleta, who paid Vasquez $300 for it. It was to prove a good investment as the shrewd Eleta engaged Ray Arcel, a veteran 72-year-old with a proven track record of success dating back some 50 years, to train Duran. Arcel had trained many world champions, including Frankie Genaro, Charley 'Phil' Rosenberg, Barney Ross, Ezzard Charles and the 1920s lightweight often bracketed with Duran as the division's best, Benny Leonard. Arcel was excited by Duran and developed a close relationship with him. He recruited Freddie Brown as assistant trainer. Another veteran, Brown had been heavyweight champion Rocky Marciano's cut man in the 1950s.

After 24 victories, Duran made his New York debut on 13 September 1971 on the undercard of the Madison Square Garden bill which featured lightweight champion Ken Buchanan's defence against former champion Ismael Laguna. Laguna was a Panamanian, like Duran, and Duran was an obvious potential challenger to the winner. The fans that night saw two outstanding performances. Champion Buchanan gave a gutsy and brilliant display of boxing skill to overcome Laguna in a superb bout, while Duran was spectacular in a different kind of way in knocking out Benny Huertas in only 66 seconds. With all eyes now on him, Duran then gave a more extended but no less stunning display when taking on the former world super-featherweight champion, Hiroshi Kobayashi, from Japan, in Panama City. Kobayashi was no match for the natural lightweight Duran, who fought with a clinical savagery that was chilling, and registered a super-impressive seventh-round knockout.

Eight months later 19,000 fans were packing Madison Square Garden, and millions more tuning in on television to see what promised to be the classic confrontation: the supremely gifted boxing of the pale Scot Buchanan against the irresistible force of the dark-haired macho man from Panama, for the world lightweight title.

Nobody was disappointed, except, of course, Buchanan and his supporters. It was a brilliant evenly fought contest in which, as the bell rang to end the 13th round, Duran appeared to have got ahead. On the way, his non-stop, snarling aggression, including a careless use of the head and a tendency to continue punching after the bell, were no more than usual Duran trademarks. But the end of the 13th round was different altogether.

Buchanan was on the ropes as the bell sounded, and Duran, with his back to the referee, unleashed a terrific blow which caught Buchanan in the groin. Buchanan himself is convinced that it was Duran's knee which delivered the dent to his foul cup that caused him to sink to the canvas in agony. Taken to his corner, he was still doubled up in pain when the buzzer sounded to warn the boxers of the start of the 14th round. Buchanan could not continue.

Referee Johnny LoBianco, who didn't see the blow, admitted it was after the bell, but claimed it couldn't have been low because the foul cup prevents a boxer being hurt by a low blow. However, when it was clear Buchanan couldn't continue, the referee gave the verdict and title to Duran on a technical knockout. The editor of the *New York Post*, Paul Sann, said that Duran had 'the best left hook to the balls I've ever seen'.

Buchanan, unusually for ex-boxers, who sink their differences in retirement, forever remained bitter about Duran, refusing to appear in a televised tribute for him years later. Duran was to agree Buchanan was the best boxer he ever met, but avoided meeting him again, an omission which Buchanan claimed cost him a fortune.

Duran became an even bigger hero in Panama than ever, with a private income tax arrangement to help maintain his riches, with some of which he bought his mother a house, to prove there was a heart of sorts in his granite make-up. Further proof that he was human came in a non-title fight in November 1972 when yet another brilliant boxer in a golden age for lightweights, Esteban DeJesus, of Puerto Rico, outpointed him in a 10-rounder at Madison Square Garden. DeJesus dropped Duran right at the start of the contest, and thereafter kept the initiative throughout. Duran's reaction to his first defeat showed more of his animal nature. He went screamingly berserk in his hotel room, and punched the walls till his hands could take no more.

Duran made three defences of his title in 1973, against Jimmy Robertson of the USA, Hector Thompson of Australia and Guts Ishimatsu of Japan, all in Panama City, and all won without serious alarms, in the fifth, eighth and tenth rounds respectively. Then Duran had to meet DeJesus again, for the title. The contest was again in Panama City. Alas for DeJesus, he experienced difficulty making the weight and as the bout continued became worn down by the heat. Despite another brilliant start by DeJesus, which saw him drop Duran again in the first minute, he could not keep on top and the referee had to rescue him in the 11th round.

None of Duran's next six challengers for his title, in contests spread over little more than two years, managed to go the distance, although three of them lasted into the 14th round, proof that Duran retained his hitting power and his desire to knock his opponent out right through the longest contests. He then met Edwin Viruet, a Puerto Rican from New York, in his 11th defence in the Spectrum, Philadelphia, and was forced to go the 15 rounds. It was the second time Viruet had taken him the distance, and seven months later brother Adolph did, too.

Duran's last defence of his lightweight title was in 1978, and fittingly was a rubber match with Esteban DeJesus. Duran's title till now had been the WBA version, the division having split during Buchanan's reign. In 1978 the WBC champion was Esteban DeJesus, so the two men were battling to unify the division. Caesars Palace, Las Vegas, was the venue. Duran paid his old adversary the respect of starting more cautiously than usual, and avoided an early knockdown. He gave his aggression full rein later to knock out DeJesus in the 12th round. DeJesus was to become addicted to drugs and, after serving a jail sentence for a killing, he contracted AIDS and died in 1989, with Duran one of his last visitors in hospital.

A year after unifying the lightweight division, Duran relinquished the title. He had developed a passion for over-indulging on food between bouts, and his weight ballooned between contests. He began campaigning as a welterweight, and included former world champion Carlos Palomino among his victims. Such was his lightweight record that in June 1980 he climbed into the ring in Montreal's Olympic Stadium to try to wrest the WBC welterweight title from the dazzling Sugar Ray Leonard, five years his junior. Leonard was being spoken of as the new boxing sensation and the match would help decide if he had yet supplanted Duran as the world's best pound-for-pound boxer.

Before 46,317 fans on a cold, damp night, Leonard's supreme self-belief led him to make a disastrous decision. Brilliantly skilful, he decided that he could beat the pumped-up lightweight Duran at his own game. His manager, Angelo Dundee, was helpless as Leonard tried to trade punch for punch with a heavily bearded macho man. Duran loved being able to get on the inside of Leonard and give him no rest from his bullying tactics. At the end of 15 rounds Leonard was a wiser man. He'd suffered his first defeat, lost his world title by unanimous decision and given Duran one of his most remarkable victories.

If Duran had retired after this contest, he would have been held in awe by boxing fans for all time. Instead, he failed to learn from Leonard's downfall, and took over from him the mantle of arrogance. Manager Carlos Eleta claimed he fixed an unusually early return fight with Leonard to try to prevent Duran destroying himself in the meantime. But it was too late to avoid Duran destroying a large part of his boxing reputation. Leonard, this time, displayed all his artistry. Halfway through he began to taunt Duran, dropping his hands and showing Duran his chin. Duran looked clumsy, and Leonard laughed at him. Halfway through the eighth Duran gave in. Saying '*No mas, no mas*' (no more) to referee Octavio Meyran, he walked out of the ring.

No doubt Duran, after his bingeing and fasting, was not fit for this contest, and retired rather than face the inevitable humiliation the later rounds would have brought, as his stamina faded. But his legend was shattered. His trainer Ray Arcel was the one who had to explain Duran's unprecedented action to the Louisiana Commission. He couldn't. He was never again to be in Duran's corner. Had Duran not received his purse in advance, it is likely that at least part of it would have been withheld by the Commission.

Duran could hardly retire now, while he was a laughing stock. Besides, at 29 he knew nothing but boxing. He moved up another weight, to light-middle, and 14 months after the Leonard debacle was challenging for a third world title, the WBC championship held by Wilfred Benitez. But Benitez was a great world champion himself, seven years younger, and more natural at the weight, and Duran was well beaten at Caesars Palace. Then Duran had to take off several pounds to fight ex-British champion Kirkland Laing in Detroit. Laing, a tricky customer, outpointed him over 10 rounds. So when on his 32nd birthday Duran challenged again for the light-middleweight title, this time the WBA version held by the unbeaten Davey Moore, it seemed like old 'Hands of Stone' was being given a last big payday. Moore was a 5–2 favourite among the betting men at Madison Square Garden.

In this contest the old Duran reappeared. He got on top, beat Moore savagely, broke his nose, and won when the referee rescued Moore in the eighth round. Duran said amidst tears: 'I've returned to be Roberto Duran. It's been a long time.' It had been just over two-and-a-half years, to be more precise, since his loss to Leonard. The 20,000 fans sang 'Happy Birthday' to him, and most of his old admirers now forgave him his single lapse.

Duran was now hotter than ever at the box-office, and was allowed to move up yet another weight and challenge the undisputed middleweight champion, Marvelous Marvin Hagler, for his crown. It appeared a mismatch, as Hagler was a magnificently muscled natural middleweight, in his prime, while Duran could be seen as a bloated, ageing lightweight. Hagler was a 4–1 favourite for the Caesars Palace showdown. But Hagler knew Duran would be merciless and unstoppable should he get the upper hand, and decided to take no chances with the old-stager. It was only in the last round or two that Hagler had the confidence to open up and assert his superiority. He took the decision clearly enough, but for the only time in his 13 successful world title bouts, he was forced to leave the verdict to the judges. This was one of Duran's bravest performances.

Duran's excursion into the middleweights cost him his WBA light-middleweight title, for failing to defend against Mike McCallum, so Duran challenged for the WBC version, now held by Thomas Hearns, another of the 1980s gallery of greats. Duran failed to get going in this encounter, was cut and dropped twice in the first round and knocked clean out in the second. It was his first knockout defeat in his 83rd contest, and another obvious point at which to retire. He was a day short of being 33.

Duran did have a rest for 18 months, and on his third contest back he was outpointed by Hagler's brother, Robbie Sims, who completed a family double over the macho man. But Duran racked up enough wins in three years to be matched with Iran Barkley for his WBC middleweight title at the Convention Center, Atlantic City. It was an outstanding contest, with Duran, badly hurt in the eighth, fighting his way back to put Barkley down in the 11th. The fight was a difficult one to score, but Duran earned the split decison. So the amazing fighting man won a world title at a fourth weight, in his 38th year. It was nearly 17 years since he had won his first world title, weighing 24lb lighter. The gap between winning different world titles was the longest in boxing history until George Foreman made his heavyweight comeback to win a version of the world crown in 1994.

The win set up another enormous payday for Duran nine months later – a third meeting with Sugar Ray Leonard for Leonard's WBC super-middleweight championship. The match was made at 2lb above the middleweight limit so as not to put at stake Duran's title, although in fact both men weighed in inside the middleweight limit. Duran earned $7½ million for his efforts at The Mirage, Las Vegas, but 'earned' is hardly the word. The fight was awful, with both men going through the motions to the disgust of the 16,000 spectators, who had paid an average of $550 each to be present. Leonard won easily on points.

The WBC took Duran's title away in 1990 as he had not defended it for nearly a year. He kept on boxing, winning some and losing a few, taking his *curriculum vitae* past 100 contests. His fights were either against up-and-coming boxers or men in decline with well-known names. On the eve of his 46th birthday in 1997 he scored his 100th victory by outpointing former WBA middleweight champion Jorge Castro, who was 16 years younger, before delirious fans in Panama. It was then announced that Sugar Ray Leonard wished to fight him for a fourth time in Australia, but Duran was in no hurry. Because he owed back taxes in the United States, he chose to fight elsewhere and, in November 1997, won in South Africa. Nevertheless he was due to challenge WBA middleweight champion William Joppy at Madison Square Garden on the undercard of the Evander Holyfield–Henry Akinwande heavyweight title match just before his 47th birthday in 1998, but the promotion was cancelled when Akinwande failed a medical. Duran would have been fighting a man more than 20 years younger for a purse most of which would have gone to the Inland Revenue. Many thought it a blessing for Duran that the fight was called off, but Duran would never think so ...

CAREER STATISTICS

World lightweight champion 1972-78
(WBA champion 1972-78, undisputed champion 1978)
WBC welterweight champion 1980
WBA light-middleweight champion 1983-84
WBC middleweight champion 1989
Colon, Panama, born Los Chorrilos, Panama
16 June 1951

1967
Mar 8 Carlos Mendoza w pts 4 Colon
Apr 4 Manuel Jimenez w ko 1 Colon
May 14 Juan Gondola w ko 1 Colon
May 30 Eduardo Morales w ko 1 Panama City
Aug 10 Enrique Jacobo w ko 1 Panama City
1968
Jan 12 Butch de Leon w ko 2 Panama City
Mar 14 Carlos Mendoza w pts 4 Panama City
Aug 25 Leroy Cargil w ko 1 Panama City
Sep 4 Eduardo Fruto w pts 8 Panama City
Sep 22 Cesar de Leon w ko 1 Panama City
Dec 7 Carlos Howard w ko 1 Panama City
1969
Jan 19 Alberto Brands w ko 4 Colon
Feb 1 Eduardo Fruto w pts 8 Panama City
May 18 Jacinto Garcia w ko 4 Panama City
Jun 22 Adolfo Osses w ko 7 Panama City
Jul 16 Serafin Garcia w ko 5 Panama City
Nov 23 Luis Patino w ko 8 Panama City
1970
Apr 5 Felipe Torres w pts 10 Mexico City
May 16 Ernesto Marcel w rsf 10 Panama City
Jul 10 Clemente Mucino w ko 6 Colon
Oct 18 Nacho Castaneda w rsf 3 Panama City
1971
Jan 5 Jose Angel Herrera w ko 6 Monterrey
Mar 31 Jose Acosta w ko 1 Panama City
May 29 Lloyd Marshall w rsf 6 Panama City
Jul 15 Fermin Soto w ko 3 Monterrey
Sep 13 Benny Huertas w ko 1 New York
Oct 16 Hiroshi Kobayashi w ko 7 Panama City
1972
Jan 15 Angel Robinson Garcia w pts 10 Panama City
Mar 10 Francisco Munoz w ko 1 Panama City
Jun 26 Ken Buchanan w rsf 13 New York
(WBA lightweight title)
Sep 2 Greg Potter w ko 1 Panama City
Oct 28 Lupe Ramirez w ko 1 Panama City
Nov 17 Esteban De Jesus l pts 10 New York
1973
Jan 20 Jimmy Robertson w ko 5 Panama City
(WBA lightweight title)
Feb 23 Juan Medina w rsf 7 Los Angeles
Mar 17 Javier Ayala w pts 10 Los Angeles
Apr 14 Gerardo Ferrat w rsf 2 Panama City
Jun 2 Hector Thompson w rsf 8 Panama City
(WBA lightweight title)
Aug 4 Doc McClendon w pts 10 San Juan
Sep 8 Ishimatsu Suzuki w rsf 10 Panama City
(WBA lightweight title)
Dec 1 Tony Garcia w ko 2 Santiago
1974
Jan 21 Leonard Tavares w rsf 4 Paris
Feb 16 Armando Mendoza w rsf 3 Panama City
Mar 16 Esteban De Jesus w rsf 11 Panama City
(WBA lightweight title)
Jul 6 Flash Gallego w rsf 5 Panama City
Sep 2 Hector Matta w pts 10 San Juan
Oct 31 Jose Vasquez w ko 2 San Jose
Nov 16 Adalberto Vanegas w ko 1 Panama City
Dec 21 Masataka Takayama w rsf 1 San Jose
(WBA lightweight title)
1975
Feb 15 Andres Salgado w ko 1 Panama City
Mar 2 Ray Lampkin w ko 14 Panama City
(WBA lightweight title)
Jun 3 Jose Peterson w ko 1 Miami
Aug 2 Pedro Mendoza w ko 1 Managua
Sep 13 Alirio Acuna w ko 3 Chitre
Sep 30 Edwin Viruet w pts 10 Uniondale, NY
Dec 20 Leoncio Ortiz w ko 15 San Juan
(WBA lightweight title)
1976
May 4 Saoul Mamby w pts 10 Miami
May 22 Lou Bizzarro w ko 14 Erie, Pa
(WBA lightweight title)
Jul 31 Emiliano Villa w rsf 7 Panama City
Oct 15 Alvaro Rojas w ko 1 Hollywood, Fl.
(WBA lightweight title)
1977
Jan 29 Vilomar Fernandez w rsf 6 Miami
(WBA lightweight title)
May 16 Javier Munoz w pts 10 Landover
Aug 6 Bernardo Diaz w ko 1 Panama City
Sep 17 Edwin Viruet w pts 15 Philadelphia
(WBA lightweight title)
1978
Jan 21 Esteban De Jesus w ko 12 Las Vegas
(World lightweight title)
Apr 27 Adolfo Viruet w pts 10 New York
Sep 1 Ezequiel Obando w ko 2 Panama City
Dec 8 Monroe Brooks w ko 8 New York
Relinquished world lightweight title

1979
Apr 8 Jimmy Heair w pts 10 Las Vegas
Jun 22 Carlos Palomino w pts 10 New York
Sep 28 Zeferino Gonzalez w pts 10 Las Vegas
1980
Jan 13 Joseph Nsubuga w rsf 4 Las Vegas
Feb 24 Wellington Wheatley w rsf 6 Las Vegas
Jun 20 Ray Leonard w pts 15 Montreal
(WBC welterweight title)
Nov 25 Ray Leonard l rtd 8 New Orleans
(WBC welterweight title)
1981
Aug 9 Mike Gonzalez w pts 10 Cleveland
Sep 26 Luigi Minchillo w pts 10 Las Vegas
1982
Jan 30 Wilfred Benitez l pts 15 Las Vegas
(WBC light-middleweight title)
Sep 4 Kirkland Laing l pts 10 Detroit
Nov 12 Jimmy Batten w pts 10 Miami
1983
Jan 29 Pipino Cuevas w rsf 4 Los Angeles
Jun 16 Davey Moore w rsf 8 New York
(WBA light-middleweight title)
Nov 10 Marvin Hagler l pts 15 Las Vegas
(World middleweight title)
1984
Stripped of WBA light-middleweight title.
Jun 15 Thomas Hearns l ko 2 Las Vegas
(WBC light-middleweight title)
1985 inactive
1986
Jan 31 Manuel Zambrano w ko 2 Panama City
Apr 19 Jorge Suero w ko 2 Panama City
Jun 23 Robbie Sims l pts 10 Las Vegas
1987
May 16 Victor Claudio w pts 10 Miami
Sep 12 Juan Carlos Gimenez w pts 10 Miami
1988
Feb 5 Ricky Stackhouse w pts 10 Atlantic City
Apr 14 Paul Thorne w rsf 6 Atlantic City
Oct 1 Jeff Llanas w pts 10 Chicago
1989
Feb 24 Iran Barkley w pts 12 Atlantic City
(WBC middleweight title)
Dec 7 Ray Leonard l pts 12 Las Vegas
(WBC super-middleweight title)
Relinquished WBC middleweight title
1990 inactive
1991
Mar 18 Pat Lawlor l rsf 6 Las Vegas
1992
Mar 30 Tony Biglen w pts 10 Buffalo
Dec 18 Ken Hulsey w ko 1 Cleveland
1993
Jun 29 Jacques Le Blanc w pts 10 Bay St Louis
Aug 17 Sean Fitzgerald w ko 6 Bay St Louis
Dec 14 Tony Menefee w rsf 8 Bay St Louis
1994
Feb 23 Carlos Montero w pts 10 Marseille
Mar 29 Terry Thomas w rsf 4 Bay St Louis
Jun 25 Vinny Pazienza l pts 12 Las Vegas
Oct 18 Heath Todd w rsf 4 Bay St Louis
1995
Jan 14 Vinny Pazienza l pts 12 Atlantic City
Jun 10 Ron Martinez w rsf 7 Kansas City
Dec 21 Wilbur Garst w rsf 4 Fort Lauderdale
1996
Feb 20 Ray Domenge w pts 10 Miami
Jun 22 Hector Camacho l pts 12 Atlantic City
Aug 31 Ariel Cruz w rsf 1 Panama City
Sep 27 Mike Culbert w rsf 6 Chester, Va.
1997
Feb 15 Jorge Castro l pts 10 Mar del Plata
Jun 14 Jorge Castro w pts 10 Panama City
Nov 15 Dave Radford w pts 8 Hammanskraal
1998
Jan 31 Felix Hernandez w pts 10 Panama City

Fights 115 Won 102 Lost 13

SUGAR RAY LEONARD

THE GOLDEN BOY

Sugar Ray Leonard was boxing's golden boy from the day he took the Olympic gold medal at light-welterweight in the 1976 Games in Montreal. On that day he announced he would not fight again, then he more or less stage-managed his own highly lucrative professional career, retiring several times but making a series of comebacks, especially to engage in big fights. At times it seemed that he couldn't be bothered with bread-and-butter contests but just wanted to collect world titles. He won championships at five different weights, a record. Many fans disliked the way he was able to dictate his own programme but they continued to pay at the box office to watch him. He represented glamour, but was no playboy. He had the steel, the character, the desire, the temperament and above all the supreme boxing skills to make himself the outstanding boxer of the 1980s.

Most things about Ray Leonard's boxing career failed to conform to the usual pattern, and his childhood was one of them. He was not the potential criminal plucked from the street by a kind-hearted policeman who took him to a gym. He was the shy, retiring child, more interested in reading, and he was pressed into boxing in order to win the respect of his father and brothers, who gave him the impression they feared he might become something of a wimp.

He was born on 17 May 1956 in Wilmington, North Carolina. His father, Cicero, and his mother, Getha, named him Ray Charles, after the blind singer, whom they admired. His mother, in particular, hoped that her son might become a famous singer, too.

When Ray was born, the parents already had three boys and a girl. They were not rich, but they managed. Cicero, who had been a keen amateur boxer when serving in the navy, worked at the local Coca-Cola plant. When Ray was four the family moved to Washington DC, and two more sisters for Ray brought the family total to nine. Seven years later the family moved again, and settled in Palmer Park, Maryland, the place with which Ray was associated as a boxer.

Ray's older brothers, Roy, Kenny and Roger, were all keen on sports, willing to try almost anything. Ray was different. He quite enjoyed hiding himself away and reading comics. He had also had some singing lessons with his sister and had an excellent voice. He sang in the church choir. The older boys in Ray's family tried to get him interested in sports, and took him along to a boys' club. He did some sparring, but was frightened and couldn't see any enjoyment in getting hurt. In fact he couldn't see the point of competitive sports at all. He enjoyed things like roller-skating and climbing, and was very fit and athletic, showing a talent for gymnastics, but he preferred swinging about on trees in the park to practising formal exercise in a gymnasium.

It was the opening of the Palmer Park Recreation Center in 1970, when Roy was 14, that finally sparked his interest in boxing. Ray's brother Roger became a Center regular, largely because he was keen on boxing and one of the volunteers helping to run the place was a former pro boxer, Dave Jacobs. When Ray's best school friend showed an interest in joining Dave's boxing classes too, Ray decided that he might as well take part with him. Ray showed no immediate aptitude, but decided to put all he had into it in order to get the approval of his brothers and his dad. In fact he over did it, in the view of David Jacobs, who wanted him to progress gradually against boys of his own size. Ray challenged an older boy who had already beaten brother Roger. Giving away around 50 lb, Ray was badly beaten up and cried in frustration. He deliberately faced bigger boys and took so much punishment that when he got home from the Center he would often go straight to bed to recover. He did it, he told an interviewer much later, to show his brothers that he was as rough as them.

Soon Ray began to do very well, particularly as a defensive boxer. He was a skinny lad with less punching power than most of those he took on but he began to enjoy it when he found that he had considerable natural ability in anticipation and countering. He began to strengthen his body by running and working out in the gym, and as he was of the age where his physique was maturing naturally, he very quickly found himself much heavier and stronger.

Everybody was amazed at the sudden development of the young boy, especially his dad and his coach Dave Jacobs. Jacobs and the Center's director, Ollie Dunlap, decided to enter some of their boxers in local tournaments. Ray now loved the edge of competition and began to win matches. He won the local Golden Gloves tournament at lightweight in 1972, when 16, and represented the USA against the USSR, and won. He entered trials to get into the US Olympic team for 1972, but was beaten somewhat controversially in a bout at local level, failing to reach the finals. He tried to get in by a different route, but suddenly all his physical efforts of the previous years overcame him and he was forced to withdraw exhausted. But he was only 16 and there was every chance of making the 1976 team for Montreal if he practised hard, and he made this his ambition.

Ray put so much into his training that his hands suffered. They became sore and inclined to swell, a problem which he was to have throughout his career. Another worry was his girlfriend's pregnancy. Juanita Wilkinson was a fellow student. The two families discussed the situation and decided that the 16-year-old Ray should be acknowledged as the father, but that the pair should not marry, at least for the time being. This was a remarkable coincidence, as the original Sugar Ray, Ray Robinson, also found himself in the same situation at a similar age. In his case the families decided that the couple should marry, but after the birth a divorce was arranged. In both cases the pregnancy resulted in the birth of a son, in Leonard's case named Ray junior.

Ray lost his form and was beaten in three contests after Ray junior was born, but nevertheless made it into the US team for the 1976 Olympics. He and his older brother Roger, who had inspired his ambition to box, were both light-welterweights by now, but Roger tried for the team as a welterweight, so that the brothers should not risk having to meet with one eliminating the other. In the event Roger lost in the final stages of the qualifiers.

Ray had by now picked up the additional 'Sugar' to his name, a recognition that some thought he might emulate the great Sugar Ray Robinson. Ray was quite proud to share the name 'Sugar Ray' with Robinson.

Sugar Ray duly reached the final of the light-welterweights at the Montreal Games, and his whole family made the journey to watch him. Ray boxed with photographs of Juanita and Ray junior in his socks. His final opponent was a good Cuban with a destructive punch, Andres Aldama, but Ray was in a different class and completely outboxed his man to win. Ray immediately announced his retirement from boxing - the first of many retirements that proved false. He was to be boxing's answer to Frank Sinatra so far as comebacks were concerned. 'I've fought my last fight. My journey is ended. My dream is fulfilled', he melodramaticallly told not only those present at Montreal but millions of stunned TV viewers back in the States.

Ray was the glamour boy of the Games, with his bright intelligence, boyish smile and confident manner. There had been offers for him to turn professional before the Games, and now there were many others. It was obvious that there was a fortune to be made by the young warrior. He was already being spoken of as the man to take over the role of Muhammad Ali as boxing's figurehead, as Ali's career began to wind down.

Ray's decision to turn pro was influenced by his father becoming ill and his mother suffering a heart attack. Juanita had been obliged to serve a paternity suit on him as a step towards receiving welfare assistance. Ray could see his earnings were to be vital to two families. Whether or not his statement that he would study at Maryland University was serious or not, the plan was ditched and he signed a professional contract. Ray's amateur record was impressive. As well as his Olympic medal, he has won three National Golden Gloves titles, the AAU title twice, and had won gold in the 1975 Pan-American Games. His figures were 155 wins to five defeats.

Janks Morton, the assistant trainer at the Recreation Center, got a lawyer, Mike Trainer, and a PR man, Charles Brotman, to draw up a plan for Ray. Ray had already decided that he would not allow one man to control his career, as he had seen the arrangement work badly with other boxers. In fact Muhammad Ali himself had warned Ray to beware of this.

Trainer set up Sugar Ray Leonard Inc, sole proprietor Sugar Ray Leonard, with a capital of $21,000 loaned by a group of friends at eight per cent interest for four years. Leonard took a weekly salary of $475. The leading trainer Angelo Dundee, who had been, and still was, an influential figure in Muhammad Ali's career, was engaged on a six-year contract from November 1976 in an advisory capacity - to oversee the training arrangements, to approve opponents and to be in Leonard's corner at contests. He was, in fact, a sort of semi-manager, and took half his usual fee, i.e. 15 per cent of Leonard's earnings. Dave Jacobs and Janks Morton would take over the day-to-day training of Leonard. In fact Jacobs had been Leonard's first trainer as an amateur and he was to be with Leonard through much of his career.

The cash involved to set up Sugar Ray Leonard Inc was, of course, minuscule in relation to his potential earnings, and in fact Ray could have paid off the loan after his first pro contest, for which he earned $40,000, a record for a newcomer. The business arrangement allowed him to control his own career, and ultimately to make more money from boxing than anybody before him, including Muhammad Ali.

Sugar Ray made his pro debut at the Civic Center, Baltimore, Maryland, on 5 February 1977. His opponent was a safe one, Luis Vega, who had 14 wins against 8 defeats. He had never been knocked off his feet, but did not possess the punch to damage Leonard. The attendance of 10,270 was a record for the venue, and CBS televised the contest to a national audience. Sugar Ray won comfortably over six rounds. He had the advantage over the vast majority of debutant boxers that he was already a national figure and the fans wanted to see his fights. He had no need to sign over a large part of himself to an influential promoter in order to get exposure in the first place. However, Leonard continued boxing mostly in the smaller venues and building up a record of good wins, graduating to eight-rounders in February 1978.

Sugar Ray gradually honed his outstanding boxing skills. His footwork, his fast two-fisted punching, his instinctive ability to out-think his opponents and his sense of tactics – of knowing when to press the button and demoralise his opponent with a bewildering spurt of virtuosity – were allied to strength, stamina and a punching power that saw nine of his first 14 opponents beaten inside the distance.

His 15th contest was an important one. He was fighting as a welterweight and met Randy Shields, ranked fourth in the world. Shields had inflicted on Sugar Ray one of his only five defeats as an amateur. The bout, in Baltimore in October 1978, saw Sugar Ray maintain a blistering pace throughout the ten rounds and stage a big final round to get a unanimous decision. The critics were impressed. There were little business snags in Sugar Ray's relentless progress, however, one of them being that at the time he beat Shields his Corporation was in dispute with Angelo Dundee over his fees, an argument that took four months to resolve. He had also lost the backing of ABC TV, who stopped showing his bouts because Mike Trainer asked too much money.

Less than a year after beating Shields, Leonard became North American welterweight champion with a stoppage of Pete Ranzany in Las Vegas. A rapid series of left jabs had Ranzany helpless on the ropes in the fourth round before Sugar Ray floored him with a right hook. When he rose, another hook sent him to the canvas again and the referee has seen enough. Then, on 30 September 1979, came the big one – the challenge for the WBC welterweight championship of the world at Caesars Palace, Las Vegas. The champion was one of the best ever, Wilfred Benitez.

Leonard was guaranteed $1 million for the contest, a record for a welterweight challenger. In fact, champion Benitez had never received more than $150,000 before this contest. This caused difficulty during the negotiations, as Benitez' manager, Jimmy Jacobs, would not allow the champion to accept less than the challenger. In the end both men received $1.2 million, naturally the first time two welters had ever taken over $1 million each from a fight. Benitez was as skilful a boxer as Sugar Ray himself. He had been light-welter champion at 17 years, 176 days old, the youngest world champion in the history of boxing. He was unbeaten after 37 contests; Sugar Ray after 25. Both men stood 5ft 10in but Leonard was bigger and had the advantage in weight, chest and reach measurements.

It turned out to be a classic contest, featuring the highest skills and sportsmanship from both sides. In fact Angelo Dundee, who should know, said it 'demonstrated all that is good in boxing'. In the third round, Benitez was momentarily dropped by a left jab from Leonard, and in the sixth a clash of heads opened a deep vertical cut on Benitez' forehead. The contest was very close, and Dundee told Leonard after 12 rounds and again before the last that he needed a big effort to make sure of the title. He made one. With half a minute to go, a left hook caught Benitez around the ear and dropped him to the canvas and, although Benitez rose and defended himself, referee Carlos Padilla stopped it with six seconds left. Leonard, who confessed he was scared senseless when before the start the boxers stared at each other with noses practically touching, was afterwards full of praise for Benitez.

Before the contest Leonard had said that he would retire afterwards having now earned enough for the rest of his life, but once champion he decided he liked the buzz too much to give up.

In 1980 Leonard knocked out British challenger Dave 'Boy' Green with what he claimed was the hardest punch he ever threw – a left hook – and then had two extraordinary contests with ex-lightweight champion Roberto Duran. In the first, the 'Brawl in Montreal', in the Olympic Stadium where he had won his gold medal four years earlier Leonard abandoned his usual style to fight toe-to-toe with the street-fighter Duran. It didn't pay off. As early as the second round Duran staggered him with a right cross and left hook and Leonard was in trouble on the ropes when the round ended. Unfortunately for him, Sugar Ray's pride, or his stubbornness, refused to allow him to change his tactics, and he kept on trying to beat Duran at his own game even while Duran was building up a points lead. Juanita, at ringside, was crying at the punishment her husband was taking, and in the eighth round she fainted. Sugar Ray didn't even notice. Duran, who loved it more the rougher it got, kept on top of Sugar Ray and took a close but unanimous decision. It was Sugar Ray's first defeat. He had ignored the advice of Angelo Dundee, who said afterwards: 'Ray's mistake was that he had it in his head that he was stronger than Duran.' After the fight Sugar Ray's face showed the signs of the severe battering it had taken, and he could hardly move from the pounding Duran had given his body. Juanita wanted him to retire, and he, too, could see little point in abusing his body further. He was rich enough, having collected around $9 million for the fight. He and Juanita went off for a long-delayed honeymoon to Hawaii and discussed his career. Leonard decided eventually he couldn't retire on this defeat, and became convinced he could beat Duran in a return. It was soon arranged.

In the return in the New Orleans Superdome, Sugar Ray fought as he should have the first time, and so demoralised Duran with first his skill, and then his taunts and laughter, that Duran gave up in the eighth round, and uttering the words '*No mas, no mas*' (no more) he retired to his corner. Sugar Ray had comprehensively avenged his first defeat. He spoke of retirement yet again, and then reversed the decision. The dithering caused a break with Dave Jacobs, who left the training team for a while. Jacobs accepted Sugar Ray's compulsion to continue. 'I know his first love is still fighting and the public acclaim that goes with it. He knows he has a god-given talent and he can't throw it away.'

After a successful defence against Larry Bonds, Leonard stepped up a division to win the WBA light-middleweight title by stopping Ayub Kalule at the Houston Astrodome. Three rights and a left dropped Kalule for the first time in his career. Under WBC rules, Sugar Ray should have been stripped of his welterweight title after winning a title in another division, but all the world wanted to see Leonard take on another great 1980s boxer, Thomas 'Hit Man' Hearns, and money, as it often does in boxing, bent the rules. The contest to unify the WBA and WBC strands of the welterweight title took place in Caesars Palace, Las Vegas, on 16 September 1981. Hearns had won all 32 of his fights, all but two inside the distance. Leonard had suffered one defeat in 31. It was billed as 'The Showdown', and Hearns was made a slight favourite. The 25,000 present saw another great match.

Hearns, the puncher, began by outboxing Leonard. In the second round he damaged Leonard's left eye. Two judges gave Leonard the third, but that was all and after five rounds Hearns was well ahead on all cards. In the sixth Leonard staggered Hearns with a left hook, but Hearns resumed his mastery and with three rounds left was so far ahead that Leonard virtually needed a knockout. In fact, in the interval between rounds, Angelo Dundee told him that he was 'blowing it'. Sugar Ray then showed his bravery and his amazing stamina. He punished Hearns for most of the 13th round, and near the end Hearns was reduced to sitting on the bottom rope and taking a count of nine. The bell saved any further catastrophe for him, but Leonard attacked in the next round and four straight lefts had Hearns in so much bother that referee Davey Pearl stopped it. Afterwards Leonard told reporters: 'I heard every word Angelo said, but I didn't respond because I already knew what I had to do.' Leonard was the undisputed welterweight champion and was being rated the best fighter in the world.

Leonard defended against Bruce Finch and then in training for his next defence again hurt the left eye that Hearns had previously hurt. A partly detached retina was diagnosed. An operation was successful, but Leonard decided it was time to give up. He was already working as a TV commentator and he called a meeting at the Baltimore Civic Center in November 1982 (for which he charged admission) to announce his retirement. He told Marvin Hagler, who was present, that a fight between them could have been worth Fort Knox, but that now it wouldn't happen.

However, 16 months later, Sugar Ray decided to make another comeback. He chose the unrated Kevin Howard as the opponent to test himself on and, for the first time in his career, was put down in the fourth round. He stopped Howard in the ninth, but immediately announced retirement again. He said he had lost all his feeling for the game.

At this time Sugar Ray was also having problems in his private life. He was now married to Juanita, the mother of his son, and a month after he beat Howard a second child, Jarrel, was born, but Sugar Ray admitted that all had not been well, and that he had taken temporary refuge in drugs.

Being out of the limelight did not suit Sugar Ray, and in 1986 he made it known that he would like to come back, but without any warm-up fights – he wanted to meet Marvin Hagler straightaway for the middleweight crown. Most thought this madness on Sugar Ray's part, as it was now over five years since his last great performance against Hearns and, even at his best he would not have been favourite against the natural middleweight Hagler, whose superb reign had already lasted six years. But a contest was arranged amid great resentment in traditional boxing circles that Leonard could come back and straightaway be given a title fight. Money had talked again. Sugar Ray was guaranteed $11 million, and the contest at Caesars Palace eventually grossed $100 million. The WBA and IBF, however, upheld normal values and stripped Hagler for refusing to meet the legitimate challenger, Herol Graham, so only the WBC title was at stake.

In the event, Sugar Ray, surprisingly fit, fashioned a perfectly judged performance. He defended well and towards the end of each round put in little spurts of flashy punches to catch the judges' eyes. He was slightly in trouble in the ninth round against Hagler's weightier punching, but kept enough in reserve to last out the 12 rounds. The verdict caused great dispute. Two judges made it close, one for each man, but the third gave it overwhelmingly to Leonard. Leonard was overjoyed. It was one of the great victories in boxing history. His brother Kenny said after the fight: 'He wanted it so bad.

That's what kept him going.' He had won a world title at three weights, beaten such outstanding rivals as Benitez, Duran, Hearns and Hagler, and was undoubtedly the boxer of the 1980s. He and a disgusted Hagler, who like many other good judges thought he'd won, both announced their retirements.

Hagler kept his word, but yet again Sugar Ray could not stay away. What urged yet another comeback was the success of his old rival Hearns, who was still sore at not getting a return with Leonard after their outstanding encounter. Leonard claimed he did not grant rematches but Hearns had now gone on to win a world title at a record fourth weight. Sugar Ray decided his own pre-eminence was now threatened, and stepped right back with yet another title fight. Canadian Donny Lalonde was the WBC light-heavyweight champion, and Leonard was allowed not only to challenge for this title, but he persuaded the WBC to inaugurate a super-middleweight championship as well and, by further persuading Lalonde to fight within the super-middleweight limit, he contrived that two world titles would be at stake in the same match. Leonard's object was to upstage Hearns and become the first boxer ever to hold a title at five weights.

The contest took place at Caesars Palace in November 1988. Sugar Ray was now in his 33rd year, Lalonde four years younger. Lalonde's right put Sugar Ray down in the fourth round – only the second knockdown of his career – but Sugar Ray shook off the effects of the punch to get on top and he knocked Lalonde down twice in the ninth round. The referee stepped in to award him the fight. Leonard was now a world champion at five weights, but it was not a new record after all; Thomas Hearns had achieved the feat three days earlier. Many thought that, as Lalonde had been forced to box at a lower weight limit than his best, his light-heavy title should not have been at stake. Nevertheless Hearns and Leonard are both credited with titles at five weights, and nobody has emulated them in the succeeding ten years.

Now, nearly eight years after their stupendous welterweight contest, Leonard and Hearns met again for Leonard's super-middleweight title. Astonishingly, with both men well past their best, Leonard pocketed $13 million, his highest payday yet, and Hearns $11 million for their Caesars Palace encounter. The result was a draw, but majority opinion was that Hearns, who dropped Leonard in the fourth and 11th rounds, was unlucky not to get the verdict. Having made such a packet for this fight, Leonard could see no reason not to collect another for meeting another old rival, Roberto Duran, in a rubber fight. This took place in December 1989, at the Mirage, Las Vegas, and was a stinker which the fans booed. There was little real action but Sugar Ray took another $13 million purse and won an easy decision (Duran was now 38), but he had to have several stitches afterwards for facial wounds.

Everybody hoped that this would be the last performance of a great boxer now clearly unable to produce the goods any more. But the last thing Sugar Ray was to lose was his self-belief. As his wife Juanita resignedly said: 'for Ray there is always one more fight'. Leonard's view was: 'if you do something well, why not do it? They tell me you can't come back every year. Maybe THEY can't but I can'. Fifteen months after the cat-calls of the Duran fight, he was back challenging Terry Norris for his WBC light-middleweight belt. Sugar Ray claimed that he wanted to fulfil an ambition by boxing at Madison Square Garden, the most famous venue in boxing. Norris was one of the best young boxers around, a fast hard-punching champion, and a faded Leonard had clearly little chance, although such was his charisma that astonishingly he was the betting favourite. Reality intruded in the second round when Sugar Ray was put on the canvas. He was down again in the seventh, but managed to last the distance, although he was beaten conclusively. It was only his second defeat, and there was really no alternative to retirement now. 'It took something like this to make me move on,' said Leonard, who was approaching 35.

Soon after his supposedly last fight, Sugar Ray's repeated squabbles with his childhood sweetheart Juanita became too much for them and they were divorced. Ray also let it be known that during his career he had had to fight his way out of a drugs problem. In 1993 Leonard married a model, Bernadette Robi. He looked after his wealth and his many business interests astutely and kept in the public eye with his pronouncements on boxing through his TV commentary work.

Yet still the itch to relive the glory continued. On 1 March 1997, after a six-year absence, he entered the ring again at Atlantic City to take on the respected Hector Camacho, who had recently conquered Duran. Camacho himself was 34, and had a son who was himself beginning a boxing career, but at least he had been boxing continuously, and was on an unbeaten run of 20 contests, having lost only three in a career of 67. Leonard, nearly 41 and by now a grandfather, said he wasn't fighting for the money, and indeed his $5 million guarantee (courtesy of pay-per-view TV) would not have added significantly to his fortune. It proved all in all a very bad impulse, because, in front of 10,324 fans, he took a battering and had to be rescued by the referee in the fifth round. 'I enjoy performing,' he said beforehand, and afterwards still wouldn't promise he would never again return, like a moth, to the bright lights.

CAREER STATISTICS

WBC welterweight champion 1979-80, 1980-82
(Undisputed world welterweight champion 1981-82)
WBA light-middleweight champion 1981
World middleweight champion 1987
WBC light-heavyweight champion 1988-89
WBC super-middleweight champion 1988-90
Palmer Park, Maryland, born 17 May 1956
1976 Olympic light-welterweight gold medal

1977

Feb 5 Luis Vega w pts 6 Baltimore
May 14 Willie Rodriguez w pts 6 Baltimore
Jun 10 Vinnie De Barros w rsf 3 Hartford
Sep 24 Frank Santore w ko 5 Baltimore
Nov 5 Augustin Estrada w rsf 5 Las Vegas
Dec 17 Hector Diaz w ko 2 Washington DC

1978

Feb 3 Rocky Ramon w pts 8 Baltimore
Mar 1 Art McKnight w rsf 7 Dayton
Mar 19 Javier Muniz w rsf 1 New Haven
Apr 13 Bobby Haymon w rsf 3 Landover
May 13 Randy Milton w ko 8 Utica
Jun 3 Rafael Rodriguez w pts 10 Baltimore
Jul 17 Dick Eklund w pts 10 Boston
Sep 9 Floyd Mayweather w rsf 9 Providence
Oct 6 Randy Shields w pts 10 Baltimore
Nov 3 Bernardo Prada w pts 10 Portland
Dec 9 Armando Muniz w rsf 7 Springfield, Ma.

1979

Jan 19 Johnny Gant w rsf 8 Landover
Feb 11 Fernand Marcotte w rsf 8 Miami
Mar 24 Daniel Gonzalez w ko 1 Tucson
Apr 21 Adolpho Viruet w pts 10 Las Vegas
May 20 Marcos Geraldo w pts 10 Baton Rouge
Jun 24 Tony Chiaverini w rsf 5 Las Vegas
Aug 12 Pete Ranzany w rsf 4 Las Vegas
(NABF welterweight title)
Sep 28 Andy Price w ko 1 Las Vegas
(NABF welterweight title)
Nov 30 Wilfred Benitez w rsf 15 Las Vegas
(WBC welterweight title)

1980

Mar 31 Dave Green w ko 4 Landover
(WBC welterweight title)
Jun 20 Roberto Duran l pts 15 Montreal
(WBC welterweight title)
Nov 25 Roberto Duran w rtd 8 New Orleans
(WBC welterweight title)

1981

Mar 28 Larry Bonds w rsf 10 Syracuse
(WBC welterweight title)
Jun 25 Ayub Kalule w rsf 9 Houston
(WBA light-middleweight title)
Relinquished WBA light-middleweight title
Sep 16 Thomas Hearns w rsf 14 Las Vegas
(World welterweight title)

1982

Feb 15 Bruce Finch w rsf 3 Reno
(World welterweight title)
Relinquished world welterweight title.

1983 Inactive

1984

May 11 Kevin Howard w rsf 9 Worcester

1985-86 Inactive

1987

Apr 6 Marvin Hagler w pts 12 Las Vegas
(World middleweight title)
Relinquished world middleweight title

1988

Nov 7 Donny Lalonde w rsf 9 Las Vegas
(WBC light-heavyweight & WBC super-middleweight titles)

1989

Relinquished WBC light-heavyweight title.
Jun 12 Thomas Hearns drew 12 Las Vegas
(WBC super-middleweight title)
Dec 7 Roberto Duran w pts 12 Las Vegas
(WBC super-middleweight title)

1990 Inactive

1991

Feb 9 Terry Norris l pts 12 New York
(WBC light-middleweight title)

1992-96 Inactive

1997

Mar 1 Hector Camacho l rsf 5 Atlantic City

Fights 40 Won 36 Lost 3 Drawn 1

THOMAS HEARNS

THE HITMAN

Although Thomas Hearns preferred his older nickname of 'Motor City Cobra', it was 'The Hit Man' which stuck. And rightly so, for Hearns in the ring was a cold, analytical, ruthless businessman who could take a man out with one shot. Reflecting now on his 20-year boxing journey, it seems the high point was the cool Las Vegas night in June 1984 when he left Roberto Duran face first on the Caesars Palace canvas in two incredible rounds. Duran had held three world titles and would go on to win a fourth, but Hearns simply blew him away with long, clean right hands that would have had the great fighters of any generations nodding in approval.

Yet as an amateur, Hearns couldn't punch. He barely stopped anyone, and when he boxed for the USA in London in 1976 he seemed lucky to outpoint England's lightweight, George Gilbody of St Helens. In 163 amateur bouts, of which he won 155, he scored only a dozen knockouts.

When he turned pro in November 1977, trainer Emanuel Steward somehow made an astonishing transformation, turning him almost overnight into one of the most chilling punchers in history.

'As an amateur he was just a super boxer,' said Steward. 'He'd jab, jab, jab, fire his right and dance away. He didn't know what a left hook was and he didn't know what leverage was. Then he started to grow and started to learn. The power was always there, but he didn't know how to use it.'

Steward and Hearns had been together since Thomas was 13. One of a family of nine children, he was born in Memphis, Tennessee, on 18 October 1958. When his father left, his mother Lois took her brood to the east side of Detroit, and by the age of 10 Thomas was learning to box at the King Solomon Gym. Three years later, he joined Steward at the Kronk.

He lost decisions to Howard Davis and Aaron Pryor in the 1976 National AAU and National Golden Gloves lightweight finals respectively, but won both titles the following year as a light-welterweight.

In only his 12th pro fight, Hearns blasted out Bruce Finch in three rounds in Detroit. Finch would go on to fight Ray Leonard for the undisputed welterweight title four years later. But it was his 15th consecutive inside-schedule victory, a 10th-round stoppage of Canadian Clyde Gray, that took him into world class, only 14 months after his debut. Gray had fought Jose Napoles, Angel Espada and Pipino Cuevas in world title fights.

Hearns was taken the distance for the first time in Philadelphia in April 1979 when Alfonso Hayman lasted the full 10 rounds, but he was soon back to his knockout habit. In May he stopped Harold Weston in six – two months earlier Weston had lasted the full 15 rounds with WBC welterweight champion Wilfred Benitez. Then Bruce Curry, who would go on to win the WBC light-welterweight title, was knocked out in three rounds.

Hearns looked all the more formidable because nothing he did seemed rushed. He rarely disposed of an opponent inside a round, because he tended to spend that time taking a look at them. But when he opened up, most failed to handle the sheer ferocity and power of his attacks. At 6ft 1in, he had reach advantages over most welterweights and his amateur experience taught him how to use that.

The last win of the year, his 24th, brought him his second 10 round points win, this time over fully blown middleweight Mike Colbert, who had seemed on the brink of a world title shot at 160lb until Marvin Hagler knocked him out and broke his jaw. Against Hearns, Colbert's jaw went again and he had to climb off the canvas four times to last the distance: a tough man!

In Detroit in March 1980, Emanuel Steward's first world champion was crowned – Hilmer Kenty, who beat Ernesto Espana of Venezuela for the WBA lightweight belt. In the chief support, Hearns stopped Angel Espada, a 32-year-old veteran who had held the WBA belt for a year, but who had been stopped twice by Pipino Cuevas in good fights. It was a huge gamble to take on the unbeaten Hearns, but he knew there was no time to waste: this was his route back.

Hearns took charge from the start, floored him twice in the third and again in round four to finish it. His fans chanted: 'We want Leonard!', who was by now the WBC champion, having dethroned Benitez. However, it was WBA champ Cuevas who filled the opposite corner in the Joe Louis Arena in Detroit when Hearns finally fought for a world title in August 1980. Cuevas, from Mexico City, was only 22 years old, but had been boxing for eight years and had been WBA champion for four. This was his 12th defence. He was strong, aggressive with a powerful hook in either hand. Fans expecting an explosive shoot-out could not have been more wrong. Cuevas backed off, hesitant and unsure of himself, and Hearns, himself still only 21, cut him down with almost casual ease with a right hand in round two.

There would be disappointments as well as incredible triumphs along the way, but the 'Hit Man' was here to stay for the next decade and a half. He defended the WBA welterweight title against three opponents: Luis Primera, Randy Shields and Pablo Baez, but while he won each of these fights by stoppage, everyone knew they were mere preliminaries to a major fight. The only question was who would be his opponent.

Sugar Ray Leonard lost the WBC belt to Duran, and then regained it with the infamous '*No mas*' fight in New Orleans. This was Sugar Ray's second fight against Duran, where he gained sweet revenge for the defeat he had suffered at Duran's hands earlier that year. This time, in November 1980, he gave Duran such a terrible time that the Panamanian gave up, saying, '*No mas, no mas*' ('No more, no more'). Benitez was winning again, but Carlos Palomino had retired.

In the end it was Leonard ... and they met in one of the fights of the decade in Las Vegas in September 1981. Leonard, because he had a higher profile, was guaranteed $8 million and Hearns $5 million, and the eventual take may have been higher: this was the first pay-per-view event in boxing history. In the crammed open air arena at Caesars Palace a crowd of 23,615 paid for seats.

Early in the fight Hearns used his long reach to outbox Leonard, raise a swelling beneath his left eye and build an early lead. In round six, the pattern changed as Leonard shook him badly with a right hand. It took the 'Hit Man' until the eighth to reassert himself, but when he hurt Leonard in the 11th it looked as if he might go on to win. However, Leonard knew he had to turn it around, and did so, with trainer Angelo Dundee warning him: 'You're blowin' it, kid. You got to knock him out.'

Leonard threw everything at a tiring Hearns and floored him at the end of round 13. He was stopped on his feet, tottering against the ropes, his legs gone, his eyes glassy, with 75 seconds left in round 14.

It was an awful blow, and while he ached for a return, he and Steward decided that at 23 he was filling out too much to go on making welterweight. In his comeback fight three months later, on the depressing Muhammad Ali-Trevor Berbick show in the Bahamas, Hearns outpointed tough Philadelphia middleweight Ernie Singletary over 10 rounds. He knocked out Mexican middleweight Marcos Geraldo in one and then stopped Jeff McCracken in the eighth in a return home to Detroit.

Finally, in December 1982 in New Orleans, he won the WBC light-middleweight title by outboxing Wilfred Benitez in a surprisingly dull fight. Benitez had enough skills to survive and Hearns had sufficient respect not to take risks. At the end judges Tony Castellano and Dick Young had Hearns way clear by five and nine points, while Lou Filippo's card was a draw at 142 each. This seemed way out of line, but the main thing in the minds of Hearns and Steward was that he was a world champion again.

Hearns boxed only once in 1983, a points decision over Scottish-born super-middle Murray Sutherland, who cut him around the left eye.

In a title defence, he outpointed Luigi Minchillo, a strong but dull Italian, over 12 rounds in Detroit in February 1984, and then Steward managed to clinch a unification fight with the WBA champion, none other than a rejuvenated Roberto Duran. Originally designed to be a double header with a WBC heavyweight title fight between Larry Holmes and Gerrie Coetzee in Nassau, it was switched to Caesars Palace when the heavyweight bout fell through. Further chaos occurred when the WBA refused to sanction the fight, and informed Duran that he would be stripped the moment he climbed through the ropes. It was absolutely ridiculous, but proved only a minor irritant. Everyone knew these were the best two 154lb fighters in the world. This was Hearns at his finest. He wobbled Duran quickly, cut him and knocked him down twice in round one. Duran had not been on the floor for 10 years, and came snarling up for round two, only for Hearns to knock him out cold, face first.

This was the era of superfights, when Leonard, Duran, Hearns and Hagler dominated, and eventually fought each other. Hearns had lost to Leonard and beaten Duran. Leonard and Duran had won one each. Hagler beat Duran and was to lose to Leonard in 1987. Hagler had outpointed Duran in November 1983. Seven months later Hearns demolished 'Hands of Stone' in a little over four minutes ... inevitably, the talk next was of a Hearns-Hagler showdown. The 'Hit Man' moved closer to it with a third-round stoppage of light-middleweight title challenger Fred Hutchings in Saginaw, Michigan, in September 1984. Then, for a guarantee of more than $5 million each, they staged one of the greatest fights ever seen on 15 April 1985. Hearns landed his shots, cut Hagler badly, took plenty in reply, and for two rounds they stood and traded. By the third Hagler was running out of time, with blood running into his eyes, but he found a shattering right that unhinged the 'Hit Man's legs and three more sent him down. He got up, but referee Richard Steele waved it off.

Hearns kept the light-middleweight title for another 18 months, defending once, unspectacularly, against Mark Medal. Much more explosive was a one-round demolition of respected middleweight James Shuler, who was to die in a road accident soon afterwards. He outpointed another tough middleweight, the iron-jawed Doug De Witt, and then in March 1987 jumped up to light-heavyweight and, in Detroit, dethroned WBC champ Dennis Andries with a tenth round stoppage. Andries, born in Buxton, Guyana, had already been British light-heavyweight champion and won a Lonsdale Belt outright. This was his second defence of the WBC title and he looked to have a big natural weight advantage. To counter this Hearns used his speed of hands and feet and caught Andries with a heavy right hand in the second round. In the third round he put the champion down and in the sixth Andries was floored three times. Andries kept trying – he still insists he was denied two knockdowns – but twice more the Hitman dropped the Englishman and it was a relief when it was stopped in the 10th round.

Hearns later relinquished the title and dropped down to middleweight, while Andries recovered and won the WBC light-heavyweight title twice more, before moving up to become British cruiserweight champion.

In the middleweight division Hagler had lost to Leonard, who had retired, leaving the titles to be split up. Hearns fought Juan Domingo Roldan for the WBC version, and knocked him out easily in the fourth.

The 'Hit Man' was a big favourite in June 1988 in Las Vegas against middleweight challenger Iran 'The Blade' Barkley from the Bronx. Barkley was a good fighter, underrated by so many, but not considered exceptional. For two rounds Hearns did as he pleased, and by the third Barkley was bleeding from gashes over both eyes. Then Barkley landed a shock right hand on Hearns' unprotected chin and followed up quickly. Hearns crashed backwards to the canvas, and was stopped.

It seemed his punch resistance had gone, a view which was reinforced in his next fight for the inaugural WBO super-middleweight title against James 'The Heat' Kinchen in November 1988. Kinchen had Hearns clinging on, his senses foggy, his legs unsteady, but could not finish him. Hearns recovered and won on points. Although nobody took the WBO seriously at the time, technically he became the first man to win world titles in five weight divisions.

After that achievement, everything else was a bonus. A fight he had yearned for was a rematch with Leonard. When it happened in Las Vegas in June 1989, they billed it as 'The War'. It was really a question of who had the most left. Pre-fight, it seemed Leonard was the more solid. In fact, he was floored twice and most felt Hearns had won. The official verdict was a draw, but Hearns considered he had proved his point. Their 1981 welterweight showdown no longer haunted him.

He won the WBA light-heavyweight belt with an emphatic points win over the dull but difficult-to-beat Virgil Hill, but lost it in a return with Barkley, who somehow outfought him over 12 rounds.

By 1993 he was a cruiserweight, and in spite of slowing with age and looking vulnerable, he retained his power. He blew away former Olympic gold medallist Andrew Maynard in one round in 1993, and added the virtually meaningless WBU belt with a first round win over club fighter Lenny La Paglia in 1995.

By the time he knocked out Ed Dalton in five rounds in January 1997, he was 38, and a shadow of what he used to be. He drifted out of boxing, although nobody could rule out the possibility of 'just one more' somewhere down the line, because when all the dust had settled, win or lose, Thomas Hearns loved to fight.

Away from the ring, he was a quiet, private man who wore his wealth well. In it, he remained one of the most popular fighters of his time.

CAREER STATISTICS

WBA welterweight champion 1980-81
WBC light-middleweight champion 1982-86
WBC light-heavyweight champion 1987
WBC middleweight champion 1987-88
WBO super-middleweight champion 1988-91
WBA light-heavyweight champion 1991-92
Detroit, born Memphis 18 October 1958

1977

Nov 25 Jerome Hill w rsf 2 Detroit
Dec 7 Jerry Strickland w ko 3 Mount Clements
Dec 16 Willie Wren w rsf 3 Detroit

1978

Jan 29 Anthony House w ko 2 Knoxville
Feb 10 Robert Adams w rsf 3 Detroit
Feb 17 Billy Goodwin w rsf 2 Saginaw

Mar 17 Ray Fields w rsf 2 Detroit
Mar 31 Tyrone Phelps w rsf 3 Saginaw
Jun 8 Jimmy Rothwell w rsf 1 Detroit
Jul 20 Raul Aguirre w ko 2 Detroit
Aug 3 Eddie Marcelle w ko 2 Detroit
Sep 7 Bruce Finch w ko 3 Detroit
Oct 26 Pedro Rojas w rsf 1 Detroit
Dec 9 Rudy Barro w ko 4 Detroit

1979

Jan 13 Clyde Gray w rsf 10 Detroit
Jan 31 Sammy Ruckard w rsf 9 Saginaw
Mar 3 Segundo Murillo w rsf 8 Detroit
Apr 3 Alfonso Hayman w pts 10 Philadelphia
May 30 Harold Weston w rsf 7 Las Vegas
Jun 28 Bruce Curry w ko 3 Detroit
Aug 23 Mao de la Rosa w rsf 2 Detroit
Sep 22 Jose Figueroa w ko 3 Los Angeles
Oct 18 Saensak Muangsurin w ko 3 Detroit
Nov 30 Mike Colbert w pts 10 New Orleans

1980

Feb 3 Jim Richards w ko 3 Las Vegas
Mar 2 Angel Espada w rsf 4 Detroit
(USBA welterweight title)
Mar 31 Santiago Valdez w ko 1 Las Vegas
May 3 Eddie Gazo w ko 1 Detroit
Aug 2 Pipino Cuevas w ko 2 Detroit
(WBA welterweight title)
Dec 6 Luis Primera w ko 6 Detroit
(WBA welterweight title)

1981

Apr 25 Randy Shields w rsf 13 Phoenix
(WBA welterweight title)
Jun 25 Pablo Baez w rsf 4 Houston
(WBA welterweight title)
Sep 16 Ray Leonard l rsf 14 Las Vegas
(World welterweight title)
Dec 11 Ernie Singletary w pts 10 Nassau

1982

Feb 27 Marcos Geraldo w ko 1 Las Vegas
Jul 25 Jeff McCracken w rsf 8 Detroit
Dec 3 Wilfred Benitez w pts 15 New Orleans
(WBC light-middleweight title)

1983

Jul 10 Murray Sutherland w pts 10 Atlantic City

1984

Feb 11 Luigi Minchillo w pts 12 Detroit
(WBC light-middleweight title)
Jun 5 Roberto Duran w ko 2 Las Vegas
(WBC light-middleweight title)
Sep 15 Fred Hutchings w ko 3 Saginaw
(WBC light-middleweight title)

1985

Apr 15 Marvin Hagler l rsf 3 Las Vegas
(World middleweight title)

1986

Mar 10 James Shuler w ko 1 Las Vegas
(NABF middleweight title)
Jun 23 Mark Medal w rsf 8 Las Vegas
(WBC light-middleweight title)
Sep: Relinquished WBC light-middleweight title.
Oct 17 Doug De Witt w pts 12 Detroit
(NABF middleweight title)

1987

Mar 7 Dennis Andries w rsf 10 Detroit
(WBC light-heavyweight title)
Aug: Relinquished WBC light-heavyweight title.
Oct 29 Juan Domingo Roldan w ko 4 Las Vegas
(WBC middleweight title)

1988

Jun 6 Iran Barkley l rsf 3 Las Vegas
(WBC middleweight title)
Nov 4 James Kinchen w pts 12 Las Vegas
(WBO super-middleweight title)

1989

Jun 12 Ray Leonard drew 12 Las Vegas
(WBC super-middleweight title)

1990

Apr 28 Michael Olajide w pts 12 Atlantic City
(WBO super-middleweight title)

1991

Feb 11 Kemper Morton w ko 2 Los Angeles
Mar: Relinquished WBO super-middleweight title
Apr 6 Ken Atkin w rsf 3 Honolulu
Jun 3 Virgil Hill w pts 12 Las Vegas
(WBA light-heavyweight title)

1992

Mar 20 Iran Barkley l pts 12 Las Vegas
(WBA light-heavyweight title)

1993

Nov 6 Andrew Maynard w ko 1 Las Vegas

1994

Jan 29 Dan Ward w rsf 1 Las Vegas
(NABF cruiserweight title)
Feb 19 Freddie Delgado w pts 12 Charlotte
(NABF cruiserweight title)

1995

Mar 31 Lenny La Paglia w rsf 1 Detroit
(WBU cruiserweight title)
Relinquished WBU title.
Sep 26 Earl Butler w pts 10 Auburn Hills

1996

Nov 29 Karl Willis w rsf 5 Roanoke

1997

Jan 18 Ed Dalton w rsf 5 Los Angeles

Fights 62 Won 57 Lost 4 Drawn 1

GEORGE FOREMAN

THE FIGHTING PREACHER

In 1973 when a 6ft 3in, 217lb package of solid muscle and surly animosity named George Foreman extended an unbeaten run of 37 contests by winning the world heavyweight title from Joe Frazier, himself previously unbeaten, by knocking him down six times in four minutes, the black-haired unshaven giant looked the most menacing fighting machine imaginable. When, in 1987, a roly-poly, cuddly, shaven-headed benign preacher called George Foreman began a boxing career by knocking over a few nohopers, he looked a joke. Only the name would have hinted to the uninitiated that this was the same man. Incredibly, after a 10-year break preaching, Foreman came back to win the world title again, and continued punching till 1997, when nearly 49 years old. His is one of the most amazing careers of all time.

George Foreman came into the world on 10 January 1949 in Marshall, Texas. His parents were J.D. Foreman, a railway worker, and Nancy Ree Foreman, who would eventually have seven children, George being the fifth. However J.D. was not George's real father, who was a man called Leroy Moorehead. It was to prevent talk that Nancy Ree moved the family to Houston, Texas, for George was to stick out a bit in the family, being quite unlike his older brother, who was ten when George was born, and his three sisters. George was much bigger for a start.

Nancy Ree and J.D. Foreman would often fight, primarily because J.D. tended to spend all his spare cash, plus some which wasn't spare at all, on drink. But the birth of George himself could not have helped too much in the situation, and his older brother and sisters certainly felt that George's arrival had exacerbated relations among the parents. They even teased him about it, telling him he was not really their brother. In fact one of their early nicknames for him was 'Mo-head', clearly based on his real father's name. Small wonder that Nancy Ree wanted to move.

The family had little money and in Houston they found digs in what they and others called the 'bloody Fifth', in reality a district called the Fifth Ward. It was a very tough part of the world, and not unnaturally little George grew up to be pretty tough too. He frequently failed to turn up at school and hung about the streets with other young no-goods looking for any sort of delinquency they could find. It was not that George had a less than caring family. His father in name, J.D., was very proud and fond of him, and his mother, brother and sisters were all religious church-goers. George rebelled against this and if forced to go to church he would spend his time ridiculing them.

When George did go to school, he liked playing American Football, where he could use his size and strength. He was very soon the 'King of the Kids' able to behave as he liked among those of his own age. He probably developed at a very young age the aggressive bullying manner which was to mark his first years in the ring.

By the time Foreman was 16 he stood over 6ft and weighed as much as some of the heavyweight champions of the past had weighed. He was a phenomenon. Luckily for him, he had avoided the worst excesses of schoolboy gangsterism. He developed a strong desire for smoking and not having money he joined some other boys in a robbery; mugging a man probably not as strong as himself. For a year or two this was his method of earning enough to satisfy his craving which, as he became a teenager, developed to embrace liquor, girls and clothes. Perhaps a victim who called the police kept George from a life of crime, because the police mounted a hunt with dogs, and a terrified George was forced to hide in fear of his life.

Eventually he was able to leave school, and his strength found him a job in the removal business until he was caught dozing on duty. He joined a community scheme called the Job Corps which sent youngsters to training centres to learn a trade. Then he met a man who was to be his salvation by persuading him to go to the gym to try boxing. How often does a variation of this story occur in the lives of the great prize-fighters? In George's case, the good Samaritan was called Doc Broadus, who was the security chief and general dogsbody at George's second posting, Parks Center, Pleasanton, California.

Unfortunately (and this is a familiar story, too) Foreman's first bout was against a smaller man who nevertheless had learned some boxing, and George felt somewhat humiliated. He went back to his old ways. Even a present of boxing shoes failed to move him and, after some violent behaviour necessitating police interest, he was on the point of being written off. Luckily for him, Doc Broadus stood up for him, and fortunately he began to win some bouts. He entered the Golden Gloves tournaments, but when eventually he was beaten, as he was bound to be sooner or later, he lost interest in boxing again.

Doc Broadus stuck behind Foreman and tried to inspire him with the idea of getting into the US Olympic team. But George graduated from the Job Corps and returned home to Houston where he lazed around drinking and smoking and got himself fined for beating up two brothers. Strangely enough, he failed the medical for induction into the army and so missed possible service in Vietnam — nobody knows why. Enter again the admirable Doc Broadus. He telephoned to find out how George was and Nancy

Ree, at her wit's end, pleaded with Broadus for help. Broadus, who could see George had the physical materials to be a boxing champion, offered to become George's manager, and he sported a one-way airline ticket back to the Pleasanton Job Corps centre where he got him a job as a cleaner and – clever touch – boxing instructor.

Foreman finally saw where his lifestyle was leading him when, at his 19th birthday party, he got drunk and gave a bad beating to a friend – and next day could remember nothing. It frightened him into giving up drinking, and smoking for good measure, and he resolved to have a serious try at boxing.

Foreman's size and strength meant that he would always win more than he would lose among the amateurs and, as he picked up some skill, he progressed. He won the Golden Gloves at San Francisco but lost in Las Vegas to a cleverer man who'd beaten him before, Clay Jones. But with Jones absent in the army, he won the national AAU tournament and did so well from then on that, after only 18 amateur bouts, he became the US representative at heavyweight in the 1968 Olympics in Mexico City.

Foreman won the Olympic gold with no difficulty and the image of the victorious fighter parading round the ring holding a tiny stars and stripes flag became one of the enduring images of the Games. He was persuaded to do this as a gesture against the earlier behaviour at the Games of Tommie Smith and John Carlos who had shocked the American nation by using the medal ceremony to raise their fists in Black Power salutes. Foreman had at first agreed to support his fellow black Americans; by changing sides he was welcomed by President Johnson and became involved in the new presidential campaign, but at the same time he found his welcome by his own people back in the Fifth Ward was distinctly cool. It would be 25 years before they would accept him with any warmth.

Foreman now turned professional and ditched Doc Broadus (his signature on a contract signed when he was 17 held no legal power). He signed a contract with Dick Sadler, trainer of big bad former champion Sonny Liston, and made his pro debut with an easy stoppage of Don Waldheim at New York's Madison Square Garden on 23 June 1969. Top of the bill that night was heavyweight champion Joe Frazier.

Sadler, Liston and even Joe Louis, who visited the camp, did a good job on the loner Foreman, keeping him focused on fighting rather than leading a promiscuous life. Sadler found enough fighters for him to knock over regularly and three years after turning pro he had despatched 36; 33 by the short route. Chuck Wepner, Greg Peralta (twice) and George Chuvalo were the best-known names on the list.

He was soon being talked of as a title challenger, and on 22 January 1973 he stepped into the ring in Kingston, Jamaica to take on Joe Frazier for the world title in what was billed as 'The Sunshine Showdown'. Despite George's imposing physique and record of mayhem, he was considered too much of a novice to beat the seasoned Frazier, who was also unbeaten and claimed among his victims the immortal Ali. Frazier was 3–1 on favourite in the betting, but looked apprehensive and, in the end, proved no match for Foreman's punching. After about two minutes a short right uppercut put Frazier down for eight. Further pounding put him down again, and when Frazier went down for a third time just before the end of the first round it was only because the 'three-knock-down' rule had been waived that the title didn't change hands there and then.

It was not long delayed. Foreman scattered Frazier's senses by punching him down twice more in the second round before a right uppercut lifted Frazier clean off his feet on his way to the canvas for the last time. When he rose he wandered about not knowing where he was and referee Arthur Mercante stopped the fight at 1 minute 35 seconds of the second. The new champion described it thus: 'I hit him with a punch, and there was a grin on his face, as if he was saying: 'Look, man, you're going to kill me'.'

This was the high point in Foreman's career. Many good judges thought he was unbeatable, and possibly the greatest champion ever seen in the ring. Before the title fight, he had shown he was developing a personality by arguing with Sadler and appointing the great Archie Moore to be his trainer. He had also married a girl named Adrienne Calhoun, who bore him a daughter 16 days before he became champion. But the marriage failed to last long. Foreman seemed intent on making people fear and hate him. He was still a bully, even though he was now champion. He was booed when he made his first defence against a no-hoper, Joe Roman. The fight was in Tokyo, for tax reasons. Roman lasted two minutes, during which there were three knockdowns, George being accused of hitting Roman as he rose from the second, but nobody took any notice. 'It was a 150 per cent mismatch', said referee Jay Edson. Foreman just scowled at the fans when declared the winner.

Before his next defence, against Ken Norton, he said he intended to kill his challenger. Norton, who was superbly equipped for a fighter and had once broken Ali's jaw, did well in the first round, which was fairly even, but when Norton was stunned by a succession of blows in the second round and forced to take a standing count, he seemed to lose heart. After another assault the referee checked his condition. When a third assault put him down for a count of five, and he looked groggy when hauling himself up, the referee stopped it. Foreman seemed disappointed at not being allowed to continue the massacre and told Ali, who was already contracted to be the next challenger, that he would kill him instead. Hints of reprisals from Black Muslims if he persisted in these threats put a stop to them.

Nevertheless there were many who seriously feared for the safety of Ali in this contest. Ali was 32, and had had some gruelling contests throughout his career. Big George still looked like a ruthless executioner, and was undoubtedly in his physical prime. It was the manner in which the good guy, Ali, beat the bully, Foreman, that has contributed to this contest becoming perhaps the greatest sporting moment of the century, and the subject of book and film.

The fight took place in Kinshasa, Zaire, on 30 October 1974, with Foreman a 7–1 on favourite but, from his point of view, it was a disaster. In the build-up Ali mixed with the fans, who loved him, and began the famous chant: 'Ah-lee, booma ya', or 'Ali kill him'. Foreman won no supporters by sulking in his penthouse with his guard dogs.

In the fight Ali baffled Foreman by not dancing and keeping out of range. Instead he invited George into him and George unloaded his bombs. Ali either evaded them, rode them, or when they landed absorbed them. It seemed a suicidal policy but while Ali did enough to keep him off balance, Foreman was unable to land the clinching blow. When round succeeded round and Ali was still in front of him George didn't know what to do. What finally happened was that Ali suddenly sprang off the ropes with two rights and a left which stunned Foreman, and a chopping right sent him slowly falling forwards to the canvas. Surprised, humiliated, exhausted, Foreman lacked the will or power to get up.

It was seen, rightly or wrongly, as the classic triumph of matador v bull, clinician v bully, intelligence v brute force. Foreman was devastated. He had numerous excuses: he was drugged, weak from weight loss, the ropes were too loose, the canvas too slow, the corner too confident, the referee too fast in the count. But, basically, he had to slink away and lick his wounds.

Just before this fight his second child, George junior, was born, the mother having to file a suit to get him to recognise the boy. He also found his own true father, and remained close to him till his death.

Foreman was certainly not finished as a boxer. After 15 months he returned with a great win over Ron Lyle. In the battle of the punchers both men were down and seemingly out in the fourth, George twice, before George delivered the pay-off in the fifth. Then he destroyed Joe Frazier again, also in five rounds.

After three more wins he tackled Jimmy Young at San Juan on what was billed as an eliminator for a challenge to Ali for the world title. Foreman's power punching gave him the edge but he tired, was knocked down in the last round and lost on points.

What happened next is extraordinary. Foreman collapsed in the dressing room and seemed to go into a trance, in which he spoke of the crucifixion and of blood on his hands and forehead. He claimed that Jesus was returning to earth in his own body. Put into intensive care, Foreman recovered in hospital, where explanations for his behaviour included heat prostration and dehydration.

But to George it was real. He described his vision on television, went to church and began praying in public. He retired from boxing, while still a powerful figure in the game. He began to sort out his personal life. By now two more women had borne him children, named Freda George and Georgetta. He took a second wife, Cynthia Lewis, thinking this would allow him to take charge of all four of his children, for whom he now wished to show proper love, but this, not surprisingly, proved a pipe-dream. So he divorced Cynthia, despite her doing all she could to maintain the partnership, like faking a pregnancy and a suicide attempt.

If this doesn't sound very Christian, George Foreman was nevertheless ordained in 1978 as a minister at the Church of the Lord Jesus Christ in Houston. However, he quarrelled with this church and built his own, his fame earning him a large congregation. He quickly acquired a third, then fourth, wife, who was already the mother of his third child, and who also bore him another son. She soon fled, but George smuggled the children back from St Lucia and then married a fifth wife, Mary Martelly, to look after them. But he lost the two children to the mother, amid a charge of child abuse, which was dropped. It was not till 1991 that he was able to see all his children regularly.

While all this was going on, he was running his church, and the George Foreman Youth and Community Center from a converted warehouse nearby. In 1986 funds were urgently needed. So Foreman, by now 315 lb and shaven-headed (after he'd ruined an attempt at self-cutting his hair) decided on a ring comeback.

On 9 March 1987, after a break of eight days short of 10 years, he stepped into a ring again at Sacramento and beat Steve Zouski. The whole thing so far as the boxing press was concerned was a joke (they labelled his Las Vegas contest with another has-been, Gerry Cooney, as 'two Geezers at Caesars'). But the public wanted to see this comical, fat, bald preacher and Foreman found that he could make easy money. A whole string of duff opponents was lined up for him and he soon cleared his money problems and built a modern full-size gym as well.

In this reincarnation he had a more benevolent image and his jokes against himself, his size and his appetite were well quoted. He drew endorsement requests for fast food and other couch-potato products. After winning 24 unexceptional contests he was put in to challenge Evander Holyfield for the latter's world heavyweight titles. At a slimmed down 257lb, Foreman was still 49lb heavier than Holyfield. He surprised everybody with a good show, lasted the distance, and was cheered throughout the last minute of the fight. The former arrogant, much-hated bully was born again as a jovial folk-hero. Furthermore, $7 million of the $85 million the fight grossed belonged to him. Now he starred in a television sitcom called *George?* No wonder he carried on.

In 1993 he earned another title shot, for the vacant WBO crown, but lost on points to Tommy Morrison. In 1994 his marketability got the near-46-year-old a shot for the WBA and IBF crown, which Michael Moorer had taken from Evander Holyfield. It is said that the last thing a fighter loses is his punch, and Foreman proved this. Taking the expected points beating from Moorer, George suddenly caught him in the 10th round with a right to the jaw and knocked him out. Foreman was a world champion again 21 years after first winning the title, easily a world record.

Foreman, of course, could hardly claim to be the best man in the world and had to pick a challenger with care. He chose the German Axel Schulz, which promptly led the WBA to strip him for not choosing a credible opponent. So the IBF title only was at stake, and in fact Schulz, in the opinion of press and spectators, did enough to win it, but the judges gave a majority verdict in Foreman's favour. At the announcement the 11,000 Las Vegas fans, who had supported George throughout, whistled in derision. Reverting to his former boorish behaviour, Foreman denigrated Schulz and said he wouldn't fight him again.

This signalled the end of Foreman's second championship reign, because when justice and the IBF demanded a return with Schulz, he relinquished the title rather than face almost certain defeat in Germany. Everybody thought this would be the end of a strange career, but George was to fight again.

He despatched an unknown and then in April 1997 took on the unbeaten Lou Savarese, US champion and winner of 36 contests. Foreman, at 48 and a grandfather, came from behind in one of the better performances of his 'second career' to win on points. He collected $4 million, better than passing round the collection plate at his church. This performance led him to take on next the dangerous Shannon Briggs. At 25, not much more than half Foreman's age, the 6ft 4in 218lb muscular warrior proved just too good. On 22 November 1997 he narrowly and controversially outpointed George, at least in the opinion of the judges. This time the press reckoned that George has been robbed of the decision. So a 28-year career ended. 'I'm happy. I'm not hurt. I'm nearly 50', said George, announcing it was all over. Perhaps a better summing-up of his extraordinary return to the ring had come four years earlier when he regained the WBA title: 'To the couch-potatoes and the big-bellies, you don't have to be old if you don't want to be'.

CAREER STATISTICS

World heavyweight champion 1973-74
WBA & IBF heavyweight champion 1994-95
Houston, Texas, born Marshall, Texas, 10 January 1949
1968 Olympic heavyweight gold medal

1969

Jun 23 Donald Waldheim w ko 3 New York
Jun 30 Fred Askew w ko 1 Houston
Jul 14 Sylvester Dulaire w ko 1 Washington DC
Aug 18 Chuck Wepner w rsf 3 New York
Sep 18 John Carroll w ko 1 Seattle
Sep 23 Cookie Wallace w ko 2 Houston
Oct 7 Vernon Clay w ko 2 Houston
Oct 31 Roberto Davila w pts 8 New York
Nov 5 Leo Peterson w ko 4 Scranton
Nov 18 Max Martinez w ko 2 Houston
Dec 6 Bob Hazelton w ko 1 Las Vegas
Dec 16 Levi Forte w pts 10 Miami
Dec 18 Gary Wiler w ko 1 Seattle

1970

Jan 6 Charley Polite w ko 4 Houston
Jan 26 Jack O'Halloran w ko 5 New York
Feb 16 Gregorio Peralta w pts 10 New York
Mar 30 Rufus Brassell w rsf 1 Houston
Apr 17 James J. Woody w rsf 3 New York
Apr 29 Aaron Easting w rsf 4 Cleveland
May 16 George Johnson w rsf 7 Los Angeles
Jul 20 Roger Russell w ko 1 Philadelphia
Aug 4 George Chuvalo w rsf 3 New York
Nov 3 Lou Bailey w rsf 3 Oklahoma City
Nov 18 Boone Kirkman w rsf 2 New York
Dec 18 Mel Turnbow w rsf 1 Seattle

1971

Feb 8 Charlie Boston w ko 1 St Paul
Apr 3 Stanford Harris w ko 2 Lake Geneva
May 8 Gregorio Peralta w rsf 10 Oakland *(NABF heavyweight title)*
Sep 14 Vic Scott w ko 1 El Paso
Sep 21 Leroy Caldwell w ko 2 Beaumont
Oct 8 Ollie Wilson w ko 2 San Antonio
Oct 29 Luis Pires w rsf 4 New York

1972

Mar 7 Clarence Boone w ko 2 Beaumont
Apr 10 Ted Gullick w ko 2 Los Angeles
May 11 Miguel Angel Paez w ko 2 Oakland
Oct 10 Terry Sorrels w ko 2 Salt Lake City

1973

Jan 22 Joe Frazier w rsf 2 Kingston *(World heavyweight title)*
Sep 1 Jose Roman w ko 1 Tokyo *(World heavyweight title)*

1974
Mar 25 Ken Norton w ko 2 Caracas
(World heavyweight title)
Oct 30 Muhammad Ali l ko 8 Kinshasa
(World heavyweight title)
1975 inactive
1976
Jan 24 Ron Lyle w ko 5 Las Vegas
(NABF heavyweight title)
Jun 14 Joe Frazier w rsf 5 Uniondale, NY
(NABF heavyweight title)
Aug 14 Scott LeDoux w rsf 3 Utica, NY
Oct 15 John Dino Dennis w rsf 4 Hollywood, Fl
1977
Jan 22 Pedro Agosto w ko 4 Pensacola
Mar 17 Jimmy Young l pts 12 San Juan
1978-86 inactive
1987
Mar 9 Steve Zouski w rsf 4 Sacramento
Jul 9 Charles Hostetter w ko 3 Oakland
Sep 15 Bobby Crabtree w rsf 6 Springfield, Mo.
Nov 21 Tim Anderson w rsf 4 Orlando
Dec 18 Ricky Sekorski w rsf 3 Las Vegas
1988
Jan 23 Tom Trimm w ko 1 Orlando
Feb 5 Guido Trano w rsf 5 Las Vegas
Mar 19 Dwight Muhammad Qawi w rsf 7 Las Vegas
May 21 Frank Lux w rsf 3 Anchorage
Jun 26 Carlos Hernandez w ko 4 Atlantic City
Aug 25 George Mijangos w rsf 2 Fort Meyers
Sep 10 Bobby Hitz w ko 1 Auburn Hills
Oct 27 Tony Fulilangi w ko 2 Marshall, Tx.
Dec 28 David Jaco w ko 1 Bakersfield
1989
Jan 26 Mark Young w rsf 7 Rochester
Feb 16 Manoel de Almeida w rsf 3 Orlando
Apr 29 J.B.Williamson w rsf 5 Galveston
Jun 1 Bert Cooper w rsf 3 Phoenix
Jul 20 Everett Martin w pts 10 Tucson
1990
Jan 15 Gerry Cooney w ko 2 Atlantic City
Apr 17 Mike Jameson w rsf 4 Lake Tahoe
Jun 16 Adilson Rodriguez w ko 2 Las Vegas
Jul 31 Ken Lakusta w ko 3 Edmonton
Sep 25 Terry Anderson w ko 1 London
1991
Apr 19 Evander Holyfield l pts 12 Atlantic City
(World heavyweight title)
Dec 7 Jimmy Ellis w rsf 3 Reno
1992
Apr 11 Alex Stewart w pts 10 Las Vegas
1993
Jan 16 Pierre Coetzer w rsf 8 Reno
Jun 7 Tommy Morrison l pts 12 Las Vegas
(WBO heavyweight title)
1994
Nov 5 Michael Moorer w ko 10 Las Vegas
(WBA & IBF heavyweight titles)
1995
Apr 22 Axel Schulz w pts 12 Las Vegas
(IBF heavyweight title)
Stripped by IBF and WBA.
1996
Nov 3 Crawford Grimsley w pts 12 Tokyo
1997
Apr 26 Lou Savarese w pts 12 Atlantic City
Nov 22 Shannon Briggs l pts 12 Atlantic City

Fights 81 Won 76 Lost 5

JULIO CESAR CHAVEZ

MEXICAN CAESAR

Julio Cesar Chavez stirred the hearts of a generation of Mexicans. One of the most accomplished pressure fighters of all time, Chavez in full flow was a joy to watch. His defeat of Edwin Rosario in 1987 was perhaps the night he put everything together, but there were so many highlights in a long career that brought him world titles from super-featherweight to light-welterweight.

Chavez was unbeaten in his first 90 fights spread over 13 years and boxed in more world championship contests than anyone else in history. The great trainer, Eddie Futch, said there was nothing particularly elaborate about what Chavez did. 'He fights you every three minutes of every round and he throws rocks,' he said.

Born in Ciudad Obregon, Sonora, on 12 July 1962, the fourth child of Rodolfo and Isabelita Chavez, he was raised in Culiacan, Sinaloa. His elder brothers were boxers, but although he spent time in the gym as a boy, he did not begin to compete until he was 16. As a youngster he added to the family income by selling newspapers on the streets, and enjoyed playing soccer. He had only 13 amateur contests and then turned professional under the guidance of his father when he was 17.

For years he was Mexico's best kept secret. But after he knocked out compatriot Mario Martinez in eight rounds for the WBC super-featherweight title at the Great Western Forum, Los Angeles, in September 1984, the world began to take notice. A sixth-round stoppage of Ruben Castillo from Arizona, was followed by a dramatic second-round knockout of the respected Roger 'Black Mamba' Mayweather. He went on to defend the WBC 130lb belt nine times, before deciding in 1987 his future lay at lightweight.

His 11th-round stoppage of Edwin Rosario in the outdoor arena at the Las Vegas Hilton in November 1987 was a textbook demonstration of relentless, merciless pressure fighting. In the end Rosario was worn down, his eye was shut and dripping blood, his gumshield fell out and he had nothing left. It was stopped.

Chavez had arrived. He beat southpaw compatriot Jose Luis Ramirez, who held the WBC version of the lightweight crown, on an 11th-round technical decision in October

1988, and then stepped up to light-welterweight, where he was more successful than ever. In May 1989 in Los Angeles, he stopped Roger Mayweather at the end of nine rounds to win the WBC 140lb belt, but it was his unification fight with IBF champion Meldrick Taylor in Las Vegas in March 1990 which sealed his greatness.

Taylor had been the boy wonder of the 1984 Olympics, a featherweight gold medallist at only 17 years of age. By 1990 he was a seasoned champion, fast and clever with a brilliant boxing brain. Chavez was Chavez. As expected, Taylor had the best of the first half, beating the Mexican to the punch. Chavez closed the gap, but going into the last seemed to be running out of time. He could not win on points. Taylor was shaken by a thudding right and another that felled him in his own corner. He hauled himself up and referee Richard Steele looked hard at him. 'Are you all right?' he said, and when no response came back: 'You're not all right.' It was stopped, and Chavez had won with TWO seconds to spare.

Taylor had a fracture of the orbital bone of the eye. The arguments about the first great fight of the 1990s would rage for some time, and Taylor complained restlessly for the rest of his career. The decision, or more likely the fight, took something away from him, for he was never as good again. It was four-and-a-half years before they fought the return, by which time Taylor was seriously faded: Chavez, also past his best, stopped him in eight.

Chavez eased his way past a series of challengers, some better than others, before his next big fight against Hector Camacho in Las Vegas in September 1992. By then the Mexican was 30, with 81 consecutive victories. Camacho had also held titles at three weights and for all his extravagant behaviour had slick skills, an iron chin – and could fight. Chavez said he would be unable to show his face in Mexico if he lost – the fight coincided with the national independence celebrations – and his fans poured into Las Vegas for what was expected to be a close, tense struggle. It was a one-sided drubbing, although Camacho's heart and ringcraft enabled him to survive the full 12 rounds.

He stopped the game Terrence Alli in six rounds in Las Vegas in May 1993, and then met the reigning WBC welterweight champion Pernell Whitaker before a crowd of more than 60,000 in the Alamodome, San Antonio. Again, it was Mexican Independence time, and the fans poured over the border. Don King billed it simply as 'The Fight'. When Chavez talked about Whitaker's 'stinking style', he acknowledged that the man from Norfolk, Virginia, another of the 1984 Olympic gold medallists, was clever, but refused to accept that his was the way to fight. Whitaker's awkward, southpaw, point-stealing made him admired, but he could never have been adored. Chavez had good rounds, but by the end seemed at best a couple of rounds behind. The judges' controversial verdict was a draw. Whitaker kept his title and Chavez his unbeaten record. America was furious. *Boxing Illustrated* ran a front cover which screamed: 'If you think the fight was a draw, don't buy this magazine!'

Back in Mexico, Chavez stopped Britain's tough but outclassed Andy Holligan with a broken nose after five, but was visibly slipping. And in January 1994, in his 91st fight, he lost when a clever, but more aggressive American, Frankie 'The Surgeon' Randall, floored him and outpointed him in Las Vegas. Four months later Don King put on the rematch, which Chavez won controversially. In the eighth round a clash of heads left him too badly cut to go on, but to the surprise of many, two of the three judges had him ahead. He won a split technical decision. For another two years he enjoyed a reprieve, beating Taylor in the long awaited return, former two-weight champion from Sacramento, Tony Lopez, and the clever Italian, Giovanni Parisi. But the cracks were widening. There were stories that his life was falling apart, helped by financial problems and marital strife.

He kept winning until the summer of 1996 when he met the new star from Los Angeles, Oscar De La Hoya, who was too sharp and fresh for him. By the fourth, Chavez's face was a bloody mask. He was stopped for the first time in his life.

He took defeat badly, and his out of the ring problems worsened. He parted from his wife Amalia, who took their three sons with her. He won low-key fights, but looked badly faded, and then drilled himself into shape and drew for his old WBC light-welterweight title against fellow Mexican Miguel Angel Gonzalez in 1998. There were reports that he would fight De La Hoya again, but by then he was past his 36th birthday with more than 100 fights behind him. Like so many others, his story was becoming sad.

CAREER STATISTICS

WBC super-featherweight champion 1984-87
WBA lightweight champion 1987-89
WBC lightweight champion 1988-89
WBC light-welterweight champion 1989-94, 1994-96
IBF light-welterweight champion 1990-91
Culiacan, Mexico, born Ciudad Obregon, 12 July 1962

1980
Feb 15 Andres Felix w ko 6 Culiacan
Mar 5 Fidencio Cebreros w pts 6 Culiacan
Apr 8 Ramon Flores w rsf 3 Navajoa
May 20 Roberto Garcia w ko 6 Guaymas
Jun 29 Jesus Garcia w ko 2 Guamuchil
Jul 18 Alberto Geraldo w pts 6 Guamuchil
Sep 5 Miguel Cebreros w pts 10 Culiacan
Sep 22 Jesus Lara w pts 10 Culiacan
Oct 13 Jesus Martinez w ko 1 Culiacan
Nov 2 Andres Felix w ko 2 Culiacan
Dec 15 Roberto Flores w ko 3 Culiacan

1981
Feb 2 Julian Gaxiola w ko 4 Tijuana
Apr 3 Miguel Ruiz w rsf 1 Culiacan
May 8 Eduardo Acosta w ko 2 Culiacan
Jun 5 Victor Games w ko 1 Culiacan
Jun 26 Fidel Navarro w ko 1 Culiacan
Jul 10 Bobby Dominguez w ko 3 Culiacan
Jul 27 Daniel Martinez w rsf 1 Tijuana
Aug 7 Jesus Lara w rsf 2 Culiacan
Aug 31 Daniel Felizardo w ko 3 Tijuana
Sep 25 Jorge Ramirez w ko 2 Culiacan
Oct 19 Carlos Bryant w ko 2 Culiacan
Nov 9 Jose Medina w ko 6 Tijuana
Dec 18 Manuel Vasquez w rsf 7 Culiacan

1982
Jan 12 Ramon Lopez w ko 1 Tijuana
Feb 8 Johnny Jensen w rsf 3 Tijuana
Feb 22 Ramon Peraza w ko 1 Tijuana
Mar 19 Juan Carlos Alvarado w ko 3 Culiacan
Apr 26 Benjamin Abarca w pts 10 Tijuana
Jul 19 Gustavo Salgado w ko 2 Tijuana
Aug 20 Santos Rodriguez w rsf 8 Culiacan
Sep 27 Jose Resendez w rsf 6 Tijuana
Oct 23 Jerry Lewis w rsf 5 Tijuana
Dec 11 Jerry Lewis w dis 6 Sacramento

1983
Feb 25 Othaniel Lopez w ko 4 Enseneda
Apr 4 Ernesto Herrera w rsf 2 Tijuana
May 1 Javier Fragoso w ko 4 San Juan
Jun 15 Romeo Sandoval w rsf 3 Los Angeles
Jul 16 Benjamin Abarca w rsf 5 Culiacan
Sep 1 Adrian Arreola w pts 10 Los Angeles
Dec 30 Armando Flores w ko 3 Mazatlan

1984
May 4 Ramon Avila w ko 6 Culiacan
Jun 13 Delfino Mendoza w ko 3 Hermosillo
Sep 13 Mario Martinez w ko 8 Los Angeles
(WBC super-featherweight title)

1985
Jan 1 Manny Hernandez w rsf 3 Mexico City
Apr 19 Ruben Castillo w ko 6 Los Angeles

(WBC super-featherweight title)
Jul 7 Roger Mayweather w rsf 2 Las Vegas
(WBC super-featherweight title)
Sep 21 Dwight Pratchett w pts 12 Las Vegas
(WBC super-featherweight title)
Dec 19 Jeff Bumphus w dis 5 Los Angeles
1986
Mar 22 Roberto Lindo w ko 2 Las Vegas
May 15 Faustino Barrios w rsf 5 Paris
Jun 13 Refugio Rojas w rsf 7 New York
Aug 3 Rocky Lockridge w pts 12 Monte Carlo
(WBC super-featherweight title)
Dec 12 Juan LaPorte w pts 12 New York
(WBC super-featherweight title)
1987
Apr 18 Francisco Tomas Da Cruz w rsf 3 Nimes
(WBC super-featherweight title)
Aug 21 Danilo Cabrera w pts 12 Tijuana
(WBC super-featherweight title)
Nov 21 Edwin Rosario w rsf 11 Las Vegas
(WBA lightweight title)
1988
Mar 5 Nicky Perez w rsf 3 Tijuana
Apr 16 Rodolfo Aguilar w rsf 6 Las Vegas
(WBA lightweight title)
Jun 4 Rafael Limon w rsf 7 Mazatlan
Aug 1 Vernon Buchanan w rsf 3 Los Angeles
Oct 29 Jose Luis Ramirez w tdec 11 Las Vegas
(WBA & WBC lightweight titles)
1989
May 13 Roger Mayweather w rsf 10 Los Angeles
(WBC light-welterweight title)
Jul 30 Kenny Vice w rsf 3 Atlantic City
Oct 9 Rodolfo Batta w ko 1 Tijuana
Oct 27 Ramon Aramburu w rsf 3 Mazatlan
Nov 18 Sammy Fuentes w rsf 11 Las Vegas
(WBC light-welterweight title)
Dec 16 Alberto Cortes w rsf 3 Mexico City
(WBC light-welterweight title)
1990
Mar 17 Meldrick Taylor w rsf 12 Las Vegas
(WBC & IBF light-welterweight titles)
Jul 5 Razor Akwei Addo w rsf 2 Madrid
Aug 18 Russell Mosley w ko 3 Culiacan
Nov 9 Jaime Balboa w rsf 4 Mazatlan
Dec 8 Kyung-duk Ahn w rsf 3 Atlantic City
(WBC & IBF light-welterweight titles)
1991
Mar 18 John Duplessis w rsf 4 Las Vegas
(WBC & IBF light-welterweight titles)
Apr 22: Relinquished IBF title.
Apr 25 Tommy Small w ko 4 Culiacan
Sep 14 Lonnie Smith w pts 12 Las Vegas
(WBC light-welterweight title)
Nov 11 Jorge Melian w rsf 4 Mexico City
Dec 15 Ignacio Perdomo w rsf 8 Hermosillo
1992
Mar 13 Juan Ramos Soberanes w ko 4 La Paz
Apr 10 Angel Hernandez w rsf 5 Naucalpan
(WBC light-welterweight title)
Aug 1 Frankie Mitchell w rsf 4 Las Vegas
(WBC light-welterweight title)
Sep 12 Hector Camacho w pts 12 Las Vegas
(WBC light-welterweight title)
Oct 31 Bruce Pearson w rsf 3 Culiacan
Dec 13 Marty Jakubowski w rsf 6 Las Vegas
1993
Feb 20 Greg Haugen w rsf 5 Mexico City
(WBC light-welterweight title)
Apr 10 Silvio Rojas w ko 3 Guadalajara
May 8 Terrence Alli w rsf 6 Las Vegas
(WBC light-welterweight title)
Oct 30 Mike Powell w ko 4 Ciudad Juarez
Sep 10 Pernell Whitaker drew 12 San Antonio
(WBC welterweight title)
Dec 18 Andy Holligan w rsf 5 Puebla
(WBC light-welterweight title)
1994
Jan 29 Frankie Randall l pts 12 Las Vegas
(WBC light-welterweight title)
May 7 Frankie Randall w tdec 8 Las Vegas
(WBC light-welterweight title)
Sep 17 Meldrick Taylor w rsf 8 Las Vegas
(WBC light-welterweight title)
Dec 10 Tony Lopez w rsf 10 Monterrey
(WBC light-welterweight title)
1995
Apr 8 Giovanni Parisi w pts 12 Las Vegas
(WBC light-welterweight title)
Jul 29 Craig Houk w ko 1 Chicago
Sep 16 David Kamau w pts 12 Las Vegas
(WBC light-welterweight title)
1996
Feb 9 Scott Walker w rsf 2 Las Vegas
Jun 7 Oscar De La Hoya l rsf 4 Las Vegas
(WBC light-welterweight title)
Oct 12 Joey Gamache w rsf 8 Anaheim
1997
Mar 29 Tony Martin w pts 10 Las Vegas
Jun 28 Larry LaCoursiere w pts 10 Las Vegas
1998
Mar 7 Miguel Angel Gonzalez drew 12 Mexico City
(vacant WBC light-welterweight title)

Fights 103 Won 99 Lost 2 Drawn 2

NIGEL BENN

THE DARK DESTROYER

Through almost ten years and 48 fights, Nigel Benn remained his own man. He chose his own path, and it took him just about everywhere a fighter could wish to go, and into one or two nightmare episodes he would have dearly loved to avoid. Like him or not, Benn earned his respect the hard way, by what he achieved in the ring.

Benn held world titles at two separate weights, fought with success on both sides of the Atlantic, had two epic struggles with Chris Eubank, and beat Gerald McClellan on that terrible night at the London Arena in 1995.

The sixth of seven sons born to a car worker at the sprawling Ford plant in Dagenham, east of London, Nigel Gregory Benn came into this world on 22 January 1964. He did some kick-boxing as a youth, and after school joined the Army, serving a grand total of four years and 256 days in the First Battalion, Royal Regiment of Fusiliers. When he emerged at 21, he joined the West Ham amateur club, whose old boys included greats like 1956 Olympic gold medallist Terry Spinks and 1960s heavyweight sensation Billy Walker. Nigel won the ABA middleweight title in 1986, and turned professional the following January, managed by Essex microchip millionaire Burt McCarthy and promoted by Frank Warren. After a short time, McCarthy retired and handed over his contract to Warren, who guided him for the next year, during which he won the Commonwealth middleweight title and developed a reputation as one of the most exciting rising stars in British boxing.

Nicknamed 'The Dark Destroyer' and always wearing black shorts and boots, he made a habit of taking opponents out quickly. Leon Morris lasted 25 seconds, Ronnie Yoe 57 and poor Ian Chantler only 16. He won the Commonwealth title by demolishing a normally durable Ghanaian, Abdul Umaru Sanda, in two rounds.

The controversial Ambrose Mendy, who was unlicensed by the British Board of Control, took over as Benn's manager. They stayed together for the next three years before – relating to an incident unconnected to boxing – Mendy was convicted of conspiracy to defraud and jailed.

By May 1989 Nigel had stormed to 22 consecutive wins, but then lost the Commonwealth title and his unbeaten record when Michael Watson knocked him out in the sixth round. Mendy's answer was to change direction. They agreed a promotional deal with Bob Arum and in October 1989 Benn made his American debut and out-pointed the rock-hard Jorge Amparo of the Dominican Republic over 10 good rounds.

In April 1990 he came good when he won the WBO middleweight title in Atlantic City. He started badly and had to climb off the canvas early on, but eventually floored the solid-chinned Doug De Witt four times for an exciting stoppage in round eight.

In his first defence he fought Iran Barkley, who had knocked out Thomas Hearns but then lost to Roberto Duran. He had also undergone surgery on his eyes, and was considered, wrongly as it turned out, to be fading. Benn was a pre-fight favourite, but nobody could have foreseen the three-knockdown, one round massacre that set Barkley, his manager John Reetz and American journalists complaining about the Englishman's roughhouse tactics. Most of Britain saw it as a case of the biter bit. Benn also publicly tore up his British Board of Control licence in protest at having to fight Barkley in the USA. The Board had refused to licence Iran to box in Britain because of his history of eye problems.

The problems with the board were ironed out quickly enough for Benn to sign for a second WBO defence against Chris Eubank at the National Exhibition Centre, Birmingham, in November 1990. The fight was magnificent, with both men drawing deep on their respective wells of courage, before Benn, with one eye almost shut, was rescued by referee Richard Steele in the ninth round.

He returned to Britain full-time, severed his connections with Miami-based trainer Vic Andreetti, and parted with Mendy when the latter was convicted. He settled in London and signed a promotional deal with Barry Hearn. He set out to chase a return with Eubank, who was also promoted by Hearn's Matchroom organisation. There were six non-title wins, two over recent challengers for Eubank's title, Dan Sherry and Sugarboy Malinga.

By now both men had moved up to super-middleweight, and in October 1992 Nigel took a calculated risk and travelled to Marino, near Rome, to challenge Italy's Mauro Galvano for the WBC version of the 168lb title (Eubank was WBO champion). Nigel made a ferocious early assault. Galvano was badly cut and at the end of round three could not go on. The Italian camp claimed the injury was caused by a butt, and wanted a technical draw, but American referee Joe Cortez stood firm and ruled it was caused by a punch, so Benn was awarded victory ... and his second world title.

The build-up to the Eubank rematch took up the next year. Finally, they met in front of 42,000 fans at Old Trafford, Manchester, in October 1993, with both titles on the line. Eubank walked to the ring with Hearn, while Benn was accompanied by his first promoter, Frank Warren. The 12 rounds were close, swaying one way and then the other. When the final bell rang, the majority at ringside favoured Benn, who was certain he had won. The result was disappointing: a fence-sitting draw. Benn stormed away, talking bitterly and without proof of dark goings-on behind the scenes.

At Earls Court in February 1994, he outpointed an inexperienced but dangerous challenger, Henry Wharton, as if he had proved something to himself against Eubank, if not to the judges. Under trainer Jimmy Tibbs, Benn had worked out a subtler defensive strategy, and could now protect a chin which, every so often, looked vulnerable.

His next defence at the NEC, Birmingham, against the solid but technically limited Paraguayan, Juan Carlos Gimenez, was marred by a riot. The violence had broken out earlier in the evening and was nothing to do with either Benn or Gimenez, but they fought with it flaring up in the background. Benn admitted it distracted him, but he won clearly anyway against an inferior opponent. In 1998, Gimenez even returned to Britain, somehow ranked No.1 contender for the WBO title, and was stopped by Joe Calzaghe.

After the relatively low-key wins over Wharton and Gimenez, Benn signed for another major showdown, at the London Arena in February 1995, against WBO middleweight champion Gerald McClellan. As most boxing fans will know, McClellan suffered tragic injuries in the fight, collapsing in his corner after he was counted out in round 10. Surgery to remove a blood clot from his brain saved his life, but he now lives at home in Illinois, where he needs 24-hour care. He is blind and almost deaf. McClellan's injury overshadowed one of the greatest fights of the decade.

By now Benn had replaced trainer Tibbs with Kevin Sanders, and the build-up to the fight also brought a distraction in the shape of a court case brought by his first trainer, Brian Lynch, who was seeking financial compensation. Benn fiercely denied owing anything, and also got himself embroiled in a public row with promoter Warren about his tax position. Warren threatened to sue Benn for not fulfilling his contractual obligations with regard to his part in publicising the show. This was the acrimonious backdrop which made most experts predict a quick, explosive win for the American.

This seemed justified when Benn was knocked through the ropes for a count of nine. Incredibly, Benn had McClellan rocking in round two, and henceforth the pace was relentless. By the fifth McClellan looked tired, in the sixth his gumshield was sent flying, and then in round eight Benn was floored for another mandatory count. With his next punch, he rocked the American, and finally in round 10, it was McClellan who went down twice, the second time for the full count. He got up, walked to his corner unaided, but then collapsed.

Benn adjusted to McClellan's injury, and returned five months later with an eight rounds retirement win over the talented but emotionally erratic Italian southpaw, Vincenzo Nardiello, who was audacious enough to plant a kiss full on Benn's lips in the preliminaries. He eventually folded and went down five times before the end.

By 1996, at the age of 32, Benn knew the end was coming. But neither he nor many others expected him to lose his title to 9–2 outsider, Sugarboy Malinga of South Africa, who was by now at least 36. But Benn's style suited the straight-punching, jab and counter tactics favoured by Malinga, and after 12 rounds, he lost a clear but – because of an eccentric piece of scoring from American judge Chuck Giampa – split decision.

Afterwards Benn said an emotional farewell to boxing and proposed to his fiancee in the ring. She accepted, and there was barely a dry eye in the house.

With hindsight, he should have left it there. He boxed twice more, both times losing inside the distance to marauding Irishman Steve Collins, and finally being booed by a near 20,000 crowd at the Nynex Arena in Manchester for his third retirement speech in eight months. This time he kept to his word and never fought again.

CAREER STATISTICS

WBO middleweight champion 1990
WBC super-middleweight champion 1992-96
London, born 22 January 1964

1987
Jan 28 Graeme Ahmed w rsf 2 London
Mar 4 Kevin Roper w rsf 1 Basildon
Apr 22 Bob Niuewenhuizen w rsf 1 London
May 9 Winston Burnett w rsf 4 London
Jun 17 Reginald Marks w rsf 1 London
Jul 1 Leon Morris w ko 1 London
Aug 9 Eddie Smith w ko 1 Windsor
Sep 16 Winston Burnett w rsf 3 London
Oct 13 Russell Barker w rsf 1 Windsor
Nov 3 Ronnie Yoe w rsf 1 London
Nov 24 Ian Chantler w ko 1 Wisbech
Dec 2 Reggie Miller w ko 7 London
1988
Jan 27 Fermin Chirino w ko 2 London
Feb 7 Byron Prince w rsf 2 Stafford
Feb 24 Greg Taylor w rsf 2 Port Talbot
Mar 14 Darren Hobson w ko 1 Norwich
Apr 20 Abdul Umaru Sanda w rsf 2 London
(Commonwealth middleweight title)
May 28 Tim Williams w rsf 2 London
Oct 26 Anthony Logan w ko 2 London
(Commonwealth middleweight title)
Dec 10 David Noel w rsf 1 London
1989
Feb 8 Mike Chilambe w ko 1 London
(Commonwealth middleweight title)
Mar 28 Mbayo Wa Mbayo w ko 2 Glasgow
May 21 Michael Watson l ko 6 London
(Commonwealth middleweight title)
Oct 20 Jorge Amparo w pts 10 Atlantic City
Dec 1 Jose Quinones w rsf 1 Las Vegas
1990
Jan 14 Sanderline Williams w pts 10 Atlantic City
Apr 29 Doug De Witt w rsf 8 Atlantic City
(WBO middleweight title)
Aug 18 Iran Barkley w rsf 1 Las Vegas
(WBO middleweight title)
Nov 18 Chris Eubank l rsf 9 Birmingham
(WBO middleweight title)
1991
Apr 3 Robbie Sims w rsf 7 London
Jul 3 Kid Milo w rsf 4 Brentwood
Oct 26 Lenzie Morgan w pts 10 Brentwood
Dec 7 Hector Lescano w ko 3 Manchester
1992
Feb 19 Dan Sherry w rsf 3 London
May 23 Sugarboy Malinga w pts 10 Birmingham
Oct 3 Mauro Galvano w rsf 3 Marino
(WBC super-middleweight title)
Dec 12 Nicky Piper w rsf 11 London
(WBC super-middleweight title)
1993
Mar 6 Mauro Galvano w pts 12 Glasgow
(WBC super-middleweight title)
Jun 26 Lou Gent w rsf 4 London
(WBC super-middleweight title)
Oct 9 Chris Eubank drew 12 Manchester
(WBC & WBO super-middleweight titles)
1994
Feb 26 Henry Wharton w pts 12 London
(WBC super-middleweight title)
Sep 10 Juan Carlos Gimenez w pts 12 Birmingham
(WBC super-middleweight title)
1995
Feb 25 Gerald McClellan w ko 10 London
(WBC super-middleweight title)
Jul 22 Vincenzo Nardiello w rtd 8 London
(WBC super-middleweight title)
Sep 2 Danny Ray Perez w ko 7 London
(WBC super-middleweight title)
1996
Mar 2 Sugarboy Malinga l pts 12 Newcastle
(WBC super-middleweight title)
Jul 6 Steve Collins l rsf 4 Manchester
(WBO super-middleweight title)
Nov 9 Steve Collins l rtd 6 Manchester
(WBO super-middleweight title)

Fights 48 Won 42 Lost 5 Drawn 1

FRANK BRUNO

BIG FRANK

Frank Bruno was blessed with a magnificent physique and a tremendously hard punch. He trained hard and conscientiously to make the most of them and his determination and perseverance took him all the way to a version of the heavyweight championship of the world. His faults were almost as obvious as his strengths: a statuesque demeanour, a stamina problem and a lack of the true fighter's instinct for survival when under pressure. These stopped him from being an all-time great, but the ups and downs of the amiable giant had British boxing fans enthralled for 14 years.

Franklin Roy Bruno was born in Hammersmith General Hospital, London, on 16 November 1961. He weighed 9lb. His father, Robert, originally from Dominica, and his mother, Lynette, had come to settle in England from Jamaica in the late 1950s. Father Robert, a warehouseman in a bakery, suffered from chronic diabetes, and mother Lynette had to work hard as a district nurse to help raise her six children, of whom Frank was the youngest. Soon after Frank was born, the family moved from Battersea to Wandsworth, south London. Lynette was a believer in big breakfasts for growing children, and so far as Frank was concerned his daily bacon, egg, sausages and fried bread built him up into the biggest lad for his age in the district. He became something of a bully and Lynette was constantly having to placate parents of other children whom Frank had beaten up. He managed to avoid serious trouble, i.e. with the police, but something had to be done with him when at Swaffham Primary School in Wandsworth he turned his attention to a teacher, punching him to the floor during a school visit to the House of Commons. He was 11, and he was expelled.

This was the last straw so far as Lynette, a Pentecostal lay preacher, was concerned, and she asked the education authorities for help with her uncontrollable son, and Frank got the luckiest break in his life. He was sent to Oak Hall School near Broadoak in Sussex, a boarding school for very difficult children run by the Greater London Council. Oak Hall was a stately Victorian country house set in 80 acres of grounds, and was restricted to 42 boys. Its facilities were excellent, and it concentrated on sports and physical skills while giving its pupils a sound basic education. Big Frank was good at most sports and got into the Sussex schools football and athletics teams, but one heated argument with a referee led to him being sent to the deputy head, where the interview degenerated into a wrestling match on the floor of the library.

Eventually Frank settled down and became a model pupil – in fact he stayed on for an extra year, until he was 17. During his time at Oak Hall he determined to become a boxer. He had boxed at Wandsworth Boys Club while at primary school, and at Oak Hall he was able to get as much training, with good gym facilities, even a punchbag, as he wanted, but while the boys could spar, they weren't allowed to take part in formal matches because of GLC rules about boxing.

Back in Wandsworth, a 17-year-old Frank had to start thinking about jobs. Without academic qualifications, he became a metal polisher and had other jobs like plumber's mate and building labourer. He realised his fists held the only way out of such a rut, and joined the Sir Philip Game Amateur Boxing Club in Croydon. Frank was soon knocking over his opponents and in fact had only one defeat as an amateur, by Irish international Joe Christle, a defeat he avenged. In 1980, 18-year-old Frank became the youngest ever winner of an ABA heavyweight title when he outpointed Welshman Rudi Pika in the Wembley final. He represented Young England, and then with 20 wins in 21 contests, decided to fight for money.

In his days as an amateur, Frank met Laura Mooney, who was to become his wife some 10 years later. As Laura herself explained in 1993 when Frank appeared on television's *This is Your Life*, they met at a roller skating park when Frank was showing off and 'a friend bet me 50 pence I wouldn't dare pinch his bum. I did, and I've been with him ever since.' Laura was 21 at the time they met and working at a children's nursery.

Frank's transition into the professional ranks hit two setbacks. First, his amateur trainer, Fred Rix, introduced him to a possible manager, Burt McCarthy, and Bruno signed a letter of intent. Unfortunately after a few months Frank decided to train with Terry Lawless at Canning Town, and a dispute developed between the two managers that was not finally decided until 1985. The courts decided that Lawless had the right to manage Bruno, which allowed him to get on with his career, but three years later Bruno had to pay McCarthy substantial damages for not fulfilling the terms of the letter of intent. Frank's second setback, which might have proved more serious, was the discovery of a rare form of short-sightedness in Frank's right eye, which made him likely to suffer from a detached retina after a blow to the head. The BBBC refused him a licence on the strength of it.

Terry Lawless sent Frank to Bogota, Colombia, to one of the few eye surgeons in the world able to operate for this condition, and the operation was successful. At last, in February 1982, the Board gave Frank a licence. His first pro bout was at the Albert Hall on 17 March 1982. Frank weighed 217lb. He had a magnificent physique, standing 6ft 3in with a 47 inch chest (51 expanded) and not an ounce of fat on him. Frank's opponent was a Mexican, Lupe Guerra, based in Nebraska. Guerra was counted out on his third trip to the canvas in the first round.

Frank's girlfriend Laura was pregnant at the time of Frank's debut, and soon afterwards his first daughter, Nicola, was born. At first Frank continued to live with his family in Wandsworth, where Laura and the baby visited, but once the tabloid papers got on to the story of the new black heavyweight hope having a white wife and a baby, Frank decided to introduce Laura and Nicola to the press. Answering questions, he said there were no plans to marry until he'd succeeded in a boxing career.

Frank had 10 contests in 1982, winning all by the quick route, only one getting beyond the second round. The public were restless because Bruno seemed to be fighting a bunch of stiffs from all parts of the world. After six opponents in 1983 had been despatched in rounds from the second to the fifth, Frank made his US debut at the Chicago De Vinci Manor, a dance hall. His contest was staged in the afternoon to allow live British television transmission in the evening. Frank impressively knocked Mike Jameson cold in the second round, earning a tribute from ace trainer Angelo Dundee: 'The best heavyweight prospect from Britain in a long, long time'.

Frank won three more fights in 1983, but the second, against Jumbo Cummings, was tough. Cummings caught Bruno with a terrific right late in the first round, and Frank was almost out on his feet when the bell rang. His corner team, managed to bring him round well enough for him to survive a dodgy second round, and then as Cummings tired Frank got on top to win by a seventh-round stoppage.

There were divided views as to whether this proved Frank could or could not take a hard punch. While the debate was going on Frank moved himself, Laura and Nicola into a four-bedroom house at Chadwell Heath, Essex, near to manager Terry Lawless's house. He also bought a Ford Granada Ghia with a six-speaker stereo system. Frank had half arrived.

After 21 fights had been won in an average of under two rounds, Frank suffered his first defeat. He was dealt it by James 'Bonecrusher' Smith, an American who later won a version of the world title. All went well for nine rounds with Bruno so far ahead going into the last that Smith needed a knockout. Suddenly he caught Bruno with a hard left hook. Bruno was completely drained and lay on the ropes while Smith crashed home 14 more punches until Bruno keeled over and was counted out. The knockout revealed Bruno's greatest flaw. He lacked the true fighter's instinct of self-preservation when hurt. Once he was under the hammer Frank did not know what to do. He just took the punches bravely.

As the contest had been shown by NBC in America, a rehabilitation course was badly needed, and it was well organised by Lawless. Less than 18 months later Frank was challenging Anders Eklund of Sweden for the European heavyweight championship. Eckland was 6ft 6in and 244lb, but a fourth-round knockout gave Frank the title. Two fights later a first-round stoppage of former WBA champion Gerrie Coetzee of South

Africa in a final eliminator for the WBA title set up Frank's first world title fight, a challenge to Tim Witherspoon at Wembley Stadium. It was Frank's 30th contest. A crowd of 40,000 packed Wembley to see if he could win. It looked promising at first, as Frank, with a five-inch reach advantage at 82 inches, kept 'Terrible Tim' on the end of his jab. He dictated the fight for five rounds, but in the sixth Witherspoon began fighting back with overhand rights, and Frank's stamina began to run out. It ended in the 11th with Frank stunned and slumped on the ropes. The referee stopped it as Lawless threw in the towel.

It was back to square one, and the management of a similar comeback to before. Three Americans were stopped, then to Frank's satisfaction a fight was fixed with veteran Joe Bugner, who had been niggling Bruno for years. Bugner had emigrated to Australia, but made a fourth comeback to the ring especially to teach Frank a lesson. The ref stopped the fight in Frank's favour just as the eighth round was ending.

Bruno then got the biggest fight of his career — a challenge for the undisputed heavyweight championship held by the feared Mike Tyson, at the Las Vegas Hilton. With 2,000 of the 9,000 present Britons who had gone to support Frank, he put up a brave show, although it was a mismatch. He was down in the first 20 seconds but got up and near the end of the first round he shook Tyson with a left hook, the first time in Tyson's professional career he had looked like wobbling. But Bruno couldn't consolidate and the end came when the referee stepped in to stop it with Bruno in trouble after a fifth-round flurry of blows from the champion. Frank's consolation was a purse of some $4 million.

Laura Mooney cradled Frank's head in her arms after the fight and tried to persuade him to retire. He didn't, but he had a break from boxing of two years. A year after the Tyson defeat, he and Laura got married at a Roman Catholic church in Hornchurch, Essex. About 3,000 well-wishers blocked the streets around the church. By now the happy couple had a second daughter, Rachel. Frank cashed in on his popularity with advertising work (HP sauce and Kleenex TV commercials) and appeared frequently as a celebrity in television shows. He got an Equity card and worked annually in pantomime.

But the lure of the ring proved too much for Frank, and in November 1991 he made a comeback, now managing himself. Inside-the-distance wins against a Dutchman, a Cuban, a South African and an American (one-time prospect Carl Williams) saw Bruno given a third chance at a world title – the WBC title held by Britain's Lennox Lewis. The contest was at Cardiff and Frank did better than many expected. His jab had him well in front after six rounds. But Lewis caught him in the seventh and, as had happened before, Bruno lost his bearings and was taking punishment on the ropes without fighting back when the referee stopped it. It was his fourth defeat.

Bruno did not give up and amazingly, after three more quick wins, he was granted a fourth title shot in September 1995 against Oliver McCall, who had shocked Lewis by taking his WBC crown. The contest, promoted by Frank Warren, was at Wembley Stadium. The Sky TV cameras were there and at last it all came right for Frank, who was now trained by George Francis. Spurred on by 30,000 fans, including Nigel Benn, who had just won his own title fight, Bruno took control from the start with jabs and overhand rights. The only question seemed to be the old one. Would his stamina last in the later rounds, especially if he were caught with a blockbuster? Midway through the 11th McCall got through with two left uppercuts and Bruno ended the round hanging on. Would it be the old story? It nearly was. Bruno was bludgeoned in the 12th and last round, and at times looked very dodgy. But his resolve never left him, and he managed to keep his arms up, block the most dangerous blows and finish a clear if weary winner. There was a tearful interview on camera, a return to the dressing room to the strains of 'Land of Hope and Glory' and a belt to show his wife, daughters, and six-month old son Franklin junior. It had taken 13 years and 44 fights since he'd turned pro, but at his fourth attempt he was a heavyweight champion of the world.

Frank had one more contest, a title defence. He met Mike Tyson again, at the MGM-Grand Garden, Las Vegas, in March 1996. The fight had been fixed as part of the deal for Bruno's title shot with McCall, Don King being the guiding hand behind both McCall and Tyson. Sky TV introduced the pay-per-view concept to Britain, and there had been talk in the trade press of the fight being worth £10 million to Bruno, so he let everybody know how put out he was that his purse was nearer £4 million. Frank trained hard and psyched himself up for the event, and was supported again by a large British contingent of fans who crossed the Atlantic to cheer him on. But Bruno, facing Tyson for the second time, could not disguise his apprehension and froze. Tyson won as he liked, the fight being stopped after 50 seconds of the third round, with Bruno sitting helpless on the bottom rope.

It was a sad end to his boxing career, but the amiable Frank retained his celebrity popularity. At 34, he had made more money than the average man could dream about. He was soon making plenty more on the after-dinner speaking circuit.

CAREER STATISTICS

WBC heavyweight champion 1995-96
London born 16 November 1961

1982
Mar 17 Lupe Guerra w ko 1 London
Mar 30 Harvey Steichen w rsf 2 London
Apr 20 Tom Stevenson w ko 1 London
May 4 Ron Gibbs w rsf 4 London
Jun 1 Tony Moore w rsf 2 London
Sep 14 George Scott w rsf 1 London
Oct 23 Ali Lukasa w ko 2 Berlin
Nov 9 Rudi Gauwe w ko 2 London
Nov 23 Georg Butzbach w rtd 1 London
Dec 7 Gilberto Acuna w rsf 1 London

1983
Jan 18 Stewart Lithgo w rtd 4 London
Feb 8 Peter Mulendwa w ko 3 London
Mar 1 Winston Allen w rsf 2 London
Apr 5 Eddie Nielson w rsf 3 London
May 3 Scott LeDoux w rsf 3 London
May 31 Barry Funches w rsf 5 London
Jul 9 Mike Jameson w ko 2 Chicago
Sep 27 Bill Sharkey w ko 1 London
Oct 11 Floyd Cummings w rsf 7 London
Dec 6 Walter Santemore w ko 4 London

1984
Mar 13 Juan Figueroa w ko 1 London
May 13 James Smith l ko 10 London
Sep 25 Ken Lakusta w ko 2 London
Nov 6 Jeff Jordan w rsf 3 London
Nov 27 Phillip Brown w pts 10 London

1985
Mar 27 Lucien Rodriguez w rtd 1 London
Oct 1 Anders Eklund w ko 4 London *(European heavyweight title)*
Dec 4 Larry Frazier w ko 2 London

1986
Mar 4 Gerrie Coetzee w rsf 1 London
Jul 19 Tim Witherspoon l rsf 11 London *(WBA heavyweight title)*

1987
Mar 24 James Tillis w rsf 5 London
Jun 27 Chuck Gardner w rsf 1 Cannes
Aug 30 Reggie Gross w rsf 8 Marbella
Oct 24 Joe Bugner w rsf 8 London

1988 inactive

1989
Feb 25 Mike Tyson l rsf 5 Las Vegas *(World heavyweight title)*

1990 inactive

1991
Nov 20 John Emmen w ko 1 London

1992
Apr 22 Jose Ribalta w ko 2 London
Oct 17 Pierre Coetzer w rsf 8 London

1993
Apr 24 Carl Williams w rsf 10 Birmingham
Oct 1 Lennox Lewis l rsf 7 Cardiff *(WBC heavyweight title)*

1994
Mar 16 Jesse Ferguson w rsf 1 Birmingham

1995
Feb 18 Rodolfo Marin w ko 1 Shepton Mallet
May 13 Mike Evans w ko 2 Glasgow
Sep 2 Oliver McCall w pts 12 London *(WBC heavyweight title)*

1996
Mar 16 Mike Tyson l rsf 3 Las Vegas *(WBC heavyweight title)*

Fights 45 Won 40 Lost 5

MIKE TYSON

IRON MIKE

When the 1990s began, Mike Tyson was simply the most feared fighter the sport of boxing had known. He was 23 years old, and undisputed heavyweight champion of the world, having won the WBA version at 20, and destroyed the claimants of the other authorities just past his 21st birthday. He had an awesome physique, including a phenomenal neck of 19½ inches, as thick and strong as some men's thighs. He entered the ring robeless, wearing simple black shorts and black boxing boots, and with an executioner's air of purposeful intent that carried more menace than King Kong and Godzilla combined. Many of his opponents were beaten by fear before any blows were exchanged. Only four of 37 had managed to be still on their feet at the final bell, mostly by subduing any violent feelings of their own in favour of self-preservation. Then, as soon as the 1990s began, everything went wrong. He lost his title to a 42–1 no-hoper in the biggest shock in boxing history, he was charged with rape, he was convicted, he served half of a six-year prison sentence, he returned to the ring after a four-year absence, regained a world title, then scandalously bit off part of an opponent's ear during a contest and was banned for a year. His outrageous behaviour guaranteed he would remain boxing's biggest-ever box-office attraction.

The bundle of animosity that became famous as Iron Mike Tyson entered the world on 30 June 1966 in the Cumberland hospital in the Bedford-Stuyvesant district of Brooklyn, New York. He weighed exactly 8½ lb. His mother was Lorna Tyson, who already had two other children, who like Mike carried her maiden name, since she and Jimmy Kirkpatrick, Mike's father, never married. Kirkpatrick was a big, strong labourer, whose legacy to Mike was the genes for the muscular development that would one day make his fortune. Kirkpatrick left the family when Mike was two years old and Lorna took her children to the nearby area of Brownsville, which had even tougher and poorer streets than those they left.

In this environment delinquency was second nature to most of the young boys, and Mike, without a father and with a mother who, however well-intentioned, couldn't control him, could not avoid the influence of the streets. But young Mike was certainly not a bully by nature and indeed throughout his life was to display glimpses of surprising sensitivity in the general picture he otherwise presented of utter callousness. The world bewildered him at times, and perhaps his shocking behaviour was a way to bring some sense into it.

His mother apart, the closest person to Mike as he grew into childhood was his sister Denise. Mike learned from her soft, girlish ways. His voice was quiet, unaggressive and with a slight lisp, which he retained to some degree even when later on he could alienate everybody inside or outside boxing by saying of a punch which broke an opponent's nose: 'I catch them there because I'm trying to push the nose bone into the brain'. Perhaps he was still reacting then to the days when his boyhood associates called him the 'little fairy boy'. There could hardly be a bigger contrast between the man who said those words in his muscled malevolent prime and the retiring, bespectacled, lisping, seven-year-old 'fairy boy', yet only a dozen years or so wrought the difference.

All his life the super-aggressive Tyson has shown a fondness for pigeons. He kept them as a boy, and legend has it that it was through a bully pulling off the head of one of his pigeons that Tyson discovered his strength and his warlike inclinations. In an unthinking fit of fury young Mike beat up the bigger boy who killed his pigeon, not only realising his power, but that he enjoyed using it.

Tyson based the rest of his boyhood on a life of crime, which was not confined to the petty theft from shops, stalls and slot-machines and the pick-pocketing in gangs normally associated with youngsters of the district. Tyson was arrested dozens of times before he was 12, and among the offences he committed was armed robbery. He was sent to a New York correction centre, the Tryon School, where the unaccustomed discipline and schooling made him an awkward rebel. But he and the school's athletic coach, Bobby Stewart, an ex-boxer, came to an agreement: Tyson would co-operate in lessons if Stewart would teach him boxing. It didn't take long for Stewart to notice the potential this amazingly strong, belligerent youngster would have as a boxer, and he arranged for him to meet a contact of his in trainer Cus d'Amato. Cus d'Amato was now 70 and in effect retired from the pro boxing game, having been made bankrupt some seven years earlier. He had been very successful in training two of his charges to win world titles: heavyweight Floyd Patterson and light-heavy Jose Torres.

When Cus D'Amato saw the 13-year-old Tyson sparring for the first time he said: 'That's the future heavyweight champion of the world'. He was living at the time in a large house in the Catskill district of New York, where he had been installed after his bankruptcy by a wealthy friend and boxing fan, Jim Jacobs, a former champion handball player. D'Amato was living there with his partner of 40 years, Camille Ewald, and was so enthusiastic about Tyson's prospects that he persuaded the authorities to allow Tyson to live in the house with himself and Camille, undertaking to make sure Tyson received an education as well as boxing training in the gym he ran above the local police station.

The arrangement worked pretty well with Tyson embarking on a successful amateur career under D'Amato's surveillance, with Teddy Atlas, a strong-man trainer, brought in to groom Tyson for professional stardom. A hitch which foreshadowed some of Tyson's later problems was overcome. Atlas was told that Tyson had abused a 12-year-old girl and, in an attempt to shock him into behaving more responsibly, he threatened Tyson with a gun. The partnership became impossible. Tyson was taken back to the Tryon School, but C'Amato quickly arranged for him to return to training under a new trainer, Kevin Rooney.

In the final trials for the 1984 US Olympic team, the 17-year-old Tyson was beaten twice by Henry Tillman, who won the place in the team and eventually the gold medal. D'Amato decided it was time his boxer turned professional.

D'Amato had carefully arranged the wherewithal to finance Tyson's launch to stardom. Jim Jacobs and Bill Cayton were the backers and subsequent joint managers of Tyson. Cayton was an advertising executive who had discovered through his business the appeal of old fight films and who, with Jacobs, had formed Big Fights Inc, buying up a huge collection of film which became the basis of a long-running TV series. Tyson liked to watch the old films, and became knowledgable about boxing history and his possible place in it. The films suggested to Tyson and his team the idea that Tyson should enter the ring in his plain black garb, like the old champions, setting himself apart from the modern trend of show-biz entrances and creating for himself the image of the no-frills destroyer.

Tyson's mother died when he was 16, and two years later, Cus D'Amato became his legal guardian. So it was a close-knit, highly professional team which was behind Tyson when he made his pro debut on 6 March 1985 at Albany, New York, against Hector Mercedes. He was not yet 19, and he won by knockout after 107 seconds. Cayton and Jacobs videoed this, and the other quick wins which followed, to compile a tape advertising Tyson for distribution to boxing people. Nothing was being left to chance.

Poor Cus D'Amato, however, was not to live to enjoy the day he became associated with his third, and perhaps greatest, world champion. He died in November 1985, aged 77. Nine days later Tyson beat Eddie Richardson, appropriately in 77 seconds. It was his 12th straight win, and ninth in the first round.

Tyson was not tall for a heavyweight, standing only 5ft 11½ in, but he weighed an adequate 220lb. D'Amato had taught him how to bob and weave and present a moving and difficult target. He mastered a fine array of hooks and uppercuts which he could throw from a variety of angles. His main assets were his hand speed, enabling him to deliver punches in swift combinations, and the terrific power of his punching. His ruthlessness in finishing off a stricken opponent was unsurpassed.

In 1986 the Home Box Office television channel in the USA was organising a tournament to unify the heavyweight championship, the purses, allied to the television revenue, being sufficient to get the champions of all bodies and the chief contenders to agree to the scheme. Such was the trail of destruction Tyson left through the ranks of heavyweight pretenders that the HBO enterprise would have been meaningless had he not been incorporated.

So it was that a mere 20 months after his debut, and a year after D'Amato died, 20-year-old Mike Tyson was challenging Trevor Berbick for Berbick's WBC championship. The 34-year-old Berbick had beaten three previous 'world' champions (he had been Muhammad Ali's last opponent), but was still a 4–1 underdog when he faced Tyson at the Hilton Center, Las Vegas. Although the convention in world title fights was that only the champion wore black, Tyson risked a fine by appearing in black as well. Berbick's answer was to enter the ring in a black hooded gown, wearing knee-length black socks.

Tyson claimed he saw the fear in Berbick's eyes at the start, and he began quickly, severely staggering Berbick in the first round. The second round was notable for the manner of Berbick's defeat. He rose from his third knockdown, delivered with an awesome left hook, to stagger right across the ring on drunken legs to crash again. Pulling himself up with the help of the ropes, he couldn't get his left ankle to hold him up, and the referee had to support him as he declared the fight over. It was a terrifying testament to Tyson's power. Tyson was the youngest man ever to hold a version of the heavyweight title, beating by 186 days Cus D'Amato's other protege, Floyd Patterson.

Four months later he outpointed James 'Bonecrusher' Smith, who took care not to join in a fight until the last 30 seconds of the last round. Smith admitted he fought only to survive, but he came nowhere near to surviving as the WBA champion. Tyson now owned two-thirds of the world's heavyweight championship.

The IBF champion, Michael Spinks, however, now opted out of the unification contests, presumably seeing a lucrative contest with 'white hope' Gerry Cooney as a better prospect than possibly losing his title and unbeaten record to Tyson. The IBF crown was declared vacant, and Tyson had to wait for a new champion, Tony Tucker (who won the IBF title by stopping Buster Douglas), before he could incorporate the IBF strand and become undisputed champion. He faced Tucker on 1 August 1987 and, despite being shaken straight away by a left hook, he outpointed Tucker to establish his right to total recognition.

Tyson then beat challenger Tyrell Biggs, prolonging the fight in order to administer a bad beating, in revenge for what he claimed was a 'lack of respect' shown him by Biggs years before in their amateur days. He then invited three prominent, beautiful women to watch him repel the challenge of veteran ex-champion Larry Holmes (which he did without difficulty): Naomi Campbell, the model, Suzette Charles, who was Miss America, and Robin Givens, an actress starring in a TV sitcom *Head of the Class.* Two weeks later he married Robin Givens, a move which radically altered both his private and boxing lives. Everything now seemed to go wrong at once.

First of all, Jim Jacobs, half of Tyson's management team, became seriously ill with leukaemia. He died a couple of days after Tyson, with new wife Givens at ringside, had easily disposed of challenger Tony Tubbs in Tokyo. Tyson had recently signed a new contract with his managers which meant that in the event of Jacobs' death, Cayton would become sole manager, but Jacobs' widow would continue to receive her husband's third of the revenue earned. Miss Givens, with the strong support of her businesswoman mother, now began to take a strong interest in Tyson's finances, telling him that not enough of his earnings were getting back to him. Her legal team alleged that Tyson had signed his last contract with Cayton and Jacobs while being kept in the dark about Jacobs' condition. They sought the contract to be declared invalid.

Meanwhile Don King, the ubiquitous promoter/manager, never happy unless he controls all the likely heavyweight champions in the world, opportunistically attended Jacobs' funeral and began a strong wooing of the Tyson family with a view to taking over Tyson's business affairs to the benefit of all (in reality himself). Meanwhile, Givens, who had claimed to be pregnant at the time of her marriage to Tyson, allowed it to be revealed through her sister that Tyson was abusing her and that as a result she had suffered a miscarriage.

All this was brewing up as Tyson prepared for his most important contest to date, a meeting with still unbeaten former IBF champion Michael Spinks, whose supporters, including *Ring* and *Boxing Illustrated* magazine, claimed he was the real champion by 'direct descent'. This contest took place at Atlantic City on 27 June 1988. It turned out to be perhaps Tyson's most impressive performance.

Fans were kept waiting over 15 minutes for the start, as both camps insisted their man was champion, and thereby entitled to be second in the ring. Eventually the New Jersey Commissioner, Larry Hazard, had to intervene and insist Spinks enter the ring first. Spinks was clearly nervous while it seemed that a hyped-up Tyson couldn't wait to get at him. A flurry of blows early in the first round put Spinks on one knee and forced him to take a mandatory count of eight. When Spinks tried to attack on the command 'box on', he was caught by a right uppercut which knocked him flat on his back, from where he tried to rise but stood no chance. He was counted out in 91 seconds. No one could now dispute that Tyson was the most efficient fighting machine in the world.

However, Tyson's next defence, against Frank Bruno, was rescheduled several times and put back in all by six months or so as Tyson's private problems mounted. He fractured his hand in a street fight with former opponent Mitch Green; he drove his wife's BMW into a tree in what many took to be a suicide bid; he threatened to hang himself after chasing his wife and her mother through a hotel lounge in Moscow, where Givens was filming; he objected to being filmed and smashed a TV camera; he appeared with Givens on a TV chat show looking drugged, and smiled foolishly and submissively while she repeated many of these stories against him, saying he was manic-depressive; he smashed up his house, threw furniture into the street and chased off his wife and her mother; he was sued for divorce; he signed a promotional contract with Don King without consulting Cayton; he sacked Kevin Rooney, his trainer since he turned professional, for siding with Cayton; he finalised his divorce after only a year and eight days of marriage, with Don King's help; and two women accused him of sexual harassment.

When Tyson eventually met and overawed Bruno, his performance was way below par, and he even allowed Bruno to stagger him with a good punch before he finished him off in the fifth round. Some good judges saw the seeds of decline in this fight, but nobody anticipated what happened next. With Tyson's problems with Cayton settled by an uneasy compromise, King was in control as Tyson fought challenger James 'Buster' Douglas in Tokyo. If any betting existed, it was at odds which made Douglas a 42–1 shot. But Tyson was under-trained, listless and drugged for venereal disease and depression. Well outboxed, he eventually caught Douglas in the eighth round with an uppercut which floored Douglas who, because of a slow referee, was given a long count (about 12 seconds), enough to save him taking any further punishment before the bell rang. Douglas recovered fully in the interval, continued as before and knocked out Tyson in the tenth, with Tyson, knocked down for the first time in his career, groping about on the canvas for a lost gumshield while the count was completed. Because of the long count earlier afforded Douglas, Don King spent days, it seemed at first with the support of the WBC, to get the verdict reversed, but the boxing world laughed at him.

Shocked by this reverse, Tyson responded well, getting himself into better shape and beginning a comeback which saw him dispose of his amateur conqueror, Henry Tillman, and the dangerous Donovan 'Razor' Ruddock twice. A multi-million dollar title fight was arranged with Evander Holyfield, who had assumed the heavyweight crown from Buster Douglas. But circumstances forced this encounter to wait for five years. Once more Tyson's reckless private life intruded.

Three weeks after his second defeat of Ruddock, Tyson went on a binge to Indianapolis, where he took a suite in a hotel near to one where the Miss Black America contest was taking place. He was introduced to the contestants, and on 19 July 1991 took one of them, 18-year-old Desiree Washington, to his room. It was 2.00 am and she alleged he raped her. Tyson was charged, came to trial, and in March 1992 was sentenced to six years imprisonment and four years' parole. As one who had lived the life of a multi-millionaire, however foolishly and wastefully, he reacted badly at first, but gradually he knuckled down and devoted himself to keeping fit, and, he claimed, to reading. He acquired new heroes (the names of Mao Tse-Tung and champion black tennis player Arthur Ashe were tattooed on his arms). He said he had been converted to Islam. He earned the maximum remission for good conduct, and was released after three years in March 1995.

Tyson was, of course, the hottest property in boxing. Everybody wanted to see the monster. The MGM Grand Garden, Las Vegas, signed him up to a six-fight deal and there was a further deal with Showtime, the pay-TV channel, leading to estimates of his first contest being worth $22 million to him. This comeback fight, on 19 August 1995, was against a soft opponent, Peter McNeeley, whose father fought Floyd Patterson for the world title in 1961. McNeeley had won 36 of his 37 fights, but it was a carefully managed record. He bravely rushed across the ring to attack Tyson crudely at the bell and, although Tyson missed with some counters, he eventually landed one to put McNeeley down. When McNeeley went down again, and rose looking groggy, his trainer Vinny Vecchione leapt in the ring to rescue him, which caused his disqualification. The contest lasted 89 seconds, and the sellout crowd of 16,737, who had paid inflated prices to see the slaughter, yelled their disapproval at being cheated of blood.

Don King was still Tyson's promoter, and in all but name his manager. In December Tyson had a second run-out, against Buster Mathis Junior, another man whose father had fought for the title. The first Buster Mathis was beaten by Joe Frazier in 1968, and had died just before his son's meeting with Tyson. Mathis was a much more credible opponent than McNeeley. The fight was switched from Atlantic City, where King was not allowed to promote because of a fraud charge hanging over him, to the Corestates Spectrum, Philadelphia. Tyson won when a short right hook started a sequence that knocked out Mathis towards the end of the third round. But he was unimpressive, and to the experts clearly a long way short of the man he was at his peak.

Nevertheless the Tyson publicity machine was rolling and, with the warm-ups out of the way, it was time to start collecting the various heavyweight titles again. First up was the WBC title, held by Frank Bruno, Tyson's victim seven years before. The immensely popular Bruno was upbeat in the run-up to the fight at the MGM Grand Garden in March 1996, and attracted many British fans to cross the Atlantic and snap up the 6–1 odds locally available against him. Unfortunately for them, a frightened Bruno was completely overawed by the occasion, and a Tyson assault in the third round had him squatting on the bottom rope from where referee Mills Lane had to rescue him. Tyson was a world champion again and went on his knees in the ring to salute Allah. Tyson's mandatory challenger for the title was Lennox Lewis, but Lewis's camp agreed to step aside, for $6 million, so that Tyson could challenge for the WBA championship.

Bruce Seldon was the WBA champion, and was expected to put up about as much resistance as Bruno when the two met at the MGM Grand Garden. An ex-convict (four years for robbery) he had three defeats in 37 contests. The odds against him were 20–1. He was called the Atlantic City Express, and was certainly very quick to grab Tyson when the fight started. He looked as anxious as Bruno, was down twice in the first round, rising each time, but the second time he shook his head and referee Richard Steele called it off at 109 seconds. The fans again hooted their displeasure. Seldon earned his biggest purse, $5 million, while Tyson picked up around $35 million.

Tyson's WBC title had not been at stake in this fight, Tyson being committed to meet Lewis for it. But now Tyson had the WBA crown, he was at liberty to defend that against Evander Holyfield, a fight which would be much bigger at the US box office than Tyson–Lewis. So Tyson decided to ditch his WBC championship.

All was now set for the big fight which should have taken place in 1989: WBC and WBA champion Tyson versus former champion Evander Holyfield. Holyfield had been a great cruiser and heavyweight champion, but had impressed in only one of his previous seven fights, suffering his only three defeats in this sequence. Significantly, after losing his titles to Michael Moorer in 1994, he had retired from boxing because of a heart condition. A year before meeting Tyson he had faced Riddick Bowe during a comeback and been stopped in the eighth, dramatically running out of steam after flooring Bowe in the sixth. Few thought a seemingly worn-out Holyfield would have the stamina to stand up to Tyson, but he trained so hard for 15 weeks and appeared so confident that initial betting odds of 22–1 on Tyson had been cut to around 6–1 on the night. Of 48 reporters polled, however, only one favoured Holyfield.

Right from the start of the bout at the MGM Grand Garden Holyfield showed that he was not intimidated by Tyson. He even stood toe-to-toe with him in the first round. Deprived of his usual psychological dominance, and faced by a confident, fast, skilful foe, Tyson quickly ran out of ideas. The contest developed into a scrappy one, with lots of holding. Tyson was 30, Holyfield 34, and both began to look tired. In the sixth round Tyson walked into a left hook from Holyfield that sent him down and sliding backwards across the canvas. He recovered and fought on bravely, but took a battering in the tenth. The effects had not worn off before Tyson was in trouble on the ropes in the 11th, and he had ceased fighting back when referee Mitch Halpern saved him from further punishment. Tyson was bitterly disappointed. It was his second defeat, but he had excuses for the first. This time he was beaten by a better, and older, man.

There had to be a return fight, and it was one of the most eagerly awaited of all time. The date was 28 June 1997, the place again the MGM Grand in Las Vegas. Both men had now had 14 world title fights, and both had won 12. Each was guaranteed $30 million. The fight had been postponed from 3 May because of a training injury to Tyson's eye. This time, of 50 boxing writers polled, 29 favoured Holyfield and 21 Tyson. Nevertheless Tyson was a narrow betting favourite at around 6–4 on.

What happened shook the world of boxing. Holyfield won the first two rounds, in which there was plenty of rough stuff. In the second a clash of heads cut Tyson's eye, causing him to complain. In the third Tyson came out without his gumshield, and was sent back for it, but after two minutes of the round he took advantage of a clinch to bite a chunk out of Holyfield's ear, and spit it on the canvas. Holyfield leapt in pain and turned his back. Referee Mills Lane, who proved much too weak to handle the fight, called a halt, and deducted two points from Tyson, but after a four-minute delay allowed the round to continue. Tyson then bit Holyfield's other ear. Astonishingly the round was allowed to end, before, in the interval, Mills Lane belatedly disqualified Tyson. The Nevada State Athletic Commission fined Tyson the maximum according to their rules, a paltry tenth of his purse, i.e. $3 million, and banned him for a year, a ban which operated in all states, and which would not be reviewed until 5 July 1998.

Tyson was now publicly derided as low-life scum, a coward, etc. But, of course, he would still be the hottest property in boxing were his licence restored. He had already earned more from boxing than any previous boxer – an estimated $200 million. In 1998 he owned six houses, including one he hardly used in Connecticut which had 61 rooms, 38 baths, and a master bedroom with five television sets. Yet he was reported to be short of liquidity, and owing $7 million in tax. He publicly confronted Don King outside a Los Angeles hotel demanding money, and allegedly kicked the promoter in the face. Lawyers are claiming that King did not account to Tyson fully and took more money from the boxer than the law allows. Tyson ditched King as promoter, although King claims he has a valid contract with Tyson to promote four more fights. While Tyson is banned this aspect is academic, but in March 1998 Tyson was reported as ready to file a $45 million fraud suit against King.

Tyson's private life is as complex as ever. Since the break-up of his marriage to Robin Givens, he has acquired four children, and is reported to be a devoted, if usually absent father. He also has a new wife, a paediatrician, Dr Monica Turner, who says he's a good guy, that he is far more intelligent than the press make out, and that she loves him for himself. His behaviour is as wild as ever, and late in 1997 he crashed riding a motorcycle, apparently having fallen asleep, and was nearly hit by a truck. He suffered broken ribs and a partially collapsed lung. He was riding without a licence, although still on parole from his recent imprisonment. In March 1998 he earned himself $3 million as an 'enforcer' at a Wrestlemania meeting before 19,000 fans in Boston. At around 240lb, he was clearly not in top condition. Film of the event shows how, after an argument, he laid out a wrestler with a swift punch, but this was 'violence' which had no doubt been carefully rehearsed.

CAREER STATISTICS

Undisputed world heavyweight champion 1987-90
WBC heavyweight champion 1986-90, 1996
WBA heavyweight champion 1996
New York, born 30 June 1966

1985

Mar 6 Hector Mercedes w ko 1 Albany
Apr 10 Trevor Singleton w rsf 1 Albany
May 23 Don Halpin w ko 4 Albany
Jun 20 Rick Spain w ko 1 Atlantic City
Jul 11 John Anderson w rsf 2 Atlantic City
Jul 19 Larry Sims w ko 3 Poughkeepsie
Aug 15 Lorenzo Canady w ko 1 Atlantic City
Sep 5 Mike Jameson w ko 1 Atlantic City
Oct 9 Donnie Long w rsf 1 Atlantic City
Oct 25 Robert Colay w ko 1 Atlantic City
Nov 1 Sterling Benjamin w rsf 1 Latham
Nov 13 Eddie Richardson w ko 1 Houston
Nov 25 Conroy Nelson w rsf 2 Latham
Dec 6 Sammy Scaff w rsf 1 New York
Dec 27 Mark Young w ko 1 Latham

1986

Jan 30 David Jaco w rsf 1 Albany
Jan 24 Mike Jameson w rsf 5 Atlantic City
Feb 16 Jesse Ferguson w rsf 6 Troy
Mar 10 Steve Zouski w ko 3 New York
May 3 James Tillis w pts 10 Glen Falls
May 20 Mitchell Green w pts 10 New York
Jun 13 Reggie Gross w rsf 1 New York
Jun 28 William Hosea w ko 1 Troy
Jul 11 Lorenzo Boyd w ko 2 Shawn Lake, NY
Jul 26 Marvis Frazier w ko 1 Glen Falls
Aug 17 Jose Ribalta w rsf 10 Atlantic City
Sep 6 Alfonzo Ratliff w rsf 2 Las Vegas
Nov 22 Trevor Berbick w rsf 2 Las Vegas
(WBC heavyweight title)

1987

Mar 7 James Smith w pts 12 Las Vegas
(WBC & WBA heavyweight titles)
May 30 Pinklon Thomas w rsf 6 Las Vegas
(WBC & WBA heavyweight titles)
Aug 1 Tony Tucker w pts 12 Las Vegas
(World heavyweight title)
Oct 16 Tyrell Biggs w rsf 7 Atlantic City
(World heavyweight title)

1988

Jan 22 Larry Holmes w ko 4 Atlantic City
(World heavyweight title)
Mar 21 Tony Tubbs w ko 2 Tokyo
(World heavyweight title)
Jun 27 Michael Spinks w ko 1 Atlantic City
(World heavyweight title)

1989

Feb 25 Frank Bruno w rsf 5 Las Vegas
(World heavyweight title)
Jul 21 Carl Williams w rsf 1 Atlantic City
(World heavyweight title)

1990

Feb 10 James Douglas l ko 10 Tokyo
(World heavyweight title)
Jun 16 Henry Tillman w ko 1 Las Vegas
Dec 8 Alex Stewart w ko 1 Atlantic City

1991

Mar 18 Razor Ruddock w rsf 7 Las Vegas
Jun 28 Razor Ruddock w pts 12 Las Vegas

1992-94 inactive

1995

Aug 19 Peter McNeeley w dis 1 Las Vegas
Dec 16 Buster Mathis w ko 3 Philadelphia

1996

Mar 16 Frank Bruno w rsf 3 Las Vegas
(WBC heavyweight title)
Relinquished WBC title.
Sep 7 Bruce Seldon w rsf 1 Las Vegas
(WBA heavyweight title)
Nov 9 Evander Holyfield l rsf 11 Las Vegas
(WBA heavyweight title)

1997

Jun 28 Evander Holyfield l dis 3 Las Vegas
(WBA heavyweight title)

Fights 48 Won 45 Lost 3

EVANDER HOLYFIELD

THE REAL DEAL

It took the boxing world a few years to get used to Evander Holyfield and to appreciate how good he was. A boxer who puts his faith in God to the extent that Evander does is unusual. When it seemed that God was allowing him to do what some thought to be miracles, they began to take notice. Now, even the most sceptical boxing scribe has to acknowledge that Evander's spirituality represents a tremendous part of his success. His near-impossible achievements include building up his body from cruiser to heavyweight without any extra flab, recovering from a heart problem which doctors said had ended his career, and intimidating super-ogre Mike Tyson into defeat. It seemed that what Evander said was true: 'I can do all things through Christ who strengthens me'.

Evander Holyfield was born at Atmore, Alabama, on 19 October 1962. The marriage of his mother, Annie Laure, to Joseph Holyfield had ended some eight years earlier, in Atlanta, soon after which Annie Holyfield had taken the four youngest of her five children to Atmore so that she could look after her mother, Pearlie Beatrice Hatton, who had suffered a stroke. During the 13 years the family lived at Atmore, Annie met Ison Coley, a big, strong lumberjack, whom she meant to marry, but it didn't work out. Coley was the father of Evander, Annie's eighth and last child. The others were Joe Ann, Eloise, James, Priscilla and Annette, from the Atlanta days, and Willie and Bernard, who were also born in Atmore. Grandmother Hatton made a good enough recovery to be able to help look after the children while Annie went to work 12 hours a day as a cook in a restaurant to help support them all. Since Grandma was confined to a wheelchair, that the youngest would obey her says much for the family discipline. When Evander was five, the whole family, including grandmother, returned to Atlanta to live with Annie's oldest daughter, Joe Ann, who had stayed there to marry Joe McCoy, and who now had three children of her own. So there were now 14 in the house.

Despite the crowding, it was a very happy house, because the whole family was deeply religious, and there was none who didn't do his or her share towards its maintanance. When a worn-out Annie had to rest after a serious heart attack aged 39, even schoolboys Evander and Bernard would search for Coca-Cola bottles to collect the nickel deposits on them and contribute a little to the purse. The family was the first Team Holyfield.

When Evander was six, a classmate introduced him to the Warren Memorial Boys Club, where there were all sorts of sporting facilities. Evander showed a natural talent in all of them, especially American Football. Aged eight, he discovered the boxing compound, forbidden to those not on the team. This was an affront to Evander, a short, chubby boy, and he determined that he would convince the coach Carter Morgan that he was tough enough to be in the team. Gradually he did, and coach Morgan became something of a father-figure to Evander. Eventually, boxing replaced football as his first love, and instead of dreaming of playing for Atlanta Falcons, his dream changed to becoming a world boxing champion.

Soon Evander was boxing his way up the junior divisions based on age to the stage where weight determines who fights whom. He won most contests, lost occasionally and, for a deeply religious lad, disgraced himself once or twice. Interestingly, in view of what happened to him in a world title fight many years later, he spat out his gum shield and bit the shoulder of one opponent who was getting the better of him. Another time he was disqualified for picking up an opponent and throwing him across the ring, wrestling style.

Evander was devastated when coach Morgan died of emphysema, but struck up a new partnership with his son, Ted, who took over his father's coaching jobs. He also began his first job, servicing aeroplanes at Atlanta's Epps Airport, where they were so proud of him they gave him an overall with 'Champ' embroidered on it. But with the expenditure, like travelling to tournaments, that his boxing demanded, Evander also took a weekend job – lifeguard at the local pool. There he met his first love, Paulette Bowden, and they were soon inseparable and living together.

As he passed through his teens, a strange thing happened to Evander. Maybe it was his fanatical training, his pumping iron, or even his daily intake of a raw eggs, milk and honey concoction, but the 18-year-old welterweight gradually began growing into a man who at 22 was 170lb of muscle. The short schoolboy was eventually to reach 6ft 2in. He won his way into the 1984 US Olympic trials as a light-heavyweight, meeting and sparring with heavyweight Mike Tyson on the way.

Before the trials, however, Evander became a father when Paulette gave birth to Evander Holyfield Junior. Evander lost in the trials, to Ricky Womack, then ranked No. 1 in the world. He was given a second chance in the box-offs. It meant he had to beat Womack in a return, and if he did so there would be a third contest, the winner representing the US in the Games. Holyfield won both his contests and was in the team.

While in training camp for the Olympics, Evander, who liked putting words to music he listened to, sang about a 'real deal', then realised the near triple rhyme of 'Real Deal

Holyfield' sounded good and tried it on his teammates. From then on he was known as 'The Real Deal'. The actual Olympics, held in Los Angeles, were not happy for him. He fought through to the semi-final against a New Zealander, Kevin Barry, and was getting the best of it in the second round when the boxers clinched. Unfortunately for Evander he didn't hear the referee call 'break' and threw a punch which knocked out Barry. He was disqualified: but he was now known all over the boxing world, and offers poured in for him to turn professional.

Evander signed with Main Events Inc, the driving force of which was Lou Duva, a former welterweight boxer. Main Events was the promoting arm of the business, which son Dan Duva, a lawyer, and other members of the family helped to run. Evander signed for $250,000 down and the promise of $2 million within four years. With his initial payment, Evander took out two mortgages for an apartment for himself and a house for his mother. Otherwise Evander was very cautious with his money.

Evander had won 160 amateur bouts (75 inside the distance) and lost only 14. Most of the 14 losses and other not too impressive performances had come when he inexplicably ran out of steam during a contest. His big worry over turning professional was his endurance. It was discovered by the Duva camp that he hoarded junk food – something he began doing when he was trying to increase his weight. Now he was a pro other methods would ultimately be found to increase his weight, but more than once late in his career he suffered again from a sudden loss of energy during a fight.

Holyfield's pro debut came on 15 November 1984, at Madison Square Garden, New York. The evening was billed as 'A Night of Gold', because each fight, except Evander's and Virgil Hill's, marked the debut of an Olympic gold medallist: Mark Breland, Meldrick Taylor, Pernell Whitaker, Tyrell Biggs. Evander's opponent was 22-year-old Lionel Byarm, a big puncher. While all but one of the other Olympic winners won inside the distance, Evander had a real battle on his hands. It was easily the best contest of the evening, with both men giving and taking some heavy punches. It was close, but Evander took a unanimous six-round decision. He was just above the light-heavyweight limit.

Evander progressed impressively, with a fifth-round stoppage of Jeff Meachum in Atlantic City in October 1985 provoking talk of a challenge to Dwight Muhammad Qawi, former light-heavyweight champion and now WBA cruiserweight champ. Qawi had been known until 1982 as Dwight Braxton, but, like Muhammad Ali, had embraced Islam and changed his name. A ruthless stoppage of contender Anthony Davis confirmed Evander's status, and on 12 July 1986 the title challenge came about in Evander's home town of Atlanta. Evander had now married Paulette, who was pregnant with their second child Ashley. He also had business interests, including a large Buick dealership.

Qawi was a fierce competitor who had learned his boxing while serving a prison sentence. He stood only 5ft 7in, seven inches shorter than Holyfield, who weighed in at

188lb. Most critics thought the experienced Qawi would be too tough for Evander, who was himself apprehensive about his ability to last 15 rounds. This became a real concern after only four rounds when Evander sat exhausted on his stool. But then, as he relates it, he prayed to the Lord for strength, and felt God flooding his body with new energy. He surprised Qawi in the fifth by the power of his fight-back. It was not over yet though. Evander's back started hurting in the sixth, and Qawi seemed to get stronger from the tenth. Evander thought seriously of accepting defeat. Qawi staged a terrific last round, but was deducted a point for low blows. It was one of the best contests of the year, and Evander took a split decision: 147–138, 144–140 and 141–143. He was the first of the USA's outstanding 1984 Olympic team to become a world champion.

Evander was proud not only that he won the title but that he showed that a devout Christian could win. 'God's people are supposed to be number one,' he said. He also believes that boxing is 10 per cent physical and 90 per cent spiritual. In his biography, *Holyfield, the Humble Warrior*, his brother Bernard relates the story of an incident that happened in their childhood, when Evander was five years old. They awoke one night to find a strange man in their kitchen in Atmore, and he reappeared each night for a week, although nobody else in the house would believe their story. On his first visit he touched the tops of their heads with his hands. Eventually mother Annie went to the kitchen, saw the tall bald-headed man and screamed, whereupon he disappeared into thin air. Grandmother Hatton said the man was an Angel from God, who by touching the heads of the boys was blessing them with God's gifts.

Champion Holyfield, who lost 15lb during the Qawi fight, recovered from his exertions in hospital, and then began to enjoy his fame. His autograph was in much demand, and he would sign 'Holyfield, Phil 4:13', a bible reference to the verse in Philippians: 'I can do all things through Christ who strengthens me'.

Evander defended his title successfully against Mike Brothers in Paris and then against his Olympic colleague Henry Tillman, who had won the heavyweight gold medal, having beaten Mike Tyson in the trials. Tillman was well beaten in Reno, the contest going to Holyfield on the three-knockdown rule when Tillman was down for the third time in the seventh round.

Holyfield's next contest was against the IBF champion, Ricky Parkey. Parkey made the mistake of taking the fight to Holyfield and an exciting slugfest developed. But it couldn't last, and the referee stepped in to give the fight to Holyfield in the third, after Parkey had been down twice.

Holyfield's objective now was to unify the cruiserweight division by beating veteran WBC champion Carlos DeLeon, who was on his third spell as champion, having won the title originally in 1980. Before they could meet, Evander repelled the challenge of two other former champions in Ossie Ocasio, who was stopped in the 11th round of a hot and humid battle in Saint Tropez, France, and Dwight Muhammad Qawi again in Atlantic City, who this time put up much less resistance then before and was knocked out in the fourth.

Carlos DeLeon lasted through to the eighth round before referee Mills Lane decided he had taken enough punishment. Mike Tyson, who was at ringside with his new wife, Robin Givens, described Holyfield as 'impressive'.

It was inevitable that Holyfield, having unified the cruiserweight division, would relinquish his titles to campaign as a heavyweight. He remains the only undisputed cruiserweight champion since the WBA joined the WBC in recognising the division in 1982. To compete among the heavyweights required Holyfield, who was comfortable at 190 lb, to bulk himself up to a fit fighting weight of 200 lb or more – easy enough to put on the extra weight but not to do so while retaining his superbly fit body, with its 31-inch waist. The heavyweights, of course, would present Evander with the chance of making several million dollars per fight, far more than he could make ruling the cruisers.

The man who supervised Evander's bulk-building was a new member of the team, Tim Hallmark. He managed to get Holyfield's weight up to 202lb for his first heavyweight contest against James Tillis at Lake Tahoe in July 1988. Holyfield easily won five rounds whereupon the ringside doctor examined Tillis and advised him not to continue. Many were unconvinced by this victory over a 31-year-old. Michael Spinks, by controversially beating an ageing Larry Holmes, had been the only champion of a lower division to win a heavyweight title, and less than three weeks before Holyfield beat Tillis, Tyson had destroyed Spinks in 91 seconds. A Tyson-Holyfield fight was now the most attractive on the horizon.

After beating two former heavyweight champions in Pinklon Thomas and Michael Dokes, the unbeaten Holyfield became No. 1 contender for the unbeaten Tyson's title in the lists of both the WBA and the WBC. Despite the procrastination of Don King, Tyson's promoter, who wanted to milk as much money as possible from Tyson before taking any risks, the fight was tentatively fixed to take place in 1990. However disaster struck for Tyson, King and, to a lesser extent, for Holyfield when a lacklustre, strife-torn Tyson lost his title to Buster Douglas in February 1990. That left Holyfield the natural challenger to Douglas and, after a warm-up knockout of Seamus McDonagh, Holyfield took on Douglas for the WBC, WBA and IBF titles in October 1990. If one ignored the upstart WBO, who began heavyweight business in 1989 by ridiculously recognising Francesco Damiani as champion, the contest was for the undisputed championship.

Tim Hallmark, who had become a close friend of Holyfield, was now supervising two trainers, two bodybuilders and a ballet instructor in his efforts to make sure Evander was at his best. He also looked after the diet. Evander trained to exhaustion, then he and Hallmark would pray together. Evander entered the ring a superb 208lb of muscle. The 6ft 4in Douglas's training, on the other hand, was said to consist of sitting in a sauna ordering room-service pizza. He entered the ring a blubbery 246lb (he had been 231 for his victory over Tyson). Fans booed when his weight was announced at the weigh-in. Even so the boxing writers were almost unanimous in selecting Douglas to win. How could a pumped-up cruiser beat the convincing conqueror of Tyson?

Before the fight, billed 'The Moment of Truth', Evander received a couple of setbacks. He was served with divorce papers from Paulette, who could cope no more with his long absences for training and the attention he received from other women, and his Buick dealership, managed for him by previous owners, went into receivership.

Evander entered the ring at the Mirage Hotel, Las Vegas, to the music of rap artist M.C. Hammer and the words 'That's why we pray, that's why we pray ... just to make it to-day'. For two rounds the much quicker Evander jabbed and danced, while Douglas crowded him, landing an occasional hard shot. In the third, Evander dodged a right uppercut and connected with a right cross flush on Douglas's chin. He crashed down, and Mills Lane waved it over when his count reached eight. 'He sure wasn't going to get up', he said.

Almost as soon as the verdict was announced, Evander's first defence was being planned. The opponent was 42-year-old former champion George Foreman, having a successful comeback campaign. Evander's greatest fear was that George, a preacher, might have even more of the '90 per cent spiritual' than he had himself. In the event, at Atlantic City, Foreman hurt Evander more than once, but the more busy Evander took an easy decision by 116–109, 117–110 and 115–112.

Holyfield desperately wanted to fight Tyson, and was delighted when the contest was scheduled for 8 November 1991 at Caesars Palace. But on 18 October Tyson hurt his ribs and pulled out. Before the match could be rescheduled, Tyson was arrested on rape charges and his subsequent conviction meant that the contest would have to wait years if it ever was to happen. After a desperate search Bert Cooper was signed as a substitute, the fight to be at the Omni in Atlanta, where Evander had won the cruiserweight title over five years earlier.

Cooper was down in the first, but had Holyfield helplessly holding on to the ropes in the third, which referee Mills Lane ruled as a knockdown, the first of Holyfield's pro career. He recovered to stop Cooper in the seventh.

Tragedy then struck in Evander's private life. His brother Willie, whom he looked up to, was shot dead in the middle of the night by his fiancee's drunken brother, who came round to the house threatening to shoot a nephew he suspected of theft, and he shot Willie instead when Willie intervened.

Holyfield's career continued when he was contracted to meet the winner of Ray Mercer v Larry Holmes, and was surprised and disappointed to find the winner was Holmes. He outpointed the 42-year-old veteran, but received a cut on the eye in the sixth, and failed to dominate. The papers were critical. He had not yet beaten a genuine challenger and had not been over-impressive against men he should have beaten easily. The $17 million Holyfield received for his efforts was not real consolation. His divorce was by now finalised, and he was separated from his children.

His next contest was certainly a real one. Riddick Bowe was 25, and unbeaten in 31 fights. Moreover, he was a genuine heavyweight whose weight often soared towards

300lb. In the contest he weighed 235lb to Evander's 206lb. In a tremendous battle, at the Thomas and Mack Center, Las Vegas, Evander possibly made the mistake of trying to out-punch Bowe. He took a bad beating in the tenth, and lost a close, but unanimous decision.

His first professional defeat shattered the 30-year-old ex-champion. He decided to retire. But as over the months his physical wounds healed, he studied film of the fight and convinced himself he could beat Bowe in a rematch. He decided that God had not let him down, but that he had let God down. Evander decided to make a comeback. Bowe was trained by Eddie Futch and managed by Rock Newaman and Evander engaged Emanuel Steward to train him.

After a disappointing and unimaginative points victory over Alex Stewart as a warm-up, Holyfield once more took the ring against Riddick Bowe. This time he was a 5–1 underdog and most critics thought there was no way he could improve enough to win. It proved to be another tremendous fight. Realising he had been out-hustled in their first meeting, Evander this time used his speed and skill in a disciplined performance. He was clearly ahead after six rounds and had cut a demoralised Bowe between his eye and nose. In the seventh there was an astonishing incident when a parasailer glided down from the ceiling and became entangled in the lights above Bowe's corner. He was immediately set upon by Bowe's handlers and clubbed with mobile phones. To cut him free, take him to hospital and get the contest restarted took 22 minutes, time for Bowe to recover much of his poise. But on the resumption Holyfield boxed as well as before and won a memorable victory, though it was only by a majority verdict. Holyfield had regained the WBA and IBF titles (by now Lennox Lewis was WBC champion). Evander was only the third (after Patterson and Ali) to win back a heavyweight title from the man who'd taken it from him.

This performance alone, against a naturally much bigger man, which had come about only because Evander changed his mind about retiring, was enough to make him one of the greatest of modern warriors. But as a heavyweight champion he was still seen as suspect, and sure enough he lost the regained titles in his first defence. Holyfield injured his arm in training but took on Michael Moorer, an ex-WBO light-heavy and heavyweight champion. After Holyfield dropped Moorer in the second round, his arm began to hurt, and he lost a majority decision.

Evander went to hospital because of dehydration, and the doctors discovered a heart problem. They told him his career was over. Evander, who wouldn't have been given medical clearance to fight anyway, retired again. But he was sure he could beat Moorer. He went to an evangelist with a reputation for divine healings, who told him he was cured. After that Evander sought conventional advice and was told his condition was improving. Eventually he had rigorous tests at the Mayo Clinic, where he was told his heart was superb. It was, to Evander, just another example of the power of God.

Holyfield's return contest was against tough Ray Mercer. Cut in the eighth, Holyfield became the first man to floor Mercer, and he won a unanimous decision. It was a tough fight, and Evander's next would test even more his new fitness as his opponent was Riddick Bowe. There was no title at stake, but this was still a big fight. At Caesars Palace, Bowe looked the more dangerous until the sixth, when a terrific left hook from Evander put Bowe down for the first time in his career. A groggy Bowe, rising at seven, looked to be ready for the knockout, but Evander then dramatically ran out of steam. He later claimed pre-fight flu as the cause, but with his man at his mercy Holyfield had no energy left. Bowe took control and floored Holyfield in the eighth, after which the referee stopped it in his favour.

Everybody assumed that Evander, aged 33, having lost three fights in his last six, and having had to overcome serious heart problems, would retire, especially when his mother died after being badly injured in a car crash in which she was the passenger, with Evander's sister Eloise driving. But, with a new trainer, Don Turner, he was already contracted to fight Bobby Czyz, a veteran who had been light-heavyweight champion nearly ten years earlier, and subsequently cruiserweight champion. For once, Evander had all the physical advantages, and won after Czyz was unable to come out for the sixth round.

By now Mike Tyson had served three years in prison, and made a ring comeback which saw him win the WBC and WBA titles in easy wins over Frank Bruno and Bruce Seldon, who offered no resistance. Tyson relinquished the WBC title rather than fight Lennox Lewis, so that Don King could accept a challenge from Evander Holyfield for the WBA title. It was the biggest fight for years, the one everybody had wanted in 1990 and 1991. Few thought Holyfield could win – a pre-fight poll of 48 reporters found 47 saying Tyson would win within seven rounds. Cablevision had to offer a special deal to viewers, who feared the fight would not last three rounds.

Tyson earned $30 million for the battle at the MGM-Grand Garden Arena in November 1996, Holyfield $11 million. Tyson weighed 222lb, Holyfield 215lb. The odds against Holyfield were at one time 22–1, but slipped to as low as 6–1 by fight time, when fans saw how confident he was, and that he would be the first Tyson opponent for many years not to be overwhelmed by his opponent's reputation. The fight was scrappy until the sixth, when cries of 'Holyfield, Holyfield' suddenly echoed round the arena. As if it were he who was suddenly intimidated, Tyson walked on to a left hook from Holyfield which knocked him backwards onto the seat of his trunks and across the ring. Tyson survived the round, but Holyfield was in control and battered Tyson in the tenth. Referee Mitch Halpern was forced to stop it in Holyfield's favour after 37 seconds of the 11th, with Tyson, not fully recovered from the tenth, taking punishment again.

Holyfield had remarried before the contest and he dropped to his knees in prayer afterwards in company with his wife, Dr Janice Itson, a specialist in pain management.

There had to be a return fight, and when it was arranged for the same venue seats were immediately snapped up for between $200 and $1,500 each. This time the pundits were more evenly divided, but the betting odds were still slightly on Tyson. Ringsiders saw a sensational event for their money, but not much of a title fight. Tyson suffered a nasty gash over his eye in the second round, and lost his self-control. In the third he bit off about half-an-inch of Holyfield's ear, spitting it onto the floor of the ring. For some reason referee Mills Lane allowed the bout to continue, deducting two points from Tyson, one each for the bite and for pushing Holyfield in the back when he turned away in pain. Tyson promptly bit Holyfield's other ear. Even then the fight was allowed to continue to the end of the round before Tyson was disqualified. 'I was beating him anyway,' said Holyfield. 'It was an easy way for him to get out of the fight.' Tyson was banned for a year. Holyfield accepted the foul gracefully (perhaps he recalled his own biting at the start of his career). The chunk of ear was rescued but could not be replaced. Evander had plastic surgery.

Evander's next contest, in the Thomas and Mack Center, Las Vegas, was in November 1997 against IBF champion Michael Moorer, the southpaw who had beaten him two years earlier. This time Moorer, a 5–2 underdog, began well and staggered Holyfield in the first round. A clash of heads cut Holyfield's eye in the second. But from then on Holyfield took control. A brave Moorer was down in the fifth, and twice in the seventh and eighth, at the end of which the ring doctor advised that the fight should be stopped. Evander earned another $20 million and was now WBA and IBF champion. 'I have two belts', he said. 'One is for the Heavenly Father, one is for Jesus, and now I need one for the Holy Spirit.' Lennox Lewis held the WBC belt, and everybody wanted to see a meeting between them. But whether Don King, who promoted the contest and had Evander under contract for another defence, would take the risk was another matter. The 35-year-old 'Humble Warrior' with his influential backers was not finished yet though. His autobiography gives 'heartfelt thanks' in the acknowledgements to 17 reverends for their prayers and encouragement.

CAREER STATISTICS

World heavyweight champion 1990-92
WBA & IBF heavyweight champion 1993-94
WBA heavyweight champion 1996-
IBF heavyweight champion 1997-
World cruiserweight champion 1988
WBA cruiserweight champion 1986-88
IBF cruiserweight champion 1987-88
Atlanta, Georgia, born Atmore, Alabama,
19 October 1962
1984 Olympic light-heavyweight bronze medal

1984
Nov 15 Lionel Byarm w pts 6 New York
1985
Jan 20 Eric Winbush w pts 6 Atlantic City
Mar 13 Fred Brown w ko 1 Norfolk
Apr 20 Mark Rivera w rsf 2 Corpus Christi
Jul 20 Tyrone Booze w pts 8 Norfolk
Aug 29 Rick Myers w rsf 1 Atlanta
Oct 30 Jeff Meachum w rsf 5 Atlantic City
Dec 21 Anthony Davis w rsf 4 Virginia City
1986
Mar 1 Chisanda Mutti w rsf 3 Lancaster, Pa.
Apr 6 Jesse Shelby w ko 3 Corpus Christi
May 28 Terry Mims w ko 5 Metairie, La.
Jul 12 Dwight Muhammad Qawi w pts 15 Atlanta
(WBA cruiserweight title)
Dec 8 Mike Brothers w rsf 3 Paris
1987
Feb 14 Henry Tillman w rsf 7 Reno
(WBA cruiserweight title)
May 15 Ricky Parkey w rsf 3 Las Vegas
(WBA & IBF cruiserweight titles)
Aug 15 Osvaldo Ocasio w rsf 11 St Tropez
(WBA & IBF cruiserweight titles)
Dec 5 Dwight Muhammad Qawi w rsf 4 Atlantic City
(WBA & IBF cruiserweight titles)
1988
Apr 9 Carlos De Leon w rsf 8 Las Vegas
(World cruiserweight title)
Jul 16 James Tillis w rsf 5 Stateline
Dec 9 Pinklon Thomas w rsf 8 Atlantic City
1989
Mar 11 Michael Dokes w rsf 10 Las Vegas
Jul 15 Adilson Rodrigues w rsf 2 Lake Tahoe
Nov 4 Alex Stewart w rsf 8 Atlantic City
1990
Jun 1 Seamus McDonagh w rsf 4 Atlantic City
Oct 25 James Douglas w ko 3 Las Vegas
(World heavyweight title)
1991
Apr 19 George Foreman w pts 12 Atlantic City
(World heavyweight title)
Nov 23 Bert Cooper w rsf 7 Atlanta
(World heavyweight title)
1992
Jun 19 Larry Holmes w pts 12 Las Vegas
(World heavyweight title)
Nov 13 Riddick Bowe l pts 12 Las Vegas
(World heavyweight title)
1993
Jun 26 Alex Stewart w pts 12 Atlantic City
Nov 6 Riddick Bowe w pts 12 Las Vegas
(WBA & IBF heavyweight titles)
1994
Apr 22 Michael Moorer l pts 12 Las Vegas
(WBA & IBF heavyweight titles)
1995
May 20 Ray Mercer w pts 10 Atlantic City
Nov 4 Riddick Bowe l rsf 8 Las Vegas
1996
May 10 Bobby Czyz w rtd 5 New York
Nov 9 Mike Tyson w rsf 11 Las Vegas
(WBA heavyweight title)
1997
Jun 28 Mike Tyson w dis 3 Las Vegas
(WBA heavyweight title)
Nov 8 Michael Moorer w rsf 8 Las Vegas
(WBA & IBF heavyweight titles)

Fights 38 Won 35 Lost 3

LENNOX LEWIS

LENNOX

An Olympic competitor at 18, and gold medalist at 22, Lennox Lewis turned professional and advanced into his 30s with only one defeat, subsequently avenged, marring his record. Yet although he held the WBC title and looked the best heavyweight in the world, boxing politics have frustrated his desire to unify the division and prove his status. The US press and fans have seemed wilfully to underrate him as various champions over the years – Bowe, Holyfield, Tyson, Moorer – have managed to avoid him while fighting each other and in between times defending their versions of titles against no-hopers in lucrative battles. Time is running out for the quiet, amiable Lewis.

Lennox Lewis's mother, Violet, was born in Port Antonio, Jamaica. Her Aunt Gee emigrated to England and in 1956 sent a one-way air ticket for Violet to join her – which she did. After working in London for some years Violet gave birth to a son, Dennis Stephen on 27 April 1962. On 2 September 1965 her second son, Lennox Claudius, was born at Queen Mary's hospital, Stratford, London. He weighed 10lb 10oz. The doctor chose the name Lennox.

Lennox was big and strong from birth, but of course Violet had to work extremely hard to bring up two boys alone, although Aunt Gee and the fathers helped. When Dennis was seven and Lennox four, Violet decided to change her life radically. She allowed Dennis to be brought up by his father, who had married, and flew to friends in Chicago where she hoped to find work. The intention was to send for Lennox, who was with Aunt Gee, when she was successful. But she had no visa to work and after a little more than a year was forced to return. Lennox had been expelled from school for punching a boy and a window. The optimistic Violet then took her son to Ontario, Canada. But Violet found it hard to keep them both and, after six months, Lewis had to return to Aunt Gee in London. He grew big (size 9 shoes at 10 years old) and boisterous, good at sports and unruly.

After five years of working and saving, Violet was at last able to send for Lennox, a thumping great 12-year-old six-footer. It was well he was strong because he took a lot of teasing at school in Kitchener, Ontario, and was always in fights. Eventually he and a pal decided to see what the local police gym was like, and Lennox was soon being taught to box. His coach was Arnie Boehm, who had been a moderate amateur boxer, and who for ten years became a father-figure to him. At first Lennox was not a muscular boy, and he was introverted. Arnie brought him out of himself, and Lennox was eager to learn.

Lennox began an amateur career and in no time was Ontario Golden Gloves champion. He had to fight older boys to get serious competition, and his first defeat, a narrow one, came at the hands of Donovan Ruddock, who also became a leading professional boxer. But Lewis was 15 and Ruddock 18.

Lennox got into the 1984 Canadian Olympic team. He was only 18, and lost in his second round bout to eventual winner Tyrell Biggs. But during his preparation he and Arnie spent eight days staying with Cus D'Amato and working out with Mike Tyson, who is nine months younger than Lennox. The two got on well and had some serious scrapping. Tyson, who didn't make the Olympic team, turned pro in 1985 and was world champion in 1986 (beating Biggs in 1987). Lewis himself received a $500,000 offer to turn pro after the Olympics, but decided to wait and have a shot at the Olympic title in 1988. Between times his performances were erratic. By the time the Olympics came round again, he had lost nine amateur bouts in around 105 contests. But in the Olympic super-heavyweight category, none of his matches reached the third round, and he won the gold medal with a second-round stoppage of Riddick Bowe, later to be world heavyweight champion.

Everybody wanted to sign Lennox to a professional contract. But Lennox was particular and was well advised by a young lawyer, John Hornewer. So many offers seemed to have drawbacks. Finally, he was persuaded (his brother Dennis first suggested it) that turning pro in England, where only Frank Bruno was a serious competitor for heavyweight attention, was a good idea. He was put in touch with the Levitt Group, and signed a five-year deal which gave him a signing-on fee of around £150,000, use of a house for him and his mother, a Mercedes, £500 a week expenses, a retainer for Hornewer and other perks, including a job in the set-up for his mother. Revenue would be split 70-30 in his favour. He would also retain a say in making career decisions. It was a fabulous deal, which also gave him Levitt employee Frank Maloney as his manager.

Maloney was a small man – 5ft 3½in, he had boxed as an amateur flyweight – and had a correspondingly small stature in boxing circles. Then a 40-year-old from the Elephant and Castle, South London, he had trained boxers with Frank Warren, been a matchmaker with Mickey Duff, and promoted small-time with Terry Marsh. He got on well immediately with Lewis, but not with the American trainer, John Davenport, who was brought in because Lennox's mother and Hornewer thought American trainers were best. Davenport kept his job for 19 contests.

Frank Maloney believed that Lewis was already good enough to fight Bruno for his first pro contest. But the real job was to find opponents from whom he could learn things, so that he could progress gradually and not scare off opposition straightaway. Al Malcolm, Midland area champion, was Lewis's first opponent, and he was knocked out in the second round in June 1989 at the Albert Hall, London. Lewis weighed 231lb. Little more than three weeks later he was in Atlantic City to stop Bruce Johnson, also in the second round.

Exactly a year after his first fight, Lewis had his 12th, and was taken the distance for the first time, by cagey veteran Ossie Ocasio, the former world cruiserweight champion.

In his 14th contest in 1990 Lewis easily stopped a courageous but outclassed Frenchman, Jean-Maurice Chanet, to take the European heavyweight title. Then, on 7 December 1990 the Levitt Group, thought to be worth £150 million, crashed. Lewis was a saleable asset, and his contract was bought by Panos Eliades, an accountant who specialises in liquidations. His company PANIX co-promotes Lewis's fights. Eliades had met Lewis and seen him box, and he kept Maloney on as manager. Lennox's brother Dennis became his personal manager.

At the time of the Levitt Group collapse, Lennox, the European champion, was contracted to meet Gary Mason, the unbeaten British champion with 33 knockouts in 35 contests. Mason had complained that he never received the same recognition that Frank Bruno, never British champion but already twice a world challenger, enjoyed. Mason had undergone surgery for a detached retina in his right eye, and had been engaged as a pundit by Sky TV. He made no secret of the fact that he thought he could beat the novice Lewis. But in reality he had little chance, especially after Lewis had trained with sparring partners wearing white crosses taped over their right eyes. In the ensuing fight Lewis concentrated on the eye and Mason was stopped in the seventh and announced his retirement.

Lewis, keeping a reasonably busy schedule, easily knocked out former world cruiserweight champion Glenn McCrory, another Sky pundit, stopped Tyrell Biggs, his 1984 Olympic conqueror, and then was taken the distance for the second time in his career by Californian Levi Billups, at Caesars Palace, Las Vegas. It was disappointing, though Lewis won by a mile. Trainer Davenport was sacked after this. Lewis thought Davenport was making him too robotic, while Maloney thought Davenport was moaning too freely about the time he had to spend away from America. A Puerto Rican, Pepe Correa, was brought in to take Davenport's place. His main claim to fame was that he had trained Sugar Ray Leonard as an amateur.

In his next contest, Lewis stopped Commonwealth champion Derek Williams in the third round to add a third title to his British and European titles. By now Lewis was being spoken of as one of the best heavyweights in the world, although Americans were reluctant to admit it. With Tyson sidelined because of his conviction for rape, it seemed Lewis might have a chance of the world title when 'semi-final' contests were fixed between champion Evander Holyfield and Riddick Bowe and between Lennox Lewis and Donovan 'Razor' Ruddock. There was a letter of intent signed by all parties that the two winners would meet for the title.

With this spur, Lewis achieved his most convincing performance to date by flooring Ruddock in the first round and twice more in the second, with Ruddock finally being unable to beat the count. Alas for Lennox, 13 days later Bowe took Holyfield's title in the other contest, and was in no way inclined to risk the championship against the man who'd beaten him in the Olympics. The agreement that the management of the four boxers had come to beforehand was not a binding contract.

So Bowe fought instead Mike Dokes, the WBA champ of 10 years before who was fighting a cocaine addiction, and the WBC decided because he would not meet a genuine contender it could not recognise Bowe. Bowe and his manager were then photographed dumping the WBC belt in a rubbish bin (it was a replica belt, which they retrieved after the photograph was taken). The WBC proclaimed Lewis champion on the strength of his victory over Ruddock. But Bowe's refusal to meet Lewis was to become a theme in Lewis's career – he found it hard to prove he was the best heavyweight around while others with championship belts were unwilling to fight him.

At least Lewis showed he was prepared to defend against genuine challengers, and the first defence of his title was against Tony Tucker, former IBF champion whose only loss in 48 contests was to Mike Tyson. Lewis won on points. He then stopped Frank Bruno in Cardiff and Phil Jackson in Atlantic City before a sensational loss to Oliver McCall. At Wembley Arena the lightly regarded McCall caught Lewis, who was usually a slow starter, with a devastating right at the start of the second round which knocked Lennox to the canvas, and although he rose groggily at six the referee, Lupe Garcia, decided he was unfit to continue.

There had been lots of unhappiness in his camp before the fight over the methods of trainer Pepe Correa, and it was decided to dispense with his services for the comeback trail. Emanuel Steward was chosen as Correa's successor. Ironically, Steward had trained McCall.

Steward saw Lennox as a perfect specimen for a heavyweight. He was 6ft 5in, and 240lb of muscle. He was well proportioned, agile, and carried a knockout punch, especially with his right. He still looked a little untutored at times, and over-anxious to land his big right, but Steward was just the man to correct this.

Meanwhile Lewis's connections had gone to court over Lewis's right to challenge the new WBC champion, Frank Bruno, who had won the title from McCall. But Mike Tyson was now out of jail and Bruno fought and lost the title to Tyson. Don King was unwilling to risk his golden nest-egg by allowing Tyson to meet the mandatory contender Lewis, but the American court decided that this must happen. Astonishingly, having won the case, Lewis then accepted $6 million from Tyson's camp to step aside, allowing Tyson to add the WBA belt to his collection by beating Bruce Seldon. The deal was that Tyson, having won, would then fight Lewis for the WBC title. But Lewis was to be foiled again. Having won the WBA belt, Tyson decided to defend that in a multi-million dollar fight with Evander Holyfield and to give up the WBC crown.

That left leading contenders Lewis and old conqueror McCall to meet for the vacant WBC title. Don King won the right to promote the fight with the highest purse bid, $9 million, but then procrastinated, Lewis picking up a forfeit of another $300,000 from King when the date passed. The right to promote then passed to Lewis's own team, who were second highest bidders at $6 million. The fight took place at the Hilton Hotel, Las Vegas, and was sensational. Lewis was well on top when, near the end of the third round, McCall burst into tears and went for a walkabout round the ring. Persuaded to come out for the fourth, he walked about in a trance, refusing to fight with tears streaming down his face. Lewis stood off. Insisting on coming out for the fifth, McCall took a few punches and then turned his back and was disqualified. McCall, who had been on drugs, had clearly been mentally unfit to fight, but so far as Lewis was concerned, he was now WBC world champion again.

While his court battles had been going on, Lennox and Panos Eliades had launched the Lennox Lewis College, in Hackney, London, initially by putting up £1 million each to get it started. It was a unique conception, its aim being to give youngsters with difficult childhoods a chance for a fresh start. Sixty pupils per year were taken on to learn trades. Lennox also sponsored Britain's first black professional golfer, golf being a game be began to enjoy himself. He also bought a racehorse, named Lennox Lewis, which like him proved to be a winner, and sponsored the Lennox Lewis Motor Racing Team.

Lennox's first defence of his regained title was against fellow-Londoner Henry Akinwande, whose boyhood was spent in Nigeria. Akinwande gave up the little-regarded WBO title to challenge Lewis. Again the fight, at Lake Tahoe, was a disaster. Akinwande, 6ft 7 in and only 4 lb lighter than Lewis, refused to make a fight of it, grabbing at every opportunity. After several exhortations to fight from referee Mills Lane and his own corner, Akinwande was disqualified in the fifth round.

Lewis, who was struggling to get the recognition he deserved in the United States, couldn't afford a third farcical fight and his next challenger, Andrew Golota, was guaranteed to be no pushover. In fact, he was a dangerous opponent, having ended Riddick Bowe's career – twice Golota had the better of the former champion only to be disqualified for blatant persistent low blows. They were the only two losses on his 30-fight record. Golota, against Lewis in Atlantic City, had no chance to do anything. Lewis nailed him with punches right from the bell, and Golota crashed down for a count of eight. He was still groggy when the fight resumed and, after another barrage of 10 or so unanswered measured blows, Golota slumped down in his corner. The referee stopped it. It was the seventh quickest win in world heavyweight title bouts. In March 1998 he defended again, winning a thriller with Shannon Briggs in five rounds in Atlantic City.

Lewis, who spends his time in Hertfordshire, Canada and Jamaica, and continues to support his college, is still desperate to unify the heavyweight division. It is scandalous the way he has been dodged by successive WBA and IBF champions. He and his management team represent what is best in boxing, and given the chance he might be able to prove he is the best in every respect.

CAREER STATISTICS

WBC heavyweight champion 1992-94, 1997-
London, born 2 September 1965
1988 Olympic super-heavyweight gold medal

1989

Jun 27 Al Malcolm w ko 2 London
Jul 21 Bruce Johnson w rsf 2 Atlantic City
Sep 25 Andy Gerrard w rsf 4 London
Oct 10 Steve Garber w ko 1 Hull
Nov 5 Melvin Epps w dis 2 London
Dec 18 Greg Gorrell w rsf 5 Kitchener, Ontario

1990

Jan 31 Noel Quarless w rsf 2 London
Mar 22 Calvin Jones w ko 1 Gateshead
Apr 14 Mike Simuwelu w ko 1 London
May 9 Jorge Dascola w ko 1 London
May 20 Dan Murphy w rsf 6 Sheffield
Jun 27 Ossie Ocasio w pts 8 London
Jul 11 Mike Acey w rsf 2 Missisauga
Oct 31 Jean-Maurice Chanet w rsf 6 London
(European heavyweight title)

1991

Mar 6 Gary Mason w rsf 7 London
(British & European heavyweight titles)
Jul 12 Mike Weaver w ko 6 Lake Tahoe
Sep 30 Glenn McCrory w ko 2 London
(British & European heavyweight titles)
Nov 21 Tyrell Biggs w rsf 3 Atlanta

1992

Feb 1 Levi Billups w pts 10 Las Vegas
Apr 30 Derek Williams w rsf 3 London
(British, Commonwealth & European heavyweight titles)
Aug 11 Mike Dixon w rsf 4 Atlantic City
Oct 31 Razor Ruddock w ko 2 London
(Commonwealth heavyweight title)
Dec: Awarded WBC heavyweight title

1993

May 8 Tony Tucker w pts 12 Las Vegas
(WBC heavyweight title)
Oct 1 Frank Bruno w rsf 7 Cardiff
(WBC heavyweight title)

1994

May 6 Phil Jackson w rsf 8 Atlantic City
(WBC heavyweight title)
Sep 24 Oliver McCall l rsf 2 London
(WBC heavyweight title)

1995

May 13 Lionel Butler w rsf 5 Sacramento
Jul 2 Justin Fortune w rsf 4 Dublin
Oct 7 Tommy Morrison w rsf 6 Atlantic City

1996

May 10 Ray Mercer w pts 10 New York

1997

Feb 7 Oliver McCall w rsf 5 Las Vegas
(vacant WBC heavyweight title)
Jul 12 Henry Akinwande w dis 5 Lake Tahoe
(WBC heavyweight title)
Oct 4 Andrew Golota w ko 1 Atlantic City
(WBC heavyweight title)

1998

Mar 28 Shannon Briggs w rsf 5 Atlantic City
(WBC heavyweight title)

Fights 34 Won 33 Lost 1

ROY JONES

PENSACOLA JONES

From the moment he was robbed in the 1988 Olympic finals, Roy Jones has spent his career fighting the system. Jones is wonderfully skilled. His talents should have given him the light-middleweight gold in Seoul, but an outrageous political decision gave the verdict instead to his embarrassed opponent, South Korean Si-hoon Park. The three judges who voted for Park – Alberto Dunn of Uruguay, Hiouad Larbi from Morocco and Robert Kasule of Uganda – were banned, but the verdict stood. Jones was given the Val Barker Trophy for the best boxer of the Games as a consolation prize, and accepted his silver medal with grace and dignity when there were those who wanted him to refuse it as a protest. He did, however, briefly contemplate retirement. 'I think that's the end of the line,' he told a TV interviewer. 'I don't want any more boxing.'

Born in Pensacola, Florida, on 16 January 1969, Jones was taught by his father, Roy Snr, from the age of six. 'You're destined to be great,' was the message he heard, as his skills developed. He won two National Golden Gloves titles, beat Frankie Liles in the Olympic trials then was robbed in the Olympic final. In the semi-finals he had out-pointed Britain's Richie Woodhall, who went on to become WBC super-middleweight champion. He earned $50,000 for his professional debut when, managed by his father, he stopped Ricky Randall in two rounds.

In his third pro fight he beat a tough contender, Ron Amundsen, in seven rounds, but his father was criticised for allegedly holding him back. In fact, he did a good job of keeping the major promoters at bay, leaving Roy to mature at his own rate. 'I wasn't going to sell him out,' said the one-time club-fighter who once fought Marvin Hagler. Roy snr. knew the pitfalls of believing one person too many in boxing. They hired a Pensacola lawyer, Stanley Levin, to help them.

It was 1992 before Roy fought in New York, and that was a brief, one-round knock-out of former WBC welterweight champion Jorge Vaca of Mexico. It brought him $75,000 and his 16th professional victory. A points win over rugged Argentine Jorge 'Locomatoro' Castro saw him go 10 rounds for the first time, and in May 1993 he was paired with Bernard 'The Executioner' Hopkins for the IBF middleweight title, which had been vacated by the weight-troubled James Toney. The fight was in Washington DC on the same bill as the heavyweight championship between Riddick Bowe and Jesse Ferguson.

Hopkins was a dangerous fighter who could punch and take one. Jones was bright enough to avoid taking him on toe to toe, and instead used plenty of movement and point-stealing jabs to make sure he won on points. He was criticised, but the tactics were perfectly suited to the occasion.

He made one defence, an unexpectedly easy two-round win over capable Thomas Tate, and then moved up to fight Toney at 168lb. By now Toney was struggling in this weight division as well, but there were those who thought he would be too strong for Jones. In fact, it was Toney who was put down in round three, outboxed and in the end outpunched in a masterclass of boxing skills. The judges' scores said it all: 119–108, 118–109, 117–111. Jones won on points to become a two-weight world champ, and acknowledged as one of the finest boxers in the world, pound for pound.

Although he courted few friends, he signed a deal with American cable TV giant Home Box Office and settled down to turn back every challenger he was given. He outclassed Antoine Byrd in one, outpunched Vinny Pazienza in six and stopped the normally durable Tony Thornton in three.

By the end of 1995 he was demanding a unification fight of some kind. He said he wanted to box Irishman Steve Collins, but nothing came of it. Collins even rang him at home, trying to make the match, but it didn't happen. Jones might have fought WBA champ Frankie Liles, who beat him as an amateur, but did not. He had periods of boredom, when he fell out of love with the game.

He was always a thoughtful man, and understood the potential horrors of the business he chose for his own. He once revealed to *USA Today* that he had often considered quitting. 'I don't want to end up punch-drunk or broke. It's scary,' he said.

He began to look towards the light-heavyweight division, stopping a protesting Merqui Sosa in two rounds in January 1996. His behaviour reached a cavalier peak five months later on the day he fought Canadian outsider Eric Lucas in a defence of the IBF super-middleweight title, when he showed such little regard for the threat posed by his opponent that he took part in a competitive basketball match. Boxing traditionalists were outraged. He stopped Lucas in the 12th round.

His last defence at 168lb was an easy second-round knockout of Bryant Brannon in New York in October 1996, and then he moved up to fight Jamaican veteran Mike McCallum for the WBC light-heavyweight belt. He won a wide decision, after which McCallum, who had fought them all, raved about Jones's ability.

'He would have beaten them all,' said the famed 'Body Snatcher', who was a couple of weeks short of his 40th birthday. Jones said he was relatively cautious because he had damaged a hand during the preparations and respected the elderly athlete before him.

'Why should I take a chance? I could have hit him a lot more, but he was The Man. Now I'm The Man ...'

After 34 straight wins, and three world titles, he had given up trying to please people for the sake of it. The politics behind the bout was confusing: it was billed for the WBC title, even though Frenchman Fabrice Tiozzo had not at that point relinquished it. Some, including HBO who covered the fight, said it was merely an interim championship. Fortunately, the position was resolved when Tiozzo moved out of the division to campaign as a cruiserweight.

In Atlantic City in March 1997, Jones's critics and detractors at last had something to celebrate: he lost the WBC light-heavyweight title on a ninth-round foul to 1992 Olympian Montell Griffin of Chicago. Jones seemed casual and out of sorts, and Griffin gave him a good test, boxing beautifully and raising a swelling on Roy's eye. After eight rounds it was close. Then suddenly Jones exploded in round nine and Griffin's legs went. He reeled across the ring and down, and then when he dropped down in a follow-up assault to clear his head, Griffin was hit twice while he was down. Jones was disqualified by veteran referee Tony Perez, a decision that was eminently fair, in spite of the criticism levelled at the official by Roy himself.

'I'm still the best,' he said. 'I'm still the best pound-for-pound fighter in the world. I'm still unbeaten. Who beat me? They gave Griffin a win when he was down crying for mercy ... I rose to the top in the Olympics and got shafted. And I rose to the top as a professional and got shafted.'

Inevitably, a rematch was made, and in August 1997 Jones took out his frustrations on an unfortunate Griffin in explosive fashion. It was all over in two minutes 31 seconds of round one.

Jones felt by now that nothing would change the way he was perceived by fight people, or the media.

'I will never get the respect I deserve from the fight public,' he said to British trade paper *Boxing News* in 1997. 'Because I don't do boxing the way they think I should do boxing ... I don't need boxing. If they want to play games, they can. I'm not a guy thirsting for attention, thirsting for money, thirsting for anything. I fight because I like to fight, but I can give it up.'

His next move was as outrageous as anything that had gone before. He said he would fight as a heavyweight. The project went so far that the 6ft 4in, 240lb Buster Douglas was mentioned as a first opponent, but his father, who had taken a back seat for some time, was said to have talked Roy around. He took a U-turn.

It was clear that he was coming to the end of the road at 29.

'There's really nothing else for me to achieve,' he said. 'Boxing's not really something I would want to stay in. It's too corrupt.'

CAREER STATISTICS

IBF middleweight champion 1993-94
IBF super-middleweight champion 1994-96
WBC light-heavyweight champion 1997 (twice)
Pensacola, Florida, born 16 January 1969
1988 Olympic light-middleweight silver medal

1989

May 6 Ricky Randall w rsf 2 Pensacola
Jun 11 Stefan Johnson w rsf 8 Atlantic City
Sep 3 Ron Amundsen w rsf 7 Pensacola
Nov 30 David McCluskey w rsf 3 Pensacola

1990

Jan 8 Joe Edens w ko 2 Pensacola
Feb 28 Billy Mitchem w rsf 2 Pensacola
Mar 28 Knox Brown w rsf 3 Pensacola
May 11 Ron Johnson w ko 2 Pensacola
Jul 14 Tony Waddles w ko 1 Pensacola
Sep 25 Rollin Williams w ko 4 Pensacola
Nov 8 Reggie Miller w ko 5 Pensacola

1991

Jan 31 Ricky Stackhouse w ko 1 Pensacola
Apr 13 Ed Evans w rsf 3 Pensacola
Aug 3 Kevin Daigle w rsf 2 Pensacola
Aug 31 Lester Yarbrough w ko 9 Pensacola

1992

Jan 10 Jorge Vaca w rsf 1 New York
Apr 3 Art Serwano w ko 1 Reno
Jun 30 Jorge Castro w pts 10 Pensacola
Aug 18 Glenn Thomas w rsf 8 Pensacola
Dec 5 Percy Harris w ko 4 Atlantic City
(USBA super-middleweight title)

1993

Feb 13 Glenn Wolfe w rsf 1 Las Vegas
May 22 Bernard Hopkins w pts 12 Washington DC
(IBF middleweight title)
Aug 14 Sugarboy Malinga w ko 6 Bay St Louis
Nov 30 Fermin Chirino w pts 10 Pensacola

1994

Mar 22 Danny Garcia w rsf 6 Pensacola
May 27 Thomas Tate w rsf 2 Las Vegas
(IBF middleweight title)
Relinquished IBF middleweight title.
Nov 18 James Toney w pts 12 Las Vegas
(IBF super-middleweight title)

1995

Mar 18 Antoine Byrd w rsf 1 Pensacola
(IBF super-middleweight title)
Jun 24 Vinny Pazienza w rsf 6 Atlantic City
(IBF super-middleweight title)
Sep 30 Tony Thornton w rsf 3 Pensacola
(IBF super-middleweight title)

1996

Jan 12 Merqui Sosa w rsf 2 New York
Jun 15 Eric Lucas w rsf 11 Jacksonville
(IBF super-middleweight title)
Oct 2 Bryant Brannon w rsf 2 New York
(IBF super-middleweight title)
Nov 22 Mike McCallum w pts 12 Tampa
(WBC Interim light-heavyweight title)

1997

Feb: Recognised as WBC light-heavyweight champion.
Mar 21 Montell Griffin l dis 9 Atlantic City
(WBC light-heavyweight title)
Aug 7 Montell Griffin w ko 1 Ledyard, Ct.
(WBC light-heavyweight title)
Nov: Relinquished WBC title.

Fights 36 Won 35 Lost 1

OSCAR DE LA HOYA

OSCAR WINNER

The fresh-faced, charismatic American 'Golden Boy' of the 1990s, Oscar De La Hoya had won world titles at four separate weights by the age of 24. There were those who said if he stayed in boxing long enough, and retained his ambition, an incredible span of championships from super-feather to middleweight could be within his grasp.

De La Hoya was a pleasure to work with: easy going, ready smiling, able and willing to talk and co-operate with the media circus in either Spanish or English. He was tall, exceptionally so when he was working in the super-featherweight division, at 5ft 11in. When he first moved into world class, he seemed, in spite of his obvious ability, almost boyishly vulnerable, yet overcame a succession of early scares to develop into a battle-hardened professional.

De La Hoya was born of Mexican parents in East Los Angeles on 4 February 1973. His mother, Cecilia, died of breast cancer at only 37 in 1990. Her last request to him was to win a gold medal at the Barcelona Olympics. His father Joel, who took him to the Resurrection Boys Club at the age of six, remained a huge influence on his career. 'He knows I'm gonna be somebody,' De La Hoya said as a teenager. 'We have our little ups and downs, but I know he wants the best for me.' Joel had been a useful professional prospect, who gave up boxing to take a steady job. 'I had to put food on the table,' he said.

At 16 Oscar was a National Golden Gloves champion at bantamweight, and his only failure between then and the Olympic lightweight gold medal at Barcelona was a points defeat by Germany's Marco Rudolph in the 1991 world championships in Sydney. He blamed himself. It was his fifth and last amateur defeat in more than 200 contests.

Even as a boy, he had a surprising wisdom. When away on American international team duty, he would take his schoolwork with him and mail it back. When he completed high school in 1991, he already had a second career planned as an architect should anything happen which prevented him succeeding in boxing.

As the 1992 Olympics approached, the pressure on him must have been intense – he was on the front pages of major sports magazines as a gold medal certainty – but he coped with it admirably, beating Rudolph on the way to the only boxing gold the USA won in Barcelona. Long before then, he had celebrity status in East Los Angeles. When he was robbed at gunpoint in 1991, the muggers returned his stolen wallet and the $150 it contained as soon as they discovered who he was.

He had trained with George Benton and Lou Duva even as an amateur, and was backed by Shelly Finkel, but when he turned pro, he opted for an incredible deal put on the table by Steve Nelson and Robert Mittleman. They paid him $500,000 in cash as a signing-on fee, a new $100,000 car, a new van for his team and half the deposit on a $500,000 four-bedroom house in a select area of Los Angeles. He was also paid $200,000 for his professional debut, a one-round win over Lamar Williams at the Great Western Forum in Los Angeles. When they fell out, Nelson and Mittleman took him to court to recover some of their investment and won a substantial settlement, but De La Hoya remained with promoter Bob Arum, with his father always there, along with his trainer since 1990, Robert Alcazar. De La Hoya left Nelson and Mittleman to take up an offer of $1.5 million from a Mexican businessman, Reynaldo Garza. In 1994, it was reported that Finkel had also began legal proceedings. In boxing, business is never simple!

De La Hoya had that thoroughbred look from the start of his pro career. 'All my fights are tests,' he said. 'They just look easy because I train so hard.' When he won the WBO 130lb title by stopping Jimmi Bredahl of Denmark on a tenth round retirement in March 1994, he was shaken along the way in between flooring Bredahl twice. He was also put down by Giorgio Campanella of Italy in his first defence in May 1994, but won in round three. These proved to be temporary worries, however. He relinquished the super-featherweight title to move up to lightweight, and became WBO 135lb champion by bombing out Jorge Paez, the colourful Mexican, in two rounds. Next challengers Carl Griffith and Johnny Avila lasted three and nine rounds respectively.

In 1995 he moved up another league, beginning by outpointing Juan 'John-John' Molina, who had been one of the best super-featherweights in the world for several years. Then Oscar blasted out Rafael Ruelas, the reigning IBF lightweight champion, in two rounds. Ruelas was normally a fast, aggressive fighter who liked to impose his will. He did well enough for a round, but once De La Hoya set to work, Ruelas was out of his depth. He was floored twice and stopped. 'My plan was never to let him get into the fight,' said De La Hoya, who had already booked a game of golf for 6 a.m. the following day. For a while he held both belts, then opted to return the IBF championship.

In September 1995 he boxed brilliantly to force former undefeated WBA super-featherweight champion Genaro Hernandez to retire with a broken nose after six rounds in the 'Battle of LA', which happened to be staged in Caesars Palace, Las Vegas! They had sparred together before Oscar won the Olympic gold, when Hernandez was already a world champ. Hernandez, criticised for quitting, said: 'I feel no disgrace. Oscar was the better fighter'.

De La Hoya was selected as the man who should take star billing when Madison

Square Garden re-opened its doors to boxing in December 1995. He outclassed Jesse James Leija, another former super-featherweight champion, in two rounds. He was superb, both in and out of the ring. It was refreshing to watch him walk into the post-fight press conference and announce with a smile: 'Ask me anything. Whatever you like. Professional or personal.' He was a publicist's dream.

By then De La Hoya and Arum were talking of a showdown with Julio Cesar Chavez, and after both had won warm-ups, and Chavez had cemented his (temporary) move from Don King to Arum, they met for the Mexican's WBC light-welterweight championship in front of a packed outdoor arena at Caesars Palace, Las Vegas, in June 1996.

It was a gruesome, one-sided spectacle, with De La Hoya drilling the shorter, slower champion from long range until by the fourth his face was a mask of blood from a dreadful two-inch cut over the left eye. Frankly, the injury saved Chavez from humiliation. The next day he acknowledged through an interpreter: 'Oscar is a good kid. He has a brilliant future ... It was Oscar's night and he beat me fair and square. No excuses.' De La Hoya was his usual polished self. 'Chavez will always be my idol, but my job is to win fights. In the ring, I had no feelings at all towards him. I feel happy, but I'm not a great champion yet. That will take many more fights, many more years.'

He took time out after that, but returned with a one-sided points win over previously unbeaten Mexican, Miguel Angel Gonzalez, in Las Vegas in January 1997.

Then came world title number four as he moved up to welterweight and challenged the horribly elusive southpaw Pernell Whitaker, who was one of Oscar's predecessors as Olympic lightweight gold medallist – in the Los Angeles games of 1984.

Whitaker was slowing by now, 33 years old and beginning to lose the hard edge of ambition. Nevertheless, he could still make anyone in the world look bad. De La Hoya won on points, without over-impressing, and Whitaker complained about the decision. Bob Arum said there would be no rematch because they had achieved what they had set out to do - take away Whitaker's WBC 147lb belt. A rematch, he said with considerable justification, simply would not sell.

In September 1997, Oscar faced wily old pro Hector 'Macho' Camacho, and won a landslide points decision in Las Vegas. Camacho's survival skills succeeded in making De La Hoya look somewhat ordinary, although he did manage to put the veteran Puerto Rican on the floor for only the second time in his long career. His main trainer, Emanuel Steward, was soon replaced by Gil Clancy, a one-time schoolteacher who had trained Emile Griffith to the world welterweight and middleweight titles in the 1960s. Clancy had been working as a TV analyst for years, before De La Hoya persuaded him that they could work together.

Oscar rounded off his year with the third defence of his WBC welterweight belt, and 15th world title fight overall, stopping Wilfredo Rivera of Puerto Rico in eight rounds in Atlantic City. Rivera was managed by none other than Robert Mittleman, De La Hoya's former co-manager, who naturally would have loved to have seen his man spring an upset.

Hand troubles emerged in the first part of 1998, which delayed a mandatory defence against Patrick Charpentier, his official challenger from France. Already Arum was looking beyond the Frenchman to a rematch with Chavez, tentatively set for September. Beyond the welterweight division, De La Hoya was also looking at a possible fight with IBF light-middleweight champion Luis Ramon 'Yori Boy' Campas of Mexico. And eventually, that middleweight division and a sixth world title remained an intriguing long distance aim.

Out of the ring, he remained as clean as he was in it. He spoke well on TV talk shows and took the time to go into schools to show children what could be achieved with hard work, attempting to persuade them to stay in school and complete their education.

'I'm very comfortable keeping an image that's good for boxing,' he said. 'We want people coming to the fights.'

He was, of course, fabulously wealthy by then with a dream home on the west side of Los Angeles worth $3.9 million. His earnings for 1997 alone were a gross $32 million. He had bought homes for his family and was developing a serious leisure habit ... golf!

CAREER STATISTICS

WBO super-featherweight champion 1994
WBO lightweight champion 1994-96
WBC light-welterweight champion 1996-97
WBC welterweight champion 1997-
Los Angeles, born 4 February 1973
1992 Olympic lightweight gold medal

1992
Nov 23 Lamar Williams w ko 1 Los Angeles
Dec 12 Cliff Hicks w ko 1 Phoenix
1993
Jan 3 Paris Alexander w rsf 2 Los Angeles
Feb 6 Curtis Strong w rsf 4 San Diego
Mar 13 Jeff Mayweather w rsf 4 Las Vegas
Apr 6 Mike Grable w pts 8 Rochester
May 8 Frankie Avelar w rsf 4 Lake Tahoe
Jun 7 Troy Dorsey w rsf 1 Las Vegas
Aug 14 Renaldo Carter w rsf 6 Bay St Louis
Aug 27 Angelo Nunez w rsf 4 Los Angeles
Oct 30 Narcisco Valenzuela w ko 1 Phoenix
1994
Mar 5 Jimmi Bredahl w rtd 9 Los Angeles
(WBO super-featherweight title)
May 27 Giorgio Campanella w rsf 3 Las Vegas
(WBO super-featherweight title)
Jul 29 Jorge Paez w ko 2 Las Vegas
(vacant WBO lightweight title)
Nov 18 Carl Griffith w rsf 3 Las Vegas
(WBO lightweight title)
Dec 10 Johnny Avila w rsf 9 Los Angeles
(WBO lightweight title)
1995
Feb 18 Juan Molina w pts 12 Las Vegas
(WBO lightweight title)
May 6 Rafael Ruelas w rsf 2 Las Vegas
(WBO & IBF lightweight titles)
Relinquished IBF lightweight title.
Sep 9 Genaro Hernandez w rsf 6 Las Vegas
(WBO lightweight title)
Dec 15 James Leija w rsf 2 New York
(WBO lightweight title)
1996
Feb 9 Darryl Tyson w rsf 2 Las Vegas
Jun 7 Julio Cesar Chavez w rsf 4 Las Vegas
(WBC light-welterweight title)
1997
Jan 18 Miguel Angel Gonzalez w pts 12 Las Vegas
(WBC light-welterweight title)
Apr 12 Pernell Whitaker w pts 12 Las Vegas
(WBC welterweight title)
Jun 14 David Kamau w ko 2 San Antonio
(WBC welterweight title)
Sep 13 Hector Camacho w pts 12 Las Vegas
(WBC welterweight title)
Dec 6 Wilfredo Rivera w rsf 8 Atlantic City
(WBC welterweight title)

NASEEM HAMED

THE YEMENI PRINCE

Naseem Hamed, the self-styled Prince from the Yorkshire steel town of Sheffield, was extravagantly talented, flamboyant in and sometimes out of the ring, and a puncher of unusual power. He was also happiest at home, and valued the base provided for him by his family and the down-to-earth if eccentric gym of his teacher, Brendan Ingle.

'He asked me what I would do if I were him,' Ingle said in a 1998 television interview. 'I said, with £12 million in the bank I wouldn't be in this game, I'd be at university or somewhere, getting myself some wisdom and education!'

But Hamed loved to box, and felt he had something to prove. 'I want to be a legend,' he said, from day one of his professional career in 1994. 'I want to win world titles at four weights and retire with £40 million.'

By the age of 24, newly married and with his first child born in June 1998, he was part of the way there. Whether or not he eventually would do all that he set out to achieve as a boy of 18, he had at least ensured that his fame was lasting, his fortune safe and his family secure.

He was born in Sheffield on 12 February 1974, the son of Yemeni parents who had settled in England. His father Sal travelled by boat through the Suez Canal from what was then North Yemen in 1958, to be followed by his wife, Caria, four years later. Sal worked in a steel mill until they had saved enough to buy a general store. Naseem was the fifth of their eight children, and no matter how successful he became and how outrageous some of his claims, his public acknowledgement of the achievement of his parents was always heartfelt. So too, his recognition of the discipline he learned because of his upbringing.

'Boxing is a 24-hour job,' he said when he spoke in a 1994 interview for *KO* magazine. 'I train three times a day, seven days a week. And my religion is one of the biggest disciplines you have to do. It's given me a law in my mind, a worshipfulness inside me. A simple way.'

Time and again, he would repeat to his public that his ability was a gift from Allah. From early in his career, his achievements were noticed in Yemen and then through the

Arabian TV channels across the Arab world. An exhibition visit to Yemen before he became a professional champion saw crowds of 10,000 visit his public workouts! Yemeni president Ali Abdulla Salah spoke to him on the telephone and sent presents, including a top of the range Mercedes. He had a set of six stamps issued in his honour.

In Britain, where boxing fans are more sceptical, his acceptance was slower, but eventually substantial, especially among the young.

When he was seven, he was sent to Ingle's gym near the family home with two of his brothers because his father was concerned about the amount of racial abuse they had to deal with. He wanted them to be able to defend themselves. Brendan Ingle, a Dubliner who settled in Sheffield, is one of the more modern 'thinking' trainers, who studies everything about the opponent in a boxing match, not just the physical side. Naseem was a natural, and his bouncy, unorthodox skills suited Ingle's teaching methods.

At 13 he won his first National Schools competition as soon as he was old enough to enter, and at 18 he was a professional. The intervening years brought Boys Clubs and Junior ABA titles, and an England vest as a 17-year-old. When he captained England against the USA, he was invited to give his team-mates a pep talk before the start. 'Well lads,' he said, with impish humour, 'You're on your own out there!'

He lost five decisions in 67 amateur contests, and then won his professional debut in Mansfield with a two-round knockout of Ricky Beard, an experienced pro from Dagenham.

In his 11th fight – a one-round trouncing of a buckle-nosed Belgian named John Miceli – he topped the bill on an ITV network show. A month later, he outclassed defending European bantamweight champion Vincenzo Belcastro over 12 rounds in Sheffield, flooring the Italian twice and then spoiling the effect by some tasteless showboating and taunting in the final round. It was inappropriate, juvenile fare and he was rightly criticised. He acknowledged it eventually: 'Maybe I did go over the top,' but felt misunderstood. He had taken to heart pre-fight speculation that he may not be able to do 12 fast rounds, and felt by behaving so exuberantly in the last that he was proving a point to his doubters. He had not, he said, intended to belittle Belcastro.

Showboating became a part of his act, and taunting a psychological ploy to be brought into use from time to time, although he almost always stressed from the Belcastro fight onwards that he had respect for his opponent ... at the very least, for daring to fight him!

After one successful European title defence, an easy three-round win over another Italian, Antonio Picardi, he moved into the super-bantamweight division and outclassed Freddy Cruz, a competent, organised fighter from the Dominican Republic, in six rounds for the WBC International belt. 'How can I hit him if I don't know where he is?' a despairing Cruz asked his corner in mid-fight.

There were five defences of the WBC's 'junior' title, but the belt mattered little. Hamed was learning all the time, and outclassing experienced fighters, some of whom were still in world class, and some of whom, like the Prince, aspired to be very soon.

All of this led to a showdown on a rainy September night at Cardiff rugby ground on 30 September 1995, when he challenged WBO featherweight champion Steve Robinson. Robinson had been champion for two-and-a-half years, but was unhappy at the contract negotiated on his behalf. Also, both Robinson and his supporters were angered by the pre-fight hype. Naseem was repeatedly stating his intention to knock Robinson out and take the title, and since Robinson had already successfully defended the title seven times since he won it, he had no intention of surrendering it to a bantamweight – champion though he might be – who was making his first appearance as a featherweight. Nevertheless, Robinson had not looked sharp for his previous two or three performances, and was some way short of his mental and physical peak when they walked down a ramp to the ring. Naseem met a hostile reception from the 16,000 crowd, but Robinson kept his cool – for the first round at least – and decided to make a cautious start: be patient; bide his time; wait for the moment. All these good intentions were his, but Hamed had used the first round to warm up a little and size up his opponent.

From the second, Robinson was tempted and taunted and when he took any kind of risk, he was punished unmercifully. He stayed on his feet until the fifth round when a four-punch combination put him down. He managed to survive the round but even the partisan crowd could see it was now only a matter of time and, after two more rounds of heavy punishment, the end came in the eighth when the Welshman went down so heavily the fight was stopped without a count being taken up. Although he had taunted a defensive and seemingly frozen Robinson in the ring, afterwards he gave him respect. Robinson went away to regroup, which took him more than two years.

Hamed had a problem with his right hand for a while after an injury in the gym, but returned to blow away Said Lawal, a Nigerian southpaw, in 35 seconds in Glasgow in March 1996.

Three months later, he received the first serious shock of his career in Newcastle when unbeaten, ambitious Puerto Rican Daniel Alicea floored him with a right hand in the opening round. Hamed bounced up unhurt and knocked Alicea cold in round two. It was a chilling finish, but British critics made much of his own knockdown.

In August 1996, he came through a tough defence against battle-hardened Mexican Manuel Medina in Dublin. Hamed insisted on fighting in spite of suffering from the after-effects of a heavy cold, but was sluggish and even though he dropped Medina in round three, was forced to concede ground, had his chin tested and his gumshield sent spinning in the middle rounds. Fortunately for him, Medina was a sharp but not hard puncher. In the 11th Hamed nailed him decisively, floored him heavily again and this time the Mexican was pulled out at the end of the round. Medina was a good fighter, who had already held the WBC and IBF belts, and who would regain the latter in 1998.

Naseem's fourth defence of the year was a second-round stoppage of the unbeaten, but physically slighter Argentine, Remigio Molina, in Manchester, and that set him up for another major fight, in February 1997 in London, against the reigning IBF featherweight champion Tom 'Boom Boom' Johnson. A proven champion, Johnson arrived in England full of confidence, only to find himself under heavy fire once the bell rang. He did shake Hamed with one countering right that made him touch down off balance – there was no count – but it was Hamed's fight all the way. He ended it with a heavy right uppercut in round eight. For all his brash talk and arrogant strutting, Hamed's 'other side' was caught by a fly-on-the-wall TV camera left running in Johnson's dressing room. It caught the young champion walking in to pay his respects quietly and sincerely to the older man he had just beaten.

Further attempts to unify the division came to nothing because of the refusal of the various organisations to work together, and the unavailability or high purse demands of the rival champions. A one–round win over his number one contender Billy Hardy was hopelessly one-sided, and was followed by another mismatch against game but unproven Argentine Juan Cabrera. After that fight, which was not approved by the IBF, he relinquished their belt rather than defend against their leading contender Hector Lizarraga.

Instead, he defended the WBO title for the eighth time with a classy, punch-picking display against a highly competent Puerto Rican counter-puncher named Jose Badillo. Trade insiders knew how good Badillo was and saw this as one of Hamed's finest displays. His southpaw right jab was never better, although there were some who griped about a lack of combination punching and his tendency to throw himself off balance when he threw his heaviest punches.

That his style had flaws was never in doubt, but when he controlled himself, was in full concentration and combined punch power with boxing ability, he was a formidable fighter.

His least controlled performance by far was his American debut in Madison Square Garden in December 1997, when he almost became the victim of his own hype. He seemed out of sorts, edgy and unsettled, although as usual he talked a big fight. American TV giant HBO allocated $1 million to market the fight, including huge billposters of Hamed overlooking Times Square. Opponent Kevin Kelley, a former WBC champion, was a dangerous contender but virtually ignored in the build-up.

However, after a ridiculous mix-up in his ringwalk which left Hamed dancing behind a giant screen for several minutes more than had been planned, round one saw him on the floor from a right hand counter. That signalled one of the most thrilling world title fights of that or any other year. When the dust settled, Hamed was still champion, courtesy of a fourth-round knockout. But both men had taken three counts, and the Englishman's pre-fight boast that he had more skills than Muhammad Ali earned him a string of derisory write-ups from American critics. For example, Budd Schulberg, the 83-year-old author of *On The Waterfront* and the Ali book *Loser and Still Champion*, said: 'It was very colourful. Hamed can hit hard, but after everything I had heard I thought he would be more elusive. Muhammad Ali at 23 would never have been hit by a jab they way Hamed was. He looks to me as if he has a lot to learn. Henry Armstrong and Sandy Saddler would have knocked him out. They would have chased him out of the ring.'

The widely respected Michael Katz of the *New York Daily News* wrote: 'Prince Naseem Hamed was on his way to being as successful as King George III in this country. He won, but he did not conquer.'

It was a stinging rebuff, following a brilliantly exciting but horribly flawed performance, which he and promoter Frank Warren attempted to cover as best they could. 'Naseem loves to fight on the edge,' said Warren, whose heart must have been in his throat for most of the 10 minutes.

At home Naseem married, then produced a far more settled performance in outpunching and stopping 37-year-old Wilfredo Vazquez of Puerto Rico, who had been WBA champion until a few weeks before the fight, which took place in front of 14,000 fans in Manchester in April. The WBA had stripped him for fighting Hamed instead of meeting his leading contender, a move which frustrated Warren, who was aware of the demand to make each fight as meaningful as possible. Vazquez caught Hamed often enough to make him think and reassess, but it was the Englishman's power which ultimately made the difference. He went down four times and by round seven had nothing left.

By the halfway point of the year in which Hamed's American adventure was to have taken off, he had fought only once – and that had been in England. There followed speculation that his second fight of 1998, scheduled for July, would also be in Britain, because it was too close to the birth of his first child to allow him to be away from home in an American training camp for a sustained spell. In fact, this was cancelled, officially because of an hand injury.

CAREER STATISTICS

WBO featherweight champion 1995-
IBF featherweight champion 1997
Sheffield, born 12 February 1974

1992
Apr 14 Ricky Beard w ko 2 Mansfield
Apr 25 Shaun Norman w rsf 2 Manchester
May 23 Andrew Bloomer w rsf 2 Birmingham
Jul 14 Miguel Matthews w rsf 3 London
Oct 7 Des Gargano w rsf 4 Sunderland
Nov 12 Peter Buckley w pts 6 Liverpool
1993
Feb 24 Alan Ley w ko 2 London
May 26 Kevin Jenkins w rsf 3 Mansfield
Sep 24 Chris Clarkson w ko 2 Dublin
1994
Jan 29 Peter Buckley w rsf 4 Cardiff
Apr 9 John Miceli w ko 1 Mansfield
May 11 Vincenzo Belcastro w pts 12 Sheffield
(European bantamweight title)
Aug 17 Antonio Picardi w rsf 3 Sheffield
(European bantamweight title)
Oct 12 Freddy Cruz w rsf 6 Sheffield
Nov 19 Laureano Ramirez w rtd 3 Cardiff
1995
Jan 21 Armando Castro w rsf 4 Glasgow
Mar 4 Sergio Liendo w ko 2 Livingston
May 6 Enrique Angeles w ko 2 Shepton Mallet
Jul 1 Juan Polo Perez w ko 2 London
Sep 30 Steve Robinson w ko 8 Cardiff
(WBO featherweight title)
1996
Mar 16 Said Lawal w rsf 1 Glasgow
(WBO featherweight title)
Jun 8 Daniel Alicea w ko 2 Newcastle
(WBO featherweight title)
Aug 31 Manuel Medina w rsf 11 Dublin
(WBO featherweight title)
Nov 9 Remigio Molina w rsf 2 Manchester
(WBO featherweight title)
1997
Feb 7 Tom Johnson w rsf 8 London
(WBO & IBF featherweight titles)
May 3 Billy Hardy w rsf 1 Manchester
(WBO & IBF featherweight titles)
Jul 19 Juan Cabrera w rsf 2 London
(WBO featherweight title)
Relinquished IBF title.
Oct 11 Jose Badillo w rsf 7 Sheffield
(WBO featherweight title)
Dec 19 Kevin Kelley w ko 4 New York
(WBO featherweight title)
1998
Apr 18 Wilfredo Vazquez w rsf 7 Manchester
(WBO featherweight title)

Fights 30 Won 30

OTHER GREATS OF THE POST-1950 ERA

Carmen Basilio

The son of an onion farmer who lived near Canastota, New York, Carmen was a rough, brawling fighter who held the undisputed world welterweight and middleweight titles. Born on 2 April 1927, he was boxing professionally by 1948. His first world title bid brought a points defeat by Kid Gavilan in 1953, but he won the welterweight crown two years later by stopping Tony De Marco in the 12th round. After beating De Marco again, he lost and regained it against Johnny Saxton, and in 1957 moved up to challenge world middleweight champion Ray Robinson in one of the fiercest battles of the decade. Basilio won on points in New York, but in the rematch in Chicago in March 1958, he was outpointed. Two stoppage defeats by Gene Fullmer foiled attempts to win the NBA title, and he also lost on points to Fullmer's rival claimant, Paul Pender, in the last of his 79 fights in April 1961. In retirement, he worked as a college physical education instructor, as a salesman and also managed a few fighters.

Joe Brown

'Old Bones' Joe Brown was a carpenter's son from Baton Rouge, Louisiana, born on 18 May 1925. He turned pro at 20, and learned the business from top to bottom before he was given his first world title shot at the age of 31, in his 87th fight, in 1956. He made sure he took it, outpointing Wallace 'Bud' Smith in New Orleans in spite of breaking a hand. Once he had the lightweight title in his grasp, he defended it with a grim determination for the next six years. He made 11 successful defences, including wins over future champions Ralph Dupas and Kenny Lane, before Carlos Ortiz outsped him over the full 15 rounds in Las Vegas in 1962, by which time he was approaching his 37 birthday. Still 'Old Bones' would not quit, boxing on until 1970, when he was 44. He had 161 fights, but at the end had little to show for them. He worked as a security guard and ran a bar. He died in 1997.

Hector Camacho

Known as the Macho Man, Hector Camacho could be insensitive, difficult and downright childish, or enormous fun. He was also a clever ring general, with a big heart and granite chin: in short he was one of the best fighters of his era. Born in Bayamon, Puerto Rico, on 24 May 1962, Camacho began boxing professionally in New York in 1980. He won the WBC super-featherweight title in 1983, the WBC lightweight crown in 1985 and the WBO light-welterweight championship in 1989. His first defeat, a controversial decision given to Greg Haugen, was not until 1991. He won his first title by knocking out Rafael Limon in five rounds, his second with a decision over Jose Luis Ramirez and his third by outboxing Ray Mancini. He also outpointed other world champions like Cornelius Boza-Edwards, Vinny Pazienza and Edwin Rosario. In 1997, he was still in top class: he stopped the elderly Ray Leonard and lost on points to WBC welterweight champion Oscar De La Hoya. It was his 69th fight and only fourth defeat.

Orlando Canizales

One of two world champion brothers from the Texan border town of Laredo, Orlando Canizales was born on 25 November 1965. A pro as a teenaged flyweight, he won the IBF bantamweight belt by stopping Kelvin Seabrooks in the 15th round in Atlantic City in 1988, and held it for the next six years, making 16 successful defences, before relinquishing it because of increasing weight problems. Although he fought on at super-bantamweight and featherweight, he was never the same force. Wilfredo Vazquez and Junior Jones both outpointed him, although he was still fighting and winning in his thirties. His brother Jose, known as Gaby, was a town sheriff in Laredo who held two other versions of the bantamweight title, the WBA and WBO.

Miguel Canto

For four years in the late 1970s, Miguel Angel Canto from Merida in Mexico, was the best flyweight in the world. Born on 30 January 1948, he turned pro in 1969, and won the WBC flyweight title in Japan in 1975 by outpointing tough southpaw Shoji Oguma. A light puncher, but beautiful craftsman, he turned back 14 consecutive challengers, a record for the flyweight division, before he lost the belt in 1979. He retired in 1982.

Sot Chitalada

A strong, hard-hitting flyweight with an iron chin and a fast, hurtful jab, Sot Chitalada was born in Chonburi, Thailand, on 24 October 1962. Trained by an Englishman, Charles Atkinson, he won the WBC flyweight title in 1984 by outpointing a Mexican, Gabriel Bernal, and dominated the division for the rest of the decade. He stopped Charlie Magri in London, was weight-drained when he lost it to Yong-kang Kim in Korea in 1988, but prepared correctly when he regained it from Kim in Thailand the following year. Atkinson said he would have been an equally great bantamweight, but his Thai management team insisted he make flyweight and Sot took off one-sixth of his body weight to do it. By 1991, it had become too much for him and he retired after two stoppage defeats by a fellow Thai, Muangsai Kittikasem.

Steve Collins

Uncompromising, strong, with good skills and a fine tactical brain, Steve Collins was the first Irishman to hold world titles at separate weights. Born in Dublin on 21 July 1964, he began his pro career in Brockton, Massachusetts, under the Petronelli brothers, working in the same gym as his hero, Marvin Hagler. He returned to Ireland, and won the WBO middleweight title by stopping Chris Pyatt in five rounds in Sheffield in 1994, but it was his two points wins over Chris Eubank in 1995 which earned him the WBO super-middleweight title and world wide respect. He also stopped Nigel Benn twice before retiring as undefeated champion in 1997 to open a gym in Dublin.

John Conteh

Acknowledged as the most talented British fighter he had ever handled by long-time manager and promoter Mickey Duff, John Conteh was WBC light-heavyweight champion for three turbulent years, 1974–1977. Conteh was born in Liverpool on 27 May 1951, and won British, Commonwealth and European titles before outpointing Jorge Ahumada of Argentina for the vacant WBC belt at Wembley in October 1974. After one successful defence against Lonnie Bennett, he fell out with Duff and his co-promoter Harry Levene and tried to go his own way. He broke his right hand in a non-title fight, had recurring out of the ring problems and was eventually stripped for failing to go through with a contracted defence in 1977. Three attempts to regain the title against Mate Parlov and Matthew Saad Muhammad (twice) failed, and he retired in 1980.

Gene Fullmer

A Mormon born in West Jordan, Utah, on 21 July 1931, he was named after world heavyweight champion Gene Tunney. He made his professional debut in 1951, took a couple of years off for army service during the Korean War, and won and lost the world middleweight title against Ray Robinson in 1957. Fullmer won NBA recognition as champion as Robinson's career began to falter in 1959, and held it until Dick Tiger deposed him in 1962. He retired in 1964 and made a fortune farming mink. A strong, rugged brawler with a solid chin, Fullmer twice boxed Carmen Basilio to a standstill, but usually relied on strength, workrate and an awkward style to carry him through. He came out ahead of Robinson by two wins to one, with one draw, and also beat fine fighters like Joey Giardello, Spider Webb, Florentino Fernandez, Wilf Greaves and Gil Turner.

Khaosai Galaxy

Perhaps the greatest fighter ever produced in Thailand, Khaosai Galaxy was born in Petchaboon, Thailand, on 15 May 1959. His twin brother Khaokor was also a world champion, but Khaosai was the more talented and more successful. He won the WBA super-flyweight crown by knocking out Eusebio Espinal in 1984 and his calm, ruthless aggression and vicious punching disposed of 19 consecutive challengers before he retired as undefeated champion at the end of 1991. His only defeat was a decision in his sixth pro fight. He remains a hero of astonishing proportions in Thailand.

Wilfredo Gomez

From San Juan, Puerto Rico, where he was born on 29 October 1957, Wilfredo Gomez was a clever, hard-hitting combination puncher who was a world champion in three weight divisions. He was mostly known as the best 122lb champion in history, who held the WBC belt from 1977 until 1982. He stopped the celebrated Mexican Carlos Zarate in his first major bout in 1978, but was stopped when he tried to step up to take on the great featherweight Salvador Sanchez. In 1984 he beat Juan LaPorte for the WBC featherweight belt, but Azumah Nelson knocked him out to relieve him of it. His final world title triumph came in 1985 when he beat Rocky Lockridge for the WBA super-featherweight crown. He lost it when Alfredo Layne stopped him the following year, and retired in 1989.

Humberto Gonzalez

'Chiquita' Gonzalez, born in the Atencio-Estadao slums of Mexico City on 25 March 1966, was an enormously popular WBC light-flyweight champion who had a great three-fight series with his biggest rival Michael Carbajal. He floored Carbajal twice and was on the brink of victory when the American turned the fight around and knocked him out in the seventh round. But in rematches Gonzalez twice used his cute boxing brain to win on points. He first won the WBC title in Korea in 1989 with a victory over Yul-woo Lee, and this butcher's son – La Chiquita was the name of the family shop – had three reigns altogether before retiring in 1995 after losing to Saman Sorjatorung of Thailand.

Virgil Hill

Virgil Hill was a neat, organised boxer who was never a superstar, but endured as a light-heavyweight champion for almost 10 years. Born in Clinton, Missouri, on 18 January 1964, he boxed out of North Dakota. The son of a plumber, he was a silver medallist in the 1984 Olympic Games and won the WBA light-heavyweight title in 1987 by knocking out Leslie Stewart of Trinidad. He was a big favourite in North Dakota, but elsewhere he was considered dull and uninspiring in spite of his obvious skills. Beset by personal difficulties, he lost his WBA belt to Thomas Hearns in 1991, but sorted himself out and regained it the following year by defeating Frank Tate. He added the IBF title by outpointing Henry Maske in 1996, but then lost both belts to Dariusz Michalczewski and seemed to have reached the end in 1998 when Roy Jones knocked him out for the first time in his life.

Eder Jofre

Eder Jofre will be remembered by the people of Brazil as a tireless politician as well as an incredibly successful boxer. Jofre, born in Sao Paulo on 26 March 1936, fought professionally for almost 20 years and lost only twice in 78 fights. They were points defeats by Fighting Harada in Japan in 1965 and 1966. Jofre won the NBA bantamweight title in 1960, and consequently was recognised as world champion after defeating Piero Rollo in 1961 and Johnny Caldwell in 1962. He retired after the second Harada defeat, but returned to the ring in 1969 and became WBC featherweight champion in 1973, at the age of 37, when he outpointed Jose Legra of Cuba. He gave up the title the following year, but boxed on until 1976. He was one of the first vegetarian world champions.

Danny Lopez

Nobody walked the edge more than hard-hitting Danny 'Little Red' Lopez, one of the most exciting of all world featherweight champions. Lopez was born in Fort Duchesne, Utah, on 6 July 1952. His elder brother Ernie was a world class welterweight, when Danny was a novice. Danny won the WBC featherweight title in the searing heat of Accra, when he outpointed defending champion and Ghanaian national hero David Kotey, in 1976. Time and again, he would look on the brink of defeat only for his big hitting to bring him through: particularly memorable were his two-round knockout of Juan Malvarez and his 15th-round win over Mike Ayala. Eventually, he was twice stopped by Salvador Sanchez and retired in 1980. A comeback in 1992 was mercifully brief.

Brian Mitchell

The Road Warrior from South Africa was a solid, all-round fighting machine who was forced to defend his WBA super-featherweight title abroad because he was a South African competing at the height of the anti-apartheid sanctions. He was born in Johannesburg on 30 August 1961, and won the WBA super-featherweight title by defeating Alfredo Layne in 1984. The WBA outlawed South Africa, but stopped short of exiling him, probably thinking that his reign would not be lengthy anyway. He defied logic, defending away from home repeatedly, including a decision over Jim McDonnell in London, and then won the IBF title in his 14th world championship bout by defeating Tony Lopez. He retired in 1995, aged 33, having lost only once in 49 fights.

Matthew Saad Muhammad

Found wandering on a Philadelphia highway, Matthew Saad Muhammad was raised by nuns in an orphanage. Only when he became a world class boxer as Matthew Franklin was his real identity traced: he was Maxwell Antonio Loach, born in Jenkintown, Pennsylvania, on 16 June 1954. Eventually, he converted to Islam and took the name Saad Muhammad. An all-or-nothing warrior, he could absorb tremendous amounts of punishment and win. His wars with Marvin Johnson were legendary. He beat Johnson for the WBC title in 1979 and turned back eight challenges until Dwight Muhammad Qawi stopped him in 1981. He boxed on until 1992.

Jose Napoles

Cuban-born and a Mexican citizen, Jose 'Mantequilla' Napoles was a wonderfully skilled welterweight champion to match the best of any other era. He was born in Santiago, Cuba, on 13 April 1940, made his professional debut in Havana in 1958 and emigrated to Mexico four years later. He had to wait until 1969 for a world title fight, when he stopped Curtis Cokes in 13 rounds in Los Angeles. With one short interruption caused by a cut eye defeat against Billy Backus, he was welterweight champion for the next six years. He lost a middleweight title bid against Carlos Monzon, and retired after losing the welterweight crown to John H. Stracey.

Azumah Nelson

The greatest fighter ever produced in Africa, Azumah Nelson was born in Accra on 19 September 1958. After winning a gold medal at the 1978 Commonwealth Games, he turned pro, won Ghanaian, African and Commonwealth titles and then in his 14th fight, lost in the 15th round to WBC featherweight champion Salvador Sanchez in New York in 1982. Two years later he won the title with an 11-round knockout of Wilfredo Gomez in San Juan. He moved up to super-featherweight in 1988, outpointing Mario Martinez in Los Angeles. For six years he remained champion, lost it to James Leija in 1994, regained it from Gabriel Ruelas and finally surrendered it to Genaro Hernandez in 1997, when he was 38. It was his 24th world championship bout.

Ruben Olivares

One of the most popular of all Mexican world champions, Olivares was a colourful, all-action battler from Mexico City (born 14 January 1947) whose career spanned almost a quarter of a century. He turned pro in 1965, and knocked out Lionel Rose of Australia in five rounds for the world bantamweight title in 1969. He had two spells as champion, then held both the WBA and WBC versions of the featherweight crown in the 1970s. His 1974 fight with Alexis Arguello was a classic. He retired in 1988 after more than 100 contests.

Eusebio Pedroza

Born in Panama City on 2 March 1953, Eusebio Pedroza was a tough, enduring WBA featherweight champion who knew every trick in the book. His first title attempt brought a shocking two-round knockout defeat against Mexican bantamweight Alfonso Zamora, but as a featherweight he was WBA champion for seven years, from 1978 when he stopped Cecilio Lastra of Spain until 1985 when Barry McGuigan outpointed him in London in his 20th defence. He made a brief comeback, which ended in 1992.

Pascual Perez

The finest flyweight of the 1950s, Pascual Perez was born in Tupungate, in the Mendoza province of Argentina on 4 May 1926. He was the flyweight gold medallist in the 1948 Olympics in London. He won the world flyweight championship in Japan by defeating defending champion Yoshio Shirai in 1954 and turned back every challenger for the next six years, including Welshman Dai Dower, whom he knocked out in one round in 1957. He lost the title to Pone Kingpetch of Argentina in 1960, but fought on for another four years. He died of liver disease on 22 January 1970, aged 50.

Lionel Rose

The first Aboriginal Australian to win a world title, Lionel Rose was born in a settlement in Drouin, Victoria, on 21 June 1948. Precociously talented, he was a professional at 16 and became a national hero when he beat Fighting Harada for the bantamweight in Tokyo in February 1968. He was still only 19. Quick and smart, he made three defences, including a decision over Britain's Alan Rudkin, before Ruben Olivares knocked him out in Los Angeles. In middle age he worked for the Department of Aboriginal Affairs.

Gianfranco Rosi

Born in Assissi, Italy, on 5 August 1957, Gianfranco Rosi was a cunning, slippery technician who had great discipline and made full use of his abilities to hold three versions of the world light-middleweight title between 1987 and 1995. He was WBC champion first, then a long-serving IBF champion and finally held the WBO belt. On the way up, he was also a two-weight European champion (at welter and light-middle) and his 65 fight career spanned almost two decades.

Vicente Saldivar

A strong southpaw with seemingly limitless stamina, Vicente Saldivar is best known in Britain for his three wins over Welsh wizard Howard Winstone. He was born in Mexico City on 3 May 1943, turned pro at 17 and won the world featherweight title by defeating Mexican-based Cuban Sugar Ramos in 1964. He retired as undefeated champion in 1967, but returned and regained the title three years later against Johnny Famechon of Australia. He lost it quickly, however, and retired in 1973. He died of heart failure in Mexico City in July 1985, aged 42.

Salvador Sanchez

One of the great featherweight champions, Salvador Sanchez was a shrewd boxer who had the great gift of making his own time in a ring. A genuine 15-round fighter, he would spend several rounds working out an opponent's style, before going to work. Born in Santiago Tianuistencio, Mexico, on 26 January 1959, he was fighting professionally at 16. His only professional defeat was in a Mexican bantamweight title fight when he was 18. He lost on points. He won the WBC featherweight title by stopping Danny Lopez in 13 rounds in 1980, and turned back nine challengers in two years, including Lopez in a rematch, Juan LaPorte, Wilfredo Gomez and Azumah Nelson. He was only 23 when he died in a car crash in Mexico on 12 August 1982.

Pernell Whitaker

As elusive a southpaw as you could wish to see, Pernell Whitaker was a bewildering, frustrating opponent who was one of the finest talents of his era. Born in Norfolk, Virginia, on 2 January 1964, 'Sweet Pea' Whitaker was Olympic lightweight gold medallist in the Los Angeles Games of 1984. After more than 200 amateur contests, he won world professional titles in four weight divisions from lightweight to light-middleweight. Apart from an outrageous decision given to Jose Luis Ramirez in France in 1988 and an equally controversial draw against Julio Cesar Chavez five years later, Whitaker beat everyone until as a veteran he was closely outpointed by the star of the next generation, Oscar De La Hoya, in 1997. Whitaker was exceptional: his victims included Ramirez in a return, Greg Haugen, Azumah Nelson, Buddy McGirt, Julio Cesar Vasquez and Jorge Paez.

Myung-woo Yuh

Born in Seoul, South Korea, on 10 January 1964, Myung-woo Yuh was a clever, strong and immensely durable. Far East boxing experts say he would have beaten the light-flyweight rivals from the West, Humberto Gonzalez and Michael Carbajal. He held the WBA 108lb title from 1985 when he outpointed American Joey Olivo until 1991 when he lost to Hiroshi Ioka of Japan. It was his only professional defeat. He beat Ioka in a rematch and retired undefeated champion in 1993 after his 21st world title fight. In a national poll he was voted the best Korean fighter of all time.

Carlos Zarate

Born in Mexico City on 23 May 1951, Carlos Zarate was a formidable WBC bantamweight champion, undoubtedly the best 118lb fighter of the 1970s. His non-title fight with celebrated Mexican rival Alfonso Zamora, who held the WBA belt, in Los Angeles in 1977 attracted enormous interest – Zarate won in the fourth round. He was WBC champion from 1976 until 1979 when he lost a mysterious decision to embarrassed stablemate Lupe Pintor. In a comeback in the late 1980s he fought both Jeff Fenech and Daniel Zaragoza for the WBC super-bantamweight title, but it was as a bantamweight in full flow that this tall, stiff and accurate puncher will be remembered.

INDEX

Numbers in bold indicate section dedicated to that boxer. Those in intalics denote captions.